T0366340

# More Praise for *Modern Portfolio Management*

"At a time when boundaries between asset classes are rapidly breaking down and hedge-fund strategies permeate traditional asset management, this book provides a superb framework to understand and analyze the broader implications of this trend in the public equity space."
—Gumersindo Oliveros, Director,
World Bank Pension Plan and Endowments

"Martin Leibowitz and his coauthors have produced a must read for financial market practitioners and researchers who want to go beyond the ABCs of 130/30 extensions. The current volume brings together the breadth of research that Leibowitz and Bova produced on active extensions, complementary work by Emrich, and a sampling of seminal contributions on active management from other authors. It is a necessary resource for pension and endowment fund managers."
—Edgar Sullivan, Managing Director,
General Motors Asset Management

# Modern Portfolio Management

*Active Long/Short 130/30*
*Equity Strategies*

MARTIN L. LEIBOWITZ
SIMON EMRICH
ANTHONY BOVA

WILEY

John Wiley & Sons, Inc.

Published by John Wiley & Sons, Inc., Hoboken, New Jersey.
Published simultaneously in Canada.

For general information on our other products and services or for technical support, please contact our Customer Care Department within the United States at (800) 762-2974, outside the United States at (317) 572-3993 or fax (317) 572-4002.

Wiley also publishes its books in a variety of electronic formats. Some content that appears in print may not be available in electronic books. For more information about Wiley products, visit our web site at www.wiley.com.

*Library of Congress Cataloging-in-Publication Data:*

Leibowitz, Martin L., 1936–
  Modern portfolio management : active long/short 130/30 equity strategies / Martin L. Leibowitz, Anthony Bova, Simon Emrich.
      p. cm. – (Wiley finance series)
  Includes index.
  ISBN 978-0-470-39853-1 (cloth)
  1. Portfolio management. 2. Asset allocation. 3. Investment analysis. I. Bova, Anthony, 1978–  II. Emrich, Simon, 1971–  III. Title.
  HG4529.5.L446 2009
  332.6–dc22                                                           2008028070

ISBN-13: 978-0-470-39853-1

Printed in the United States of America

10  9  8  7  6  5  4  3  2  1

*This volume is dedicated to all those whose support nurtured our careers over the years and made this work possible.*

# Contents

# Foreword
## The High and Low of 130/30 Investing

"There are two ways to make money in the stock market. You can buy low and sell high, or you can sell high and buy low." With this short statement, California Public Employee Retirement System (CalPERS) entered the world of long/short investing.

I made this statement in the middle of a presentation to the CalPERS board of trustees several years ago. At that time, CalPERS was considering an internal active long/short equity product. The CalPERS investment staff prepared a detailed agenda item for the pension fund trustees that explained how:

- Custodians lent out shares to prime brokers on behalf of their customers,
- Securities lending generated fee revenue to the pension fund,
- Hedge fund managers borrowed these shares from the prime brokers to establish their negative alpha bets,
- The short rebate worked, and
- Collateral must be maintained at the prime broker, as well as many other details.

Midway through the presentation, I realized that the amount of detailed information that the staff had prepared was beginning to build into an unwieldy pile for the fund trustees. It was at the point that I decided to distill into two sentences the essence of what the investment staff wanted to accomplish.

Was this statement an oversimplification? Perhaps. Did it convey the exact nature of what the investment staff wanted to do? Definitely. With this anecdote behind us, the real question remains: Why did CalPERS enter the world of long/short investing? To understand this issue, we need to look at a problem common to many investors, not just pension funds.

## BETA GRAZERS DRESSED UP LIKE ALPHA HUNTERS

In his great article on alpha hunters and beta grazers, Marty Leibowitz demonstrates that the asset management industry can be broken down into two simple camps: those that generate active returns—demonstrating a level of portfolio manager skill—and those that generate returns that mostly match the market return.[1] Even more bluntly, beta grazers are those asset managers that do little more than capture the systematic risk premium associated with an asset class. Passive/index managers are the classic example of a beta grazer, whereas hedge fund managers are often thought of as the best example of alpha hunters.

However, there are many beta grazers out there that try to disguise themselves as alpha hunters. Consider Exhibit F.1. This is a long-only active equity manager whose stated benchmark is the S&P 500. This manager currently has several billion dollars of assets under management. Consider how neatly this manager tracks the broad stock market. The beta of this active portfolio is 1.000 (yes, I really did carry out the beta calculation to three decimal places) and the R-Square measure is 0.994. More visually, notice that compared to the S&P 500, this active manager produces a nice straight line.

This is one of the first lessons of beta management: Beta grazers are linear in their performance. By this, I mean that when you compare a beta grazer to its benchmark, you should see a straight line of the type presented in Exhibit F.1. The straighter the line, the more the active manager is a beta grazer despite any claims to the contrary.

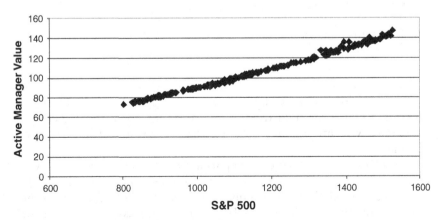

**EXHIBIT F.1**   Large-Cap Active Equity Manager: Beta = 1.000, R-Square = 0.994

In addition, this alpha hunter maintains well over 200 positions in its portfolio, many held for risk management purposes. This means that many of the stocks in the portfolio are not held for their alpha generating capability, but rather, are held passively to balance the portfolio back to the benchmark. There is no conviction with respect to the bulk of the securities in this portfolio; many of the stocks held are there to capture the systematic risk premium associated with the S&P 500.

Unfortunately, the performance of this product matches its hidden beta grazer status. It has consistently underperformed the S&P 500 for the last five years by about 55 to 60 basis points (bps) per year—approximately equal to its management fee of 55 bps and trading costs of about 10 bps per year.

## THE CURRENT BUSINESS MODEL FOR ASSET OWNERS AND ASSET MANAGERS

Unfortunately, the current business model for most asset owners (pension funds, endowment funds, retail investors, and high net worth investors) as well as for asset managers is: beta trumps alpha.

- Most investors first make the strategic allocation to broad asset classes.
- Then asset managers are directed to squeeze alpha out of the asset owner's strategic benchmarks. But the strategic benchmarks are designed to be efficiently constructed to measure risk premiums associated with different asset classes.
- As a result, alpha and beta are packaged together in traditional long-only products.
- The result is frequently much more beta than alpha (see Exhibit F.1).
- And, alpha risk budgets are typically spent in the most efficient markets, like large cap equity.

To break out of this conundrum, a new business model must be established: Alpha is sought independently of beta:

- Alpha should not be captive to beta.
- Alpha risk budgets should be spent in the least efficient markets:
  - High yield, distressed debt, private equity, small cap, emerging markets, absolute return, real estate, corporate governance.
  - These subasset classes have the least efficient benchmarks and, therefore, the highest alpha content.

So what does this really mean? Investors must break away from the traditional asset allocation model of trying to extract alpha from beta drivers.

■ Beta grazers are not designed to outperform the market—they provide efficient exposure to broad asset classes, and should capture these risk premiums as cheaply as possible.

Conversely, alpha hunters are designed to outperform the market, often without regard for *benchmark boxes*—style boxes should be used when an investor believes that it has the least amount of talent or insight to add value.

■ Investors must reduce their reliance on beta grazers to generate excess returns.
■ In seeking active returns, asset owners should commit their investment capital to those sub-asset classes where asset managers have the best opportunity to add value—look for the cracks in between benchmark boxes.

130/30 products are a natural extension away from benchmark boxes. They seek to exploit the cracks that exist between the more efficient long-only market and the less efficient short market. When an active manager conducts research to construct an active portfolio, she inevitably comes across good and bad stock bets. In the traditional benchmark box of the long-only world, the negative information concerning the bad stock bets cannot be fully exploited. 130/30 products allow asset owners and asset managers to break out of this way of thinking to fully exploit an active manager's information set.

## THE FUNDAMENTAL LAW OF ACTIVE MANAGEMENT

The added value produced by portfolio managers can best be summarized by the Law of Active Management. This law was first proposed by Richard Grinold and later expanded by Clarke, de Silva, and Thorley[2]:

$$IR = IC * TC * \sqrt{Breadth} \qquad F.1$$

where IR is the information ratio of an active manager measured *ex post* by

$$\alpha/\sigma_\alpha \qquad F.2$$

where $\alpha$ is the excess return generated by the portfolio manager, and $\sigma_\alpha$ is the active risk taking or tracking error (TE) of the manager.

IC is the information coefficient of the portfolio manager. It is a measure of manager skill and typically gauged by

$$\text{Correlation (Forecasted returns, Actual returns)} \qquad \text{F.3}$$

TC is the transfer coefficient, where TC $\leq$ 1.0. This is a measure of how efficiently an active manager can translate her active bets into portfolio positions. Any amount of friction in the financial markets with respect to implementing an active portfolio position (portfolio constraints, trading costs, market impact, opportunity, cost) will reduce the TC below the value of 1.

Breadth is the number of independent bets that the active manager places in the portfolio.

Equation F.1 represents the calculus of active management. Every active portfolio manager is beholden to this rule. For example, a portfolio manager can develop a deep insight into a specific sector or industry, such as biotechnology. For her, the number of independent bets in her portfolio will be limited by her knowledge of this one industry; the breadth will be small. However, her IC should be large as she extracts as much competitive information from a smaller investment opportunity set. Conversely, other portfolio managers will follow several industries to increase the number of active bets (breadth) that they may place into the portfolio. Their trade-off is that their IC is likely to be smaller because they are trying to extract an informational advantage over a larger pool of investment candidates.

Exhibit F.2 summarizes the Fundamental Law of Active Management, and the several moving parts that can have an impact on portfolio

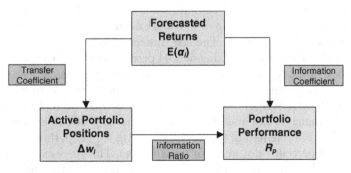

**EXHIBIT F.2**   The Generation of Information Ratios (IRs)

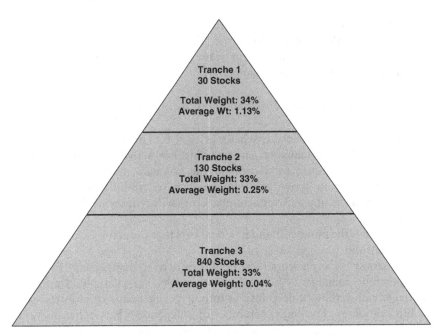

**EXHIBIT F.3**   The Capitalization of the Russell 1000 Stock Index

performance. The single largest constraint in active portfolio management is the long-only constraint. It is estimated that this constraint alone can reduce the TC by up to 40 percent.[3]

The limitation of the long-only constraint can best be demonstrated by Exhibit F.3. This exhibit shows a breakdown of the capitalization weighted Russell 1000 stock index, a common equity benchmark. One-third of the capitalization of this index is represented by only 30 stocks, where the average contribution to the capitalization of the index is 1.13 percent. The second tranche is made up of 130 stocks, with an average cap weighting in the index of 0.25 percent. The last tranche of the index consists of 840 stocks, with an average weighting of 0.04 percent. In fact, the median weight for a stock in the Russell 1000 stock index is 0.04 percent.

For active portfolio management, overweights in the portfolio must be funded with underweights. With the long-only constraint in place, the most a portfolio manager can underweight a stock in the portfolio is by its weight in the index. For one-half of the stocks in the Russell 1000, this underweight is only 0.04 percent—not much of an active bet. This forces an active manager to sell down more stocks from the first two terciles to fund the active overweights in the portfolio. Or, even more clearly, consider a portfolio

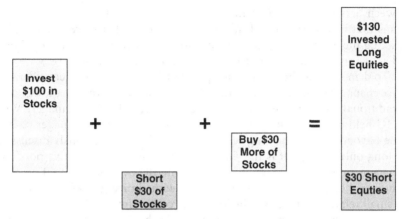

**EXHIBIT F.4**   Breaking Free of the Long-Only Constraint

manager whose strongest active overweight is with respect to a stock in the first tercile, whereas her most negative bet is with respect to a stock in the third tercile. This means that her ability to fund her strongest overweight is constrained to only 0.04 percent from the most negative underweight.

This problem is by no means limited to the Russell 1000 index. The median weight of a stock in the S&P 500 is only 10 basis points. The smallest 250 companies in the S&P 500 have an index weight of less than 10 basis points.

Exhibit F.4 demonstrates the advantage of relaxing the long-only constraint for 130/30 products. Additional funding is created for active overweights in the portfolio through the use of 30 percent short positions. The 30 percent short positions also increase the leverage of the portfolio. The total exposure to the market is 160 percent—the combination of both 30 percent short active positions with 130 percent long active positions.

Furthermore, the relaxation of the long-only constraint in 130/30 portfolios allows a manager to increase her IR along two dimensions. First, according to Equation F.1, the active manager can increase the number of active bets in the portfolio—expanding the breadth. In addition, the manager can increase the size of her bets—in effect, increasing her IC.

The improvement in the IR of an investment manager follows from the concavity of the return versus risk trade-off common to all actively managed investment products. For both traditional actively managed products and 130/30 products, an increase in TE ($\sigma[\alpha]$) leads to an increase in expected excess returns ($E[\alpha]$). With the long-only constraint in place, the relation between active risk taking and expected alpha is not proportional. This means that increases in risk lead to smaller and smaller increases in alpha. Relaxing the long-only constraint leads to a better trade-off between return and active risk taking. Exhibit F.4 demonstrates this trade-off.

To demonstrate the power and appeal of 130/30 investing, consider two active managers who have the same skill level as measured by the IC: one, a traditional long-only manager, and the other, a 130/30 manager. With the IC held constant, there are two ways for the 130/30 manager to add value beyond that of the long-only manager. First, as previously discussed, the long-only constraint is the single greatest constraint on active portfolio management and can reduce the TC (and the IR) by more than 40 percent. Although there are more costs associated with shorting stocks, these costs are small relative to relaxing the long-only constraint.[4]

Second, the breadth can be expanded by the 130/30 manager. In fact, the breadth can be expanded in two directions. First, more active long-only bets can be placed into the portfolio because the active manager now has the ability to short stocks to fund long positions that might otherwise not be implemented. Second, negative alpha bets that were previously limited through the long-only constraint may now be executed for the portfolio.

The simple mathematics of Equation F.1 demonstrate that if you can increase the TC or the breadth of the portfolio while holding the IC (manager skill) constant, the IR will increase. It really is not a fair fight between a long-only manager and a 130/30 manager.

## CORPORATE GOVERNANCE AND 130/30 INVESTING

Large institutional investors such as CalPERS are keen proponents of good corporate governance of public companies. Yet, the asset management industry, similar to any industry, is subject to good and bad corporate governance and the movement toward alpha/beta separation has improved the governance of this industry. Unfortunately, the existing paradigm for most of the asset management industry is still benchmark driven. Although benchmarks are a useful tool for performance measurement, they are also a significant constraint that reduces the IR of active managers. To achieve consistent alpha, investors must think outside the benchmark in the construction of their portfolios.

Consider a manager that is benchmarked to the S&P 500. This manager is allowed an active risk budget of 5 percent (TE of 5%). This means that the remaining 95 percent of the risk of the portfolio is geared to nothing more than matching the volatility of the benchmark. Why pay active management fees for the 95 percent that does nothing more than track the S&P 500? Again, this gets back to the governance in the asset management industry.

Here is another observation. Ten years ago—even five years ago—an active manager who went 130 percent long and 30 percent short would have called himself a hedge fund manager and typically charged a 2 percent management fee and a 20 percent incentive/profit sharing fee. With the advent of 130/30 products, with most of these products coming from the long-only side of the asset management industry, it is no longer enough for a hedge fund manager to short stocks to demand a 2 and 20 fee structure. Simply, 130/30 products have brought a better form of pricing governance to the asset management industry.

Managers of 130/30 products typically charge a management fee of 0.50 percent to 1.5 percent and a modest profit sharing fee—a far better governance arrangement with the client than a hedge fund would ever establish. Indeed, with the growing number of 130/30, 150/50, and 200/100 products coming to the market, one really has to question whether an equity long/short hedge fund can maintain its 2 and 20 pricing structure.

In summary, 130/30 products have brought transparency into the world of long/short investing, and this is one way to improve the governance in the asset management industry. A clear identification of what is beta and what is alpha goes a long way toward establishing fair and proper pricing. Transparency is a key element of every good governance regime and it can mitigate four risks associated with the *asymmetric relationship* between asset owners and asset managers:

- Asset managers have much better information as to their true level of skill or alpha-producing ability, as measured by their IC, because the IC is not directly observable by asset owners. The implication is that it is incumbent upon asset managers to make their investment process as transparent as possible to the asset owners, which will lead to more efficient pricing of investment products.
- Furthermore, this asymmetry of information between asset managers and asset owners is exacerbated because the investment process or risk taking by the asset manager is not perfectly observable by the asset owners. It is only after the asset manager has produced a return stream and the beta components have been accounted for that alpha can be observed. Therefore, *ex ante*, asset managers have much better information about their alpha-producing skills, whereas *ex post* asset owners need to observe this skill.

- Asset owners only get a snapshot of their portfolio at any point in time. The amount or risk that is embedded in the portfolio, as well as the investment process by which the portfolio was constructed, may not be transparent.
- Asset managers know how much beta they deliver with their alpha. In the traditional governance structure, asset owners receive a combination of alpha and beta from asset managers. In fact, because many asset managers are still driven by benchmark-style investing, there is much more beta than alpha in their investment products. This leads to beta grazers dressed up like alpha hunters.

## CONCLUSIONS AND A CAUTIONARY NOTE

130/30 investing has grown in popularity, acceptance, and demand. There are several reasons for the surge in this style of investing.

First, smart investors want more active risk taking. As Exhibit F.1 demonstrates, what is sold as active management can often turn out to be a disguised beta grazer. Active risk taking has declined significantly over the last several years as the dispersion across stocks has decreased. Although most investors would say that they want less rather than more dispersion in their portfolio returns, greater dispersion in stock returns provides larger opportunities for active managers to add value. The long-only constraint locks an active manager into an environment of lower dispersion.

Second, both asset owners and asset managers have come to understand the Fundamental Law of Active Management and its implications for long-only portfolios. The long-only constraint is now widely recognized as the most limiting constraint on the ability for an active manager to generate excess returns.

Finally, less constrained investing has become much more accepted. Hedge funds, absolute return managers, private equity, credit derivatives, commodities, and other forms of alternative assets have expanded the investment opportunity set for asset owners. 130/30 products are the natural extension for both traditional active managers seeking less constrained portfolio management, as well as hedge fund managers moving into more mainstream asset management.

We should note that not all is apple pie with 130/30 strategies; there are additional risks. These strategies appeal both to asset managers and asset owners, but there are many moving parts associated with 130/30 strategies. The most important piece is the ability to borrow stock from a prime broker from which to sell short. Stock can sometimes be hard to borrow, particularly those stocks that are in the lower capitalization range. Also, borrowed stock can be recalled by its owner, forcing the portfolio manager to cover her short position before maximizing the value of her position. In fact, 130/30 managers can sometimes be subject to short squeezes in which the covering of their short positions in the open market results in quick increases in the price of the underlying stock and a reduction of the short sale profits. And, short positions, in theory, can have unlimited risk associated with them because the stock price can—again, in theory—increase forever. This last criticism is a favorite one of consultants to throw out in their resistance to long/short strategies, but with the increase of intelligent risk management and trading systems, this risk is significantly minimized.

These cautionary notes are not meant to diminish the appeal of 130/30 strategies. They are simply meant to indicate that although 130/30 strategies have the potential to add significant value, there are also some additional risks associated with their implementation. However, these risks are far outweighed by the opportunity to improve the IR of the asset manager. Their potential is real and valuable. Furthermore, 130/30 products have brought better pricing governance to at least one part of the alternative investment universe—long/short hedge fund investing. So, understand the risks, but enjoy the benefits.

Mark Anson
President and Executive Director
of Investment Services
Nuveen Investments, Inc.

# NOTES

1. See M. Leibowitz, 2005, "Alpha Hunters and Beta Grazers," *Financial Analysts Journal*, September/October.
2. See R. Grinold, 1989, "The Fundamental Law of Active Management," *The Journal of Portfolio Management*, Spring, pp. 30–37; and R. Clarke, H. de Silva, and S. Thorley, 2002, "Portfolio Constraints and the Fundamental Law of Active Management," *Financial Analysts Journal*, September/October, pp. 48–66.
3. See Clarke, de Silva, and Thorley, 2002.
4. See M. Leibowitz, 2005, "Alpha Hunters and Beta Grazers," *Financial Analysts Journal*, September/October.

# Structure of the Book

This book is divided into four parts.

Part One includes Chapter 1, "Active 130/30 Extensions and Diversified Asset Allocations," by Martin Leibowitz and Anthony Bova. It describes the key features of active extension (AE) strategies and highlights their ability to improve an equity portfolio's alpha at the cost of increased tracking error (TE).

Part Two, written by Simon Emrich, consists of two chapters: Chapter 2, "Active Extension—Portfolio Construction," and Chapter 3, titled "Managing Active Extension Portfolios." A framework is developed that separates a portfolio into a part that is responsible for benchmark returns and one responsible for the excess, alpha-driven returns. In a long-only portfolio, the active component is asymmetric, consisting of a relatively concentrated long position in the overweights and a relatively diversified short position in the underweights. As the long-only constraint is relaxed, both the risk and return in the portfolio increase. First, the weight in the alpha component can be simply scaled up. This will increase the risk and return of the portfolio proportionately, so the risk-adjusted return will not change. Second, the structure of the alpha component can be changed to take the alpha views better into account. Emrich also presents empirical evidence of the non-normality of stock returns over time. These fat tails have important implications for the risk management of AE portfolios.

Part Three is a compilation of various articles written by Martin Leibowitz and Anthony Bova that were published as Morgan Stanley Portfolio Notes over the 2005 to 2008 period. These articles address various aspects of the AE approach to equity management. Each Note is intended to be self-contained, so that the reader can focus his or her attention on specific areas of immediate interest. As a consequence, there is some degree of overlap across these papers.

Chapter 4, "Active Extension Portfolios: An Exploration of the 120/20 Concept," was the first article written by Leibowitz and Bova on AE. The increased flexibility for active equity management that AE provides allows a wider range of alpha-seeking opportunities for both traditional and quantitative management. Active extensions open the door to a fresh set of actively chosen underweight positions that are limited in long-only portfolios. With proper risk control, an AE should entail TE that is only moderately greater than that of a comparable long-only fund.

Chapter 5, "Alpha Ranking Models and Active Extension Strategies," shows how alpha ranking models can be useful for analyzing the structure of AEs (as well as providing useful insights for traditional long-only strategies). With a moderately declining alpha ranking, AE provides increasing alpha/TE ratio (information ratio [IR]) benefits that begin to peak with short percentages somewhere in the 40 to 60 percent region. For a more concentrated ranking model, the optimal shorting percentage is in the 10 to 20 percent range.

Chapter 6, "The Tracking Error Gap," explores the difference between theoretical projections of the TE and actual TEs seen in practice. This TE gap is usually due to some form of correlation or factor effect across the active positions. If the TEs from active equity management are truly uncorrelated, they are likely to be beta dominated and, therefore, play a very minor role in the standard volatility of the overall fund. However, there is a danger that such correlation/factor effects could accumulate across managers and represent a more significant source of fund-level risk.

Chapter 7, "Correlation Effects in Active Extension 120/20 Strategies," explores how factor correlations can affect the potential rewards from AEs. These correlations, even at a minimal level, can have a significant effect on the TE and can, therefore, have a meaningful impact on portfolio performance. In AE portfolios, these correlations may lie within the long positions, within the short positions, and/or between the long and short positions. One of the benefits of AE is the opportunity to use the short positions to offset factor effects within the long portfolio. Such offsets can sharpen the intended exposures by removing extraneous risk factors, thereby leading to materially improved IRs.

Chapter 8, "Alpha Returns and Active Extensions," presents empirical evidence that a wide range of active portfolios can be approximated by exponentially declining alpha rankings and position weightings. The actual sequential weights seen in practice provide confirmation that portfolios are at least roughly structured along these lines. These alpha/weighting models can be used to explore how AEs (and active portfolios in general) can generate alpha returns subject to prescribed risk limits.

Chapter 9, "An Integrated Analysis of Active Extension Strategies," looks at the impact of various weighting patterns for long and/or short active positions. With the assumption of a constant residual volatility for each active position, the theoretically optimal weighting for each position should be proportional to its alpha ranking. However, one key finding is that for a moderately declining alpha ranking, the alpha/TE ratio is little changed by different, but still reasonable, weighting patterns.

Chapter 10, "Portfolio Concentration," further explores how various active weighting patterns relate to different alpha rankings. It turns out that higher alphas and still near-optimal IRs can be derived from weights that are significantly more concentrated than the theoretically optimal. Because most funds have significant unused capacity for active risk, more concentrated active structures can enhance the alpha prospects while sustaining near-optimal IRs. Optimal solutions are usually defined in terms of a maximum IR of alpha to TE, but there may be situations in which a sponsor may seek a greater alpha at the expense of a higher TE and a lower IR.

Chapter 11, "Generic Shorts in Active 130/30 Extensions," discusses the use of customized generic shorts in AE portfolios. Active portfolios often embed factor exposures that are less than fully productive in alpha terms. An appropriate basket of generics can limit unwanted factor effects, lower TEs, and improve IRs. These generics can be thought of as style/sector-specific instruments, such as exchange-traded funds (ETFs) or tailored baskets that are tied to an existing factor in the long-only portfolio. Even though these generic shorts may have zero alphas, they can still provide benefits in terms of providing reinvestable funds and correlation offsets.

Chapter 12, "Beta-Based Asset Allocation," demonstrates that U.S. equity is the primary risk factor in most U.S. institutional portfolios. The explicit equity percentage is exposure as an inadequate risk gauge of beta risk. The correlations of each asset class with U.S. equities can provide an implicit beta measure that can be used to determine a fund's total beta. This total beta approach suggests that most U.S. institutional funds share three surprising characteristics:

1. Total volatilities in the 10 to 11.50 percent range,
2. 90 percent or greater correlation between fund performance and U.S. equities, and
3. Total implicit beta values between 0.55 and 0.65.

Chapter 13, "Beta Targeting: Tapping into the Appeal of 130/30 Active Extensions," shows how having a well-defined beta, even if different from the beta-1 standard, can provide 130/30 extension-like characteristics. The essential feature is having a targeted beta that can act as an expected value, together with a sufficiently low beta volatility. This expectational form of beta targeting allows a broader range of active equity strategies to fall in the AE category. Beta-targeted strategies also help to more clearly identify the true level of alpha performance.

Chapter 14, "Activity Ratios: Alpha Drivers in Long/Short Funds," focuses on a fund's activity level—the aggregate weight of all meaningfully sized active long and short positions as the determinant of the basic alpha characteristics. It turns out that the IR depends largely on the activity ratio (AR)—the short activity divided by the long activity. With a given AR, the expected alpha and TE both increase (or contract) proportionally with the long activity level acting as a scaling factor. Thus, funds with the same AR can be viewed as simply rescaled versions of one another with respect to their intrinsic alpha-producing potential. By moving from active to generic positions, or vice versa, a fund can adjust its activity levels to achieve a given AR and activity scale. With beta and AR flexibility, some long/short funds can be reshaped to serve as more generalized versions of a 130/30 or 150/50 AE.

Chapter 15, "Generalizations of the Active 130/30 Extension Concept," discusses a number of generalizations of the basic AE format that offer the promise of higher alphas while still retaining the AE's essential structural features and risk characteristics. These generalized AE-Plus strategies may not necessarily have a 100 percent net exposure or beta target of 1. The key to this broader extension umbrella is to establish a well-defined beta-target, which may be smaller than beta-1, and a stable net investment basis (even though that need not be 100 percent). It is the clear-cut distinction between beta and alpha risk that represents the hallmark of such generalized AE-Plus funds.

Part Four reproduces, in chronological order, papers that were published from 1998 to 2008 in external journals, such as the *Financial Analysts Journal, Journal of Portfolio Management,* and *Journal of Investment Management.*

Numerous authors have contributed to the theory and methodology of long/short strategies. Part Four contains two papers from three groups of the most influential authors on this topic. Their unique perspective should aid the reader in better understanding the complexities around this important topic. These authors discuss both long/short investing in general as well as hone in on the particular issues that arise from active 130/30 extension portfolios. Each group of authors has chosen both a classic paper that discusses key principles of long/short investing, and a more contemporary paper that reflects their more recent thoughts. The three papers from 1998 to 2004 reflect the earlier work of these influential authors on long/short active equity and the origins of the 130/30 concept.

Bruce Jacobs and Ken Levy derived formulas for optimal active long/short portfolios. The relative sizes of the active and benchmark exposures depend on the investor's desired residual risk within the framework of a minimum variance active portfolio. They also show that all long and short positions must be simultaneously integrated in the construction of optimal long/short portfolios. The correlations between long and short positions play a large role in determining the risk of a portfolio.

Richard Grinold and Ronald Khan focused on their Fundamental Law of Active Management and its role in determining the IR of a portfolio. They show empirically how the movement into long/short investing offers significant benefits over long-only investing. Long/short implementations are particularly advantageous when the universe of assets is large, asset volatility is low, and the strategy has high active risk. The long-only constraint induces capitalization biases, limits the manager's ability to act on good insights, and reduces the efficiency of active strategies relative to enhanced index (low-risk) long-only strategies.

Roger Clarke, Harindra de Silva, Steven Sapra, and Steven Thorley extended Grinold and Kahn's Fundamental Law of Active Management with the development of the portfolio transfer coefficient. They show that the ability to take even modest short positions provides an important structural advantage that can improve the information efficiency of traditional long-only portfolios. Investors do not need to relax the long-only constraint completely to reap substantial benefits as relaxing the constraint by just 10 to 20 percent can be advantageous. This modest relaxation of the long-only constraint results in a disproportionate improvement in the information transfer from security valuation to active portfolio weights.

It was the convergence of these insights that leads to the realization that the 20 percent level of shorting in a 120/20 fund can become broadly acceptable while still capturing a large percentage of the benefits available from more flexible long/short portfolios.

The later 2007 to 2008 papers present the more recent thinking of these authors and their associates who have played such a key role in the development of this area. In addition, we have included several journal articles by Leibowitz and Bova that relate to AE and related issues.

# Acknowledgments

The authors would like to acknowledge Morgan Stanley, generally, and Research Management, specifically, for their encouragement and support of these studies on 130/30 active extension. The development of this concept was greatly facilitated by early writers who explored how loosening the long-only constraint could lead to a much wider range of risk-controlled equity portfolios. This extraordinary analytic background was framed by such thought leaders as Rob Arnott, Peter L. Bernstein, Roger Clarke, Harinda de Silva, Richard Grinold, Thomas Hewett, Bruce Jacobs, Ronald Kahn, Kenneth Levy, Robert Litterman, Harry Markowitz, Richard Michaud, Kenneth Winston, and many others.

We are especially grateful to the authors and their co-authors who have made their landmark journal articles available for publication in this volume. These papers have continuing relevance within the investment field, and their inclusion surely represents a substantial contribution to the value of this volume.

This book would not have gotten to the starting gate without the initiative, vision, and "push" of Bill Falloon. Helen of Troy may have launched many ships, but Bill Falloon has surely launched even more books—and hopefully for better causes! In addition, we must express our gratitude to the many wonderful people at Wiley who put forth a very special effort—Emilie Herman, Laura Walsh, Meg Freeborn, and all those others who worked behind the scenes to bring this work to fruition in a timely fashion.

Finally, the authors would like to thank the many clients and colleagues who helped to forge the ideas and to shape the practice of this exciting new initiative in active investment management.

# Introduction

# Evolution of the Active Extension Concept

The early motivation behind the development of active extensions (AEs) came from plan sponsors who wanted to generate more active returns from their basic equity allocation. In a number of cases, these plans were intrigued by the attractive performance results of various long/short and market neutral strategies. However, most investment offices and their boards were not yet prepared to embrace high levels of shorting and forgo the benchmark-centric discipline of traditional long-only portfolios.

The benefits of moving to a long/short framework had been well described by several theoretical and empirical studies published by Jacobs and Levy (1993, 1995, 1999, 2006), Kahn and Grinold (2000a, b, c), and others. In 2002, building on these earlier studies, Clarke, de Silva, and Thorley (2002) introduced the concept of the "transfer coefficient" that could measure how efficiently active insights are projected into a given portfolio structure. Their study showed that a significant enhancement of the transfer coefficient could be achieved by having the flexibility to short a modest 20 percent of the original asset value. With productive active insights and appropriate risk discipline, the higher transfer coefficient should translate into enhanced alpha returns.

Moreover, this benefit could be achieved while maintaining the key risk characteristics of long-only funds, that is, 100 percent net long, a beta-1 target, and a relatively modest tracking error (TE). In addition to this theoretical argument, funds that had been previously long-only found this 20 percent figure to represent a more palatable "baby step" into the new realm of shorting.

In a 120/20 fund, the basic 100 percent long-only format is extended by allowing shorts amounting to 20 percent of the original asset value, with the 20 percent proceeds being reinvested back into new or existing long positions. The shorting/reinvestment process is carried out to maintain the same beta-1 value as the original long-only portfolio. The resulting portfolio is thus 120 percent gross long and 20 percent gross short. Hence, the designation: 120/20 fund.

Virtually every equity market is highly concentrated, with a small number of stocks with large capitalizations and a much larger number of lower-capitalization companies. In a long-only portfolio, the ability to take significant underweight positions is usually limited to the small number of stocks with large capitalizations. By allowing a limited facility to short stocks within a risk-controlled framework, 120/20 strategies allow more significant views to be expressed in the lower-cap stocks.

The return enhancement benefits for these strategies are derived from a number of interacting sources:

1. More appropriate sizing of previously existing active underweights across the broader range of securities having low percentage weights within the reference index;
2. The additional opportunities in the low capitalization (and less intensively researched) companies that become "freshly" available because they are now candidates for significant active underweighting;
3. New or enhanced active long positions funded by reinvestment of the short proceeds;
4. Portfolio benefits from a wider "breadth" of potential active positions on both an overweight and underweight basis;
5. Use of shorts to offset unproductive sector and style effects within the long portfolio (and vice versa);
6. More intensive active positions made possible by removing extraneous factors and sharpening the focus on key decision parameters.

## THE EVOLUTION OF ACTIVE EXTENSION: THE CALPERS BREAKTHROUGH

One story told by a manager at an industry conference was about how his firm got involved in AE. The firm had been using the same methodology to run both a large base of long-only assets and a much smaller market neutral portfolio. Over a recent period, the market-neutral fund had generated better returns. An existing client who was only involved with their long-only product asked how they could achieve the superior performance of the market-neutral fund. When the manager replied that all the client had to do was simply to switch his fund to the market-neutral product, the client responded that his board would never accept that high level of shorting.

The manager then asked whether they might consider a little shorting— 10 percent, 20 percent? After some analysis, it became evident that a significant (and actually disproportionate) benefit could be obtained by allowing only 20 percent shorts within a properly deigned management framework.

As concerns receded about the ability of previously long-only managers to efficiently manage a subportfolio of shorts, 120/20s morphed into 130/30s and 140/40s, and even the occasional 175/75s. At this point, the majority of portfolios fall into the 130/30 to 150/50 range. As more varied levels of shorting became common, these funds soon became known by more generic names such as "active extensions." The term active extension (AE) was coined to convey that, rather than being a quantum leap into alternative assets, these strategies were designed as an incremental "extension" of the risk structure of standard active long-only funds.

A major breakthrough occurred in February 2006, when the $212B California Public Employees' Retirement System (CalPERS), under the leadership of Mark Anson, approved the issuance of a Request-for-Proposal for US AE managers. To date, $3B has been deployed by CalPERS into AE strategies. This "Sacramento Blessing" provided comfort to other US pension funds that relaxing the long-only constraint within this risk-controlled framework was an acceptable way to pursue higher levels of alpha.

## BOTH QUANT AND FUNDAMENTAL STYLES

Quantitative managers were the first to become significantly involved in AE, and they continue to represent the majority of assets under management. For the "quants," moving from long-only to AE was relatively easy because their models already provided ranking scores for a large universe of stocks. Active positions in the more highly ranked securities could always be appropriately sized by overweights. However, within long-only portfolios, the lower rankings could be expressed through minimal or zero holdings. For smaller capitalization stocks, such nonholdings represented a frustrating limit on the more severe underweightings called for by the quant models.

With the flexibility to short, these portfolios could now put in place underweight positions that were more appropriate for these low-scored securities. The cash proceeds from the short sales could then be reinvested into their more highly scored stocks.

For fundamental managers, rankings are typically expressed more implicitly in terms of conviction "tiers." With the underweights in a fundamental portfolio, the question arises of whether the manager is actively avoiding certain stocks or using the (generally fragmented) underweights simply as a source of funds.

Fundamental managers typically have more concentrated portfolios without the "breadth" found in quant portfolios. However, fundamental managers can certainly take advantage of the other benefits available in an AE framework—"fresh" underweights, enhanced and sharpened long positions, offset correlations,and so forth. Indeed, in some ways, the offset potential from the shorts may be even more valuable to fundamental managers who want to more precisely shape their concentrated exposures.

To this date, a relatively small number of fundamental managers have implemented AE strategies and have generally experienced good results. The more significant trend involves the larger number of both quantitative and fundamental managers that have "seeded" products internally and are intensively considering launching various AE products.

Many of the early AEs represented sponsor-initiated conversions of existing long-only mandates. Sponsors who already had a current relationship with active equity managers generally felt comfortable with their risk-control procedures and their ability to produce positive alphas over the long term. In essence, these sponsors were eager to enhance the alpha returns from the existing allocations to these managers. From the manager viewpoint, AEs call for a wider range of active positions and more intensive monitoring for the short positions. The reward was a deeper relationship with the sponsor and higher fees. The move to AE also opened the door to the potential for performance fees. As AE becomes more widely accepted, the earlier sponsor "push" gave way to managers playing more of a role in proposing conversions or using their experience to attract new relationships.

The already implemented AEs represent a significant trend, but it is even more impressive to see the large pipeline of both quantitative and fundamental products expected to come to the market over the next few years.

## THE FUND-LEVEL CONTEXT

It is worth trying to understand the basis for the evident attractiveness of the AE concept. At the outset, there is the increasingly pressing need to extract higher alphas from the basic equity allocation—an allocation that remains sizable in even the most diversified portfolios. There is also the related desire to tap into the typical fund's unused capacity for taking productive active risk. The AE framework is specifically designed to have TE that is largely uncorrelated with the underlying equity beta risk. With most institutional portfolios having beta as the overwhelmingly dominant risk factor, such uncorrelated TE risks are suppressed and translate only weakly into fund-level risk.

By applying a standard return/covariance matrix to a range of policy portfolios seen in practice, this beta effect can be seen to be the source of three common-risk characteristics shared by most funds: (1) total volatilities ranging from 10 to 11 percent, (2) a 90 percent or greater correlation with US equity movements, and (3) total "correlation-based" betas between 0.5 and 0.65. These high total beta values account for an overwhelming percentage of fund volatility. With funds all having similar total beta values, and with these betas accounting for most of the fund-level volatility, it is not surprising that virtually all funds have similar levels of volatility risk.

Given beta's central role, it is obviously important for an investment strategy to have the greatest possible clarity on its beta benchmark and for any incremental active risk to be reliably uncorrelated with the dominant beta risk. Active 130/30 extension strategies fit neatly into both these criteria. The beta is well defined, usually at the same beta-1 value as the standard long-only equity portfolio. This beta-1 specification allows AEs to be viewed as residing within the traditional equity space. Moreover, in the AE design, the alpha is clearly delineated so that the associated TE should be basically uncorrelated with the beta risk.

With this minimal beta correlation, any increased TE from AE should have only a small impact on fund-level volatility. Moreover, most institutional funds have far less active management than could be readily accommodated within their overall volatility limits. The challenge is to find active strategies that are:

- Productive (i.e., have the expectation of positive alpha over the long term), and
- Risk "contained" (i.e., where there is a definitive beta target and where the TE, even if sizable, has a reliably low correlation with the underlying beta risk).

It may be helpful to see where AE lies along a spectrum of strategies that stretches from indexing up to the most aggressive forms of macro management.

Beta "grazing" through passive indexing is the most alpha-free form of equity investment. A more active form is alpha hunting to capture skill-based incremental returns relative to a tightly specified benchmark. The TE may vary, but both the alpha return and TE are clearly intended to be defined within a benchmark-centric framework. A rather different approach entails moving beyond the traditional asset class boundaries to "gather" the higher returns available in new asset classes. This alpha gathering may or may not be "benchmark-centric," depending on the level of active management and the extent to which the fund's policy portfolio incorporates the new assets. Finally, there is the "foraging" for excess returns however and whenever they can be found. With this ultimately boundary-free flexibility, relative return and alphas obviously become harder to identify or measure.

Within this spectrum, AEs fall solidly within the benchmark-centric "alpha hunting" category.

## AE-PLUS GENERALIZATIONS

It can be argued that it is the constrained nature of alpha hunting that accounts for much of AE's appeal. With its beta-1 equity risk, its 100 percent net long base, and its clearly delineated alphas, AE represents only an "incremental" expansion of the standard forms of long-only active equity. Indeed, it is these more familiar and more comfortable features that enable AE strategies to be kept within the basic equity allocation rather than having to be thrust into the generally smaller allocation dedicated to "alternatives."

As noted earlier, TE that is largely uncorrelated with the fund's dominant beta risk will have very little impact on fund-level volatility risk. (This fund level effect is one reason why the information ratio should not constitute the sole yardstick for judging the benefits from a given AE).

The basic motivation behind the AE initiative was the desire for more alpha return without taking on directional leverage or moving too far afield from standard equity management. To pursue higher alphas usually entails accepting higher TEs. However, as long as the mandates are reasonably diversified across management styles, the suppressive effect of the dominant beta will continue to hold for TEs considerably greater than the 3 to 4 percent associated with the typical 130/30 AE. This raises the question of whether more intrinsically active benchmark-centric strategies can still be accommodated within the general AE guidelines. It turns out that there are a number of generalizations of the basic AE format that offer the promise of higher alphas while retaining AE's essential structural features and risk characteristics so acceptable.

These generalized AE strategies may not necessarily have a 100 percent net exposure or beta target of 1. The key to this broader "extension" umbrella is to establish a well-defined beta-target, which may be smaller or larger than beta-1, and a stable net investment basis that need not be 100 percent. The targeted beta level could also be set at different levels, and it may not have to coincide with the net long position. One example of such generalized "AE-Plus" funds may be a 175/75 structure that remains 100 percent net long but has a somewhat lower beta of 0.7. This strategy may have the appeal for funds seeking higher alphas while reducing their overall beta exposure. Another AE-plus format may have the same 0.7 beta but with a 130 percent gross long and 60 percent gross short for a 70 percent net long position.

Rather than being a rigidly fixed value, the beta target can be more of a design objective that may vary from period to period. As long as the average realized beta matches the target value, it can be shown that the fund volatility will closely approximate the estimated level over time. With a stable beta target, an AE-plus strategy can be viewed as benchmark-centric with well-defined risk characteristics and clearly delineated alphas. Clarity of the beta risk level and the clear-cut distinction between beta and alpha risk represent the hallmarks of a generalized AE fund.

Many long/short managers as well as long-only managers have portfolio styles that are not pinned to specific beta values. However, their strategies often rotate around some average beta value. Such funds could be brought within the generalized AE framework by simply formalizing this preexisting average as a "beta target." This beta target need not be rigidly realized in every period, as long as it can be construed as a reasonable average value. With this flexibility, the managers can retain their basic investment style and have a basis to access the evident appeal of the AE framework.

In the course of time, one may expect to see convergence between the various types of long/short equity strategies. Benchmark-centric alpha-hunting strategies may come to encompass a wider range of long-only and long/short strategies. In addition to fitting within a fund's dominant beta risk, well-defined beta targets sharpen the measurement of both skill-based active alphas and the associated TEs. The resulting better delineation of alphas can facilitate the earlier and more reliable identification of the true level of skill embedded in a given performance history.

## REFERENCES

Clarke, R., H. de Silva, and S. Thorley. 2002. "Portfolio Constraints and the Fundamental Law of Active Management." *Financial Analysts Journal*. September/October.

Grinold, R. C., and R. Kahn. 2000a. "The Surprising Large Impact of the Long-Only Constraint." *Barclays Global Investors Investment Insights*. May.

Grinold, R. C., and R. Kahn. 2000b. "The Efficiency Gains of Long-Short Investing." *Financial Analysts Journal*. November/December.

Grinold, R. C., and R. Kahn. 2000c. "Active Portfolio Management: Quantitative Theory and Applications." McGraw Hill.

Jacobs, B. I., and K. N. Levy. 1993. "Long/Short Equity Investing: Profit from Both Winners and Losers." *Journal of Portfolio Management.* Fall.

Jacobs, B. I., and K. N. Levy. 1995. "More on Long-Short Strategies." *Financial Analysts Journal.* March/April.

Jacobs, B. I., and K. N. Levy. 1999. "Long/Short Portfolio Management: An Integrated Approach." *Journal of Portfolio Management.* Winter.

Jacobs, B. I., and K. N. Levy. 2006. "Enhanced Active Equity Strategies: Relaxing the Long-Only Constraint in the Pursuit of Active Returns." *Journal of Portfolio Management.* Spring.

# Active 130/30 Extensions and Diversified Asset Allocations

CHAPTER **1**

# Active 130/30 Extensions and Diversified Asset Allocations

**Anthony Bova**
Vice President
Morgan Stanley, Research

**Martin Leibowitz**
Managing Director
Morgan Stanley, Research

**V**irtually all asset allocations have risks that are dominated by a 90 percent or greater correlation with equities. This high correlation acts as an 800-pound equity gorilla lurking behind the multiasset façade of even the most diversified allocations. The dominance of equities as risk factors is generally known, but their many significant implications have yet to be fully incorporated into either the theory or the practice of investment management. One such implication relates to the opportunity for return enhancement from active extension (AE) 130/30 strategies.

Benchmark-centric equity strategies such as active 130/30 extensions aim to have tracking errors (TE) that are largely uncorrelated with equities. Within equity-dominated allocations, these uncorrelated TEs should have little impact on fund-level volatility risk. Positive alpha opportunities from these strategies can, therefore, be particularly valuable because they can significantly increase the fund's total return with only minor increases in the overall volatility or other forms of beyond-model risk. Moreover, because such strategies relate to the basic equity assets, they help minimize any stress beta effects from short-term correlation tightening.

Active extension strategies can be designed to fit within a sponsor's existing allocation space for active U.S. equity with TEs only moderately greater than that of a comparable long-only fund. The expanded

**11**

footings can open the door to a fresh set of active underweight positions and provide a wider range of alpha-seeking opportunities for both traditional and quantitative management. AE mandates are often conversions of pre-existing relationships in which the sponsor has grown comfortable with a manager's alpha-seeking skills, organization infrastructure, and risk-control procedures.

A growing body of studies has addressed the potential performance benefits that can be obtained by loosening the standard long-only constraint. The early work of Jacobs and Levy (1993, 1995, 1999, 2006) on risk-controlled, long/short equity portfolios created a body of literature that served as a foundation in this area. A further dimension was analytic framework for active management developed by Grinold (1989, 2005), Grinold and Eaton (1998), and Grinold and Kahn (2000a,b,c). In recent years, the 130/30 strategy has been the direct focus for an increasing number of theoretical studies, including key papers by Clarke, de Silva, and Thorley (2002, 2004, 2005) and Clarke (2005), with further contributions on this specific topic by Jacobs and Levy, Grinold and Kahn, as well as various studies by numerous other authors (Michaud, 1993; Arnott and Leinweber, 1994; Brush, 1997; Litterman, 2005; Markowitz, 2005; Bernstein, 2006; Emrich, 2006; Winston and Hewett, 2006). Two recent articles by Jacobs and Levy (2007a,b) provide a comprehensive review of how AE compares with traditional long-only and market-neutral strategies. The current authors have also published a series of papers from 2006 to 2007 on various topics related to AE (Leibowitz and Bova, 2006a, 2007f), including articles in the *Journal of Portfolio Management* (Leibowitz and Bova, 2007b) and *Journal of Investment Management* (Leibowitz and Bova, 2007d).

At the outset, it should be noted that there are important preconditions and cautionary points for achieving value-additive AE. First, the portfolio must be able to access positive long alphas. Second, it must have the risk discipline necessary to maintain the beta target and a reasonable level of TE. Third, the alpha productivity must be extendable into the short area. Shorting differs significantly from long-only management in a number of important ways, including higher transaction and maintenance costs, the available level and continuity of liquidity, the need for more intensive monitoring and risk control, and so on. To realize the potential benefits from AE, the management organization must also have the ability to establish short positions in a risk-controlled, operationally secure, and cost-efficient fashion.

The first section of this part describes the key features of AE strategies and highlights their ability to improve an equity portfolio's alpha at the cost of increasing TE. There are a number of considerations, such as position size limits, use of generics versus active positions, and so on, that come into play when analyzing AE strategies and that can affect the results. The second section discusses AEs from the point of view of the asset owner as a way to add alpha to the overall fund return with only modest increases in overall fund risk. The higher TE from AE can be shown to be largely submerged within the beta risk that dominates the volatility of the overall fund. Moreover, AE strategies should be able to avoid the equity-correlated TEs and stress betas that could complicate the risk structure of other forms of active management.

## ACTIVE MANAGEMENT WITH ALPHA RANKING MODELS

In a benchmark-centric management process, a portfolio is structured to maintain a targeted beta relative to the stated benchmark. An active position is then based on the expectation of a positive return in excess of the security's beta-adjusted return. Portfolio managers generally have some formal or informal process for classifying these prospective active positions in a descending sequence based on their expected excess return. Alpha ranking models can be used to approximate such classifications. The base case ranking model in Exhibit 1.1 is based on an exponential alpha decay with a beginning alpha of 5 percent that declines to 1.5 percent by the 25th position.

An active position is established by assigning a differential weight to the security that is above (or below) its weight in the benchmark. Note that even in long-only portfolios, active positions can take the form of either overweights or underweights. However, the exposition is greatly simplified by treating the long-only active positions as if they were all overweights. The long-only portfolio, therefore, consists of 25 active positions, each having a 2 percent weight for a net activity level of 50 percent. The remaining nonproactive component of the portfolio is assumed to serve as a source of funds, as well as to help maintain the fund's target beta.

The alpha contribution of each active position is represented by the product of its alpha (from the alpha ranking model) and its 2 percent active weight. The sum of all such alpha contributions adds up to the expected portfolio alpha. As shown in Exhibit 1.2, for the 25 position long-only portfolio, the cumulative alpha attains a level of 1.5 percent.

The key for both fundamental and quantitative managers in moving from a long-only to an AE portfolio is to have some sort of alpha ranking system. For quantitative managers, this is quite easy because their models

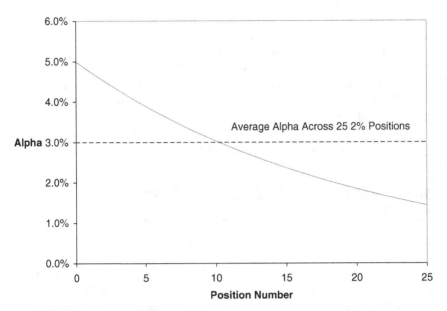

**EXHIBIT 1.1**   Alpha Ranking Model
*Source:* Morgan Stanley Research

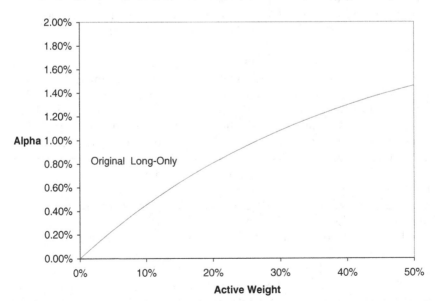

**EXHIBIT 1.2**   Portfolio Alpha
*Source:* Morgan Stanley Research

typically already rank all stocks in their universe. However, for fundamentals managers, the ranking system may be more implicitly expressed in terms of conviction tiers. The question for fundamental managers becomes whether they were actively avoiding certain stocks by underweighting them, or simply using these underweights as a source of funds.

## TRACKING ERROR MODELS

With the target beta pinned down by assumption, the remaining source of volatility risk is the portfolio's TE. The three factors that determine the TE are the residual volatilities of each position, the portfolio weightings, and the correlations or factor effects that exist between the positions.

At the security level, the TE is simply the residual volatility of the excess return; that is, the standard deviation of the security's return above or below its beta-adjusted market return. At the portfolio level, when the portfolio beta is tightly targeted at 1, the TE measures the deviation of portfolio returns around the benchmark.

With uncorrelated positions in the long-only portfolios, projected TEs in the range of 1 to 2 percent will be well below the observed TEs of 4 percent or higher seen in most actively managed portfolios. This discrepancy between the observed TEs and the theoretical uncorrelated values implies that there is typically some degree of correlation among the various positions. These correlations, even at a minimal level, can have a significant effect on the TE and can, therefore, have a meaningful impact on portfolio performance.

Exhibit 1.3 shows how the TE grows as positions are added to the long-only portfolio under assumed pairwise correlations ($\rho_L$) of zero and +0.05. For the 25-position long portfolio, the TE ends up at 2 percent for the uncorrelated case, and at 3 percent for an assumed +0.05 pairwise correlation among all 25 active positions. Thus, it takes only a slight increase in pairwise correlation to generate significant increases in the TE.

## THE ACTIVE EXTENSION

The ability to take short positions provides access to a fresh set of underweights. These new underweights are assumed to have alphas that coincide with the corresponding long-only alpha ranking model, less some given shorting cost, taken to be 0.50 percent in the base case example. The shorter, dashed line that starts at a 4.50 percent alpha in Exhibit 1.4 schematically depicts a 30 percent AE. In essence, these new underweights are picking off

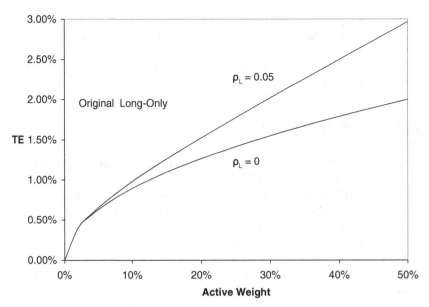

**EXHIBIT 1.3**  Uncorrelated versus Correlated TE
*Source:* Morgan Stanley Research

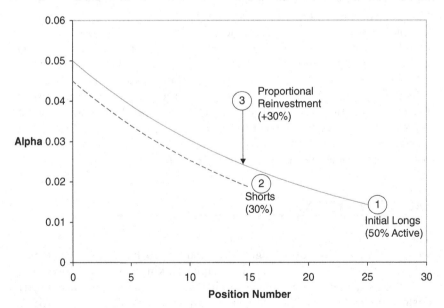

**EXHIBIT 1.4**  AE: Proportional Reinvestment
*Source:* Morgan Stanley Research

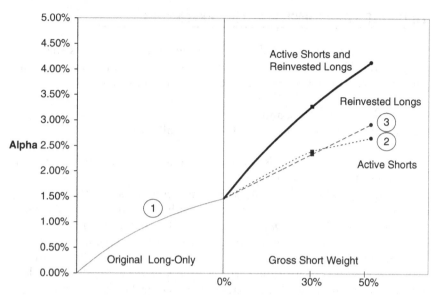

**EXHIBIT 1.5**   Alpha versus Gross Short Weight
*Source:* Morgan Stanley Research

the early cream of the alpha ranking curve. The gross short weight determines the number of 2 percent positions in the short portfolio while adding proportionally to the size of the 25 long positions.

Exhibit 1.5 displays the build of the cumulative alpha from the (1) initial long-only portfolio (25 position/50% active weight), (2) the new active shorts, and (3) the enhanced long position funded by the reinvested proceeds. With the combination of the added short alphas and proportional reinvestment into the long alphas, the portfolio alpha rises from 1.5 percent in the long-only case to 3.3 percent for the 30 percent extension, and 4.1 percent for the 50 percent extension.

The size of potential alpha improvement often seems disproportional given the modest 30 percent or so level of extension. This seemingly high alpha effect becomes more understandable when the extension percentage is placed in the context of a portfolio's activity level. A long-only portfolio with a 100 percent gross weight will typically have active weights in the 50 to 60 percent range. Thus, a combination of a 30 percent AE and a corresponding 30 percent reinvestment has the potential to double the activity level of the original long-only portfolio. Indeed, it was a recognition of this high-powered impact of even a 120/20 extension that motivated some of the early interest in these strategies.

## TRACKING ERROR UNDER ACTIVE EXTENSION

As the extension process adds new positions and/or augments the active weights, the TE increases accordingly. In the earlier discussion of the long-only portfolio, there were two different correlation assumptions:

1. Totally uncorrelated, and
2. A pairwise correlation of +0.05 between all positions.

The uncorrelated case is the most optimistic, leading to significantly smaller TEs than the correlated case.

In moving to the AE, this discussion on correlations becomes somewhat more complicated. The most conservative path would be to assume positive correlations of +0.05 *within* the long portfolio ($\rho_L$) and *within* the short portfolio ($\rho_S$). By itself, this assumption would lead to significantly greater TEs, as the short weight expands. However, with a long/short portfolio structure, the treatment of the correlation $\rho_{L,S}$ *between* the short and long positions can also have a meaningful impact on the TE.

Exhibit 1.6 displays three different cases of correlations between the longs and shorts. In the case, $\rho_{L,S} = +0.05$, the new short positions reinforce the factor risks present in the long portfolio. The TE expansion is much more

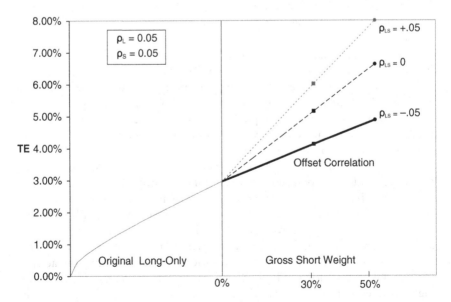

**EXHIBIT 1.6**   TE and the Long/Short Correlation
*Source:* Morgan Stanley Research

severe due to the continued emphasis on the same factor risks. With a zero pairwise correlation between the longs and shorts, they are assumed to be subject to different factor risks. The independence of the two factor risks materially reduces the TE. With a $-0.05$ offset correlation between the long and short positions, the short offsets act to significantly lower the TE. This offset case shows one of the potential benefits of AE as the short portfolio takes out unproductive factor effects within the long portfolio, such as an excessive size or growth bias.

With a positive correlation between the longs and shorts ($\rho_{L,S} = +0.05$), the portfolio is essentially reinforcing its risk exposures, which leads to significant increases in TE. At 30 percent extension, the TE rises to 6 percent, as more correlated positions are added to the portfolio. With a zero pairwise correlation between the longs and shorts, the TE is slightly lower at 5.2 percent for the 30 percent extension. However, to achieve the lowest possible TE curve, short positions are needed that can act as offsets to the longs ($\rho_{L,S} = -0.05$).

## INFORMATION RATIOS

Exhibit 1.7 combines the alphas and TEs from Exhibits 1.5 and 1.6 to form alpha/TE or information ratio (IR) curves for each scenario. With $\rho_{L,S} = +0.05$ and $\rho_{L,S} = 0$, the IRs rise at the outset, peak at 0.55 and 0.63 at extension weights of 20 percent and 30 percent, respectively, and then decline slightly with further extensions. In the $\rho_{L,S} = -0.05$ case, the TE drops significantly due to the offsetting correlation, enabling the IR to rise to 0.79 for a 30 percent extension and ultimately reaching 0.85 at a 50 percent weight.

Exhibit 1.8 plots these same three correlation cases in alpha versus TE space. All cases have the same 3.3 percent alpha at 30 percent and 4.1 percent alpha at 50 percent. However, the TEs are quite different, with the $\rho_{L,S} = +0.05$ and $\rho_{L,S} = 0$ both exceeding a TE of 5 percent, even before reaching the 30 percent extension level. In contrast, the $\rho_{L,S} = -0.05$ maintains a TE below 5 percent even for a 50 percent extension. Thus, it can be seen that AE strategies can benefit significantly by making good use of this offset potential.

## USING GENERICS IN ACTIVE EXTENSION

One of the key benefits from AE is derived from the opportunity to augment both the active long and short positions in the portfolio. However, there may be situations when limited active opportunities are on either the long or the short side, resulting in a need to complete with generic investment vehicles. Generic investments that correspond to the equity benchmark can

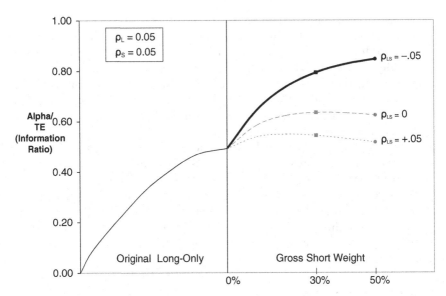

**EXHIBIT 1.7**   Alpha/TE Ratio for Different Long/Short Correlations
*Source:* Morgan Stanley Research

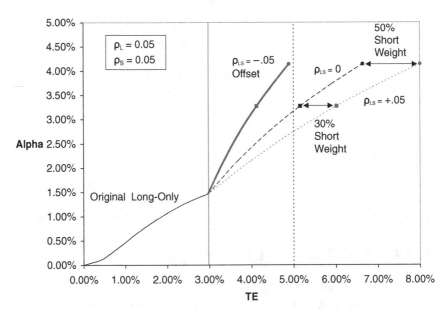

**EXHIBIT 1.8**   Alpha versus TE for Different Long/Short Correlations
*Source:* Morgan Stanley Research

either generate proceeds (if short) or consume investment funds (if long). Thus, they can be used to keep the net exposure at 100 percent and fund beta at 1. At this point, it is assumed that such generics have neither alpha nor TE effects (Leibowitz and Bova, 2007g,h).

Exhibit 1.9 shows the TEs for the base case with both active longs and active shorts (SA/LA) together with two extreme generic cases. An offset correlation of $\rho_{L,S} = -0.05$ is now assumed throughout. The top curve represents a short generics/long actives (SG/LA) case where generics are shorted to provide funds for active reinvestment in the long positions. Because these generic shorts are assumed to create no offset to the long positions, the TE is quite high. At the other extreme, the lower curve reflects the case where shorts are invested actively but the proceeds must be invested in generic longs. In this case, the active shorts do provide an offset to the original long portfolio, while the generic longs are TE-free. Consequently, this short actives/long generics (SA/LG) case has TEs that are even lower than the original long-only portfolio.

The alpha curves in these two generic cases are the same as the short-only and reinvested long-only alpha curves in Exhibit 1.5. By combining these

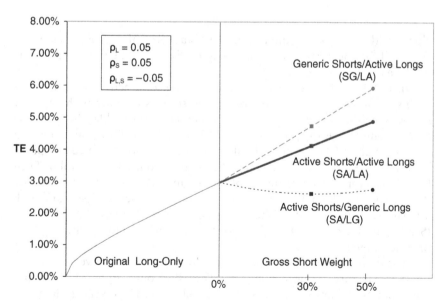

**EXHIBIT 1.9**   TE versus Short Weight: Generics on the Short and/or Long Sides
*Source:* Morgan Stanley Research

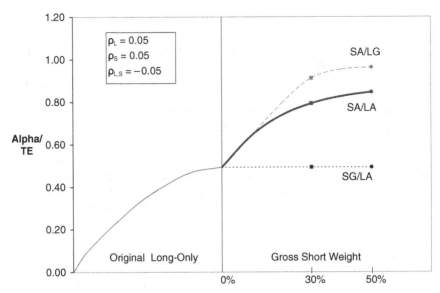

**EXHIBIT 1.10**   Alpha/TE versus Short Weight: Generics on the Short and/or
Long Sides
*Source:* Morgan Stanley Research

alphas with the TEs in Exhibit 1.9, one obtains the alpha/TE IR shown in
Exhibit 1.10 for a range of short weights. Exhibit 1.11 plots these same
results as alphas versus TEs.

In Exhibit 1.10, the base AE case (SA/LA) with active investment on
both sides has the benefit of the two alpha sources together with TEs that
fall between the two extreme cases. This combination enables the base case
to dominate the short generics (SG/LA) case at every TE for all extension
weights of up to 50 percent. It should be noted that this SG/LA case approximates the results from leveraging the original long-only portfolio. Such
leveraging simply sustains the IR of the original long-only as evidenced by
the flat line in Exhibit 1.10. With the two sources of active alphas and with
a lower TE from the offset effect, it is no surprise that that the AE model
(SA/LA) attains much higher IR ratios than the original long-only portfolio
or its leveraged SG/LA version.

The comparison of the base AE case with the short active/long generics (SA/LG) case is more complex. The short-only alpha curve is not
much different from the reinvested long-only case. However, as shown in
Exhibit 1.9, the combination of the short offset and the lack of additional
long positions lead to TEs that are actually lower than the original long-only

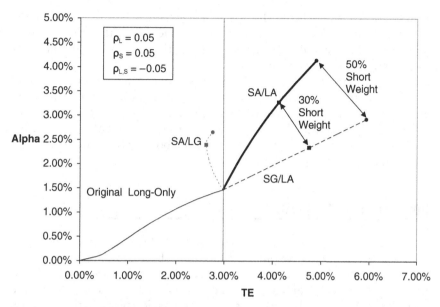

**EXHIBIT 1.11** Alpha versus TE: Generics on the Short and/or Long Sides
*Source:* Morgan Stanley Research

portfolio. The low TEs drive the IR curves for this SA/LG case to levels well above that of the basic AE. In Exhibit 1.10, these higher IRs naturally look quite appealing at first glance.

However, the situation looks quite different when the focus moves from Exhibit 1.10's IR graph to the more fundamental alpha versus TE graph in Exhibit 1.11. Here, the basic AE model (SA/LA) has the same curve as seen earlier, whereas the SG/LA case has the straight line projection expected from a proportional increase (i.e., simple leveraging) of the long-only portfolio.

The long generics case (SA/LG) is quite unusual for a return versus risk graph. Unlike curves where higher alphas are attained with greater TEs, this long generic case curves to the left. This seemingly peculiar shape results from the powerful TE reduction obtained when the offset from the short actives is combined with the lack of new actives on the long side. This result is instructive in that it demonstrates some basic principles about the use of IRs in situations in which additional leverage is limited or simply not available.

The preceding discussions treated generics as providing the basis for either the entire short extension or the entire reinvestment. The basic AE design requires the short extension proceeds and the reinvested funds to be matched in size and in beta values. In practice, there will often be gaps in the availability of viable active opportunities for one side or the other. Generic investments can help fill these gaps and bring the net funding and net beta values into the required balance.

Today's market contains a wide range of liquid generic instruments tied to specific sectors. This range of generic instruments allows for more targeted applications of offset hedging that can address undesired factor exposures in the active positions. When applied on a partial basis to either the short or the long side, sector generics can improve IRs, both by reducing the TE and by facilitating more focused active positions.

## POSITION SIZE CONSTRAINTS

The original long-only portfolio consisted of 25 active positions, each with a 2 percent fixed weight. A 50 percent short extension would raise these weights to 4 percent, which may exceed the tolerable position limit. Exhibit 1.12 presents alpha versus TE graphs for two cases in which the reinvestment is limited by these position size considerations. In the first case,

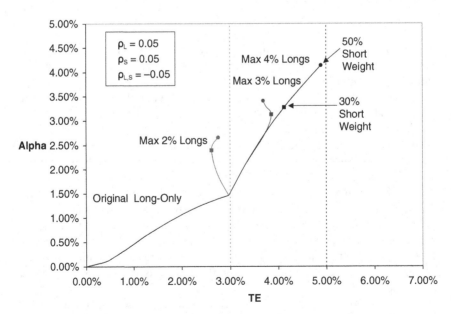

**EXHIBIT 1.12**   Alpha versus TE with Position Size Limits
*Source:* Morgan Stanley Research

the active long position size is capped at 2 percent; that is, the active longs are not allowed to grow beyond the 2 percent size in the original long-only portfolio. This case coincides with the short actives/long generics (SA/LG) case discussed earlier in this chapter, where all short proceeds are reinvested in beta-maintaining generic longs. In the second case, the active longs are subject to a 3 percent maximum position limit. With a 50 percent extension, only half of the new proceeds could be reinvested in active positions. The remaining half of the proceeds would then have to be deployed into generic long investments.

For the 2 percent position limit, the original long portfolio has already reached the maximum weight, and all short proceeds have to be reinvested generically. Without active reinvestment on the long side, the new shorts would be the sole alpha source at all extension levels. With the 3 percent long position limit, the reinvestment adds proportionally to the 25 long positions up until a 25 percent short weight. At higher extension percentages, the additional proceeds are reinvested in generic longs that have neither an alpha nor a TE impact. This 3 percent limit does not affect the portfolio alpha prior to a 25 percent extension, but reduces the alpha buildup for higher short weights.

These position limits and the associated reduction in the active weights actually have a beneficial effect on the TE. With the 2 percent limit, the TE declines from outset and then turns up slightly past 30 percent. With a 3 percent position limit, the TE initially coincides with the base SA/LA case, but diverges downward beyond the 25 percent short weight. It is at first surprising to see TEs turn downward as active short positions are added. This downward TE path results from the power of the short offsets that have yet to be overridden by active reinvestment on the long side, or by the accumulating correlating positions on the short side.

As shown in Exhibit 1.12, the highest IRs are attained in the 2 percent limit case in which the greater TE reduction overrides the lower alphas. The net result is an IR that reaches 0.91 at 30 percent; however, this low TE range has alphas that are not very productive. In situations such as AEs, where leverage is not an option, high IRs may not lead to satisfactory alphas. For example, at the 30 percent extension with this 2 percent position limit, the high IR of 0.91 applies to such a low TE that the alpha rises only to 2.4 percent. By comparison, even with its lower IR of 0.79, the base AS/AL case with 4 percent position limits provides an alpha of 3.3 percent. The alpha differential becomes even more dramatic for the 50 percent extension, where in spite of its higher IR, the 2 percent position limit case provides an alpha of only 2.7 percent, far less than the 4.1 percent obtained with the 4 percent limit.

## BEYOND THE INFORMATION RATIO

In recent years, the IR has become a standard measure of relative performance. In the AE space, a common approach is to plot the IR as a function of the extension percentage. The peak or near-peak is then taken as the optimal level of extension. However, as illustrated in the preceding discussion of Exhibits 1.10 through 1.12, high IRs may not always be the best guide to the high alphas, especially when there are multiple investment constraints.

Exhibit 1.12 can be used to illustrate a situation in which the acceptable TE tolerance is 5 percent or lower. There may be little problem as long as the TE remains within this 5 percent bound. With a 30 percent or even 50 percent extension, the 4 percent position case could then acceptably move toward an expected alpha in the 3 to 4 percent range. In contrast, the 2 percent position limit case (with the generic long reinvestment) has much higher IRs at all extension weights up to 50 percent, but it can never generate TEs above 3 percent. Without exogenous leverage, this case cannot take full advantage of the allowable 5 percent TE limit, so that its high IR falls well short of providing the higher alphas.

These results raise a number of questions about the very nature of IRs as a yardstick. The key point is that higher IRs do not always lead to better alphas. For IRs that are leveragable, the highest IR will lead to the highest alpha for a given TE. But the whole motivation behind the AE model is to seek enhanced alpha potential with relatively modest extensions of the traditional long-only model. Consequently, for this problem (as for many other investment situations), direct leverage is simply ruled out. Without the possibility of exogenous leverage, high IRs can be quite misleading as the route toward finding the best alphas.

## FUND LEVEL RISK EFFECTS

(For a fuller discussion of this topic, see Chapter 24.) The preceding sections have dealt with how AEs can lead to improvements in the equity portfolio's alpha at the cost of increasing TE. To this point, the discussion has taken place strictly within the confines of the individual equity portfolio. From the point of view of the asset owner or the fund sponsor, the situation is quite different and, in many ways, more compelling. As long as the risk control discipline can assure that a beta of 1 is being maintained and that exogenous sources of risks are excluded, the increased TE from the AE will be the only additional source of volatility risk at the fund level. In such a situation, the extension's alpha adds, on a weighted basis, to the overall fund return, while the higher TE can be shown to be largely submerged within the beta risk that dominates the volatility of the overall fund.

The policy allocations of a wide range of institutional funds have surprisingly similar risk characteristics. Exhibit 1.8 shows two examples—a traditional 60/40 portfolio B and a modern portfolio C that is diversified into a wide range of asset classes.

The funds' risk characteristics in Exhibit 1.13 are derived from a standard return/covariance matrix that provides an estimation of the volatility of each asset class and the correlations between any two-asset classes. In particular, it specifies the correlation of each asset class with a U.S. equity benchmark. This correlation can be combined with the ratio of the asset's volatility to the equity volatility to develop an implicit beta. This implicit beta represents a correlation-based estimate of the asset's mean response to changing equity returns.

The correlation-based implicit betas for each asset class are shown in Exhibit 1.13. A total beta for a given fund can then be found by weighting the implicit betas by their respective percentage allocations. Thus, portfolio B has a total beta of 0.65, consisting of its 60 percent explicit equity allocation and 0.05 from the 40 percent bonds that have an implicit beta of 0.14. In the highly diversified portfolio C, the total beta value of 0.57, consisting

**EXHIBIT 1.13** Typical Diversification Does Not Materially Change Fund Volatility: 90 Percent-Plus Comes from Equity

|  | Correlation-Based Implicit Beta | B | C |
|---|---|---|---|
| U.S. Equity | 1.00 | 60% | 20% |
| U.S. Bonds | 0.14 | 40% | 20% |
| International Equity | 0.77 |  | 15% |
| Emerging Mkt Equity | 0.76 |  | 5% |
| Absolute Return | 0.28 |  | 10% |
| Venture Capital | 0.59 |  | 10% |
| Private Equity | 0.98 |  | 10% |
| Real Estate | 0.07 |  | 10% |
| Total |  | 100% | 100% |
| Total Volatility |  | 11.17 | 10.45 |
| Correlation with U.S. Equity |  | 96.7% | 90.4% |
| Total Beta |  | 0.65 | 0.57 |

*Source:* Morgan Stanley Research

of 0.20 from the 20 percent direct equity and a further 0.37 from all the correlation-based betas of the nonequity asset classes.

## Three Volatility Surprises

In comparing the fund-level risk characteristics of portfolios B and C at the bottom of Exhibit 1.13, three surprises immediately present themselves. The first surprise is that, despite the vastly different levels of diversification, portfolios B and C have total volatilities that are nearly the same.

The second surprise is that the total betas for these two very different funds again are quite close, 0.65 and 0.57, respectively, for portfolios B and C. If you were to look at a wide spectrum of asset allocations across U.S. pension funds, foundations, and endowments, you will find that both total betas and total volatilities fall within quite narrow ranges: 0.55 to 0.65 for the total betas, and 10 percent to 11.5 percent for the volatilities.

The third surprise is found by taking the total beta value and multiplying by the 16.50 percent volatility that the covariance model assigns to U.S. equities. When this product is divided by the fund volatility, the result is the percentage of the total volatility that can be ascribed to the fund's equity exposure. For portfolios B and C, these percentages are $(0.65 \times 16.50\%)/11.17\% = 97\%$ and $(0.57 \times 16.50\%)/10.45\% = 90\%$, respectively. Thus, an overwhelming percentage of the volatility risk in these two funds is derived from their comovement relationship with equities. This dominating beta role can be seen across a wide swath of institutional (and individual) portfolios.

This percentage of equity-based volatility can also be interpreted as the correlation of the fund with movements in the equity market. This powerful and pervasive beta dominance at the fund level has major implications for the potential role of AEs and other benchmark-centric strategies that are tightly targeted to a well-defined equity benchmark.

## PASSIVE IMPLICIT ALPHAS

Exhibit 1.14 shows how fund B's expected return of 5.85 percent and fund C's 7.08 percent is derived from the weighted expected return of the component assets. The return components can also be broken down into a risk-free base rate of 1.50 percent, and return premiums of 4.35 percent for fund B, and a significantly higher 5.85 percent for fund C. The return premiums can then be further parsed into one component associated with the asset's implicit beta component, and a second component consisting of the remaining expected return specified in the return/covariance model. The beta-based

**EXHIBIT 1.14**  Diversification Raises Fund Return through Implicit Alphas

|  | Expected Return | Correlation-Based Implicit Alpha | B | C |
|---|---|---|---|---|
| U.S. Equity | 7.25 |  | 60% | 20% |
| U.S. Bonds | 3.75 | 1.47 | 40% | 20% |
| International Equity | 7.25 | 1.33 |  | 15% |
| Emerging Mkt Equity | 9.25 | 3.36 |  | 5% |
| Absolute Return | 5.25 | 2.14 |  | 10% |
| Venture Capital | 12.25 | 7.37 |  | 10% |
| Private Equity | 10.25 | 3.14 |  | 10% |
| Real Estate | 5.50 | 3.58 |  | 10% |
| Total |  |  | 100% | 100% |
| Total Expected Return |  |  | 5.85 | 7.08 |
| Total Beta × |  |  | 0.65 | 0.57 |
| Equity Premium |  |  | ×5.75 | ×5.75 |
| Beta Return |  |  | 3.76 | 3.29 |
| Risk-Free Rate |  |  | 1.50 | 1.50 |
| Implicit Alpha |  |  | 0.59 | 2.29 |

*Source:* Morgan Stanley Research

return component is simply the multiple of the implicit beta and the equity return premium. The second component has the form of an implicit alpha; that is, the remaining return that can be accessed by *passively* investing in the given asset class.

As seen in Exhibit 1.14, the weighted sum of these implicit alphas adds to only 0.59 percent in portfolio B. On the other hand, the implicit alphas for portfolio C accumulate to a sizable 2.29 percent, accounting for a large part of portfolio C's higher return relative to portfolio B.

The actual numerical values will, of course, vary with the selected return/covariance model. The covariance results tend to be relatively robust across the various models used in practice, although there may be more variability in the return assumptions. In this regard, the implicit alpha values will depend on the risk parameters assumed for equities, with lower equity risk premiums leading to higher implicit alphas.

It should be emphasized that these implicit alphas are quite different from active alphas. Implicit alphas are derived from a passive investment in an asset class that captures the expected return embedded in the return/covariance model. These passive alpha returns are obtainable without any unique skills or structural advantages. They represent a nonzero-sum reward for moving the portfolio from its current allocation into a less constrained and more diversified posture that provides higher expected returns.

It should also be noted that Exhibits 1.13 and 1.14 have the somewhat startling implication that diversification as typically practiced by institutional funds does not really reduce total volatility, but rather serves to enhance expected returns.

## BEYOND-MODEL DRAGON RISKS

The preceding discussion suggests that, at the fund level, asset classes with positive implicit alpha can provide a higher expected return with little impact on total volatility. This raises the question as to why this apparently free lunch should not be pursued more vigorously. A related question is why allocations are not more concentrated on the single highest alpha source, rather than having the weight to alternatives fragmented over multiple alpha assets. This same issue arises from an unconstrained optimization process that invariably produces initial allocations with overtly unacceptable concentrations in one or more alternative assets.

In practice, pension funds, endowments, and foundations often use a process that could be described as tortured optimization, based on the mean/variance approach first suggested by Harry Markowitz in the 1950s (Markowitz, 1959). The resulting allocations are naturally highly dependent on both the assumptions in the covariance matrix and on the constraints established for each asset class. Torturing refers to the common practice of sequentially manipulating these constraints to achieve portfolios that are theoretically optimal, but that also satisfy the more ephemeral criterion of being palatable. Whether determined in advance or as part of the process, constraints play a key role in determining the ultimate allocation.

The allocation into any alternative asset is always subject to a variety of constraints, some well founded and well articulated, and others that may be more subtle and/or simply convention based. Some considerations that are frequently put forward for setting these position limits include:

- Underdeveloped financial markets,
- Liquidity concerns,
- Limited access to acceptable investment vehicles or first-class managers,
- Problematic fee structures,
- Regulatory or organizational strictures,
- Peer-based standards,
- Headline risk,
- Insufficient or unreliable historical data.

The term dragon risks aptly captures the cornucopia of concerns that lead to these constraints. This expression is taken from a paper by Cliff Asness (2002), referring to the medieval mapmaker's characterization of uncharted territories as places where dragons may dwell. The basic issue here is the critical divide between modelable probabilities and the more fundamental uncertainty about the validity of any model. This distinction has been discussed at some length in the work of Peter Bernstein (1996) and Frank Knight (1964).

As funds diversify into alternative assets, they incur three forms of risk:

- Implicit betas,
- Modeled alpha volatility,
- Beyond-model dragon risks.

The implicit beta at the fund level is often preserved through the purchase of a mid-beta alternative asset using a mid-beta combination of bonds and equity. Indeed, this is why the typical diversification creates only minimal changes in the fund's total beta or overall volatility risk.

If the passive investments are coincident with the benchmark used for gauging the allocation's performance, the alpha volatility should not engender any TE relative to the policy portfolio. Moreover, the modeled alpha volatility should be uncorrelated with the dominant beta exposure. With the alternative assets having such fragmented allocations, the fund's dominant beta risk will overwhelm the volatility effect from modeled TEs (as long as they remain uncorrelated with each other). The beyond-model risks are more problematic because they are harder to formally assess and control. The standard approach is to set what seems to be reasonable constraints on each alternative asset, and trust that the resulting fragmented allocation represents an acceptable balance of risk and return.

Thus, regardless of any optimization results based upon a given return/covariance matrix, it tends to be these beyond-model dragon risks that determine the percentage weight ultimately assigned to the nontraditional asset classes.

## ACTIVE ALPHAS

To this point, I have not focused on any return/risk characteristics other than those associated with passive investments in the various asset classes. The implicit alphas are fundamentally different from the various forms of active alphas derived from superior security selection, better portfolio construction, uncovering high-performing managers, unique access to desirable investment vehicles, and so on. Active alphas are intrinsically skill-based and theoretically zero-sum in nature. Benchmark-centric and AE strategies depend upon skilled active management to generate their anticipated positive alphas.

A benchmark-centric strategy has a TE that is intended to be independent of the targeted beta volatility, and hopefully has few sources of beyond-model risk. This situation is quite different from the beyond-model concerns associated with nontraditional asset classes, where the standard covariance model will almost surely be viewed as only partially describing all the potential dimensions of risk. For example, any simple covariance assumptions for real estate or commodities can hardly be interpreted as capturing the entire constellation of risks associated with such investments. However, a benchmark-centric process should theoretically be able to provide risks that can be segregated into a targeted beta risk, an orthogonal TE component, and relatively few beyond-model concerns.

The first column in Exhibit 1.15 summarizes the return and risk characteristics for portfolio C with only passive investments. The third column, labeled $C^{**}$, shows the case in which the 20 percent passive equity is transferred to four 5 percent active 130/30 mandates, each having the 3.3 percent alpha and 4.1 percent TE described in the earlier base case example. The active equity increases the returns by $20\% \times 3.3\% = 0.66\%$, or from 7.08 percent to 7.74 percent. The beta remains the same at 0.57 because one of the requirements for benchmark-centric active management is that the equity portfolio's beta retains the original target value of 1. If the four managers' 3 percent TE are uncorrelated (an admittedly ideal case), the total fund TE becomes $\sqrt{4}^{*}5\%^{*}4.1\% = .41\%$

Even if the active 130/30 strategies have some level of correlation, the net effect on the total fund risk would still be negligible. At the same time, it should be pointed out that the 0.41 percent TE could be a source of departure from the short-term returns of the policy portfolio.

With equity beta being the overwhelming short-term risk factor for most U.S. institutional funds (Leibowitz, 2004; Leibowitz and Bova, 2005b), it can be seen that positive alpha sources that are uncorrelated with beta are particularly valuable. The key is to find active sources of positive alphas that are highly risk-controlled relative to a specific benchmark, with a benchmark that has a stable equity beta, and where the active TE around this benchmark is reliably uncorrelated with equity beta.

However, whereas the total volatility is the standard measure of fund risk, there are other risk concerns that deserve mention. In addition to the beyond-model dragon risks described earlier, there are other risks associated with the fund's ultimate ability to fulfill its (possibly complex) set of liabilities. This issue of surplus risk is a critically important factor in many

**EXHIBIT 1.15** Long-Only Active Equity Adds Active Alpha with Minimal Volatility Impact

|  |  |  | C | C** |
|---|---|---|---|---|
|  | Alpha | TE | Passive | 130/30 |
| Passive U.S. Equity | 0% | 0% | 20% | – |
| Active 130/30 Extension | 3.3% | 4.1% | – | 20% |
| Passive U.S. Bonds | 0% | 0% | 20% | 20% |
| Passive Alpha Core | 0% | 0% | 60% | 60% |
| Expected Return |  |  | 7.08 | 7.74 |
| Active Alphas [1.5% Alpha on 20% Long-Only] |  |  | – | 0.30 |
| AE Incremental Alpha [1.8% Alpha on 20% AE-30%] |  |  | – | 0.36 |
| Total Volatility |  |  | 10.45 | 10.46 |
| Passive Long-Term Volatility |  |  | 10.45 | 10.45 |
| Added TE: Four 5% 130/30 AEs with 4.1% Independent TE |  |  | – | 0.41 |
| Added Total Volatility |  |  | – | 0.01 |

*Source:* Morgan Stanley Research

settings, but one that would take the discussion far afield from the asset-only focus of this paper.

## RISK AS RISK TO THE POLICY PORTFOLIO

One question raised by this analysis is why most funds have total fund volatilities that fall within the same 10 to 11 percent range.

Following significant market movements, the common practice among institutional funds is to automatically rebalance back to the set policy portfolio. The standard rationale for such behavior typically takes the form of either an appeal to efficient markets theory or some version of buy low/sell high. In fact, it can be argued that both these rationales are fundamentally flawed (Leibowitz and Hammond, 2004). Nevertheless, the policy portfolio exerts a strong gravitational pull that results in a virtually uniform acceptance of automatic rebalancing.

This strong reluctance to being forced to shift away from its policy portfolio may play an underappreciated role in setting the fund's risk tolerance and in shaping its policy portfolio in the first place. When an institution shifts to a lower-risk allocation, it departs from the policy portfolio that was previously considered to represent an optimal allocation. Institutional funds are understandably reluctant to move away from these pre-established policy portfolios. Indeed, their rebalancing behavior is specifically geared toward sustaining this portfolio structure. Most institutional managers would view it as most unfortunate if the fund were to be forced by an extreme market movement—or by the fund's investment committee—to abandon its presumably optimal approach and shift into a lower-risk strategy.

Potential trigger points for such mandated shifts lurk in the background of every investor's mind and can act (possibly subconsciously) as fence posts that define the outer limits of tolerable risk. These fence posts may also play a feedback role in setting the policy portfolio's overall risk level in the first place. For example, suppose adverse movements of 15 to 20 percent are considered to be the tolerable outer limit of the risk envelope. A fund may then reasonably want to control the prospect of any such triggering event by reducing this probability to a minimal level. It can be shown that a combination of reasonable shortfall constraints leads total betas in the 0.55 to 0.65 range and portfolio volatilities of 10 to 11 percent, that is, exactly where risk levels are located in practice (Leibowitz and Bova, 2005a).

Under the banner of diversification, funds adopt different mixes of active alpha hunting and/or implied alpha gathering that they find suitable as a way of enhancing their expected return. However, there seems to be a surprising commonality in their determination to avoid roughly the same level of catastrophic risk. With the equity beta serving as the dominating risk factor for virtually all institutional funds, it is likely that any such catastrophic event would be the result of—or at least associated with—a major equity downturn. Consequently, it may not really be too surprising that total fund betas have been generally found to lie in the narrow range of 0.55 to 0.65.

## CORRELATION TIGHTENING AND STRESS BETAS

The standard covariance data that project these 10 to 11 percent volatilities is based on a performance history that necessarily has a concentration on normal times. A fund's true risk tolerance tends to be more determined by this perceived need to alter the strategic allocation—even when further market deterioration is assessed to have a relatively low probability. Another related facet of extreme downside risk may be the prospect of a decline in asset (or surplus) value so severe and so persistent as to erode a fund's capability to fulfill its liabilities without extraordinary sponsor contributions (Leibowitz and Bova, 2007a). It is at precisely these juncture points of maximum stress that standard asset relationships break down and the original risk estimates become invalid.

To be realistic, any risk reduction strategy must address these potential tail events. With equity being the dominant factor even under normal times, it is almost sure to play a crucial role at the points of maximum duress. There are many challenges in trying to estimate equity movements under such tail events and the interasset correlations that may then prevail. In discussions of these prospective events, one often hears the comment that, under such adverse conditions, "all correlations go to one." However, there is rarely any serious analysis of the covariance and volatility effects implied by such extreme extrapolations.

The concept of correlation tightening provides a more measured way to gain some insight into these effects. By assuming varying forms of correlation tightening across asset classes, one can explore how stress conditions might affect different allocations. Any such study would, of course, be plagued by myriad degrees of freedom. However, with equities as the dominant risk factor, the problem can become more manageable by focusing only on tightening correlations between equities and other asset classes. This approach leads to what may be called stress betas for each asset class. For a given allocation, these values will then build to a stress beta for the fund as a whole. Exhibit 1.16 shows the stress betas for portfolios B and C under a 25 percent correlation tightening, where the residual volatilities are assumed to be kept constant.

With normal-times covariance data and the associated normal beta values, most U.S. funds tend to have roughly the same 10 to 11 percent projected level of volatilities. However, unlike this common range for normal times volatility, stress betas can affect different allocations very differently. As shown in Exhibit 1.16, it is the more diversified funds that tend to be severely strained by stress betas that far exceed their normal betas. Naturally, when stress betas come into play, the underlying equity volatility also tends to increase markedly.

The traditional 60/40 funds have stress betas that essentially match their normal betas. In a more diversified fund, the lower correlations across the assets tend to moderate volatility under normal times. However, under market duress, these correlations tighten, resulting in a higher percentage of an asset's volatility being transmitted to the overall fund level. Thus, it is ironic that, in comparison with the traditional 60/40, diversified allocations

**EXHIBIT 1.16**  Effect on Beta of 25 Percent Increase in Correlations—Residual Volatility Constant

|  | Original Beta | Stress Beta | Allocation Percentages B | Allocation Percentages C |
|---|---|---|---|---|
| U.S. Equity | 1.00 | 1.00 | 60% | 20% |
| U.S. Bonds | 0.14 | 0.18 | 40% | 20% |
| International Equity | 0.77 | 1.25 |  | 15% |
| Emerging Mkt Equity | 0.76 | 1.03 |  | 5% |
| Venture Capital | 0.59 | 0.77 |  | 10% |
| Private Equity | 0.98 | 1.80 |  | 10% |
| Absolute Return | 0.28 | 0.39 |  | 10% |
| Real Estate | 0.07 | 0.09 |  | 10% |
| Initial Beta |  |  | 0.65 | 0.57 |
| Stress Beta |  |  | 0.67 | 0.78 |
| % Beta Increase |  |  | 2% | 36% |
| Stress Volatility |  |  | 11.42 | 13.61 |
| Stress Correlation with U.S. Equity |  |  | 96.8% | 94.4% |

*Source:* Morgan Stanley Research

may actually experience a much larger gap between the losses under stress times as opposed to the estimated losses under normal times.

## SHORT-TERM RISK AND LONG-TERM RETURNS

The prospect of such stress events—and the impact of the stress betas that they may induce—clearly deserves serious consideration in any comprehensive risk plan (Leibowitz and Bova, 2008).

At the same time, these short-term beta-driven risks must be balanced against the prospect of longer-term returns from diversification. The initial correlations embedded in the covariance matrix are based primarily on short-term price changes. Over longer periods, the correlations may be quite different. For example, the relationship between developed and emerging market equities may be quite tight under a sudden down move. However, over the long term, regional decoupling could lead these two markets to behave more independently, and an emerging market allocation may, therefore, serve as a powerful diversifier over the long term.

It should be noted that, theoretically, pension funds and certain other institutional funds are ideal vehicles for pursuing long-term investment returns. Diversified portfolios have the potential to provide both passive and active expected returns above and beyond the returns derived from the beta relationship. The most desirable assets for this purpose would be those that combine the prospect of incremental passive returns and/or positive active returns that are relatively uncorrelated with equities (or where the equity component can be reliably stripped out). Over time, the accumulation of these incremental returns can provide a sizable cushion against beta-based risks.

The incremental risk from AE should, theoretically, remain uncorrelated with equity movements, both in normal times as well as in periods of market turmoil. In this regard, it may enjoy certain advantages relative to other forms of active management that are embedded in more stress-vulnerable asset classes.

## THE ALPHA/BETA MATRIX

The alpha/beta matrix in Exhibit 1.17 attempts to classify the various forms of portfolio management styles using an alpha/beta template.

In an earlier work (Leibowitz, 2005), a rather anthropomorphic classification was used to describe different categories of alpha-seeking behavior:

- The beta grazers are the index funds that passively feed off the return premiums that are broadly available to all.
- The gatherers are funds that expand their allocation by diversifying, but passively, into a wider range of asset classes with the intention of accessing the implicit alphas.
- The alpha hunters are the active managers that aggressively seek excess returns from the exercise of superior investment skill. In contrast to gathering, such hunting is an intrinsically zero-sum activity.
- The foragers venture forth and seek returns wherever these can be found.

All of these return-seeking pursuits can prove valuable if successfully pursued, but they differ materially in the character of the risks entailed—and nature of their fund-level effects.

Benchmark-centric alpha hunting should ideally have risks that take the form of a moderate level of uncorrelated TE. These modest TE additions should have little impact at the fund level volatility.

The gathering of implicit alphas in new asset classes may entail a substantial degree of uncorrelated TE. However, the more significant risk in expanded diversification arises from the beyond-model dragon risks.

**EXHIBIT 1.17** Fund Level Alpha/Beta Structures

| Metaphor | Betas | Management Styles | Nature of Alphas | Fund Volatility | Model Risk | TE vs. Policy | Stress Betas |
|---|---|---|---|---|---|---|---|
| Beta Grazing | Stapled | Passive Investing in Broad Equity/Fixed Income Markets | Risk Premium | Fundamental Source | Very Low | Zero | Zero |
| Alpha Hunting | Beta-Targeted | Risk-Controlled Active Equity Market Neutral Market Neutral Some Hedge Funds | Active Management | Low | Low | Moderate | Very Low |
| Alpha Gathering | Correlation-Based | Diversification into New Asset Classes | Implicit Correlation-Based Passive Alphas | Low | High | Low | High |
| Alpha/Beta Foraging | "Free Range" Betas | Beta-Agnostic Opportunistic Investment Some Hedge Funds Macro Funds | Intense to Hyper Active | High | High | High | High |

*Source:* Morgan Stanley Research

These risk factors may not be formalized, but they reveal themselves at the fund level through the de facto limits imposed on nontraditional asset classes.

Free-range foraging can incur any and all these forms of risk. However, the fund-level impact depends on the intensity of the risks and percentage of the overall allocation deployed in each form of active management.

Clearly, these activities can be mixed and matched. For example, an alpha-gatherer fund may well elect—at the outset or subsequently—to become a hunter and pursue active alphas within the new asset classes.

The basic message is that benchmark-centric active management will have only a minimal impact on fund level volatility if:

- Its beta is tightly stapled to the targeted value.
- The TE is uncorrelated with the fund's dominant beta exposure.
- The TE-associated relative return deviations over the short term are manageable.
- No other significant sources of volatility risk correlate with the TE.
- Few, if any, sources of other nonmodeled risks exist.

If a reliably positive alpha can be accessed with such minimal impact on total volatility risk, it would seem to be desirable to accept the additional TE (which should be quite modest at the fund level) in exchange for alpha enhancement.

## CONCLUSION

The basic message is that when its design goals are realized, active 130/30 extension falls into the realm of benchmark-centric alpha hunting. The discussion in this chapter illustrates the key drivers that enable an AE to be productive:

- Fresh active underweights from the ability to short,
- Enhanced opportunities for active long positions that are more sizable and/or broader in range,
- Reduction in TE from potential offset of unintended factor exposures,
- More sharply focused (and possible more sizable) active positions afforded by the offset potential,
- Ability to use generics, especially sector-based generics, to help fill gaps in active opportunities.

These features play a role in both fundamental and quantitative management strategies, but their relative importance can obviously vary (Leibowitz and Bova, 2007e). For example, the greater breadth of active opportunities may play a greater role in a highly diversified quantitative approach, whereas the ability to shape the exposures in a concentrated portfolio may be more significant for a bottom-up fundamental manager.

Of course, the benefits from AE, as with all active management, are dependent on the ability to generate reliably positive alphas on a risk-adjusted basis and to do so at reasonable costs (especially including shorting costs). The corresponding downside is that AE generally leads to some modest increase in TE and would exacerbate the adverse effects of any negative alphas.

One key driver for the growth of AE has been the desire from U.S. institutional funds to seek incremental alphas that can significantly affect their overall returns. United States equity is an asset class that will always have a sizable allocation, even in diversified portfolios. In addition, as an asset class, equities have a number of advantages for active alpha hunting. The techniques for shorting and for extending long-only risk control to AE formats are relatively straightforward. There is the advantage of a large cadre of both quantitative and fundamental managers that have significant performance records, reliable operational procedures, credibility in terms of their risk control, and well established institutional relationships. Indeed, most AE 130/30 assignments to date have been literal extensions of pre-existing relationships with a long-only manager.

From another point of view, for many institutional investors, AE strategies enable access to the benefits of shorting and return enhancement, given only a modest expansion of the traditional risk control framework. Moreover, AE strategies are indexed to well-defined equity benchmarks so that the alpha performance is clearly delineated. Although yet to be seen in practice, this alpha clarity, together with the availability of highly liquid derivatives and overlay vehicles, suggests that AE strategies may well be used as a portable alpha source in the future (Leibowitz and Bova, 2007c).

Within the framework of institutional funds, the fact that equity is such a dominating risk factor has special implications for AE as an intensive benchmark-centric form of active investment within the equity asset class.

The volatility risk of U.S. institutional funds is 90 percent or more dominated by their explicit—and implicit—equity exposure. AEs are designed to maintain the targeted beta relative to the original long-only benchmark, with the primary source of additional risk being increased TE from the larger number of active positions. In a properly risk controlled setting, such TE should be uncorrelated with equities. Because total equity exposure is overwhelmingly dominant at the fund level, the additional TE from AEs will be swamped in the standard sum-of-squares calculation. The net result is that the positive alphas derived from an AE will add to the fund's expected return, with only a minimal impact on the fund's overall volatility. Moreover, because it relates to the basic equity asset class, AE strategies should, theoretically, be able to avoid stress beta effects.

In other diversifying asset classes (i.e., non-U.S. equity), active management is typically measured relative to the corresponding passive benchmark. The resulting alphas and TEs are then determined with reference to this asset class benchmark, and performance evaluation usually occurs within these confines of the specific asset class. Consequently, the TEs from even well-controlled active management in nonequity assets may be statistically independent of their primary benchmark, but may still correlate with U.S. equities, that is, credit-tilted strategies in fixed income or export-tilted approaches within emerging markets. With equity being the overwhelmingly dominant risk factor at the fund level, such equity-correlated TEs could significantly add to the fund level volatility risk. Moreover, under conditions of market stress, short-term tightening of the covariance structure across diversifying asset classes could further exacerbate this adverse fund-level effect.

In contrast, the alpha component of AE strategies is specifically designed to be orthogonal to U.S. equity risk, and so the associated TEs should be relatively free from the beta correlation and stress effects that could complicate risk control at the fund level.

Equity-based AE has the benefits of being resident in an efficient asset class that also happens to be the dominant risk factor in virtually all institutional (and many individual) portfolios. At the same time, it should be pointed out that the alphas that can be hunted in a highly efficient, but intensely competitive, asset class can be distinctly different from alphas that may be hidden in a less-efficient asset class.

## REFERENCES

Arnott, R. D., and D. J. Leinweber. 1994. "Long-short Strategies Reassessed." *Financial Analysts Journal*. September/October.

Asness, C. 2002. As cited in the "NACUBO Endowment Study." *NACUBO Business Officer*. April.

Bernstein, P. L. 1996. *Against the Gods: The Remarkable Story of Risk*. John Wiley & Sons, Inc.

Bernstein, P. L. 2006. "The Points of Inflection Revisited." *Economics and Portfolio Strategy*. January.

Brush, J. S. 1997. "Comparisons and Combinations of Long and Long/Short Strategies." *Financial Analysts Journal*. May/June.

Clarke, R. 2005. "Portfolio Constraints and the Fundamental Law of Active Management." *Society of Quantitative Analysts Half-Day Fall Seminar: Advances in Optimization and Portfolio Construction.* November.

Clarke, R., H. de Silva, and S. Thorley. 2002. "Portfolio Constraints and the Fundamental Law of Active Management." *Financial Analysts Journal.* September/October.

Clarke, R., H. de Silva, and S. Sapra. 2004. "Towards More Information-Efficient Portfolios." *Journal of Portfolio Management.* Fall.

Clarke, R., H. de Silva, and S. Thorley. 2005. "Performance Attribution and the Fundamental Law." *Financial Analysts Journal.* September/October.

Emrich, S. 2006. "Alpha-Beta Separation and Short Extension Portfolios." *Morgan Stanley Quantitative and Derivatives Strategy.* June.

Grinold, R. C. 1989. "The Fundamental Law of Active Management." *Journal of Portfolio Management.* Spring.

Grinold, R. C. 2005. "Implementation Efficiency." *Financial Analysts Journal.* September/October.

Grinold, R. C., and K. Eaton. 1998. "Attribution of Performance and Holdings." *Worldwide Asset and Liability Modeling.*

Grinold, R. C., and R. Kahn. 2000a. "The Surprising Large Impact of the Long-Only Constraint." *Barclays Global Investors Investment Insights.* May.

Grinold, R. C., and R. Kahn. 2000b. "The Efficiency Gains of Long-Short Investing." *Financial Analysts Journal.* November/December.

Grinold, R. C., and R. Kahn. 2000c. "Active Portfolio Management: Quantitative Theory and Applications." McGraw-Hill.

Jacobs, B. I., and K. N. Levy. 1993. "Long/Short Equity Investing: Profit from Both Winners and Losers." *Journal of Portfolio Management.* Fall.

Jacobs, B. I., and K. N. Levy. 1995. "More on Long-Short Strategies." *Financial Analysts Journal.* March/April.

Jacobs, B. I., and K. N. Levy. 1999. "Long/Short Portfolio Management: An Integrated Approach." *Journal of Portfolio Management.* Winter.

Jacobs, B. I., and K. N. Levy. 2006. "Enhanced Active Equity Strategies: Relaxing the Long-Only Constraint in the Pursuit of Active Returns." *Journal of Portfolio Management.* Spring.

Jacobs, B. I., and K. N. Levy. 2007a. "20 Myths about Enhanced Active 120-20 Strategies." *Financial Analysts Journal.* July/August.

Jacobs, B. I., and K. N. Levy. 2007b. "Enhanced Active Equity Portfolios are Trim Equitized Long-Short Portfolios." *Journal of Portfolio Management.* Summer.

Knight, F. H. 1964. *Risk, Uncertainty, and Profit.* New York: Century Press. Originally published in 1921.

Leibowitz, M. L. 2004. "The $\beta$-Plus Measure in Asset Allocation." *Journal of Portfolio Management.* Spring.

Leibowitz, M. L., and P. B. Hammond. 2004. "The Changing Mosaic of Investment Patterns." *Journal of Portfolio Management.* Spring.

Leibowitz, M. L. 2005. "Alpha Hunters and Beta Grazers." *Financial Analysts Journal.* September/October.

Leibowitz, M. L., and A. Bova. 2005a. "Convergence of Risks." Morgan Stanley Research. April.

Leibowitz, M. L., and A. Bova. 2005b. "Allocation Betas." *Financial Analysts Journal*. July/August.

Leibowitz, M. L., and A. Bova. 2006a. "Short-Extension Portfolio: An Exploration of the 120/20 Concept." Morgan Stanley Research. January.

Leibowitz, M. L., and A. Bova. 2007a. P/Es and Pension Fund Ratios." *Financial Analysts Journal*. January/February.

Leibowitz, M. L., and A. Bova. 2007b. "Gathering Implicit Alphas in a Beta World." *Journal of Portfolio Management*. Spring.

Leibowitz, M. L., and A. Bova. 2007c. "Beta Targeting: Tapping into the Appeal of 130/30 Active Extensions." Morgan Stanley Research. April.

Leibowitz, M. L., and A. Bova. 2007d. "Active Extensions: Alpha Hunting at the Fund Level." *Journal of Investment Management*. Third quarter.

Leibowitz, M. L., and A. Bova 2007e. "Portfolio Concentration." Morgan Stanley Research. July.

Leibowitz, M. L., and A. Bova. 2007f. "Active Return Drivers in 130/30 Extensions." Morgan Stanley Research. August.

Leibowitz, M. L., and A. Bova. 2007g. "Activity Drivers: Alpha Drivers in Long/Short Funds." Morgan Stanley Research. October.

Leibowitz, M. L., and A. Bova. 2007h. "Generic Shorts in Active 130/30 Extensions." Morgan Stanley Research. November.

Leibowitz, M. L., and A. Bova. 2008. "Stress Risks within Asset and Surplus Frameworks." Morgan Stanley Research. January.

Litterman, B. 2005. "Are Constraints Eating Your Alpha?" *Pensions & Investments*. March.

Markowitz, H. 1959. *Portfolio Selection: Efficient Diversification of Investments*. John Wiley & Sons, Inc.

Markowitz, H. M. 2005. "Market Efficiency: A Theoretical Distinction and So What?" *Financial Analysts Journal*. September/October.

Michaud, R. O. 1993. "Are Long-Short Equity Strategies Superior?" *Financial Analysts Journal*. November/December.

Winston, K., and T. Hewett. 2006. "Long-Short Portfolio Behavior with Barriers Part 1: Mechanism." *Q Conference Presentation*. Spring.

# The Role of Quantitative Strategies in Active 130/30 Extensions

# Active Extension—Portfolio Construction

**Simon Emrich**
Executive Director
Morgan Stanley
Institutional Equity Division

**A**ctive extension (AE) (e.g., 130/30) portfolios have been positioned as extensions to existing long-only active portfolios. They have the same objectives, but because of the relaxation of the critical long-only constraint, AE portfolios can express those objectives better—namely, the combination of benchmark exposure with excess return generating active positions.

The theoretical rationale for AE is well established, for example, by utilizing Clarke, de Silva, and Thorley's Fundamental Law of Active Management argument (Clarke, de Silva, and Thorley, 2002). In this chapter, we discuss the actual implementation of an AE portfolio, and the key differences between AE and active long-only portfolios. We also introduce a general framework for the analysis of benchmark-relative portfolios and use this framework to show the typical characteristics of long-only portfolios. We then show how the relaxation of the long-only constraint allows a number of different changes to the portfolio structure and discuss the relative merits of these changes.

## A FRAMEWORK FOR ANALYZING ACTIVE BENCHMARK-RELATIVE PORTFOLIOS

Active benchmark-relative portfolios, whether long-only or AE, have two objectives that often conflict. On the one hand, these portfolios should deliver the benchmark return through beta. On the other hand, they should deliver something on top of the benchmark return: an alpha.

Delivering the benchmark return requires tracking of the benchmark. In the simplest case, this can mean simply replicating the benchmark composition. More typically, tracking a benchmark involves the identification of the key systematic risk drivers for the benchmark's return and the construction of a more concentrated portfolio that gives exposure to the same systematic risk drivers.

Delivering alpha requires deviations in the portfolio structure from that of the benchmark—we have to take active bets. These can be either on a bottom-up stock level, or on a top-down level, such as sector, size, style, or regional exposures.

In many cases, the two objectives are combined, and a portfolio is characterized by its expected or realized excess return as well as its tracking risk relative to the benchmark. This makes it more difficult to differentiate between risk and return contributions coming from the first or the second objective. This also makes a comparison between the characteristics of long-only and AE portfolios more challenging.

We, therefore, introduce an explicit nominal separation of an existing portfolio $p$ into a core, market exposure component $c$ that is responsible for tracking the benchmark $b$, and a portion that is responsible for delivering alpha $a$. This can be done for any portfolio. The benchmark, the portfolio, and the portfolio components can be expressed as vectors of individual asset weights—$v_b$, $v_p$, $v_c$, and $v_a$, respectively—with a representative asset weight of $v$ for asset $i$.

Conceptually, the portfolio is the core component that a benchmark-relative investor would hold in the absence of alpha views. Trivially, that portfolio may simply be the benchmark—implemented through a passive index portfolio, exchange-traded funds (ETFs), or futures, where appropriate. More typically, this core portfolio will be more concentrated than the benchmark (e.g., an optimized basket) because it is generally possible to capture the key return drivers of a benchmark with a relatively concentrated portfolio.

Because the portfolio, as a whole, is evaluated relative to the benchmark, the $c$ portion of it will always be fully invested. This means that $w_c = \sum v_{c,i}$, the sum of individual asset weights in $c$, will always sum to 1. In the absence of borrowing, the sum of individual asset weights in the portfolio $p$, $w_p$ will also be equal to 1. This means that the alpha portfolio $a$ will necessarily be a cash-neutral, long/short portfolio with the sum of individual asset weights equal to 0. We scale the asset weights in the $a$ portfolio such that the sum of long weights and that of short weights are equal to 1, and denote the inverse of the scaling factor by $w_a$.

The portfolio's asset weights can then be decomposed as

$$v_p = v_c + w_a v_a$$

Portfolios are constructed such that they maximize the expected risk-adjusted return, subject to constraints. In the framework just introduced, constraints can have an impact on the feasible set of both $v_c$ and $v_a$. Liquidity constraints, concentration constraints, or limits on the total number of assets held in the portfolio, for example, can affect the feasible set of both $v_c$ and $v_a$. Constraints defined relative to the benchmark, such as maximum active positions in individual bottom-up assets, or top-down asset classes, such as sectors, will affect the feasible set of $v_a$.

A long-only constraint (i.e., $v_{p,i} \geq 0$ for all $i$) is special because it affects the feasible set of $v_a$, as well as $w_a$. Relaxing the constraint, as happens in AE portfolios, affects the feasible of both these variables. We can turn an existing portfolio into an AE portfolio simply by scaling up the active weights (that is, by increasing $w_a$), or we can change the structure of the active weights $v_a$ within the now-greater feasible set. As we will see later in this chapter, scaling the existing active weights will not change the risk-adjusted excess returns of the portfolio (in the terms of the Fundamental Law of Active Management, the transfer coefficient does not change), although changing the structure of active weights can change the risk-adjusted excess returns.

We can use the framework of separating a portfolio into a benchmark tracking and an excess return generating component to gain a deeper understanding of the sources of risk and return in the portfolio. Denote by $R$ the vector of asset returns (either historical or expected) and by $\Sigma$ the covariance matrix of these asset returns. The returns of a component (e.g., the portfolio itself) are then given by $r_p = v_p R$, while its volatility is given by $\sigma_p = v_p' \sum v_p$, and the covariance between two components (e.g., $c$ and $a$) is given by $\sigma_{c,a} = v_c' \sum v_a$.

We can then decompose the excess return of the portfolio, $r_{p-b}$, and the tracking risk, $\sigma_{p-b}$, into components due to the separate portions:

$$r_{p-b} = r_{c-b} + w_a r_a$$

$$\sigma_{p-b}^2 = \sigma_{c-b}^2 + w_a^2 \sigma_a^2 + 2 w_a \sigma_{c-b,a}$$

The first component represents the return and risk due the component $c$ mistracking the benchmark $b$. Careful portfolio construction should minimize this component—most of the return and risk should come from the active bets taken in the $a$ portfolio. This is measured by the second term. Risk has a third term, which expresses the cross correlation of the mistracking of term $c$ and the active bets taken in portfolio $a$. As an example, many benchmark tracking portfolios have a large-cap bias because it is generally possible to capture the key risk drivers in a benchmark with relatively few large-cap names. If the active asset selection in the $a$ portfolio is predominantly in the small-cap space, we would expect the cross correlation between benchmark mistracking in $c$ and active risk in $a$ to be negative.

## THE STRUCTURE OF ACTIVE LONG-ONLY PORTFOLIOS

We use the framework to characterize typical benchmark-relative active long-only portfolios. This will set the scene for the extension of such long-only portfolios through the relaxation of the long-only constraint.

The structure of benchmark-relative active long-only portfolios and the feasible set of active weights are driven by the structure of the benchmark itself. Given the long-only constraint $v_{p,i} \geq 0$ for all assets $i$, active under-weights in each asset $i$ are limited by the benchmark weight $v_{b,i}$. For example, Exhibit 2.1 shows the distribution of constituent weights for the Standard & Poor's (S&P) 500 as of December 31, 2007.

The pattern of benchmark weights for the S&P 500 is typical of capitalization-weighted benchmarks. The index is dominated by relatively few large-cap names. As of December 31, 2007, 120 names in the S&P 500 had a weight that was greater than the 0.2 percent weight of an equally weighted benchmark. The 20 names with a weight of greater than 1 percent in the benchmark accounted for around 31 percent of the total market capitalization of the index.

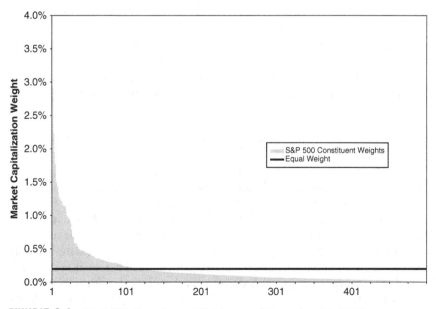

**EXHIBIT 2.1**   S&P 500 Constituent Weights as of December 31, 2007

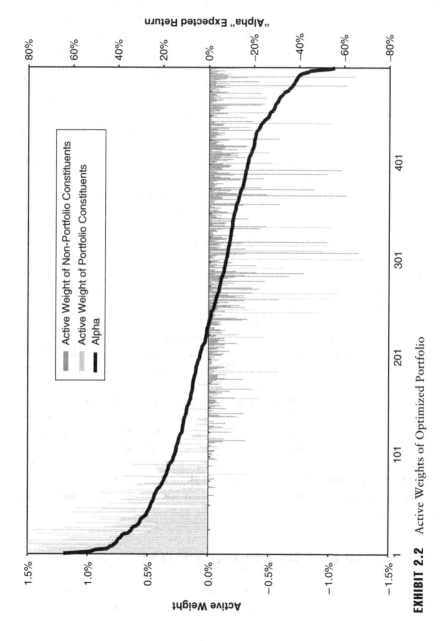

**EXHIBIT 2.2** Active Weights of Optimized Portfolio

This concentration in large-cap names has implications for the structure of a typical portfolio's active weights. For most index constituents, meaningful active underweights are not possible in a long-only portfolio because their weight in the benchmark is very small. As an example, Exhibit 2.2 shows the active weights of a pro forma optimized portfolio of S&P 500 constituents, based on randomly generated alphas or expected returns.[1]

The active weights show a characteristic distribution. The names with the highest expected excess return are significantly overweight, with overweights of up to 1.5 percent. The remaining stocks, including many with still somewhat positive alpha, are mostly not represented in the portfolio at all. They are maximally underweight. Because of the distribution of market cap weights, there is very little correlation in the size of the underweight and the size of the negative alpha for these names. This means that the information in the alpha is represented suboptimally in the portfolio—the only information exploited is that these names are not among the highest alpha names because, in that case, they would have been significantly overweight.

We typically measure the activeness of a portfolio by its tracking risk relative to a benchmark. In this case, the tracking risk is around 5 percent by construction. Alternatively, we can use the framework to determine activeness in terms of the active weights in the portfolio. Assuming that all active positions in this portfolio are alpha driven, we can model the portfolio as a benchmark replicator, plus a pure alpha long/short component. The weight of this component, calculated as $w_a = 0.5 \sum |v_{p,i} - v_{b,i}|$, is around 68 percent for our example portfolio.

Using the framework, the active component $a$ of the portfolio consists of a relatively concentrated long position in the overweights, and a relatively diversified short position in the underweights. This is particularly true for more active portfolios—so-called enhanced index portfolios—that tend to combine a diversified core portfolio with a relatively large number of small active weights, and typically exhibit less asymmetry in their active weight structure.

This asymmetric structure of the active portfolio has implications for the tracking risk contribution of the long and short side, respectively. In particular, the overweights will typically contribute a greater portion of the overall idiosyncratic risk of the portfolio than the underweights. We will return to this point in the next chapter when we consider the management of AE portfolios.

## MOVING FROM LONG-ONLY TO ACTIVE EXTENSION

Given the structure of market capitalization weighted benchmarks, benchmark-relative active long-only portfolios will often not be able to fully represent the available alpha information because underweights are bounded below by the long-only constraint. Therefore, relaxing the long-only constraint enables us to improve the exploitation of the alpha insights, particularly on the short/underweight side. This improvement comes both from the ability to take the alpha view fully into account, and to hedge out (systematic) risks in a more targeted manner.

How big is the improvement in risk-adjusted returns? How far should the long-only constraint be relaxed? The answer will clearly depend on the precise situation. However, the framework we introduced earlier enables us to characterize the range of outcomes. In particular, the optimal gross exposure ratio (e.g., 120/20, 130/30, etc.) will depend on the precise circumstances.

In our framework, we distinguish between the component $c$ of the portfolio that is responsible for benchmark returns and the component $a$ that is responsible for the excess, alpha-driven return. As the long-only constraint is relaxed, we can increase the risk and return in the portfolio. First, we can simply scale the $a$ component by increasing $w_a$. This increases the risk and return of the portfolio proportionately so the risk-adjusted return will not change. Also, we can change the structure of the $a$ component to better take our alpha views into account.

As a result of either of these changes, the gross exposure ratio will change. Exhibit 2.3 shows the trade-off between more and better alpha, that is, between changing $w_a$ and changing the structure of $a$, schematically.

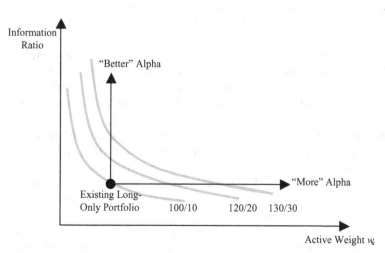

**EXHIBIT 2.3** The Trade-off between More and Better Alpha

Starting from an existing long-only portfolio, we can change the activeness of the portfolio by changing $w_a$. This means simply scaling up existing active bets; for example, by increasing the overweights further and going short the relevant index instrument. The active weight increases by moving horizontally from the initial portfolio, but the risk-adjusted return (the information ratio [IR]) will not change. At the other extreme, we can keep the active weight $w_a$ unchanged, but better exploit our negative alpha views by changing the structure of $a$. This means moving up vertically from the initial portfolio.

In either case, the gross exposure of the portfolio will change. The precise shape of the iso-exposure curves will depend on the degree to which the gross exposure constraint is binding. As an example, the constraint is likely to be less binding for relatively low, active-risk, enhanced-index portfolios than for more concentrated, high-tracking-risk portfolios. The shape and location of the iso-exposure curves will also depend on the structure of the original long-only portfolio. For example, if this portfolio is the result of an optimization process such that the risk-adjusted excess return (the IR) of the portfolio is maximized, the iso-exposure curve would be truncated. Lowering the active weight $w_a$ and changing the composition of the active basket would not improve the IR. Exhibit 2.3 depicts a generic case in which the existing long-only portfolio is not IR maximized.

In addition to the extreme, orthogonal cases of more and better alpha, any point in between on the iso-exposure curves is also reachable. Which point is optimal? This clearly depends on the degree to which the gross exposure constraint limits the exploitation of positive and, in particular, negative alpha views. Much of the literature focuses on the potential for better alpha (i.e., moves in a vertical direction). On a more practical level, depending on the alpha quality, the breadth of alpha, and, of course, the investor demands, more alpha may be more appropriate. We will return to this point in the next chapter, where we look at the issues associated with calculating expected IRs in the presence of non-normal returns.

According to this framework of separating active portfolios into a benchmark-tracking portion $c$ and an alpha-generating portion $c$, both long-only portfolios and AE portfolios should be seen as particular points on a two-dimensional continuum. The dimensions are the quality of the activeness, as measured by the IR, and the quantity of the activeness, as measured by the weight $w_a$ of the active basket.

This means that a particular gross exposure, such as 130/30, does not correspond to a unique portfolio structure. There is a whole set of portfolios with this gross exposure, all located on an iso-exposure curve in the

IR/active weight space. Which portfolio on this curve is chosen is a function of the inputs, in particular the alpha quality. We view the separation between the benchmark tracking component $c$ and the alpha-generating component $a$ as providing significant additional insight. By extension, this separation can then more directly address the question of the optimal gross exposure level. We expect that in the medium term, the discussion in the industry will move away from the choice of optimal exposure levels, and toward the optimal combination of IR and active weight.

## BENCHMARK REPRESENTATION

What about the portfolio component $c$? Based on the discussion earlier in this chapter, this notional component of the portfolio gives beta, or exposure, to the portfolio's benchmark. Trivially, this can be achieved by full benchmark replication. In practice, full replication is usually not necessary for active benchmark-relative portfolios, and may be counterproductive on a transaction cost-adjusted basis. Typically, we find that there is a relatively small number of systematic return drivers in a benchmark (e.g., as measured by a predicted risk model). These drivers may include sectors or style factors, such as value, growth, and size. If we choose a sufficiently diversified subset of stocks from the benchmark, which gives exposure to the same risk factors as are present in the index, we can achieve market exposure with a substantially reduced number of stocks. The resultant core portfolio $c$ will have tracking risk to the benchmark, but most of this risk will be idiosyncratic.

In many active benchmark-relative portfolios, this mistracking component of overall tracking risk is combined with the active tracking risk. For long-only portfolios, in particular, this can lead to a suboptimal beta representation—to fund active overweights, the portfolio becomes overly concentrated. This means that the market risk may not be adequately captured in the portfolio. This mistracking is, by assumption, not alpha generating—the expectation of $r_{c-b}$ is zero. This component of tracking risk is, therefore, a deadweight loss, incurred due to the long-only constraint, and leads to overall lower IRs.

Note that this is a separate issue from the inefficiencies in the *active* portion $a$ that arise from a long-only constraint, which were discussed earlier. There, the issue was that negative alpha views can only be suboptimally exploited due to the market capitalization distribution of typical benchmarks.

If the long-only constraint is removed, for example through AE, the pressure to introduce mistracking in the component $c$ in order to fund active overweights is lessened. There is more active weight available on the long side, funded by the newly introduced shorts.

This means that moving from long-only to AE allows for the lowering of the deadweight loss tracking risk that comes from the mistracking of component $c$ versus the benchmark. This can improve the IR of the overall portfolio's active positions. The construction of benchmark-tracking portfolios is a well-researched process. It typically involves the identification of the key return drivers in a benchmark, as well as a stock selection and weight optimization process to minimize the active exposure to these return drivers relative to the benchmark.

For AE portfolios, there is an additional consideration that comes from the interaction between the positions in the benchmark tracking component $c$ and the active component $a$, particularly if the portfolio is constructed under a fixed-gross-exposure constraint. Predicted risk models, which represent the key systematic return drivers in a benchmark, reduce the dimensionality of the covariance matrix between stock returns. There are typically far fewer systematic return drivers than there are stocks in a benchmark. The lower dimensionality of the covariance matrix means that there will typically exist a whole set of optimal benchmark-tracking portfolios for a given set of constraints, particularly if the number of stocks allowed in the portfolio is limited.

If there is a constraint on the gross exposure of the overall portfolio, it can be beneficial to choose the constituents of the component $c$ such that many of the short positions of the component $a$ are represented. This increases the scope for increasing the active weight $w_a$ because the short positions of the component $a$ can initially be funded by selling out of the benchmark tracking component $c$.

## CONSTRUCTING ACTIVE EXTENSION PORTFOLIOS

In this chapter, we introduced a framework for analyzing and constructing active benchmark-relative portfolios. We argued that separating the benchmark-tracking component $c$ from the alpha-generating component $a$ was beneficial for portfolio construction, both in terms of risk attribution and to ensure that alpha was optimally represented in the portfolio.

Separating a portfolio into those components provides a way to pinpoint both the opportunities and the issues involved in moving from a long-only to an AE framework. We showed that this move provides scope for more alpha by increasing the active weight of existing alpha-driven active positions, and for better alpha by changing the structure of the alpha component. AE can be located anywhere in the continuum defined by those two parameters.

Thinking about AE portfolios in this framework gives investors a clearer delineation of the sources of the efficiency gain (in terms of increased IR) that results from relaxing the long-only constraint. In particular, we can identify cases in which better alpha, achieved by changing the structure of the active positions, may not be the optimal answer. We discuss this possibility in greater depth in the next chapter, where we consider issues around the management of AE portfolios.

## NOTES

1. For illustrative purposes, we randomly generated alphas, or expected excess returns, for each S&P 500 constituent, using a normal distribution with mean zero and standard deviation of 20 percent. We then constructed a portfolio with a predicted tracking risk of 5 percent versus the S&P 500 that maximized the alpha.

## REFERENCES

Clarke, R., H. de Silva, and S. Thorley. 2002. "Portfolio Constraints and the Fundamental Law of Active Management." *Financial Analysts Journal.* September/October.

# CHAPTER 3

# Managing Active Extension Portfolios

**Simon Emrich**
Executive Director
Morgan Stanley
Institutional Equity Division

In the previous chapter, we characterized active extension (AE) portfolios (and active benchmark-relative portfolios, generally) in terms of a two-dimensional continuum. The gross exposure of active portfolios is a function both of how much alpha we want (in terms of active weight) and how good the alpha should be (in terms of the information ratio [IR]). Compared to long-only active portfolios, AE portfolios provide scope for both "more" and "better" alpha—the active weight can be greater, and the composition of the active weights can better reflect the expected alphas.

Most AE managers will fall somewhere between those two extremes by taking new bets in areas of the portfolio where expected alpha opportunities were insufficiently represented in the long-only case, and scaling up existing bets where the long-only constraint was less binding. This decision will be driven by the maximization of expected risk-adjusted returns.

In this chapter, we take a closer look at the risk component of constructing long-only and AE portfolios. We argue that the empirical distribution of returns means that, in many cases, the incremental risk from taking on short positions is greater than that predicted from a typical linear factor model due to the non-normality of returns. This non-normality affects both the long and the short side; however, portfolio managers typically have greater experience managing the risk from non-normality on the long side than on the short side. Moreover, we show that the contribution of tail events to risk on the short side is more idiosyncratic than that on the long side.

Based on our analysis, the management of AE portfolios requires fundamentally different risk monitoring tools than long-only portfolios. In many cases, this means that the balance between more and better alpha is tilted toward scaling up existing positions as we move from long-only to AE, rather than adding on new, concentrated bets.

In the previous chapter, we decomposed active benchmark-relative portfolios into a benchmark-tracking portion and an active portion. We showed that for typical long-only active portfolios managed against typical market capitalization weighted benchmarks, active positions are asymmetric—relatively few, significant overweights are funded and counterbalanced by a relatively large number of maximally underweight stocks (i.e., those benchmark constituents not held in the portfolio). Because underweights can exceed the benchmark weight, the asymmetry of the active positions for AE portfolios can be reduced. This is the basis for "better" alpha.

## MEASURING AND MANAGING PORTFOLIO RISK

To understand the implications of relaxing the long-only constraint on portfolio and tracking risks, we need to analyze the sources of portfolio volatility. In the previous chapter, we showed by analyzing a portfolio's stock weights one can decompose the tracking risk of a portfolio into a benchmark mistracking portion, an active risk component, and a cross correlation term.

We generally measure the risk of equity through its volatility. This means that calculating the risk of a basket of equities requires both the volatility of each stock and their correlation with each other. These metrics are generally modeled as arising from a few systematic risk sources, as well as idiosyncratic, stock-specific risk sources. There are many different modeling approaches for systematic risk sources, from simple capital asset pricing models (CAPMs) that assume a single-market risk factor, to more detailed, multifactor models, such as those coming out of the arbitrage pricing theory (APT), and proxy models, such as the Fama-French approach.[1]

Regardless of the economic theory underlying the risk models, the basic structure of these linear factor models is always the same: The covariance matrix of stock returns is the sum of systematic and idiosyncratic components. Denoting the exposures (factor loadings) of stocks to each postulated systematic return driver by $\beta$, the covariance matrix of factor returns by $\sigma_F$, and the idiosyncratic variance matrix of stock returns by $\sigma_\varepsilon$, the covariance matrix $\Sigma$ is given by

$$\Sigma = \beta^T \sigma_F \beta + \sigma_\varepsilon$$

This common formulation makes a number of assumptions. For our purposes, it assumes that returns on both the stock level and the systematic factor level are (log) normally distributed. This enables us to characterize stocks based solely on their (expected) returns, and on their covariance matrix, without having to consider higher moments, such as skew or kurtosis. Calculation of portfolio risk, and optimization of portfolio weights, is much more straightforward under this assumption of normality because the first-order conditions of the optimization problem can be derived in closed form.

## OUTLIERS AND THE ASSUMPTION
## OF IDIOSYNCRATIC NORMALITY

How reasonable is the assumption of multivariate normality? Normality in factor and stock returns refers to a normal distribution over time. Under this assumption, the distribution of a sample of one return observation from each stock at a time $t$ will also be normally distributed. Exhibit 3.1 shows the empirical cross-sectional distribution of monthly Morgan Stanley Capital International United States (MSCI US) constituent returns for the period 1996 to 2007. The distribution is truncated at ±3 standard deviations, with the cumulative probability density of the tails aggregated for return observations beyond those points. We also show the implied normal distribution of cross-sectional returns, using the empirical cross-sectional standard deviation over the period.

We can clearly reject the hypothesis that cross-sectional returns were normally distributed over this period. There are significant fat tails, with monthly returns in excess of ±3 standard deviations much more likely than would be expected under a normal distribution.

These outliers are approximately symmetrically distributed in both tails. In fact, as Exhibit 3.2 shows, the outliers are also distributed relatively persistently over time. The exhibit shows the number of outlier stocks within the MSCI US on a monthly basis, together with the expected number of outliers if stock returns were cross-sectionally normally distributed.

The one-month return to outlier stocks over this period has been significant—on average, around ±38 percent. There were slightly more positive than negative outliers over the period.

These outlier returns can have a number of possible causes. On the negative outlier side, profit warnings have played a significant role, particularly in more volatile sectors such as information technology or consumer discretionary. On the positive outlier side, in addition to positive earnings surprises, takeovers, or leveraged buyouts (LBOs) have also played a significant role.

These outliers have been market characteristics since at least 1996. They have been a challenge for portfolio management, particularly in risk

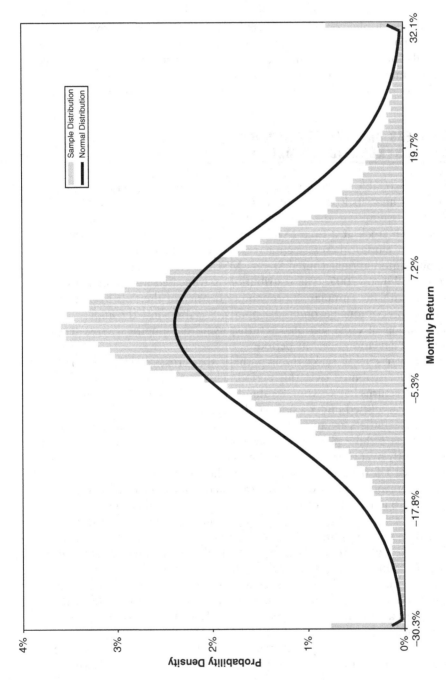

**EXHIBIT 3.1** The Empirical Cross-Sectional Distribution of Monthly MSCI US Stock Returns (1996–2007)

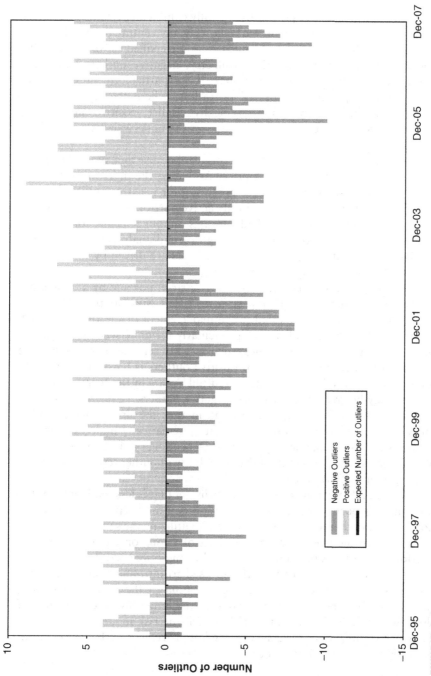

**EXHIBIT 3.2** The Number of Monthly Outlier Stocks in MSCI US (1996–2007)

control. Long-only active portfolios typically exhibit an asymmetry between overweights and underweights—a relatively concentrated set of signifi- cant overweights is funded by a much more diversified set of (maximally) underweight stocks. Given this asymmetry, negative outliers in the rel- atively few significant overweights have been particularly important for these types of portfolios. For AE portfolios, where the asymmetry be- tween over- and underweights is typically smaller, positive outliers also become important because they may impact the underweights, particularly the shorts.

Outliers are, by definition, hard to predict because they typically involve idiosyncratic shocks to a stock's price. Arguably, the investment manage- ment industry has more experience preparing for negative outliers because these have been important for long-only active portfolios, the most common form of investment portfolios. Bad earnings announcements, for example, should in principle be predictable through careful analysis of a company's fundamentals. Critically, most negative outliers are driven by idiosyncratic events affecting the company alone.

Positive outliers, in contrast, are often driven not just by a company's characteristics, but by another party's decisions, such as the decision to launch a takeover bid. This makes the management of the risk from such positive outliers more challenging, particularly for underweights. Although there are a number of approaches, such as LBO screens, a comprehensive list of stocks with the potential of positive outliers is hard to compile. As a result, the possibility of unanticipated tail events in the form of positive outliers may be greater than that for negative outliers.

Outliers in idiosyncratic returns mean that the linear factor models introduced in the previous section might systematically underestimate the volatility and tracking risk of portfolios. Depending on the capability of the alpha process to take account of the probability of outlier returns, this might be particularly relevant for AE portfolios.

Because AE portfolios have a constraint set that is less binding than that for long-only portfolios, the information ratio of the AE portfolio should be not lower than that for a long-only portfolio utilizing the same alpha source. By scaling up the over- and underweights of a long-only portfolio, an AE portfolio can always maintain the IR of the long-only portfolio.

If the opportunities of the AE are used to introduce new bets in the portfolio (what we referred to as better alpha in the previous chapter), the IR should increase when compared to the long-only case. However, if the new bets increase the outlier risk, and if the risk model used does not account for this outlier risk, the expected improvement in the IR might not be realized *ex post* if outliers occur.

## ACCOUNTING FOR OUTLIER RISK

How can we estimate the potential impact of outlier risk on *ex post* realized IRs, and hence decide on the optimal construction process for AE portfolios? Non-normality (the so-called fat tails) are a frequent problem in finance. A number of possible approaches have been developed that typically involve the use of higher moments (skew and kurtosis, in particular) and the development of risk measures taking account of the non-normality of returns. Value at risk (VaR) is an early example of such measures, but is often seen as unsatisfactory given its focus on a certain part of the return distribution only. More recently, the focus has been on the development of risk-adjusted return measures that take account of the non-normality of returns and can serve as replacement for the IR.[2]

However, many of these approaches may not be appropriate for the problem at hand. Although outliers occur persistently over time, the likelihood of any one stock on both sides of the distribution being an outlier stock over the next time period is quite low. Modeling the potential fat tailedness of individual stock returns, for example by assessing the likely kurtosis (and skew), can thus be problematic because the incidence of outliers in a particular stock is very low.

Instead, we advocate an adjustment in the aggregate portfolio's tracking risk forecast, taking account of the potential impact of outliers. The impact will critically depend on both the stock selection process (the alpha sources), and the portfolio construction process.

Historical analysis shows that outliers are unevenly distributed across the universe of stocks. In the MSCI US, for example, outliers have historically been concentrated in certain sectors (in particular, information technology and consumer discretionary), in the mid- to smaller-cap segment, and in stocks that would be classified as Growth. If an alpha process places particular emphasis on active stock selection in these segments of the market, the impact of outliers on *ex post* realized tracking risk may be greater than if the process focuses on other segments.

We propose classifying the universe of stocks along the three dimensions of sector, style, and size. For each possible combination of these classes, we can estimate both the probability of outlier events occurring, and the expected magnitude of returns conditional on an outlier event. Depending on the size of the universe, this approach can give more statistically significant estimates of the potential impact of outliers than trying to model them on a stock level. In principle, we can estimate the probability and the expected magnitude separately for positive and negative outliers. There may be cases in which these are meaningfully different for certain segments of the market.

For simplicity, we abstract away from these differences, and instead estimate the *absolute* expected magnitude of returns conditional on an outlier event.

Assuming that outlier events are independent from each other, we can calculate a three-dimensional matrix "cube" of expected impact of outliers, calculated by multiplying the probability of outliers in a specific segment of the market with the expected magnitude of conditional returns. The dimensions of the cube will be the number of sectors $l$, the number of styles $m$, and the number of market capitalization buckets $n$. This is another form of idiosyncratic returns. However, unlike the idiosyncratic returns in standard linear factor models, these represent the specific, non-normal component of a stock's return that is due to outlier events.

For computational simplicity, we can transform this matrix cube into a square, diagonal matrix of dimension $l \times m \times n$, with the diagonal elements corresponding to the entries in the matrix cube. Call this matrix $\sigma_o$. We also define a binary factor-loading matrix $\beta_o$, which maps each stock in the universe to its characteristics combination (sector, style, and market capitalization bucket).

This formulation allows us to extend our expected *ex post* covariance matrix of stock returns:

$$\Sigma = \beta^T \sigma_F \beta + \sigma_\varepsilon + \beta_o^T \sigma_o \beta_o$$
$$= \Sigma_F + \sigma_\varepsilon + \Sigma_o$$

The first two terms are given by a linear factor risk model (which assumes normality in returns); the last term reflects the contribution of the estimated outlier risk.

Because the three risk terms are assumed to be independent from one another, we can rewrite the risk decomposition introduced in the previous chapter in terms of the three risk terms:

|  | Mistracking Risk | Active Risk | Cross Risk | |
|---|---|---|---|---|
| $\sigma_{p-b}^2 =$ | $v_{c-b} \Sigma_F v_{c-b}^T$ | $+ w_a^2 v_a \Sigma_F v_a^T$ | $+ 2 w_a v_a \Sigma_F v_{c-b}^T$ | Systematic Risk |
|  | $+ v_{c-b} \sigma_\varepsilon v_{c-b}^T$ | $+ w_a^2 v_a \sigma_\varepsilon v_a^T$ | $+ 2 w_a v_a \sigma_\varepsilon v_{c-b}^T$ | Idiosyncratic Risk |
|  | $+ v_{c-b} \Sigma_o v_{c-b}^T$ | $+ w_a^2 v_a \Sigma_o v_a^T$ | $+ 2 w_a v_a \Sigma_o v_{c-b}^T$ | Outlier Risk |

Our focus is on the new, third row of this decomposition and, in particular, on the contribution of outlier risk to the active risk term. We further split this term into contributions from overweights and underweights by defining two new vectors $v_a^+$ and $v_a^-$, which contain the positive and negative active weights, respectively. The term is then given by

$$w_a^2 v_a \Sigma_o v_a^T = w_a^2 v_a^+ \Sigma_o v_a^{+T} + w_a^2 v_a^- \Sigma_o v_a^{-T}$$

The two components of this term are quadratic in the weights $v_a$. This accentuates the contribution to outlier risk from large active weights compared to that from small active weights, everything else being equal.

We argued earlier that AE portfolios typically reduce the asymmetry between the structure of overweights and of underweights. Because the short component of AE portfolios allows us to take underweights that are greater than the benchmark weight, we would expect stocks with a large negative alpha to show greater underweights than in a long-only active portfolio using the same alpha source.

The reduction in asymmetry will typically increase the contribution to tracking risk coming from outliers on the underweight side. To the extent that this outlier risk is not captured by the risk model utilized, this may mean that the *ex post* realized tracking risk in the presence of outliers may be greater than anticipated.

This can have an impact on the *ex post* realized IR as well. Depending on the structure of the active positions in the portfolio, the impact can be significant. In terms of our earlier distinction between AE allowing for both more and better alpha, this impact may reduce the attractiveness of changing the structure of the active positions unless the outlier risk can be properly accounted for.

## MANAGING OUTLIER RISK

Outlier risk presents some unique challenges to the management of AE portfolios. Assuming that the linear factor model used to predict tracking risk is equally valid for both overweights and underweights, managing the portfolio's tracking risk based on the linear factor model presents no new challenges when compared to the case of a long-only portfolio. However, outliers do present new challenges.

Outlier risk management involves two components. First, outlier risk has to be anticipated, at least in aggregate terms. The previous section outlined an approach to estimate and control for this risk. The second component is the day-to-day management of the portfolio, and the response to outliers should they occur.

Many portfolio managers have stop-loss rules in place that are intended to close out or reduce positions that contribute significantly negatively to performance. Stop-loss rules can be a valuable risk control tool; however, in many cases, they do not deal adequately with outlier risk. Outliers, as defined earlier in this chapter, tend to be driven by idiosyncratic shocks, such as a bad earnings report or mergers and acquisition (M&A) activity. In many cases, the price response to such shocks is instantaneous; outlier risk is often gap risk, something that stop-loss rules cannot control. In many cases, stop-loss rules can prevent worse losses in case the stock drifts up or down further following the gap, but they cannot control the gap itself.

This inability to protect from gap risk, which forms a large part of outlier risk, makes the anticipation of outliers so important. We have to be aware of the potential impact on both performance and tracking risk, and compare this impact to that on long-only portfolios.

Because positive outliers may be more challenging to anticipate, given our earlier discussion, limiting their potential impact on the portfolio may often be given a greater weight than the exploitation of alpha ideas. In practice, this means that even if we have the ability to reduce the asymmetry between overweight and underweight positions in an AE portfolio, we may choose not to do so in certain segments of the market. Instead, we may opt to keep the structure of relatively few, concentrated overweights coupled with a relatively diversified basket of underweights (including the net shorts).

In terms of our portfolio decomposition framework, this means that certain segments of the active long/short portfolio will continue to resemble a "portable alpha" portfolio. Short positions are represented by broad, benchmark-replicating instruments, such as sector ETFs. This means that for those segments of the market, the focus is on more rather than better alpha.

## MANAGING ACTIVE EXTENSION PORTFOLIOS

In this chapter, we argued that AE portfolios introduce some unique challenges to the portfolio manager. Although much of the framework of risk-controlled alpha generation that is familiar from long-only portfolios carries over to AE portfolios, the potential structural differences in the latter can lead to some significant new issues.

We argued that these issues are particularly related to the presence of outliers in the cross-sectional return distribution, driven by idiosyncratic shocks to individual stock prices. The impact of these outliers on portfolio return and risk may be disproportionately greater in AE portfolios than in long-only portfolios, particularly if the structure of the active weights is changed. Greater concentration in the underweight positions may lead to significantly higher outlier risk contribution.

This outlier risk is by definition hard to manage because it is driven by idiosyncratic shocks. Moreover, many of the common risk management approaches, such as stop-loss rules, may not provide sufficient protection from the impact of this outlier risk. Instead, we need to form expectations of the possible impact of this outlier risk on the overall portfolio and choose an appropriate active weight structure to manage this impact. In many cases, this may lead to a preference of more alpha, rather than better alpha.

## NOTES

1. The literature on equity risk premia is vast. CAPM was developed by Sharpe, Lintner, and Black—see Sharpe, William, "Capital Asset Prices: A Theory of Market Equilibrium under Conditions of Risk," *Journal of Finance*, 19/3, September 1964; Lintner, John, "The Valuation of Risk Assets and the Selection of Risky Investments in Stock Portfolios and Capital Budgets," *Review of Economics and Statistics*, 47/1, February 1965; and Black, Fischer, "Capital Market Equilibrium with Restricted Borrowing," *Journal of Business*, 45, July 1972. See Fama, Eugene and Kenneth French, "The Cross-Section of Expected Stock Returns," *Journal of Finance*, 47/2, June 1992, for a discussion of the so-called Fama-French Approach. Arbitrage pricing theory was introduced in Ross, Stephen, "The Arbitrage Theory of Capital Asset Pricing," *Journal of Economic Theory*, 13/3, 1976.
2. For an example for such an approach, see Cherny, Alexander S. and Dilip B. Madan, "On Measuring the Degree of Market Efficiency," January 2007. Available at SSRN: http://ssrn.com/abstract=955472.

# Special Topics Relating to Active 130/30 Extensions

# CHAPTER 4

# Active Extension Portfolios: An Exploration of the 120/20 Concept

**Anthony Bova**
Vice President
Morgan Stanley, Research

**Martin Leibowitz**
Managing Director
Morgan Stanley, Research

A ctive extensions (AEs) such as 120/20 strategies offer increased flexibility for active equity management. The expanded footings provide a wider range of alpha-seeking opportunities for both traditional and quantitative management.

Active extension strategies can be designed to fit within a sponsor's existing allocation space for active U.S. equity management. With proper risk control, an AE may entail a tracking error (TE) that is only moderately greater than that of a comparable long-only fund.

Active extensions open the door to a fresh set of actively chosen underweight positions. With long-only funds, significantly sized underweights are limited to stocks with very large market capitalizations, with the remaining underweights being scattered (sometimes with less attention) across a broad range of stocks.

A carefully implemented AE can expand relationships with existing managers. A sponsor may want to draw upon those active managers who

---

Originally published as part of the *Morgan Stanley Portfolio Notes*, January 18, 2006.

have already been vetted in terms of their alpha-seeking skills, organization infrastructure, and risk-control procedures.

Active extensions can facilitate and sharpen a number of standard active management techniques; for example, more specific relative value trades, selective weight enhancement, industry and sector positioning, and so on.

The special challenges and costs involved in the shorting process should not be underestimated. Many long-only managers are initially daunted by shorting's costs and need for significantly different approaches to valuation, execution, monitoring, and risk control.

## RATIONALE FOR ACTIVE EXTENSIONS

Active equity management can be enhanced through a moderate loosening in the long-only constraint, allowing up to 20 percent of a fund to be shorted. In general, these 120/20 techniques use this shorting facility to *extend* the universe of active management opportunities, rather than acting as a leveraging mechanism for taking more concentrated long positions. For this reason, the term *short extension* seems like a more reasonable expression to capture the key distinguishing feature of the 120/20 concept and its variants.

At the outset, it should be noted that shorting differs significantly from long-only management in a number of important ways, including transaction and maintenance costs, the available level and continuity of liquidity, the more intensive monitoring and risk control requirements, and so on.

A key feature of the 120/20 strategy is that it maintains the basic risk characteristics of benchmark-centric long-only funds:

- The 20 percent short is offset by a beta-equivalent 20 percent long position to preserve the beta posture, and
- The overweight and underweight positions are structured to keep the TE within reasonable bounds.

Within these risk constraints, the 20 percent short extension opens up a broader range of active alpha opportunities, with the objective of improving the ratio of active return relative to the associated TE.

The total beta accounts for over 90 percent of the total volatility of most U.S. pension funds, foundations, and endowments. Moreover, this total beta dominance occurs even with very highly diversified allocations having as little as 15 to 20 percent weightings in U.S. bonds and equities. Given this central role for the beta factor, the function of each asset class within a policy allocation can be analyzed in terms of its implicit or explicit beta value, beta variability, passive and/or active alpha variability, and other associated dragon risks. By maintaining a general congruence along these risk dimensions, short-extension portfolios can be viewed as a modest variant of traditional equity as an asset class.

Thus, unlike shorting vehicles that tend to have beta values that are either untargeted or deliberately varied, a short extension's well-defined beta value allows it to basically occupy the same allocation space as long-only equity funds.

The recent studies of the 120/20 portfolio have drawn upon new developments in the theory of active management. These academic studies generally employ an elegant, but somewhat complex, approach to address the broad sweep of problems associated with multiple portfolio constraints. The strategy here is to focus more narrowly on the opportunity enhancement feature of the 120/20 strategies, using a simple alpha-ranking model to characterize the active management process. This model is applied to a basic short-extension example that was chosen primarily for illustrative purposes, and should not be construed as being representative of any specific extension strategy. Although this approach represents an admittedly less comprehensive treatment than the referenced studies, it does capture the fundamental appeal of AE strategies for sponsors and for both traditional active and quantitative equity managers.

For sponsors, the 120/20 concept is a relatively modest move toward expanding the opportunities for an active manager that the sponsor already believes has the skill set to generate positive alphas. Moreover, this potential alpha enhancement can be pursued within a disciplined framework that retains absolute and relative risk controls that are comparable to those provided by the sponsor's existing long-only managers.

For active managers that would like to organically expand their alpha-seeking process, the short-extension technique offers the prospect of a differentiated, higher value-added service.

## THE CAPITALIZATION STRUCTURE OF THE EQUITY MARKET

It is well known that virtually every equity market is highly concentrated, with a small number of very large-cap names, a moderate number of reasonably large-cap names, and a very large number of lesser capitalization companies. Taking the S&P 500 index as an example, Exhibit 4.1 presents, in descending order, the capitalization for each stock as a percentage of the total S&P 500; that is, the first stock, Exxon Mobil, has a market capitalization of 3.2 percent, the second-largest stock, GE, 3.1 percent, and so on.

Capitalization rank has broad implications for a stock's performance characteristics, although some key variables exhibit surprisingly modest sensitivity to the capitalization level. For example, Exhibit 4.2 displays the

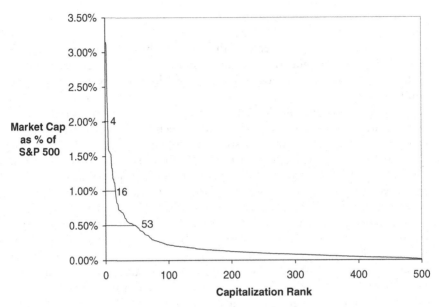

**EXHIBIT 4.1**   Market Cap Percent of S&P 500 Stocks
*Source:* Morgan Stanley Research

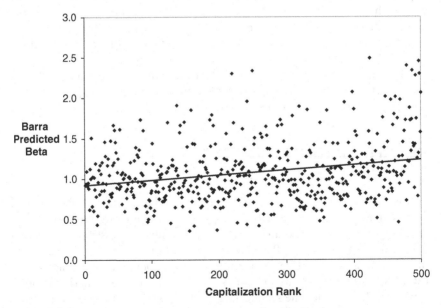

**EXHIBIT 4.2**   Barra Predicted Beta versus Capitalization Rank
*Source:* Morgan Stanley Research

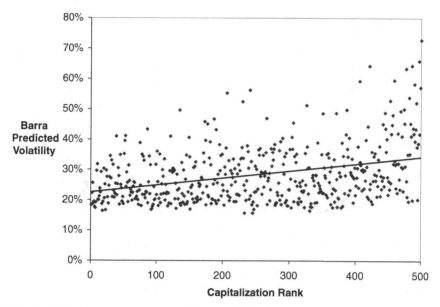

**EXHIBIT 4.3** Barra Predicted Volatility versus Capitalization Rank
*Source:* Morgan Stanley Research

*ex ante* Barra betas for each stock across the capitalization structure. As we can see from the scattergram, these betas are indeed all over the place, but with only a moderate trend toward higher betas at the lower capitalizations.

Similarly, if we look at the Barra estimates of total volatility, the scattergram in Exhibit 4.3 shows that, in contrast to what might have been expected, overall volatility increases only moderately as we move toward smaller capitalization.

Exhibit 4.4 shows the *alpha volatility*—the residual volatility after extracting the stock's beta-based co-movement with the market as a whole. Again, there is a modest increase in alpha volatility with smaller capitalization. However, it is interesting to see that even the large-capitalization stocks seem to have a surprising amount of this idiosyncratic volatility relative to their Barra beta.

## AN ALPHA OPPORTUNITY MODEL

To explore the potential advantages of the AE, it is helpful to have a model for active management opportunities as a function of capitalization structure. Even though we could argue with the specific details of any such

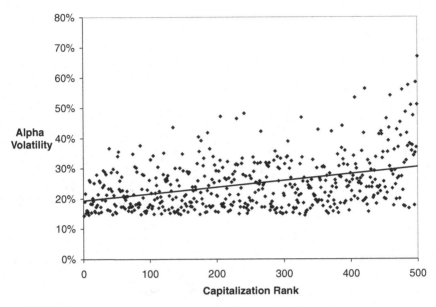

**EXHIBIT 4.4**  Alpha Volatility versus Capitalization Rank
*Source:* Morgan Stanley Research

model, the broad outlines can serve to illustrate the key points involved in AE.

By showing the number of analysts' earnings estimates, Exhibit 4.5 provides a rough gauge of the level of research coverage across the capitalization structure. Research coverage does appear to have a discernible trend, with the larger names being more intensely covered. This scattergram may understate the level of research intensity in that, for a given number of estimates, the larger companies may be subject to more intense and more comprehensive analyses.

In the following discussion, we shall assume that there is no distinction between the coverage on the long or the short side, even though many would argue that the dominance of long-only asset managers leads to a far more intense focus on buy versus sell opportunities.

We often hear the argument that the very largest caps offer less opportunity for truly fresh insights, implying that there may be more alpha potential in the lower caps. However, at some point, with ever lower capitalizations, the issue of liquidity will arise. Liquidity is a function of trading volume that, in turn, tends to be related to market capitalization. Of course, the need for liquidity is very dependent on the nature and size of the fund

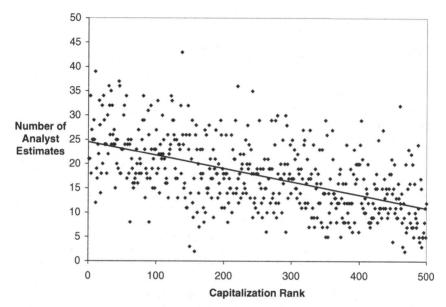

**EXHIBIT 4.5** Research Coverage versus Capitalization Rank
*Source:* Morgan Stanley Research

in question (e.g., larger funds with shorter horizons require more liquidity, smaller funds with longer horizons may require less). Exhibit 4.6 makes the point that the better active opportunities are likely to be found in that swath of the capitalization spectrum where the liquidity is ample but the research coverage is not too intense.

Benchmark-centric active managers tend to have limits in terms of both their minimum and their maximum position size. The maximum size serves as one form of risk control, whereas the minimum helps keep the monitoring span within reasonable bounds. Under these fairly standard sizing conditions, the long-only mandate allows for positive overweights across the entire capitalization spectrum. However, negative views can only be expressed by underweight positions that are limited in size by a stock's benchmark weight. Thus, underweight opportunities are restricted to very large-cap stocks. As schematically illustrated in Exhibit 4.7, the market's cap structure means that long-only funds are foreclosed from a wide range of potential underweights.

One of the benefits of the flexibility to take short positions is that it opens the door to this region of potentially opportunity-rich underweights. To gauge the benefits of this flexibility, a framework is needed that is descriptive of the active management process.

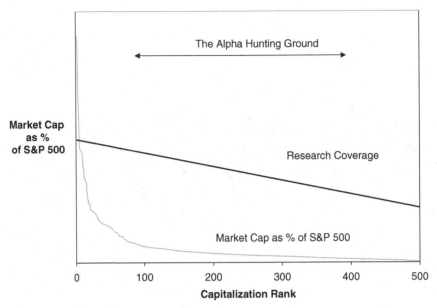

**EXHIBIT 4.6**   Where to Search for Alpha
*Source:* Morgan Stanley Research

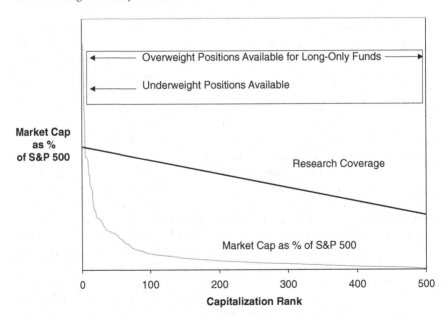

**EXHIBIT 4.7**   Search for Alpha for Long-Only Fund Is Limited
*Source:* Morgan Stanley Research

## AN ACTIVE MANAGEMENT MODEL

In contrast to the more theoretical analyses with score-based variable weights, we will use a more basic model with a fixed weight of 2 percent for all active positions, whether underweights or overweights. In practice, most funds have a standard weight for their active positions. Indeed, in those cases where they have smaller positions, they may act as a first step in the direction of a deeper analysis and a firmer conviction that might ultimately lead to the full standard position size.

With funds that are strictly long-only (i.e., without access to futures or other derivatives), the overweight positions must be balanced against the complementary underweights that serve both as funding sources and as mechanisms for beta control. As such, the underweights are generally *not* equivalent in active content to the overweights. There may be a wide dispersion in the size of these nominal underweights, but it would be misleading to view all of them as truly active positions. For many reasons, the basic orientation of most active portfolio managers is a focus on the selection of the overweight positions.

One of the motivations behind the 120/20 AE is to enable the portfolio manager to exploit a broader range of potentially attractive underweight positions. Suppose a fund is granted the freedom to short up to 20 percent of its assets, subject to maintaining a high level of beta control and a limited TE. The portfolio construction can then deploy 20 percent of its asset size in newly available underweights and then use the additional 20 percent funds generated for a comparable set of additional overweights. At the 2 percent position size that we have assumed, this translates into 10 new active underweights and 10 new active overweights.

## THE ALPHA RANKING MODEL

To evaluate the benefits of this portfolio extension, assume that the best overweight offered an expected alpha of 5 percent, and that the remaining positions could be arrayed in sequence of decreasing alpha. Exhibit 4.8 displays such orderings, with the decline in alpha proceeding in two phases.

The first phase consists of the best 25 positions, with the alpha eroding from the highest 5 percent down to an alpha of 3 percent by the 25th ranked position (i.e., 60% of the first alpha). After this first phase, the subsequent positions undergo a second phase of more rapid decay, with the 50th position having an alpha of only 1 percent (i.e., about 33% of the 26th position's alpha).

As shown in Exhibit 4.9, with this two-phase ranking model, the total portfolio alpha will rise with additional positions, but at a decreasing rate.

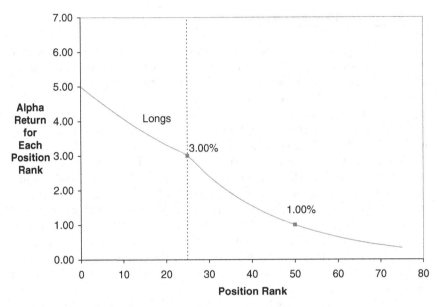

**EXHIBIT 4.8**   A Two-Phase Model of Alpha Rankings
*Source:* Morgan Stanley Research

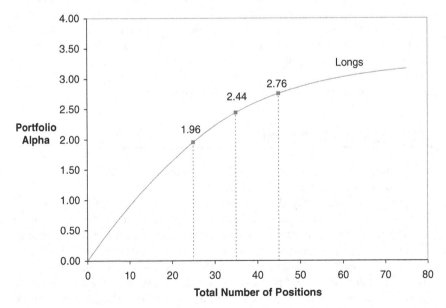

**EXHIBIT 4.9**   Cumulative Portfolio Alpha for Given Number of Positions
*Source:* Morgan Stanley Research

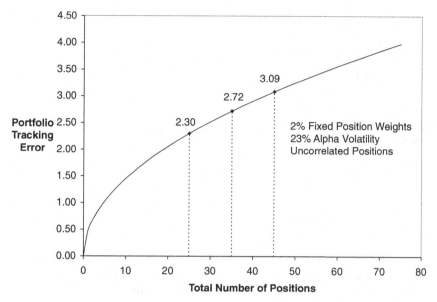

**EXHIBIT 4.10**   Portfolio TE for Given Number of Positions
*Source:* Morgan Stanley Research

In terms of TE, if the positions have statistically independent TE (assumed to be 23%), the well-known square root of N rule applies, leading to the portfolio TE shown in Exhibit 4.10.

Combining the portfolio alpha from Exhibit 4.9 together with the TE from Exhibit 4.10 leads to Exhibit 4.11, which plots the portfolio alpha as a function of the TE for varying numbers of positions.

At this point, we make a further assumption that the portfolio manager will have a maximum number of positions that he can thoughtfully establish and monitor. Indeed, one characteristic of an active manager's style is this maximum number of active positions and the percentage of the portfolio that they comprise. Our base-case example consists of a long-only manager having 25 overweight positions, each with a 2 percent weight. The remaining 50 percent of the assets serve as nonspecific underweights configured so as to maintain the unit-beta posture.

## AN ACTIVE EXTENSION MODEL

The preceding alpha ranking model can be adapted to a fund having a limited flexibility to take short positions. Assume that the manager now

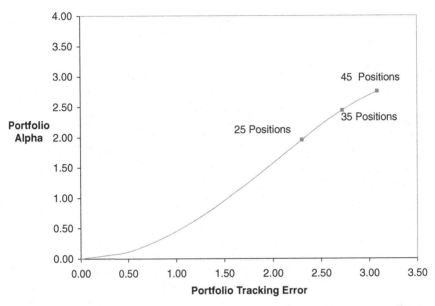

**EXHIBIT 4.11**   Portfolio Alpha as Function of TE for Long-Only Funds
*Source:* Morgan Stanley Research

achieves the right to short up to 20 percent of the fund's asset size. With the position size kept constant at the 2 percent level, this 20 percent shorting option allows for 10 new underweights. The added fractional costs involved in the short side can be modeled by assuming that the best short position has an alpha somewhat lower than the best long position. If we take a 0.50 percent decrement for this effect, the best new underweight will have an alpha of 4.50 percent. For simplicity, the subsequent underweight position can then be viewed as subject to the same percentage erosion as applied to the overweights (Exhibit 4.12). These 10 new underweight positions now represent a fresh source of high-quality alpha that could contribute 0.81 percent to the total portfolio alpha. In essence, these new underweights are picking off the early cream of the alpha ranking curve.

It well might be argued that the alpha quality ranking of the short positions because they are generally underpursued, should be higher than the ranking curve used for overweights. However, there are serious pragmatic infrastructural and risk-control problems associated with the short side, quite apart from all the behavioral biases and limited shorting experience

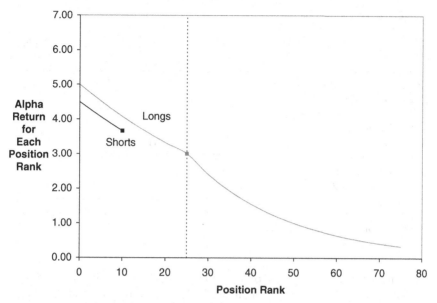

**EXHIBIT 4.12**  Alpha Rankings for Short Positions
*Source:* Morgan Stanley Research

of long-only managers. Managers who have moved into shorting stocks for the first time frequently point out that the process proves far more difficult than they anticipated. (Indeed, the recent trend of long/short hedge funds to launch long-only funds has been frequently ascribed to the difficulties in finding good shorts.)

After frictional costs, the proceeds from these shorts could be deployed to establish 10 new long positions. Because the 25 best overweight positions have already been taken, these additional 10 will have to represent lesser ranked opportunities. In other words, these new (short-funded) overweights will consist of alpha returns from the 26th to 35th ranked positions in Exhibit 4.8. The 35-position overweights will now provide cumulative alpha of 2.44 percent (Exhibit 4.9).

The question might be raised at this point as to why not simply increase the sizing of the more attractive overweight positions. Quite apart from how this greater concentration might lead to increased TE, the pragmatic fact is that most traditional managers are limited to a certain maximum position size.

**EXHIBIT 4.13**  AE Model

|  | Total Number of Positions | Alpha | Tracking Error | Alpha/ TE Ratio |
|---|---|---|---|---|
| Long-Only Funds with 25.2% Positions | 25 | 1.96 | 2.30 | 0.85 |
| Long-Only Funds + next 10.2% Positions | 35 | 2.44 | 2.72 | 0.90 |
| Top New + next 10.2% Short Positions | +10 | +0.81 | | |
| Total Active Extension Portfolio of 45.2% Positions | 45 | 3.25 | 3.09 | 1.05 |

*Source:* Morgan Stanley Research

The net portfolio effect from the 20 percent AE is a move from 25 long overweights to 35 long overweights *and* 10 fresh short underweights (i.e., a total position count of 45). As summarized in Exhibit 4.13, this extension in position count, together with the mining of a rich set of underweight opportunities, leads to a portfolio alpha of 3.25 percent, a significant increase from the 1.96 percent of the original long-only portfolio. At the same time, the TE increases to 3.09 percent versus 2.30 percent for the long-only case. The active return/risk ratio rises to 1.05, compared with 0.85 for the long-only case.

It should also be noted that the total positions increase from 25 to 45 represents an 80 percent change (i.e., far greater than the 20% amount shorted). This greater position count derives from the assumption that the 20 percent shorts and the new overweights will only be taken against explicit alpha opportunities, whereas the original 100 percent fund had only 50 percent of its assets devoted to truly active positions.

Exhibits 4.14 and 4.15 compare the alphas for the long-only and the short-extension portfolios as a function of position count and TE, respectively.

Finally, Exhibit 4.16 moves beyond the 120/20 case to depict the ratio of portfolio alpha to TE as a function of various extension levels. This curve rises rather rapidly as it moves from the original long-only portfolio to the 20 percent extension and then starts to bend over as it moves toward larger short-extension levels, with the lower incremental alphas on both the long and the short side.

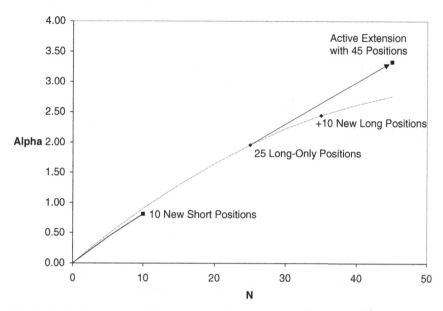

**EXHIBIT 4.14** Portfolio Alpha as Function of Number of Positions
*Source:* Morgan Stanley Research

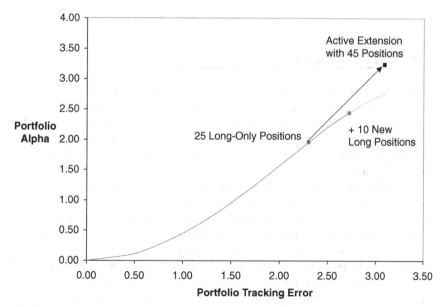

**EXHIBIT 4.15** Portfolio Alpha as Function of TE
*Source:* Morgan Stanley Research

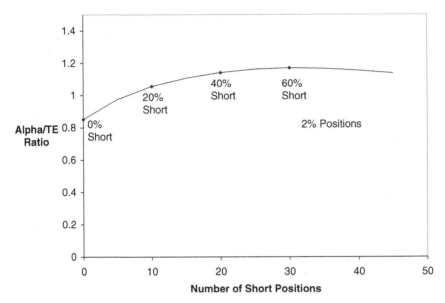

**EXHIBIT 4.16**   Alpha/TE Ratio versus AE
*Source:* Morgan Stanley Research

## OTHER APPLICATIONS

In addition to the position expansion previously described, the AE can facilitate and sharpen a number of standard management techniques. Thus, relative value trades on two or more specific securities can be more precisely shaped. Moreover, the augmented proceeds can enable priority positions to be better-sized, even within the initial bounds on maximum position size.

In addition, the additional footings, both on the long and the short side, can be deployed in a mix of active/generic modes. This flexibility could be useful in a wide variety of applications (e.g., more refined relative value trades both within and among different industry and sector groups). Moreover, even for a prescribed set of initial long-only positions, the broader footings could provide the needed flexibility to achieve better beta control and tighter benchmark tracking. Thus, in such an application, an AE may actually (and somewhat ironically) result in a lower TE for a prescribed initial set of long-only positions.

## CAVEATS AND GENERALIZATIONS

As noted at the outset, our numerical example was chosen primarily for purposes of simplicity and clarity. There are many additional factors and myriad complications that would come to bear in any actual portfolio context. At the same time, the issues that differentiate short positions from long positions should not be underestimated. In particular, there are multiple formats for implementing the shorting process, with considerable variation in transaction costs and other frictions (e.g., the fraction of short proceeds that become available for reinvestment).

Our analytical model was deliberately based on a highly restrictive set of assumptions—a fixed position size, a common TE, redeployment of short proceeds into the long tail, comparable long/short ranking models, and so on. The alpha ranking model can be extended to overcome many of these limitations. For example, the weighting could be scaled to each position's prospective return/risk ratio, whereas the portfolio TE could be optimized relative to a specific parameter for risk tolerance or to some general utility function. It would also certainly be desirable to have a more refined treatment of the differences between long and short positions. However, in this model, we have tilted toward simplicity in addressing the challenge of capturing the key elements of the concept without overburdening the exposition.

In summary, an AE, reasonably sized and properly risk-controlled, can occupy the same allocation space as traditional long-only equity funds while providing significant additional flexibility for alpha-seeking active management.

# CHAPTER 5

# Alpha Ranking Models and Active Extension Strategies

**Anthony Bova**
Vice President
Morgan Stanley, Research

**Martin Leibowitz**
Managing Director
Morgan Stanley, Research

**A**lpha ranking models can be useful for analyzing alternative structures for both long-only and long/short portfolios. With active extension (AE) portfolios, the alpha ranking model can also help determine the number of active short positions that should be taken. At some point, the incremental benefit in portfolio alpha will fall below the increase in tracking error volatility (TEV), and the alpha/TEV curve will begin to turn down.

With a moderately declining alpha ranking, the AE provides increasing benefits that provide peak improvement in the alpha/TEV ratio of about 30 percent. The optimal short percentage lies somewhere in the 40 to 60 percent region.

For a "concentrated" ranking model with very high initial alphas followed by an intense decay process, the optimal shorting percentage is in the 10 to 20 percent range, with about the same 30 percent improvement. A highly concentrated ranking model would also argue for a smaller number of positions in the basic long-only portfolio.

Active extensions can provide valuable improvements in the alpha/TEV ratio across a wide range of portfolio characteristics. However, there are also situations where the various costs and frictions can outweigh the benefits.

---

Originally published as part of the *Morgan Stanley Portfolio Notes*, May 16, 2006.

The preconditions for productive AEs include an efficient shorting procedure, an effective risk control discipline, and a credible prospect of being able to generate truly positive alpha values.

## LONG-ONLY ALPHA RANKING MODELS

Three distinct alpha-ranking patterns are displayed in Exhibit 5.1. The first begins with an alpha of 5 percent and then declines exponentially to 2 percent at the 25th position. The second model is a simple flat pattern with all alphas fixed at 3.50 percent. The third model represents a highly concentrated set of good opportunities, with an initial alpha of 13 percent but subject to rapid exponential decay that reduces the alpha to 1 percent by the 15th position.

As shown in Exhibit 5.2, all three models were calibrated to have the same cumulative alpha of 1.75 percent for a portfolio with 25 position weights of 2 percent.

In terms of tracking error (TE), if the 2 percent positions have statistically independent TE (assumed to be 23%), then the well-known square root of N rule applies, leading to the same portfolio TE for all three cases, as shown in Exhibit 5.3.

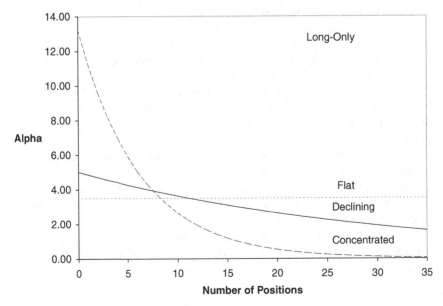

**EXHIBIT 5.1**  Long-Only Alpha Ranking Models
*Source:* Morgan Stanley Research

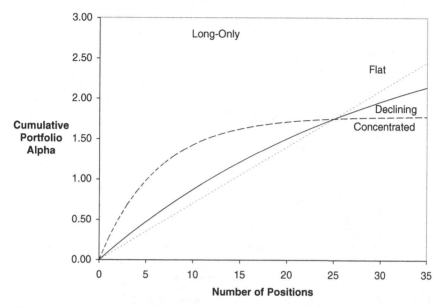

**EXHIBIT 5.2**   Cumulative Portfolio Alpha for Given Number of Positions
*Source:* Morgan Stanley Research

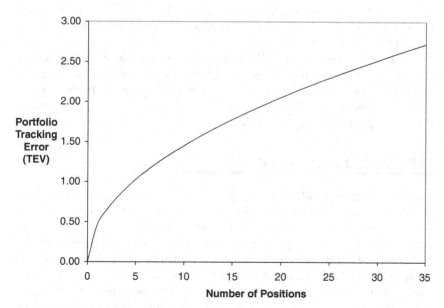

**EXHIBIT 5.3**   Portfolio TE for Given Number of Positions
*Source:* Morgan Stanley Research

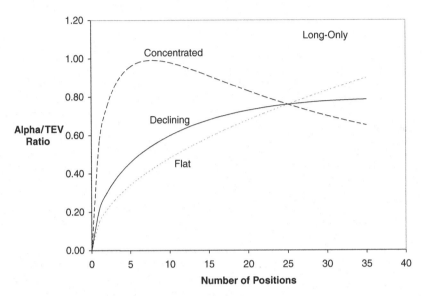

**EXHIBIT 5.4** Alpha/TEV Ratio for Given Number of Positions
*Source:* Morgan Stanley Research

The portfolio alpha and TEs from Exhibits 5.2 and 5.3 can be combined to calculate the alpha/TEV ratio as a function of the position count (Exhibit 5.4) and the TEV (Exhibit 5.5).

In the flat case, the alpha/TEV ratio increases as the alpha from each new position overwhelms the added TE. In the declining alpha case, the alpha/TEV ratio begins to flatten around the 20th position. In the concentrated case, the alpha/TEV ratio peaks quickly after 5 to 10 positions and then subsequently decreases rapidly.

## ADDING THE ACTIVE EXTENSION

The preceding long-only alpha ranking models can be adapted to a fund that has a limited flexibility to take short positions. An AE with 2 percent underweights is now assumed to be added to a fixed a long-only portfolio consisting of 25, 2-percent positions. The added fractional costs involved in the short side can be modeled by taking a 50 basis point (bp) decrement for each short position versus the corresponding long position. The underweight positions are assumed to be subject to the same percentage erosion as the corresponding long-only alpha ranking model. Exhibit 5.6 displays both the long and short rankings for the declining alpha case.

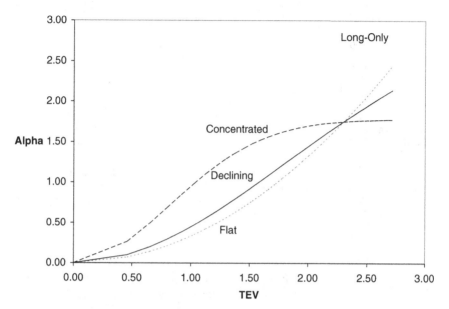

**EXHIBIT 5.5**   Portfolio Alpha versus TEV
*Source:* Morgan Stanley Research

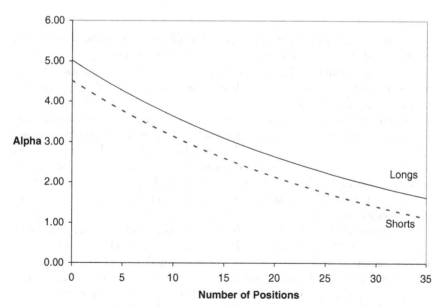

**EXHIBIT 5.6**   Long and Short Declining Alpha Ranking Model
*Source:* Morgan Stanley Research

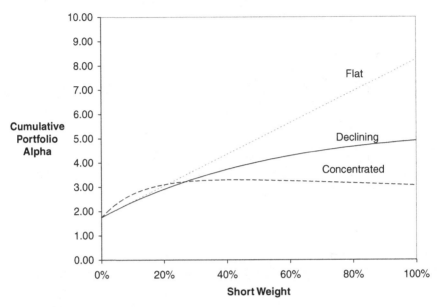

**EXHIBIT 5.7**  Cumulative Portfolio Alpha versus AE
*Source:* Morgan Stanley Research

Assuming a fixed 2 percent weight for all active positions, each short position will result in 2 percent cash proceeds that can be used to fund a new 2 percent long position. However, to be conservative, we have assumed these new long positions come from the lower-ranked 26th to 35th opportunities on the long-only alpha curves.

Exhibit 5.7 displays the portfolio alpha for all three cases as a function of increasing extension levels. Not surprisingly, the constant alpha case results in an upward sloping curve. In the declining case, the portfolio alpha flattens as the 100 percent short weight is approached. The concentrated case results in a portfolio alpha that peaks out in the 20 to 30 percent range and then decreases slightly due to the negative alpha levels that occur at the higher extension levels.

Incorporating the higher TE from the short positions and new longs yields the alpha/TEV curves in Exhibit 5.8. The alpha/TEV ratio increases in the declining alpha case as we move from 0 percent to 40 percent and remains relatively flat until it begins to fall after 60 percent. The concentrated case peaks in the 10 to 20 percent AE range and subsequently declines. As with the cumulative portfolio alpha, the (unrealistic) flat case results in a continuously upward sloping alpha/TEV ratio.

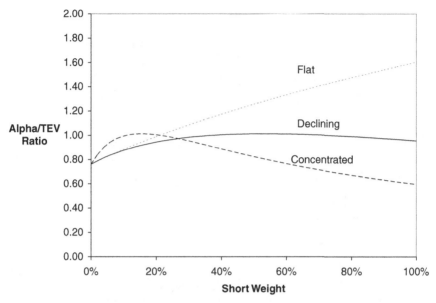

**EXHIBIT 5.8**  Alpha/TEV Ratio versus AE
*Source:* Morgan Stanley Research

## GREATER SHORTING COSTS

The short positions thus far have been assumed to carry a 50 basis point higher cost than the long positions. Managers who have moved into shorting stocks for the first time frequently point out that the process proves more difficult than they anticipated. Thus, the cost of shorting is an important factor in analyzing the impact of moving from a long-only to an AE portfolio. Exhibits 5.9 and 5.10 display the declining and concentrated alpha cases for shorting costs of 50, 100, and 200 bp.

For the declining-alpha case, the AEs with costs of 50 bp and 100 bp both generate peak alpha/TEV ratios at short weights of 40 to 50 percent. With short costs of 200 bp, the extension strategy peaks earlier around a 30 percent short weight and then actually falls below the long-only portfolio at a short weight of 70 percent. In the concentrated alpha case, the AE portfolios all peak with short weights in the 10 to 20 percent range, and fall below the long-only portfolio's alpha/TEV ratio when a 40 to 60 percent short is reached.

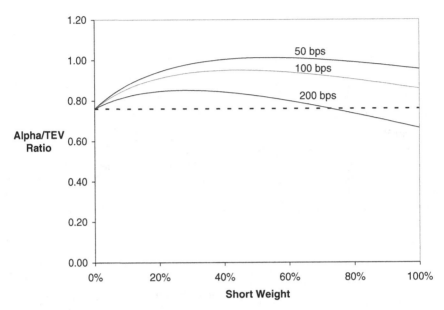

**EXHIBIT 5.9**  Declining Alpha/TEV Ratio for Various Short Costs
*Source:* Morgan Stanley Research

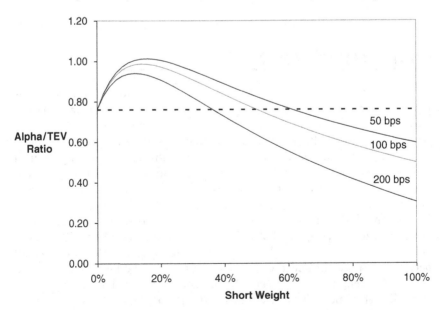

**EXHIBIT 5.10**  Concentrated Alpha/TEV Ratio for Various Short Costs
*Source:* Morgan Stanley Research

## A DOUBLY CONCENTRATED PORTFOLIO

The AE process thus far has started after the first 25 long positions (i.e., at a 50% active weight). Given the alpha ranking model in the concentrated case, the question can be raised as to whether it would be more beneficial to start with a more compact long portfolio before adding short positions. From Exhibit 5.4, the alpha/TEV ratio in the long-only case attains its maximum level at eight positions (16% active weight). Adding the short positions from this point yields the alpha/TEV graph in Exhibit 5.11. The peak alpha/TEV ratio is now 70 percent higher than the long-only ratio.

## PRECONDITIONS FOR ACTIVE EXTENSIONS

For most alpha ranking models based on positive alpha values, the move to an AE portfolio will make sense, although the best short weight may vary significantly. However, when the alpha expectations are low, the frictional costs associated with shorting can seriously erode the benefits of the extension portfolio. Exhibit 5.12 displays an alpha ranking model for a very low

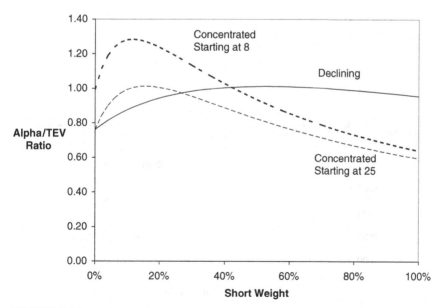

**EXHIBIT 5.11** Concentrated Alpha/TEV Ratio versus AE
*Source:* Morgan Stanley Research

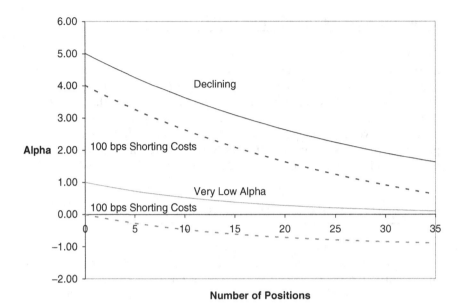

**EXHIBIT 5.12**  Alpha Ranking Model for Declining Cases
*Source:* Morgan Stanley Research

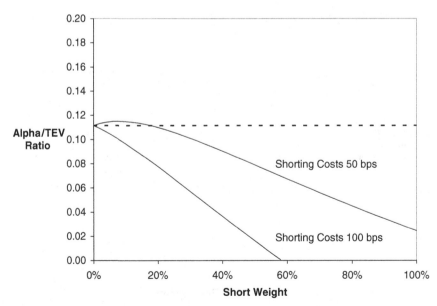

**EXHIBIT 5.13**  Alpha/TEV Ratio for Declining Cases
*Source:* Morgan Stanley Research

alpha expectation beginning at 1 percent and declining as the number of positions increase.

As this lower-alpha portfolio begins to add short weights, it experiences only a small increase in the alpha/TEV ratio versus the long-only portfolio. As shown in Exhibit 5.13, at 100 bp shorting costs, obviously only negative values are derived from any short positions.

Active extensions can provide valuable improvements in alpha/TEV ratios across a wide range of portfolio characteristics. However, there obviously are also situations in which the various costs and frictions can outweigh the benefits. The preconditions for a productive AE include an efficient shorting procedure, an effective risk control discipline, and a credible prospect of being able to generate truly positive alpha values.

# CHAPTER 6

# The Tracking Error Gap

**Anthony Bova**
Vice President
Morgan Stanley, Research

**Martin Leibowitz**
Managing Director
Morgan Stanley, Research

T he relative weights of long-only equity funds typically fall within a narrow range. The maximum overweight is usually stated, thereby allowing for reasonable estimates of the number and average size of a portfolio's active positions.

A theoretical tracking error volatility (TEV) can then be calculated using the standard assumption of uncorrelated residuals. For example, a portfolio with 50 active positions having an average 1 percent relative weight would have a theoretical TEV of around 1.5 to 2 percent.

In practice, actual TEVs of active equity funds often rise above 4 percent (i.e., far greater than the theoretical projection). This TEV gap is usually due to some form of correlation or factor effect across the active positions.

A large TEV gap raises questions about implied correlations/factor effects. Are they intentional or coincidental, chronic or occasional, beta-based or residual-based, alpha-producing or alpha-eroding?

For U.S. institutional portfolios that are almost always beta-dominated, weakly correlated TEVs will have a minimal impact at the overall fund level. However, multiple sources of correlated active risks, factor effects, and/or beta gaps may build to a point where they can constitute a significant risk increment.

Originally published as part of the *Morgan Stanley Portfolio Notes*, May 18, 2006.

## IMPLICIT BETAS AND BETA DOMINATION

As long as higher residual TEVs are uncorrelated, they will be dominated by the "total beta" risk—the combination of the explicit equity allocation together with the implicit beta contributed by all other assets classes based on their assumed co-movement with equities. Over 90 percent of a fund's volatility can generally be accounted for by this total beta exposure to U.S. equity. This overriding degree of beta domination holds even for those institutional portfolios that have low equity allocations, and have diversified into a broad array of alternative asset classes. This total beta effect will even swamp multiple nonbeta volatility risks inherent in generic allocations to alternative asset classes, as well as the risks associated with active management. Beyond the standard volatility, alternative asset classes do contain other risk factors (dragon risks) that cannot be subsumed and that consequently should play a key role in framing the allocation limits.

On one hand, the residual TEVs from active equity management, especially if truly uncorrelated, are also likely to be beta dominated and, hence, play a very minor role in the standard volatility of the overall fund. On the other hand, high observed TEVs tend to be evidence of some form of correlation or factor effect. As with any intentional or coincidental beta gaps, such factor effects could accumulate across managers (and possibly even across asset classes) and come to represent a more significant source of fund-level risk. However, an even more important basis for analyzing high TEVs is that the associated correlation/factor effects can often provide valuable signals regarding the consistency and characteristics of the active management process.

## THE KEY CHARACTERISTIC OF POSITION SIZE

One data point not given its proper recognition is that equity portfolios typically have a characteristic size range for the relative weight of their active positions versus the corresponding benchmark weight. There is usually a well-defined maximum size for these relative weights, ranging from 0.50 percent for highly controlled portfolios, to 2 percent for more aggressive funds, and only rarely reaching or exceeding 5 percent even for the most concentrated portfolios. There is generally also a minimum position size: For traditional active (i.e., nonquantitatively driven) portfolios, even the smallest proactive overweights (or underweights) will be sized at 0.25 percent or higher. Of course, there may be smaller positions that are not fully proactive that serve as sources of funds, transitional positions, and/or play some part in the beta control process.

Thus, apart from the most concentrated portfolios, there will be a limited variation in the *active* position size, with the average position size tending to be approximately 1 to 2 percent for traditional portfolios. Indeed, given that the maximum position size is generally disclosed, the average position size can usually be estimated with some degree of accuracy. This estimated average position size can then serve as a basis for interpreting the signals provided by an observed portfolio TEV. This fixed-weight approach can be readily expanded to incorporate some weighting sequence that declines from the maximum to the minimum size (which should theoretically be based on a sequence of alpha opportunities with declining Sharpe ratios).

## UNCORRELATED TRACKING ERRORS

In their classic works on active management (Grinold, 1989; Grinold and Kahn, 2000; Grinold, 2005), Grinold and Kahn pointed out that the projected tracking error (TE) from uncorrelated overweights will be the square root of the number of positions multiplied by the weighted residual risk. For a residual risk of 23 percent, this basic result is displayed in Exhibit 6.1, which shows the TE for a fixed position size of 1 percent. The points

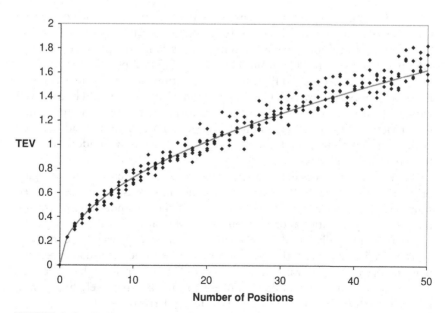

**EXHIBIT 6.1**  Monte Carlo Simulations—TEV versus Number of Positions
*Source:* Morgan Stanley Research

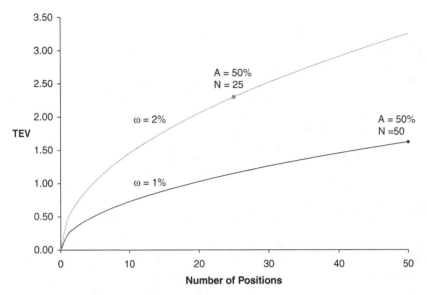

**EXHIBIT 6.2**  TEV versus Number of Positions
*Source:* Morgan Stanley Research

scattered along the curve represent the outcomes from a series of Monte
Carlo simulations. Notice how the range of these scatter points widens as
the number of positions increases. With 50 positions, the projected TEV of
1.63 percent is seen to fall within the range of 1.5 to 2 percent cited earlier.

Exhibit 6.2 compares TEV curves for position sizes of 1 and 2 percent.
For 2 percent positions, the same 50 percent activity level would be achieved
with 25 positions, and would lead to a 2.30 percent TEV. (The remaining
nonproactive 50 percent is assumed to serve as a source of funds as well
as helping to maintain the fund's beta target—possibly with added support
from derivative overlays.)

This model assumes that the active positions may be either underweights
or overweights. The TEV relative to the benchmark is, therefore, derived
solely from the alpha volatility of the overweights or underweights (rather
than from any intentional or unintentional beta gap).

In fundamentally based active portfolios, an activity level that comprises
more than 50 percent of the portfolio would be rather unusual, especially
without the use of leverage or derivatives. Thus, even though 50 percent
activity may seem like a modest number, it is actually relatively high for an
all-cash portfolio that is foreclosed from using derivatives.

Exhibit 6.3 combines these results and relates these TEVs to position
sizes that range up to 10 percent. To obtain the 4 percent or higher TEs that

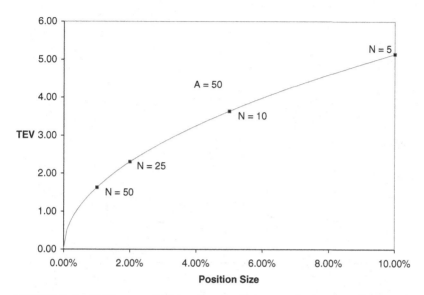

**EXHIBIT 6.3** TEV versus Position Size for 50 Percent Activity Level
*Source:* Morgan Stanley Research

are not uncommon among active funds, Exhibit 6.3 shows that uncorrelated positions would need to have extraordinarily high individual weights—on the order of 6 percent or higher. If the average positions are smaller than this 6 percent, an observed 4 percent TEV must be associated with either higher activity levels than the assumed 50 percent or with some degree of correlation among the various positions.

## CORRELATION EFFECTS

Exhibit 6.4 focuses on the case of 1 percent positions to examine how the concept of pairwise correlation $\rho$ could help explain high observed TEV levels. Exhibit 6.4 shows that even a slight increase in pairwise correlation leads to significant increases in the projected TE. For example, with a 50 position portfolio, the TEV moves close to 3 percent when the correlation jumps to 0.05.

Exhibit 6.5 relates the expected TEVs as a function of the full range of (positive) pairwise correlations. The solid curve reflects the theoretical expected values for the correlated TEV (see the formulation in the Technical Appendix), whereas the scatter plot reflects a series of Monte Carlo simulations. As we would expect, the range of the scatter points becomes more compressed as the correlation approaches $\rho = 1$.

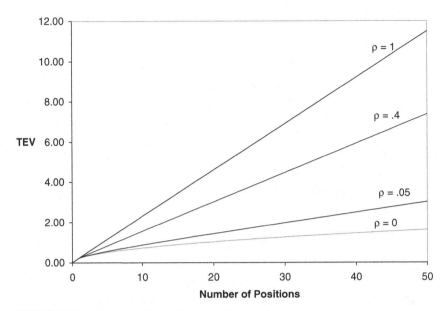

**EXHIBIT 6.4**   TEV at Different Pairwise Correlation Levels
*Source:* Morgan Stanley Research

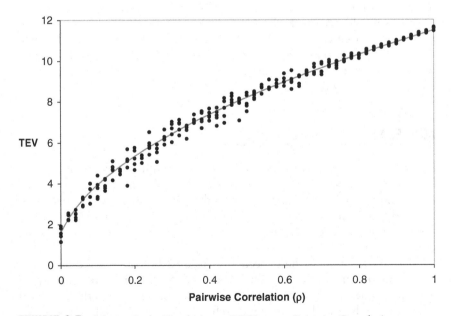

**EXHIBIT 6.5**   Monte Carlo Simulations—TEV versus Pairwise Correlations
*Source:* Morgan Stanley Research

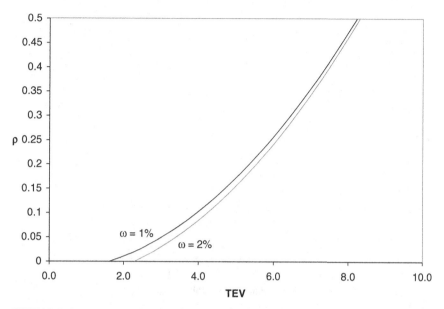

**EXHIBIT 6.6** Pairwise Correlation Levels versus TEV
*Source:* Morgan Stanley Research

In Exhibit 6.6, the axes are reversed, the TEV becomes the independent variable, and the vertical axis now represents the implicit correlation needed to generate a specified TEV. The implicit correlations are plotted for both 50 fixed positions of 1 percent and 25 positions of 2 percent (i.e., keeping the activity level fixed at 50%). For the 1 percent positions, an observed 4 percent TEV implies a roughly 0.1 correlation, whereas a 6 percent TEV calls for an implied correlation of 0.25. It is interesting to see that the implied correlation is largely determined by the TEV itself—for an activity level fixed at 50 percent, the position size of 1 percent versus 2 percent has only a minor impact.

## A SIMPLE FACTOR MODEL

The concept of a "factor effect" (F) can also be used as an alternative, and perhaps more intuitive, measure of correlation (one simple factor model is described in the Appendix, later in this chapter). The concept here is that, in addition to their baseline volatility, the active positions generate an aggregate factor effect of some magnitude. In actuality, this factor effect may be a composite of a variety of common subfactors. Exhibit 6.7 plots this factor/correlation relationship, and the factor effect can be seen to basically rise with the correlation, without any dependence on the position size.

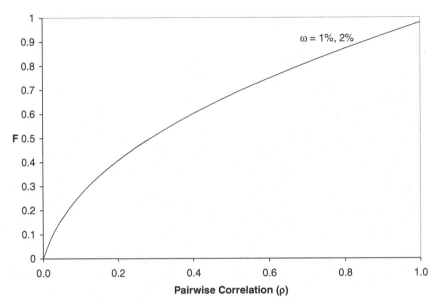

**EXHIBIT 6.7**   Factor Effect versus Pairwise Correlations
*Source:* Morgan Stanley Research

In Exhibit 6.8, the factor effect volatility is derived directly from the portfolio TEV. In this case, the position size can make a significant difference, especially in the lower TEV levels. However, for any observed TEVs greater than 4 percent, it is evident that some factor effect becomes the dominating source of residual volatility.

## SOURCES OF HIGH TRACKING ERROR

In the preceding section, we assumed that the fund is able to maintain perfect beta control relative to its benchmark. Consequently, the TEV is derived solely from the accumulation of the residual risks associated with active positions. Of course, in general, beta control is rarely perfect, and significant TE can arise from beta gaps that are intentional, coincidental, or accidental in nature.

It should be noted that there are highly developed procedures for analyzing a fund's sequence of return over time to identify various style factors. Such returns-based analysis can provide a much deeper and more granular insight into a portfolio's structure. However, returns-based analysis typically requires a rich set of historical performance data. In contrast, the thrust of

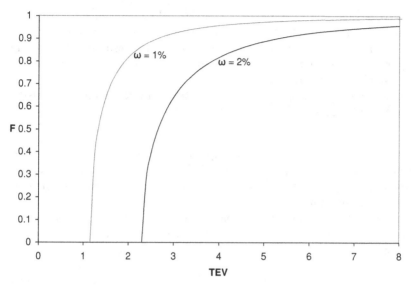

**EXHIBIT 6.8** Factor Effect versus TEV
*Source:* Morgan Stanley Research

this chapter is to point out that even just the single value of a fund's TEV can serve as a surprisingly valuable signal for a probing examination of the management process.

In fairness, it should be pointed out that high TEVs can result from intentionally large position sizes that enable more weight to be dedicated to higher alpha prospects. Although this concentration generates higher TEVs, it may also lead to more desirable alpha/TEV ratios. In a multi-asset, multimanager allocation within a beta-dominated fund, any active TEV will be compressed by the beta effect and end up having very little impact on the fund-level volatility. Thus, a sizable alpha, even when associated with a high TEV, may prove very beneficial to the fund's overall return/risk ratio.

## HIGH TRACKING ERRORS AS A PROBE

For any given position size, however, higher than projected TEVs may still raise a number of questions such as the following:

- Is the TEV due to a sizable beta gap?
- If the beta gap is an important TEV source, does it represent an intentional timing decision?

- If so, is such timing an intrinsic feature of the management process, or an occasional foray under perceived extreme market conditions?
- Did the beta gap arise coincidentally, such as the result of a bottom-up portfolio construction with a concentrated focus on alpha seeking, or an implicit timing decision?
- If the beta gap is accidental but identified, was there a deliberate decision to be beta agnostic?

The fundamental question that applies to such situations is whether prospective beta gaps will be controlled, with limited occurrences, or whether the fund can be expected to continue to generate random beta variability in the future.

If the high TEV cannot be explained in terms of a beta gap, the potential for some other correlation/factor effects could lead to the following questions:

- Is the portfolio manager aware of the factor effect?
- Does it arise from an intentional sector tilt?
- Is such a sector tilt an intrinsic or an occasional component of the management process?
- Is there a discipline for identifying and controlling such sector and factor exposures?
- Could the alpha production be materially enhanced by higher level of attention to these sector effects?

## THE LONG/SHORT FUND CONTEXT

The preceding discussion addressed the TEV and the correlation/factor effects within the context of long-only funds. Of course, the active positions in long-only funds may be underweights as well as overweights. However, given the capitalization structure of most equity market benchmarks, the long-only constraints severely limit the number of proactive underweight positions. In situations where active underweights become more significant, such as in 130/30 active extension (AE) strategies, the same form of analysis is also applicable. In fact, because of the potential for offsetting positions, there generally will be an opportunity for improved TEV control. Moreover, such control can become quite valuable with the larger number of positions, and the larger gross footings that are characteristic of AE portfolios.

## APPENDIX

A portfolio consisting of N independent over- or underweight positions with residual risks $\sigma$ relative to the benchmark will have a TEV of

$$TEV = \sqrt{N}\omega\sigma$$

where $\omega$ is the fixed percentage weight of each position.

If the portfolio has an activity level A of proactive positions, the number of positions can also be expressed as

$$N = \frac{A}{\omega}$$

The remaining nonactive positions are assumed to be a source of funds and/or to play a role in maintaining the portfolio's beta target (possibly with the help of derivative overlays as needed).

The TEV can then be related to the position size by

$$\begin{aligned} TEV &= \sqrt{N}\omega\sigma \\ &= \sqrt{\frac{A}{\omega}}\omega\sigma \\ &= \sqrt{A}\omega\sigma \end{aligned}$$

This formulation assumes that all active positions are uncorrelated. If there exists a pairwise correlation $\rho$, if $X_i$ is a normally distributed random residual with zero mean and variance $(\omega\sigma)^2$, the correlated TEV becomes

$$\begin{aligned} [TEV(\rho)]^2 &= E\left\{\left[\sum_{i=1}^{N}X_i\right]^2\right\} \\ &= E\left\{\sum_{i=1}^{N}X_i^2 + \sum_{i\neq j}X_iX_j\right\} \\ &= NE\{X_1^2\} + N(N-1)E\{X_1X_2\} \\ &= N(\omega\sigma)^2 + N(N-1)\rho(\omega\sigma)^2 \end{aligned}$$

or

$$TEV(\rho) = \omega\sigma\sqrt{N + N(N-1)\rho}$$
$$= TEV(0)\sqrt{1 + (N-1)\rho}$$

This correlated TEV can also be expressed in terms of the activity level A:

$$TEV(\rho) = \omega\sigma\sqrt{\frac{A}{\omega} + \frac{A}{\omega}\left(\frac{A}{\omega} - 1\right)\rho}$$
$$= \sigma\sqrt{A\omega + A\omega\left(\frac{A}{\omega} - 1\right)\rho}$$
$$= \sigma\sqrt{A\omega + A(A - \omega)\rho}$$

Because $A \gg \omega$, the correlated TEV can be approximated by

$$TEV(\rho) \cong \sigma\sqrt{A\omega + A^2\rho}$$
$$= TEV(0)\sqrt{1 + \frac{A}{\omega}\rho}$$

This relationship can be reversed to find the implicit pairwise correlation $\rho(TEV)$ that would give rise to an observed TEV:

$$[TEV]^2 = \sigma^2[A\omega + A(A - \omega)\rho]$$
$$\left[\frac{TEV}{\sigma}\right]^2 \frac{1}{A} = \omega + (A - \omega)\rho$$

or

$$\rho(TEV) = \left\{\left[\frac{TEV}{\sigma}\right]^2 \frac{1}{A} - \omega\right\}\frac{1}{(A - \omega)} \quad N\omega\sigma \geq TEV \geq \sqrt{N}\omega\sigma$$
$$\cong \left[\frac{TEV}{\sigma A}\right]^2 - \frac{\omega}{A}$$
$$\cong \left[\frac{TEV}{\sigma A}\right]^2$$

In terms of the number of positions N:

$$\rho\,(\text{TEV}) = \left\{ \left[ \frac{\text{TEV}}{\sigma} \right]^2 \frac{1}{N\omega} - \omega \right\} \frac{1}{(N\omega - \omega)}$$

$$= \frac{1}{(N-1)} \left\{ \left[ \frac{\text{TEV}}{\sigma\omega} \right]^2 \frac{1}{N} - 1 \right\}$$

The pairwise correlation can also be related to a common factor effect f that correlates with the residual returns $X_i$:

$$\tilde{X}_i = \omega \left[ \tilde{f} + \tilde{\varepsilon}_i \right]$$

where $\tilde{\varepsilon}_i$ is independent of $\tilde{f}$ and each other, and where both $\tilde{\varepsilon}_i$ and $\tilde{f}$ have zero means.

Because the square of the two component volatilities must add to the original residual variance $\sigma^2$:

$$E\left\{ \tilde{X}_i \right\} = \omega^2 \sigma_f^2 + \omega^2 \sigma_{\varepsilon_i}^2$$

$$= \omega^2 \sigma^2$$

so that

$$\sigma = \sqrt{\sigma_f^2 + \sigma_\varepsilon^2}$$

The TEV for the portfolio then becomes

$$\text{TEV}^2 = E\left\{ \left[ \sum_{i=1}^{N} \tilde{X}_i \right]^2 \right\}$$

$$= E\left\{ \sum_{i=1}^{N} \tilde{X}_i^2 + \sum_{i \neq j} \tilde{X}_i \tilde{X}_j \right\}$$

$$= \omega^2 E\left\{ \sum_{i=1}^{N} \left( \tilde{f} + \tilde{\varepsilon}_i \right)^2 + \sum_{i \neq j} \left( \tilde{f} + \tilde{\varepsilon}_i \right) \left( \tilde{f} + \tilde{\varepsilon}_j \right) \right\}$$

$$= \omega^2 \left[ \mathrm{NE}\left\{ \tilde{f}^2 \right\} + \mathrm{NE}\left\{ \tilde{\varepsilon}^2 \right\} + \sum_{i \neq j} \left[ \mathrm{E}\left\{ \tilde{f}_i^2 \right\} \right] \right]$$

$$= \omega^2 \left[ N\sigma_f^2 + N\sigma_\varepsilon^2 + N(N-1)\sigma_f^2 \right]$$

$$= \omega^2 \left[ N^2\sigma_f^2 + N\sigma_\varepsilon^2 \right]$$

or

$$\mathrm{TEV} = \omega\sqrt{N^2\sigma_f^2 + N\sigma_\varepsilon^2}$$

$$= \omega\sqrt{N^2\sigma_f^2 + N\left(\sigma^2 - \sigma_f^2\right)}$$

$$= \omega\sqrt{N\sigma^2 + N(N-1)\sigma_f^2} \qquad \sigma \geq \sigma_f$$

The factor relationship has a similar form to the result obtained for pairwise correlation. In fact, from the form of the TEV expression, it is evident that the same TEV value can be obtained by either assuming a pairwise correlation $\rho$ or by an equivalent factor volatility $\sigma_f(\rho)$:

$$\sigma_f(\rho) = \sigma\sqrt{\rho}$$

Thus, if a factor effect $F(\rho)$ can be defined as the fraction of the total TEV associated with the factor volatility:

$$F(\rho) = \frac{\omega\sqrt{N(N-1)\sigma_f^2}}{\mathrm{TEV}}$$

$$= \frac{\sqrt{N(N-1)\sigma_f^2}}{\sqrt{N\sigma^2 + N(N-1)\sigma_f^2}}$$

$$= \frac{\sqrt{N(N-1)\left(\frac{\sigma_f}{\sigma}\right)^2}}{\sqrt{N + N(N-1)\left(\frac{\sigma_F}{\sigma}\right)^2}}$$

$$= \frac{\sqrt{(N-1)\rho}}{\sqrt{1 + (N-1)\rho}} \qquad 1 \geq \rho \geq 0$$

This $F(\rho)$ measure has the desirable characteristic of being equal to zero for zero correlation, and proceeds to 1 as either $\rho$ approaches 1 or N becomes large and $\rho > 0$. Also, note that the factor effect depends only on N and $\rho$, not the position size $\omega$.

And because $\sigma_f$ can also be expressed in terms of TEV:

$$\sigma_f = \sqrt{\frac{\left(\frac{TEV}{\omega}\right)^2 - N\sigma^2}{[N(N-1)]}}$$

We can also obtain F(TEV) as a function of TEV:

$$F(TEV) = \frac{\omega\sqrt{N(N-1)}}{TEV} \bullet \sqrt{\frac{\left(\frac{TEV}{\omega}\right)^2 - N\sigma^2}{[N(N-1)]}}$$

$$= \sqrt{1 - \frac{N\omega^2\sigma^2}{TEV^2}}$$

which also leads to

$$F^2(TEV) = \frac{\left[TEV^2 - TEV^2(0)\right]}{TEV^2}$$

## REFERENCES

Grinold, R. C. 1989. "The Fundamental Law of Active Management." *Journal of Portfolio Management*. Spring.

Grinold, R. C., and R. Kahn. 2000. "Active Portfolio Management: Quantitative Theory and Applications." McGraw Hill.

Grinold, R. C. 2005. "Implementation Efficiency." *Financial Analysts Journal*. September/October.

# CHAPTER 7

# Correlation Effects in Active 120/20 Extension Strategies

**Anthony Bova**
Vice President
Morgan Stanley, Research

**Martin Leibowitz**
Managing Director
Morgan Stanley, Research

Active extensions (AEs) of active equity portfolios can improve both the cumulative alpha and the alpha/tracking error volatility (TEV) ratio. The preconditions for productive AEs include an efficient shorting procedure, an effective risk control discipline, and a credible prospect of being able to generate truly positive alpha values.

Active extension strategies can be designed to fit within a sponsor's existing allocation space for active U.S. equity management. With proper risk control, an AE may entail tracking error (TE) that is only moderately greater than that of a comparable long-only fund.

Correlation effects materially increase the TE and lower information ratios (IRs) of both long-only and AE portfolios. It is, therefore, important to try to minimize any correlation effects.

Active extension portfolios can provide a natural offset to adverse correlations. This offset feature can be valuable across a wide range of alpha-ranking models.

Active extensions can be particularly productive for situations in which the portfolio alpha is the primary consideration, as long as the associated TE falls within certain bounds.

Originally published as part of the *Morgan Stanley Portfolio Notes*, June 15, 2006.

Even when dealing solely with long-only portfolios, projected TEVs fall in the range of 1 to 3 percent, well below the observed TEVs of 4 percent or higher seen in most actively managed portfolios. This discrepancy between the observed TEVs and the theoretical uncorrelated values implies that there is typically some degree of correlation among the various positions. These correlations, even at a minimal level, can have a significant effect on the TEV and can, therefore, have a meaningful impact on portfolio performance.

In AE portfolios, these correlations may lie within the long positions, within the short positions, and/or between the long and short positions. One of the benefits of an AE is the opportunity to use the short positions to offset factor effects within the long portfolio. Such offsets can sharpen the intended exposures by removing extraneous risk factors, thereby leading to materially improved IRs.

## LONG-ONLY ALPHA RANKING MODELS

A basic assumption throughout this chapter is that the fund is able to maintain a strict benchmark-centric structure; for example, that the portfolio is constructed so as to maintain a beta value of 1 relative to its benchmark. The active management then consists of choosing overweight and/or underweight positions that are expected to generate a certain alpha return.

Exhibit 7.1 displays three distinct alpha-ranking patterns for the long-only portfolio:

- A simple flat pattern with all alphas fixed at 3.50 percent,
- A moderately declining exponential ranking that begins with a 5 percent alpha for the position with the highest expected alpha and falls to 2 percent by the 25th position, and
- A highly concentrated ranking with an initial alpha of 13 percent, but subject to a rapid exponential decay that reduces the alpha to 1 percent by the 15th position.

As shown in Exhibit 7.2, all three models were calibrated to have the same cumulative alpha of 1.75 percent for a portfolio with 25 long positions, each having a 2 percent weight.

The correlation model used in Exhibit 7.3 shows the TEV effect of pairwise correlations in the context of long-only portfolios for the current case of long portfolios with 2 percent position sizes, each with a residual volatility of 23 percent. As shown in Exhibit 7.3, it takes only a slight increase in pairwise correlation to generate significant increases in the TEV. For a 25-position portfolio, the TEV moves from 2 percent in the uncorrelated

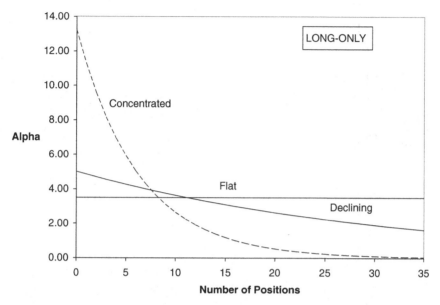

**EXHIBIT 7.1**  Long-Only Alpha Ranking Models
*Source:* Morgan Stanley Research

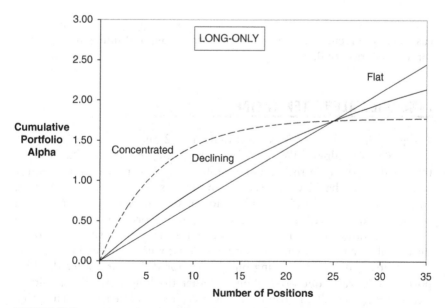

**EXHIBIT 7.2**  Cumulative Portfolio Alpha for a Given Number of Positions
*Source:* Morgan Stanley Research

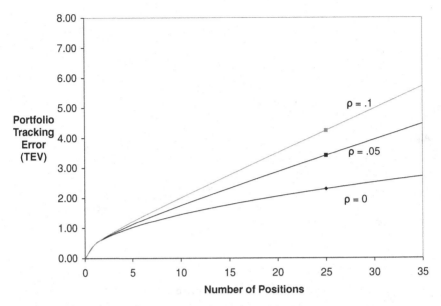

**EXHIBIT 7.3**   Portfolio TE for a Given Number of Positions
*Source:* Morgan Stanley Research

case to 3.5 percent at a 0.05 pairwise correlation, and jumps to 4 percent for a correlation of 0.10.

## LONG-ONLY ALPHA/TEV RATIOS

The portfolio alpha and TEs from Exhibits 7.2 and 7.3 can be combined to calculate the alpha/TEV ratio for each ranking model as a function of the position count. In the declining alpha case, shown in Exhibit 7.4, the uncorrelated alpha/TEV increases as more positions are added. With a correlation of 0.10, the alpha/TEV ratio remains at levels that many would consider unattractive. A more reasonable 0.05 correlation results in an alpha/TEV ratio that starts to flatten around the 15th position (although the cumulative portfolio alpha continues to rise with additional positions).

At first glance, this leveling out of the alpha/TEV ratio after the 15th position may raise questions about whether the long portfolio should be structured to the full 25 positions. However, it should be noted that with a 0.05 pairwise correlation, the 25-position TEV is still well below 4 percent. At the same time, as shown in Exhibit 7.2, the portfolio alpha for this ranking model continues to rise with the higher position counts. For situations in

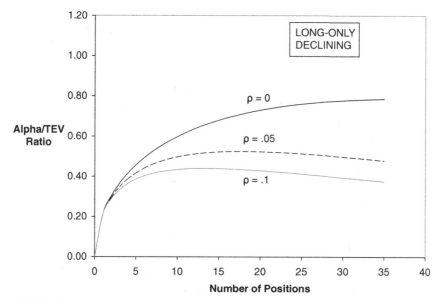

**EXHIBIT 7.4** Alpha/TEV Ratio for Declining Alpha Rankings
*Source:* Morgan Stanley Research

which such TEVs are quite tolerable, the investor may well opt for the higher alpha portfolio even without any corresponding improvement in the alpha/TEV ratio itself.

In the concentrated case, shown in Exhibit 7.5, the alpha/TEV ratio peaks quickly at attractive levels for both the correlated and the uncorrelated cases. It is no surprise that, for the concentrated alpha ranking, a tight portfolio with only five to eight positions appears optimal in terms of both the alpha/TEV ratio as well as the cumulative portfolio alpha.

In the flat case with a zero correlation, shown in Exhibit 7.6, the alpha/TEV ratio increases as the alpha from each new position overwhelms the added TE. With a 0.05 or 0.10 correlation, the alpha/TEV curve still rises as more positions are added, but now at a decreasing rate.

## ADDING THE ACTIVE EXTENSION

The preceding long-only alpha ranking models can be adapted to a fund that has some degree of flexibility to take short positions. An AE with 2 percent underweights is now assumed to be added to the long-only portfolio with its 25, 2 percent positions. The underweight positions are assumed to be

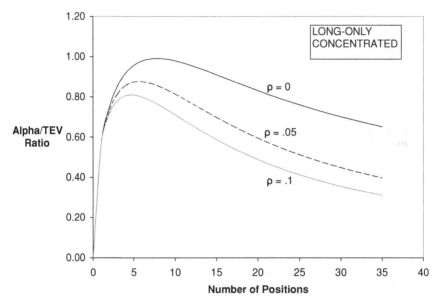

**EXHIBIT 7.5**  Alpha/TEV Ratio for Concentrated Alpha Rankings
*Source:* Morgan Stanley Research

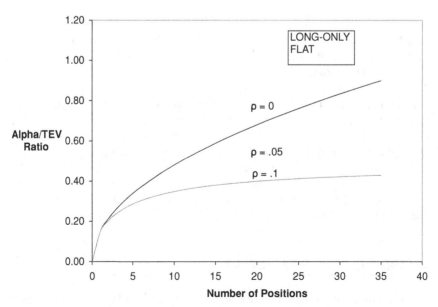

**EXHIBIT 7.6**  Alpha/TEV Ratio for Flat Alpha Rankings
*Source:* Morgan Stanley Research

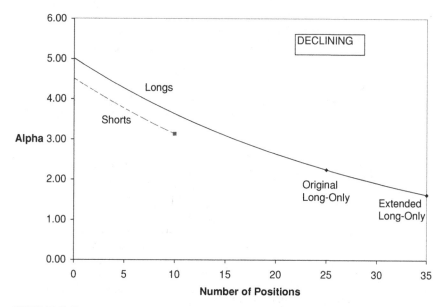

**EXHIBIT 7.7**   Long and Short Declining Alpha Ranking Model
*Source:* Morgan Stanley Research

subject to the same percentage erosion as the corresponding long-only alpha ranking model. The added fractional costs involved in the short side are modeled by taking a 50 basis point (bp) decrement for each short position versus the corresponding long position. Exhibit 7.7 displays both the long and short rankings for the declining alpha case.

Assuming a fixed 2 percent weight for all active positions, each short position will result in 2 percent cash proceeds that can be used to fund a new 2 percent long position. However, to be conservative, it is assumed that a maximum 2 percent constraint prevents further investment into the first 25 high-alpha long positions. The proceeds from the shorts, therefore, must be deployed into the lower-ranked long opportunities that lie beyond the 25th position.

## OFFSETTING LONG/SHORT CORRELATIONS

The basic long-only correlation model applies when all positions have a common pairwise correlation. Just as a uniform positive correlation can have a material TEV-increasing effect, so the opportunity for offsetting

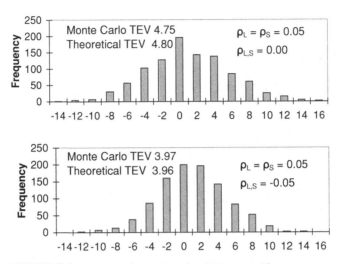

**EXHIBIT 7.8**  TE Simulation Results: 20 Percent Short Weight

*Source:* Morgan Stanley Research

negative correlations can act as a major TEV-reducing factor. In theory, such offsets could be present within the long portfolio itself. However, for the sake of simplicity, only positive correlations are assumed to exist *within* the longs and *within* the shorts, whereas the offsetting negative correlations are assumed to occur only *between* the shorts and longs.

To analyze AEs with such offsetting correlations, a more structured model is needed. The Appendix at the end of this chapter develops a theoretical formula for these more complex TEVs.

To demonstrate the impact of offsetting correlations, two Monte Carlo simulations were run for the case of a 20 percent short weight—one without correlation between the longs and shorts, and another with a negative (−0.05) correlation. Both simulations contained positive 0.05 correlations within the longs and within the shorts. Exhibit 7.8 displays the resulting histograms. The top histogram with a zero correlation between the longs and shorts has a wider distribution of TEs and, hence, a larger TEV than the bottom histogram with an offsetting correlation. Exhibit 7.8 also shows that the simulated TEV results are generally in accord with the expected TEVs derived from the theoretical formula.

Exhibit 7.9 uses the results from the TEV formula to show the impact of various short-to-long correlations as the short weight increases. The three cases all assume a positive 0.05 correlation within the longs and the shorts,

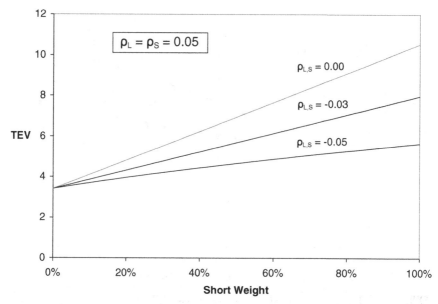

**EXHIBIT 7.9** TEV versus Short Weight for Various Offset Correlations
*Source:* Morgan Stanley Research

but differ in the short-to-long correlations. The TEV-reducing effect of these offsets is clearly evident.

Exhibit 7.10 focuses on AE weights of 20 percent and 40 percent to show the TEVs as a function of the pairwise correlation between the longs and shorts. The solid curves reflect the theoretical expected values. The scatter points along the curve for the 20 percent case reflect a series of Monte Carlo simulations. The tightness of the fit provides comfort as to the robust quality of the offset TEV formula as developed in the Appendix.

## INFORMATION RATIOS FOR ACTIVE EXTENSIONS

The three alpha-ranking models can be combined with the TEV formula to develop alpha/TEV IRs for AEs.

Exhibit 7.11 presents the ratios for the moderately declining alpha ranking. With positive correlation of 0.05, the IR for the basic 25-position long-only portfolio ratio is 0.51. With varying AEs added from that point, the long-to-short correlation can be seen to play a key role. With a zero offset correlation, the AE provides only modest benefits. However, with an

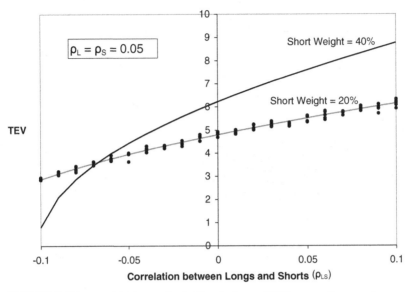

**EXHIBIT 7.10** Model Monte Carlo Simulations—TEV versus Short-to-Long Correlations
*Source:* Morgan Stanley Research

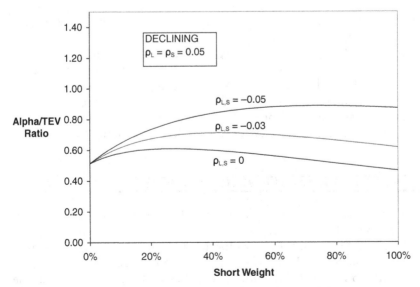

**EXHIBIT 7.11** Alpha/TEV Ratio versus AE for Declining Alpha Case
*Source:* Morgan Stanley Research

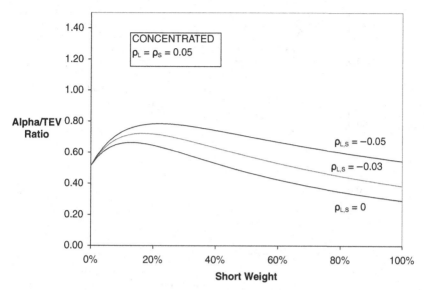

**EXHIBIT 7.12** Alpha/TEV Ratio versus AE for Concentrated Alpha Case
*Source:* Morgan Stanley Research

offsetting −0.05 correlation, the AEs can raise the IR from the long-only's 0.51 to a peak value of 0.90 for short weights in the 50 to 80 percent range. With the more moderate offset of −0.03, the ratio reaches a peak value of around 0.70 for short weights of 30 to 50 percent.

As shown in Exhibit 7.12, for the concentrated case, the IR curves have a more pronounced maximum, ranging from 0.65 to 0.80, but with short weights falling in a much tighter range of 15 to 25 percent.

Finally, the less realistic, flat alpha ranking shown in Exhibit 7.13 results in a continuously upward sloping ratio for the two offset cases. With a zero short-to-long correlation, the curve starts to flatten out around the 80 percent short weight and a ratio around 0.75.

## ALPHA-FOCUSED INVESTMENT

In practice, the alpha/TEV ratio may not always serve as a totally sufficient gauge of portfolio value. For typical asset allocations, the TE from any component portfolio is likely to have only a minimal impact on the

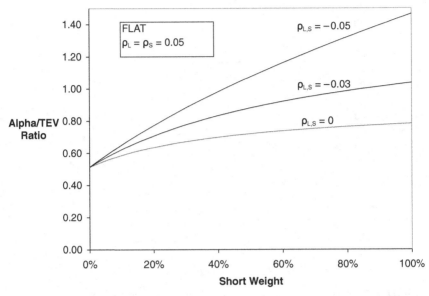

**EXHIBIT 7.13**  Alpha/TEV Ratio versus AE for Flat Alpha Case
*Source:* Morgan Stanley Research

overall fund volatility. Although the TE may be important for other reasons, including as an informational signal relating to risk discipline, consistency, process reliability, and so on, there certainly are situations in which lower alpha/TEV ratios could be exchanged for higher returns as long as the TEV remained within some reasonable bound. In such situations, AEs can lead to significantly enhanced alphas. Exhibit 7.14 illustrates the alpha enhancement for the declining alpha case. As an example, for a TEV limit of 4 percent, the alpha is increased by 1 to 2 percent, depending on the degree of offset correlation provided by the short positions.

## CONCLUSION

The key finding, which is perhaps best illustrated in the more realistic moderately declining alpha ranking, is that unproductive positive correlations can seriously elevate the TEVs and erode the alpha/TEV ratios for long-only portfolios. Consequently, there is a significant benefit to reducing any unintended or alpha-inefficient correlations. Improved alphas and

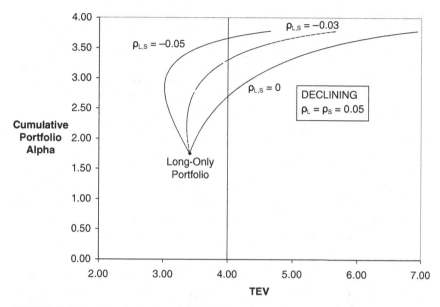

**EXHIBIT 7.14**   Cumulative Portfolio Alpha versus TEV for Declining Alpha Case
*Source:* Morgan Stanley Research

better IRs can then be obtained from appropriately sized AEs, provided that the proper risk discipline is maintained, the total shorting costs are sufficiently modest, and management can truly deliver credibly positive alphas. In addition, if the shorts can be selected to offset undesirable correlations within the long portfolio, even further ratio improvement may be attained.

## APPENDIX

In Chapter 6, "The Tracking Error Gap," the following algebraic expression was developed for the TEV of an N-position portfolio, with each position having a weight $\omega$, a residual volatility $\sigma$, and a pairwise correlation $\rho$:

$$\text{TEV}(\rho) = (\omega\sigma)\sqrt{N + N(N-1)\rho}$$

**EXHIBIT 7A.1**　Correlation Matrix for AE Portfolios

| | | Longs | | | | | Shorts | | | | |
|---|---|---|---|---|---|---|---|---|---|---|---|
| | | 1 | 2 | 3 | · · · | $N_{L1}$ | 1 | 2 | 3 | · · · | $N_S$ |
| Longs | 1 | 1 | $\rho_L$ | $\rho_L$ | · · · | $\rho_L$ | $\rho_{LS}$ | $\rho_{LS}$ | $\rho_{LS}$ | · · · | $\rho_{LS}$ |
| | 2 | $\rho_L$ | 1 | $\rho_L$ | | | $\rho_{LS}$ | $\rho_{LS}$ | $\rho_{LS}$ | | |
| | 3 | $\rho_L$ | $\rho_L$ | 1 | | | $\rho_{LS}$ | $\rho_{LS}$ | $\rho_{LS}$ | | |
| | · | · | | | | | · | | | | |
| | · | · | | | | | · | | | | |
| | · | · | | | | | · | | | | |
| | $N_{L1}$ | $\rho_L$ | | | | 1 | $\rho_{LS}$ | $\rho_{LS}$ | | | $\rho_{LS}$ |
| Shorts | 1 | $\rho_{LS}$ | $\rho_{LS}$ | $\rho_{LS}$ | · · · | $\rho_{LS}$ | 1 | $\rho_S$ | $\rho_S$ | · · · | $\rho_S$ |
| | 2 | $\rho_{LS}$ | $\rho_{LS}$ | $\rho_{LS}$ | | | $\rho_S$ | 1 | $\rho_S$ | | |
| | 3 | $\rho_{LS}$ | $\rho_{LS}$ | $\rho_{LS}$ | | | $\rho_S$ | $\rho_S$ | 1 | | |
| | · | · | | | | | · | | | | |
| | · | · | | | | | · | | | | |
| | $N_S$ | $\rho_{LS}$ | $\rho_{LS}$ | | | $\rho_{LS}$ | $\rho_S$ | | | | 1 |

For AE portfolios consisting of $N_L$ long positions and $N_S$ short positions, a comparable model would require identifying three distinct correlations regimes:

- $\rho_L$ within the $N_L$ longs,
- $\rho_S$ within the $N_S$ shorts,
- $\rho_{LS}$ *between* the short and the long positions.

The correlations matrix would have the structure shown in Exhibit 7A.1. Because all positions have a common variance $(\omega\sigma)^2$, the TEV $(\rho_L, \rho_S, \rho_{LS})$ for an AE portfolio can be found by simply enumerating all the pairs:

1. $N_L$ with $\rho_L = 1$,
2. $[N_L^2 - N_L]$ with $\rho = \rho_L$,
3. $N_S$ with $\rho_S = 1$,
4. $[N_S^2 - N_S]$ with $\rho = \rho_S$,
5. $2N_L N_S$ with $\rho = \rho_{LS}$.

This enumeration leads to the expression:

$$\text{TEV}\,(\rho_L, \rho_S, \rho_{LS}) = (\omega\sigma)\,\sqrt{N_L + N_L(N-1)\rho_L + N_S + N_S(N-1)\rho_S + 2N_LN_S\rho_{LS}}$$

It is interesting (and comforting) to see that when all the $\rho$s are the same, the previous formula devolves to the simple one for a homogenous portfolio, for example,

$$
\begin{aligned}
\text{TEV}\,(\rho, \rho, \rho) &= (\omega\sigma)\,\sqrt{N_L + N_L(N-1)\rho + N_S + N_S(N-1)\rho + 2N_LN_S\rho} \\
&= (\omega\sigma)\,\sqrt{(N_L + N_S) + \rho\left[N_L^2 - N_L + N_S^2 - N_S + 2N_LN_S\right]} \\
&= (\omega\sigma)\,\sqrt{(N_L + N_S) + \rho\left[(N_L + N_S)^2 - (N_L + N_L)\right]} \\
&= (\omega\sigma)\,\sqrt{N + \rho\left[N(N-1)\right]}
\end{aligned}
$$

where now $N = N_L + N_S$.

Moreover, for extreme values of $\rho$, the formula provides the well-known result:

$$\text{TEV}\,(0, 0, 0) = (\omega\sigma)\,\sqrt{N}$$

and

$$\text{TEV}\,(1, 1, 1) = (\omega\sigma)\,N$$

# CHAPTER 8

# Alpha Returns and Active Extensions

**Anthony Bova**
Vice President
Morgan Stanley, Research

**Martin Leibowitz**
Managing Director
Morgan Stanley, Research

The relaxation of the long-only constraint within equity portfolios and the subsequent move into an active extension (AE) 120/20 strategy can lead to material improvements in both alpha returns and alpha/tracking error volatility(TEV) ratios. These potential benefits can be estimated by combining an alpha ranking system, a position weighting function, and a tracking error (TE) model.

There is empirical evidence that the structure of a wide range of active portfolios can be approximated by exponentially declining alpha rankings and position weightings. These alpha/weighing models can be used to explore how AEs (and active portfolios, in general) can generate alpha returns subject to prescribed risk limits.

Additional benefits from AE portfolios include the ability to offset unproductive correlations and to facilitate specific pair trades between long and short positions. Such offsets can sharpen the intended risk exposures, and lead to higher alpha/TEV ratios.

Moving into a risk-controlled AE will generally not have a significant impact on the fund level volatility. Because most U.S. institutions'

Originally published as part of the *Morgan Stanley Portfolio Notes*, August 31, 2006.

portfolios are overwhelmingly beta dominated, any incremental TEV will be submerged by this beta effect. Active extensions that provide positive alphas can, therefore, significantly increase the fund's total return with only a minimal impact on the overall volatility.

The preconditions for realizing any of these benefits are a credible basis for producing positive alphas in both long and short portfolios, a high level of risk discipline, an ability to minimize and/or offset unproductive correlations, and an organizational ability to pursue AEs in a benchmark-centric, cost-efficient fashion.

## ALPHA RANKING AND PORTFOLIO WEIGHTING MODELS

The standard measure for the value added from active management is the alpha/TEV ratio. The first step in analyzing this ratio is to create an alpha ranking model. Portfolio managers generally have some formal or informal process for classifying their prospective active positions into a descending sequence based upon their level of conviction. Alpha ranking models can be used to approximate such classifications. These alpha ranking models may take a variety of forms depending on the style of the investment fund and/or perceived opportunities in the market. Our base case ranking model is based on an exponential alpha decay with a beginning alpha of 5 percent that declines to 2.24 percent at the 25th position.

In theory, with a constant residual volatility, the optimal weighting for each position should be proportional to its alpha ranking. The actual sequential weights seen in practice provide empirical evidence that portfolios are at least roughly structured along these lines. Exhibit 8.2 displays the sequence of position weights for a sample of long-only funds. The top line represents the gross weights, whereas the bottom line shows the active weights (i.e., the difference between the gross weight and benchmark weight). The middle dotted line is an exponential weighting function that begins at a 3 percent weight. This theoretical weighting function has approximately the same decay rate as the alpha ranking model in Exhibit 8.1.

## CORRELATION EFFECTS

The three factors that affect the TEV are the residual volatilities of each position, the portfolio weightings, and the correlations that exist between the positions.

Using the exponential weighting model from Exhibit 8.2, our baseline long-only portfolio was constructed to have 25 proactive positions with a net activity level of 50 percent. The remaining nonproactive component

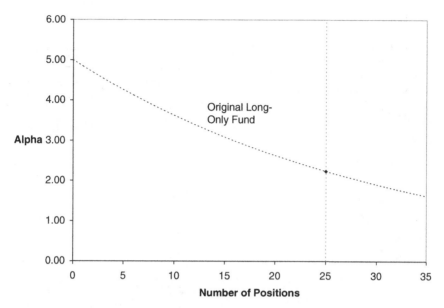

**EXHIBIT 8.1**  Alpha Ranking Model
*Source:* Morgan Stanley Research

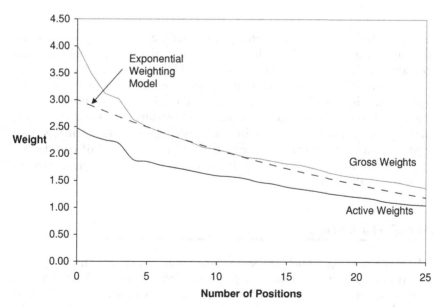

**EXHIBIT 8.2**  Gross and Active Weighting Functions for Long-Only Portfolios
*Source:* Morgan Stanley Research

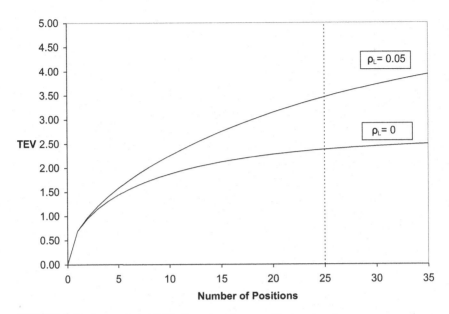

**EXHIBIT 8.3**    Long-Only TEV: Correlated versus Uncorrelated
*Source:* Morgan Stanley Research

of the portfolio serves as a source of funds as well as helping to maintain the fund's target beta. After the 25th position, the active weight remains constant for any additional long positions added to the portfolio.

Exhibit 8.3 compares the TEVs for the long-only portfolio under assumed pairwise correlations ($\rho_L$) of zero and 0.05. In calculating the TEVs, we assume throughout a constant residual volatility of 23 percent for all active positions. For the 25-position long portfolio, the TEV increases from 2.38 percent for the uncorrelated case to 3.46 percent for a 0.05 correlation. It only takes a slight increase in pairwise correlation to generate significant increases in the TEV.

## ALPHA/TEV RATIOS

The alpha ranking model can be combined with the exponential weighting function to generate a cumulative portfolio alpha. Exhibit 8.4 displays this portfolio alpha as a function of the TEVs from Exhibit 8.3. In the uncorrelated case, the alpha continues to rise as more positions are added to the portfolio while the TEV stays within a 2 to 2.5 percent range. This suggests that under the assumption of a zero correlation, more positions should

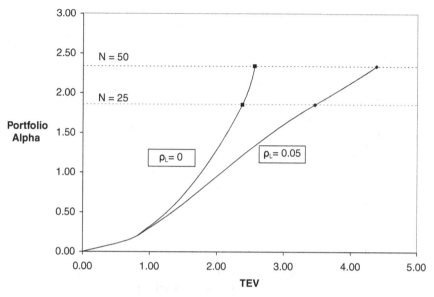

**EXHIBIT 8.4** Long-Only Alpha versus TEV: Correlated and Uncorrelated
*Source:* Morgan Stanley Research

continue to be added to the portfolio because the cumulative alpha increases faster than the portfolio's TEV. This is also evidence that to get TEVs greater than 3 percent (which is what is observed in actively managed, long-only, equity portfolios), there must exist some degree of positive correlations among the long positions.

With a 0.05 correlation, the alpha and TEV increase at nearly the same rate as more positions are added to the portfolio, leading to a roughly constant alpha/TEV ratio. In this situation, the investor may sacrifice a higher TEV (if it can be tolerated) for the higher alpha portfolio even without any corresponding improvement in the alpha/TEV ratio.

## THE ACTIVE EXTENSION

The ability to take short positions provides access to a fresh set of underweights. In the following analysis, these new underweights are assumed to have alphas that coincide with the corresponding long-only alpha model, less some given shorting cost. Exhibit 8.5 schematically depicts a 20 percent AE. The short portfolio is based on an alpha ranking model that follows the original long-only 5 percent declining alpha ranking model, but with a 0.50 percent reduction to account for shorting costs. This model also

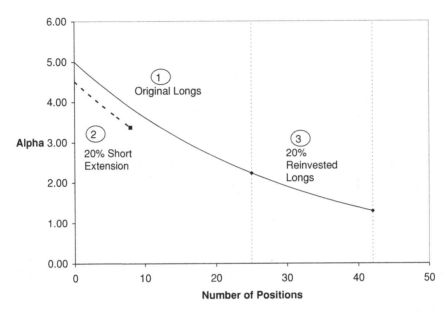

**EXHIBIT 8.5**  Alpha Rankings for Short Positions
*Source:* Morgan Stanley Research

assumes that the short portfolio follows the same exponential weighting model as the long portfolio. The proceeds generated by the shorts are then reinvested into the new long positions.

The proceeds from the shorts could theoretically be reinvested to increase the weight invested in the highest-alpha long positions. However, most portfolios will have already established their maximum allowable weight in these high-ranked positions, so we take the more conservative approach and reinvest the proceeds starting with the 26th ranked long position.

Note that because of the frontend loading from the exponential weightings, the 20 percent extension is achieved with only eight new short positions. The 20 percent funds are then reinvested into new longs from the 26th to 42nd position, in which the position weight was assumed to be fixed at the 1.2 percent minimum.

Exhibit 8.6 displays cumulative portfolio alpha as a function of the total number of positions for the long-only and a 120/20 portfolio. The biggest boost in alpha comes from the eight new short positions that come from the early part of the alpha ranking model. The 17 new longs consist of the tail end of the alpha ranking model and weighting function. Because these are lower-grade alpha sources, these new longs do not provide as significant a benefit as the new shorts.

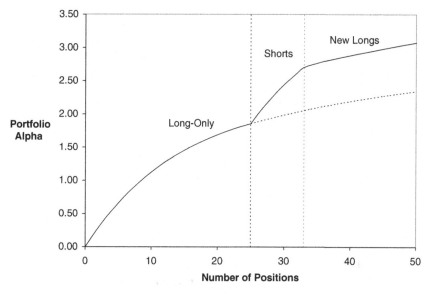

**EXHIBIT 8.6** AE Impact on Portfolio Alpha
*Source:* Morgan Stanley Research

As an empirical test for how these exponential models apply to actual portfolios, Exhibit 8.7 displays the weighting functions for an admittedly small sample of AE funds that have reported their holdings to the Security and Exchange Commission (SEC). Like the long-only funds, both the longs and shorts in the AE funds follow a pattern that can be approximated as an exponential decay.

The exposures and beta values for this sample of AE funds along with a sample of SEC-reporting market-neutral (MN) funds are shown in Exhibits 8.8 and 8.9. It can be seen that the AE funds are closely aligned to the target 100 percent net exposure, and have betas that remain close to 1. Not surprisingly, the MN funds all have net long exposures and net betas close to zero.

## OFFSETTING LONG/SHORT CORRELATIONS

The basic long-only correlation model applies when all positions have a common pairwise correlation. Just as a positive correlation can have a material TEV-increasing effect, so the opportunity for offsetting negative correlations can act as a major TEV-reducing factor. In theory, such offsets

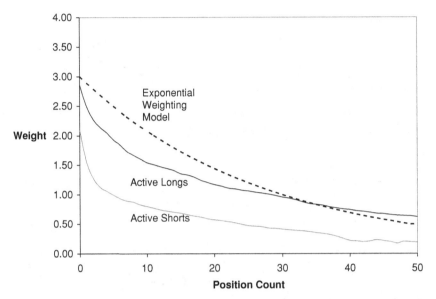

**EXHIBIT 8.7**  Weighting Functions for AE Portfolios
*Source:* Morgan Stanley Research

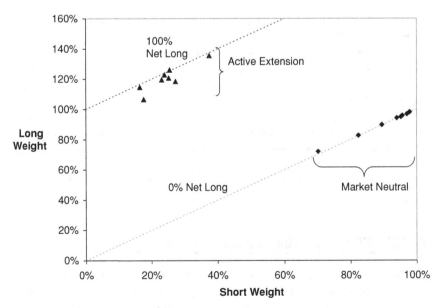

**EXHIBIT 8.8**  Long and Short Exposures for AE and MN Funds
*Source:* Morgan Stanley Research

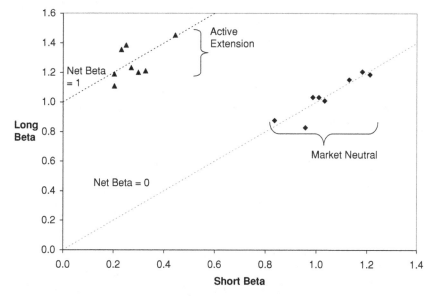

**EXHIBIT 8.9** Long and Short Betas for AE and MN Funds
*Source:* Morgan Stanley Research

could be present within the long portfolio itself. However, for the sake of simplicity, only positive correlations are assumed to exist *within* the longs and *within* the shorts, whereas the offsetting negative correlations are assumed to occur only *between* the shorts and longs.

Exhibit 8.10 shows impact of various correlation effects. The top three lines all assume a positive 0.05 correlation within the longs and within the shorts, but differ in the short-to-long correlations. The TEV-reducing effect of these offsets is clearly evident as the −0.05 offset curve moves toward the uncorrelated case.

The alpha ranking models from Exhibit 8.5 can be combined with the TEVs in Exhibit 8.10 to calculate the alpha/TEV ratios at various short weights. With positive correlation of 0.05, the information ratio (IR) for the basic 25-position long-only portfolio ratio was 0.54. With varying AEs added from that point, the long/short correlation can be seen to play a key role. With a zero offset correlation, the AE provides only a modest increase in the IR to 0.63. However, with an offsetting −0.05 correlation, the AEs can raise the IR to 0.92 for short weights in the 40 to 60 percent range. With the more moderate offset of −0.03, the ratio reaches a peak value of around 0.74 for short weights of 30 to 50 percent. For the uncorrelated situation, the AE improves the alpha/TEV ratio from 0.78 for the long-only portfolio

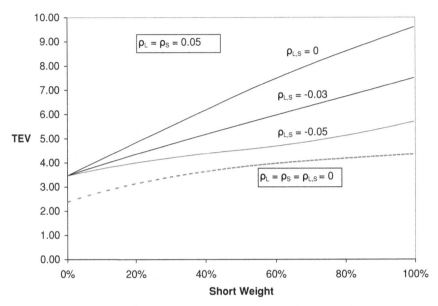

**EXHIBIT 8.10** Correlation Effects: TEV versus Short Weight
*Source:* Morgan Stanley Research

to a peak value of 1.10 for short weights in the 60 to 80 percent range (Exhibit 8.11).

Clearly, any AE strategy is critically dependent on an efficient facility for selecting, implementing, and maintaining the short portfolio. If shorting costs become too high, the resulting alpha degradation would eliminate any benefits from AE.

The alpha/TEV ratio is an important metric, but it may not always serve as a sufficient gauge of portfolio value. It also makes sense to look separately at the two components of this ratio. Exhibit 8.12 presents the results from AE in alpha versus TEV space. If a fund had a maximum TEV it was willing to tolerate, the extension could add a significant alpha increment to the return from the long-only portfolio (even with a zero offset between internally correlated longs and shorts).

## FUND LEVEL EFFECTS

For typical asset allocations, it is well known that the TEV from a moderate-sized component portfolio is likely to have only a minimal impact on the

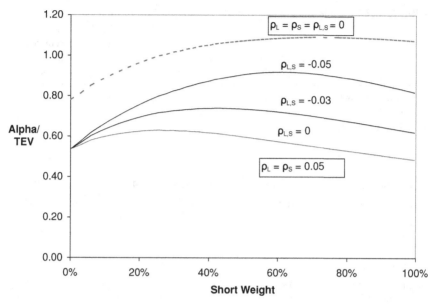

**EXHIBIT 8.11** Alpha/TEV versus Short Weight
*Source:* Morgan Stanley Research

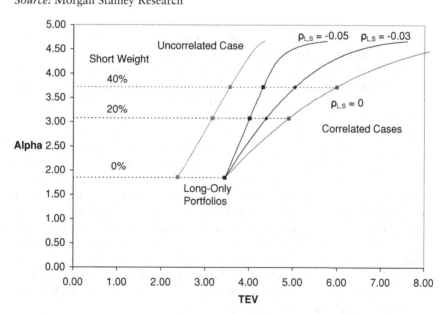

**EXHIBIT 8.12** Alpha versus TEV for Various Offset Correlations
*Source:* Morgan Stanley Research

**EXHIBIT 8.13** Alpha Enhancement with Minimal Volatility Increase

| | Benchmark Portfolio | Active Long-Only | Correlated AE Case without Offset | Correlated AE Case with Offset |
|---|---|---|---|---|
| U.S. Equity Passive Benchmark | 60% | | | |
| U.S. Equity Active – Long-Only | | 60% | 40% | 40% |
| Active Extension – 40% Short Weight | | | 20% | 20% |
| U.S. Bonds | 40% | 40% | 40% | 40% |
| Total | 100% | 100% | 100% | 100% |
| Total Beta | 0.65 | 0.65 | 0.65 | 0.65 |
| Expected Return | 5.85 | 6.96 | 7.36 | 7.36 |
| Alpha | | 1.11 | 1.51 | 1.51 |
| TEV | | 2.08 | 2.62 | 2.26 |
| Total Volatility | 11.17 | 11.36 | 11.48 | 11.40 |

*Source:* Morgan Stanley Research

overall fund volatility. Therefore, many institutional portfolios may care more about the portfolio alpha than the alpha/TEV ratio.

Exhibit 8.13 provides an example of how AEs can affect performance characteristics at the overall fund level. The first column represents the passive benchmark portfolio with a 60 percent equity/40 percent bond allocation. The second column replaces the 60 percent passive equity benchmark with 60 percent active long-only equity.

The move of the 60 percent equity allocation from a passive index into long-only active management increases the total volatility modestly from 11.17 to 11.36 percent. However, the total portfolio return increases by a significant 1.11 percent (i.e., 60% of the active alpha of 1.85%). The next two columns show the effect of moving 20 percent of the active equity into a correlated AE with a short weight of 40 percent. (To be conservative we have assumed that the TEVs of the AE and long-only active equity are fully correlated.) Without any long/short offset, the portfolio return increases by 0.40 to 7.36 percent, with the portfolio volatility only moving from 11.36 to 11.48 percent. With offsets, the return remains at 7.36 percent whereas the volatility declines to 11.40 percent.

The reason that there is not a significant increase in the portfolio volatility in Exhibit 8.10 is because this portfolio (as with most U.S.

institutions' portfolios) is beta dominated, and any additional TEV is submerged by this beta effect. Moving to an active management posture or to an AE will generally not have a significant impact on the overall volatility of the fund—one beta-dominated asset is just being replaced with another. The only question then becomes whether these active management processes can reliably generate positive levels of expected alpha.

## CONCLUSION

Active extension can be viewed as an extended form of traditional active equity management that has the potential to materially improve both portfolio alphas and alpha/TEV ratios by:

1. Creating access to a fresh crop of active underweight opportunities,
2. Reinvesting the short proceeds in productive new longs (even if they are of lower alpha rank), and
3. Providing offsets that reduce unproductive correlations and facilitate return-enhancing pairing opportunities.

The preconditions for realizing any of these benefits are a credible basis for producing positive alphas in both long and short portfolios, a high level of risk discipline, an ability to minimize and/or offset unproductive correlations, and an organizational ability to pursue AEs in a benchmark-centric, cost-efficient fashion.

# CHAPTER 9

# An Integrated Analysis of Active Extension Strategies

**Anthony Bova**
Vice President
Morgan Stanley, Research

**Martin Leibowitz**
Managing Director
Morgan Stanley, Research

The interest in active extension (AE) strategies has grown significantly as both investment sponsors and asset managers have sought enhanced levels of positive alpha. Active extension strategies provide the potential for incremental alpha by accessing fresh underweights, reinvesting the short proceeds, facilitating offsets against unproductive correlations, and creating more sharply focused pairing opportunities.

With appropriate risk control, a 130/30 strategy can be literally viewed as a simple extension of traditional equity management rather than as a quantum leap into the more complicated space allocated to alternative assets.

This chapter develops a new integrated methodology to incorporate variable weighting functions. With this more comprehensive methodology, the proportional weightings that are more optimal can now be explored.

Proportional weighting turns out to have only a minor effect for the more typical portfolio structures. For the base case example, a 20 percent AE with an optimal proportional weighting raises the 1.85 percent long-only alpha to 3.02 percent, only slightly higher than the 2.91 percent alpha obtained with fixed 2 percent weights.

---

Originally published as part of the *Morgan Stanley Portfolio Notes*, July 27, 2006.

Correlation effects can have a major impact on the risk/reward ratios of both long-only and 130/30 long/short extensions. Positive correlations or factor effects significantly exacerbate portfolio tracking error volatility (TEV). A properly structured AE can offset this correlation effect and provide enhancements that are comparable to the uncorrelated case.

In this chapter, we depart from this fixed weight assumption and explore the impact of various weighting schedules on both long-only and long/short portfolios. With the assumption of a constant residual volatility for each active position, the theoretically optimal weighting for each position should be proportional to its alpha ranking. The exploration of various exponential weighting patterns helps to ascertain whether the earlier fixed-weight results could be significantly improved under more optimal active weightings.

One key finding is that for our base case of a moderately declining alpha ranking, the alpha/TEV ratio is little changed by different weighting functions. For the more extreme case of a highly concentrated alpha ranking, a similarly concentrated weighting schedule can lead to a material improvement in the alpha/TEV ratio. However, such concentrated weightings may not be practical for most portfolio situations because they call for exceptionally large weights in a small number of positions.

## EXPONENTIAL WEIGHTING FUNCTIONS

As alternatives to the assumption of a fixed 2 percent weight, Exhibit 9.1 displays two exponential weighting functions—the first beginning at 3 percent for the initial position with the highest alpha and declining to 1.2 percent for the 25th position, and the second beginning at 7.5 percent and declining to 0.2 percent for the 25th position. These three weighting functions were calibrated to keep the activity level across the first 25 positions at 50 percent. After the 25th position, the active weight remains constant as additional active positions are added to the portfolio.

Exhibit 9.2 shows the cumulative active weights for increasing position counts. One can see that the weighting functions have been normalized to provide a 50 percent active weight for the basic long-only case of 25 active positions.

Exhibit 9.3 displays the TEVs for the different weighting functions under the assumption of a zero correlation between the positions. There are large differences in the path that the TEV takes as more positions are added, but both the more reasonable 2 percent fixed and 3 percent initial weightings end up in the 2.30 to 2.40 percent TEV range.

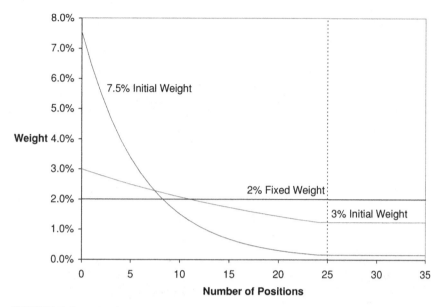

**EXHIBIT 9.1** Weighting Functions
*Source:* Morgan Stanley Research

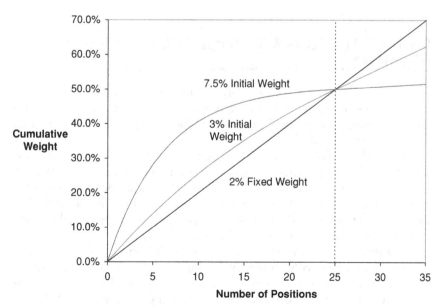

**EXHIBIT 9.2** Cumulative Weightings
*Source:* Morgan Stanley Research

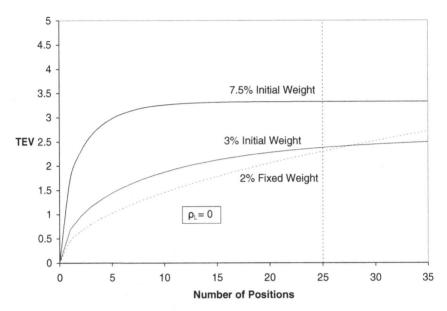

**EXHIBIT 9.3** TEVs for Weighting Functions
*Source:* Morgan Stanley Research

## CORRELATION EFFECTS AND EXPONENTIAL WEIGHTINGS

Correlation effects are considerably complicated with variable weighting functions. However, for the exponential weightings examined in this chapter, it is possible to develop a formula for the expected TEV with given pairwise correlations.

Given the complexity of this formula, it is helpful to validate the formula values by using a Monte Carlo simulation that proceeds directly from the underlying joint probability distributions. For a 25-position long-only portfolio with a 3 percent initial weighting function, Exhibit 9.4 shows that the scatter of the Monte Carlo outcomes fits tightly to the projected formula values across a wide range of pairwise correlations.

The formula can now be used to assess the TEV impact of pairwise correlations interacting with variable weighting functions. Exhibit 9.5 displays the three weightings for a long-only portfolio with a 0.05 pairwise correlation between the long positions. The correlation effect raises the TEVs for all three weightings, with the more accelerated 7.5 percent initial weighting schedule naturally developing greater TEVs. For the 25-position long

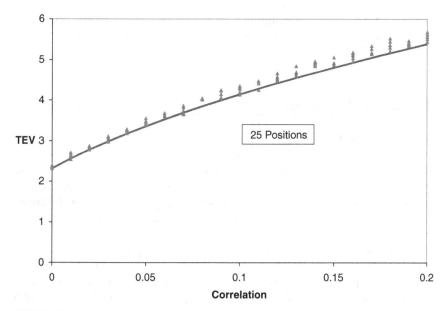

**EXHIBIT 9.4** Simulation and Formula Results for 3 Percent Initial Weighting
*Source:* Morgan Stanley Research

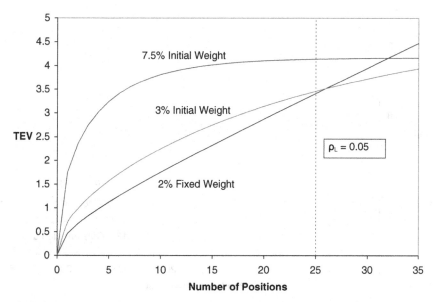

**EXHIBIT 9.5** TEV for Long-Only Weighting Strategies with Pairwise Correlation
*Source:* Morgan Stanley Research

portfolio with a 3 percent initial weighting, the TEV increases from 2.38 percent for the uncorrelated case (Exhibit 9.3) to 3.46 percent for a 0.05 correlation (Exhibit 9.5).

## ALPHA RANKING MODELS

Three alpha ranking patterns are displayed in Exhibit 9.6. The first begins with an alpha of 5 percent and declines exponentially to 2.24 percent at the 25th position. The second model is a simple flat pattern with all alphas fixed at 3.50 percent. The third model represents a highly concentrated set of exceptional opportunities, with an initial alpha of 13 percent, followed by a rapid exponential decay that reduces the alpha to 1 percent at the 15th position.

With both the declining and the concentrated alpha ranking, the better alphas occur in the earlier positions. Thus, the more accelerated weightings should be expected to provide higher portfolio alphas at the outset. This result is evident in Exhibit 9.7, which displays the cumulative portfolio

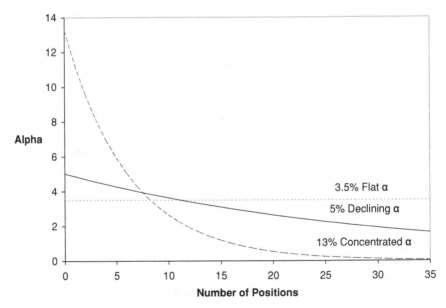

**EXHIBIT 9.6** Long-Only Alpha Ranking Models
*Source:* Morgan Stanley Research

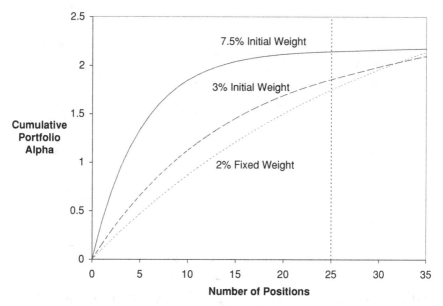

**EXHIBIT 9.7** Cumulative Portfolio Alpha for Declining Alpha Case
*Source:* Morgan Stanley Research

alpha for the 5 percent declining alpha model under the four weighting scenarios. As with TEV, the portfolio alpha accumulates somewhat faster with higher initial weightings, but ends having roughly the same values by the 25th to 35th position.

## ALPHA/TEV RATIOS

Exhibit 9.8 combines the preceding results to form the standard alpha/TEV ratio for the base case of a 5 percent declining alpha ranking.

The 3 percent weighting function provides weights that are proportional to this alpha ranking. Given the assumption of a constant tracking error (TE) for each position, this 3 percent weighting should be optimal and provide the best ratio. From Exhibit 9.8, it is evident that for both the uncorrelated and the 0.05 correlated case, the 3 percent weighting does, in fact, generate better ratios than the fixed 2 percent weights assumed in earlier studies. (To avoid clutter, the 7.5% weighting is not shown, but it also has ratios that fall well below those from the 3% weighting.)

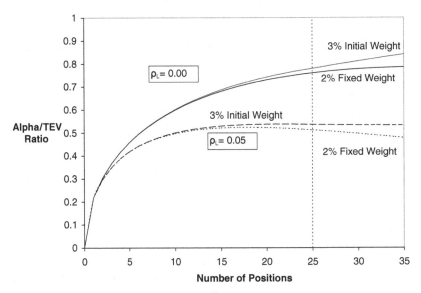

**EXHIBIT 9.8**   Alpha/TEV Ratio for Long-Only 5 Percent Declining Alpha Case
*Source:* Morgan Stanley Research

Another key point is that for a 5 percent declining alpha ranking, there is very little difference between the ratio curves for the 2 percent fixed weights and for the more optimal 3 percent initial weighting function. Thus, for all intent and purposes, the results obtained previously with the simple 2 percent fixed weight can be seen to remain generally valid. This observation holds for both the uncorrelated and correlated long-only cases shown in Exhibit 9.8.

Exhibit 9.8 also shows that a 0.05 correlation has a significant impact on the alpha/TEV ratio that becomes increasingly severe at the higher position counts.

Exhibit 9.9 presents these results in tabular form for the 25 position long-only portfolios. The differential weighting functions have no effect on portfolio alpha for the 3.5 percent flat alpha case. For the 5 percent declining alpha case, the more front-end loaded weightings generate somewhat greater portfolio alphas. The different weightings have a significant impact only for the extreme case of the 13 percent concentrated alphas.

The TEVs are unaffected by the alpha model, but they are highly sensitive to both the weighting function and the assumed correlation. One general observation is that front-end loading can itself lead to a certain form of positive correlation. (In the limit, a positive correlation of 1 will be tantamount to a single-position portfolio.)

**EXHIBIT 9.9** Long-Only 25-Position Portfolios

| Alpha Ranking Model | 3.5% Flat Alpha | | | 5% Declining Alpha | | | 13% Concentrated Alpha | | |
|---|---|---|---|---|---|---|---|---|---|
| Weighting Function | 2% Fixed | 3% Initial | 7.5% Initial | 2% Fixed | 3% Initial | 7.5% Initial | 2% Fixed | 3% Initial | 7.5% Initial |
| PORTFOLIO ALPHA | 1.75 | 1.75 | 1.75 | 1.75 | 1.85 | 2.14 | 1.75 | 2.20 | 3.65 |
| *TEV* | | | | | | | | | |
| $\rho_L = 0$ | 2.30 | 2.38 | 3.32 | 2.30 | 2.38 | 3.32 | 2.30 | 2.38 | 3.32 |
| $\rho_L = .05$ | 3.41 | 3.46 | 4.13 | 3.41 | 3.46 | 4.13 | 3.41 | 3.46 | 4.13 |
| *ALPHA/TEV* | | | | | | | | | |
| $\rho_L = 0$ | 0.76 | 0.74 | 0.53 | 0.76 | 0.78 | 0.64 | 0.76 | 0.92 | 1.10 |
| $\rho_L = .05$ | 0.51 | 0.51 | 0.42 | 0.51 | 0.53 | 0.52 | 0.51 | 0.64 | 0.88 |

*Source:* Morgan Stanley Research

## OPTIMAL WEIGHTING EFFECTS

When these effects are combined into an alpha/TEV ratio, certain predictable patterns begin to emerge. As noted earlier in this chapter, given our assumption of a constant residual volatility, the maximum alpha/TEV ratio should be obtained with position weights that are proportional to each position's alpha expectations. The optimal (or near-optimal) weightings are 2 percent fixed for the 3.5 percent flat alphas, a 3 percent initial weight for the 5 percent declining alpha case, and a 7.5 percent initial weighting for the 13 percent concentrated alpha case.

This ratio optimality is quite evident in the 5 percent declining alpha model, in which the best ratios, 0.78 and 0.53 for $\rho_L = 0$ and $\rho_L = 0.05$, respectively, are both obtained with the near-optimal 3 percent initial weighting. However, the key point is that all the ratios in this 5 percent declining alpha case differ only slightly. This result suggests that for this alpha ranking case, the use of alternative weightings would have little effect on the earlier correlation results based on the 2 percent fixed weightings.

The 2 percent fixed weighting becomes questionable only when we move to the concentrated alpha rankings. A concentrated alpha ranking model will generally argue for front-end loaded portfolios with the majority of the active weight concentrated in the first 10 positions. This high level of concentration may be descriptive of some hedge funds or certain types of intensely active funds. However, such concentrations are hardly commonplace among risk-controlled, benchmark-centric, long-only funds or the AEs that are the subject of this chapter.

It is well known that proportional weightings provide more theoretically optimal alpha/TEV ratios. However, results for the 25-position long-only portfolio in Exhibits 9.8 and 9.9 suggest that a fixed weighting is quite satisfactory in dealing with the moderately declining alpha models that characterize standard forms of active equity management.

## THE ACTIVE EXTENSION

The ability to take short positions provides access to a fresh set of underweights. In the following analysis, these new underweights are assumed to have alphas that coincide with the corresponding long-only alpha model, less some given shorting cost. A shorting cost of 0.50 percent is used in the numerical examples, but it should be clearly noted that higher shorting costs could seriously erode the return benefit from any AE.

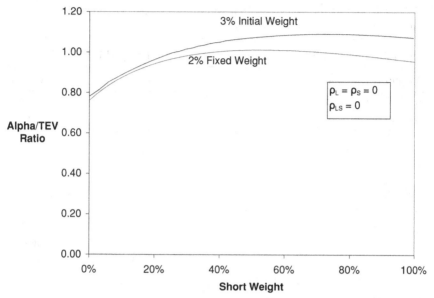

**EXHIBIT 9.10** Alpha/TEV Ratio for AE 5 Percent Declining Alpha
Case
*Source:* Morgan Stanley Research

The proceeds from the shorts could theoretically be reinvested to boost the weight of the highest-alpha long position. However, most portfolios will have already established their maximum allowable weight in these high-ranked positions, so we take the more conservative approach and reinvest the proceeds starting with the 26th ranked long position.

For the 5 percent declining alpha ranking with fully uncorrelated positions, Exhibit 9.10 shows that AEs can lead to significantly improved alpha/TEV ratios. Again, it can be seen that the 3 percent initial weighting function provides the best ratio curve, but one that is only slightly different from the 2 percent fixed weight case until the higher short weights are reached. For the optimal 3 percent weighting, the ratios rise rapidly from 0.78 at 0 percent short weight to 0.96 and 1.05, for short weights of 20 and 40 percent, respectively. The improvement peaks at 1.10 for short weights in the 50 to 70 percent range.

Exhibit 9.11 is a tabular presentation of results for the uncorrelated case with 20 and 40 percent extensions.

Exhibit 9.12 presents the results of the different weighting functions for the two other alpha ranking models. As expected, the best ratios are

**EXHIBIT 9.11**  20 and 40 Percent Extensions for 5 Percent Declining Alpha: Uncorrelated Case ($\rho_L = \rho_S = \rho_{LS} = 0$)

| Alpha Ranking Model | 5% Declining ALPHA | | |
|---|---|---|---|
| Weighting Function | 2% Fixed | 3% Initial | 7.5% Initial |
| PORTFOLIO ALPHA | | | |
| Long-Only | 1.75 | 1.85 | 2.14 |
| 20% Short/Long | 2.91 | 3.02 | 3.11 |
| 40% Short/Long | 3.72 | 3.83 | 3.87 |
| TEVs | | | |
| Long-Only | 2.30 | 2.38 | 3.32 |
| 20% Short/Long | 3.09 | 3.13 | 4.25 |
| 40% Short/Long | 3.71 | 3.64 | 4.68 |
| ALPHA/TEV | | | |
| Long-Only | 0.76 | 0.78 | 0.64 |
| 20% Short/Long | 0.94 | 0.96 | 0.73 |
| 40% Short/Long | 1.00 | 1.05 | 0.83 |

*Source:* Morgan Stanley Research

**EXHIBIT 9.12**  20 and 40 Percent Extensions for Flat and Concentrated Alpha: Uncorrelated Case ($\rho_L = \rho_S = \rho_{LS} = 0$)

| Alpha Ranking Model | 3.5% Flat Alpha | | | 13% Concentrated Alpha | | |
|---|---|---|---|---|---|---|
| Weighting Function | 2% Fixed | 3% Initial | 7.5% Initial | 2% Fixed | 3% Initial | 7.5% Initial |
| PORTFOLIO ALPHA | | | | | | |
| Long-Only | 1.75 | 1.75 | 1.75 | 1.75 | 2.20 | 3.65 |
| 20% Short/Long | 3.05 | 2.89 | 2.37 | 3.11 | 3.84 | 5.82 |
| 40% Short/Long | 4.35 | 3.80 | 2.98 | 3.31 | 4.18 | 6.94 |
| TEVs | | | | | | |
| Long-Only | 2.30 | 2.38 | 3.32 | 2.30 | 2.38 | 3.32 |
| 20% Short/Long | 3.09 | 3.13 | 4.25 | 3.09 | 3.13 | 4.25 |
| 40% Short/Long | 3.71 | 3.64 | 4.68 | 3.71 | 3.64 | 4.68 |
| ALPHA/TEV | | | | | | |
| Long-Only | 0.76 | 0.74 | 0.53 | 0.76 | 0.92 | 1.10 |
| 20% Short/Long | 0.99 | 0.92 | 0.56 | 1.01 | 1.23 | 1.37 |
| 40% Short/Long | 1.17 | 1.04 | 0.64 | 0.89 | 1.15 | 1.48 |

*Source:* Morgan Stanley Research

obtained with the optimal weighting functions—2 percent fixed for the 3.5 percent flat alpha and 7.5 percent for the 13 percent concentrated alpha ranking. Moreover, the weighting effects are more pronounced than with the 5 percent declining alpha case. For the 3.5 percent flat alpha, the optimal 2 percent fixed weighting provides a modest improvement over the 3 percent initial weighting. However, for the extreme (but atypical) case of the 13 percent concentrated alphas, the front-end loaded 7.5 percent initial weighting does provide materially better ratios.

## OFFSETTING LONG/SHORT CORRELATIONS

In contrast to the uncorrelated case, unproductive correlations and factor effects within the longs and/or the short portfolios can increase the TEV, and seriously impair the alpha/TEV ratio of both the initial long portfolio and any AEs. Consequently, an important benefit of AEs is the potential for providing efficient offsets against such unproductive correlations.

Consideration of variable weighting functions adds a considerable degree of analytic complication. By focusing only on weighting functions that have an exponentially declining form, we were able to develop a formula that addresses this more general problem.

Because of the TEV formula's complexity when applied to AEs with offsetting correlations, another Monte Carlo simulation was performed for the purposes of validation. In Exhibit 9.13, the formula was used to develop the solid curve, whereas the scatter points represent outcomes from the Monte Carlo simulations. With reassurance from this close fit, we can use the formula to explore a broader range of TEV scenarios.

Exhibit 9.14 focuses on the 5 percent declining alpha and 3 percent initial weighting to illustrate the material impact of an offset when a 0.05 correlation exists *within* the longs and the shorts. With a −0.05 offset, the AE raises the ratio from the long-only 0.53 to 0.75 at a 20 percent short weight to 0.86 at a 40 percent short weight, and ultimately to a peak of 0.92 at around a 60 percent short weight. Exhibit 9.15 provides a tabular presentation of these results for this base case for AEs of 20 and 40 percent.

Exhibit 9.16 extends the summary presentation of these results to include 120/20 and 140/40 AEs for the other two alpha ranking models. The more simplistic flat alpha ranking model has ratios that are roughly comparable to the 5 percent declining model. Although the 13 percent concentrated alpha ranking does not apply for most AE situations, the summary values are also presented in Exhibit 9.16, both for

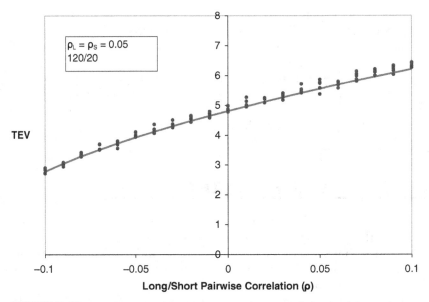

**EXHIBIT 9.13**　3 Percent Initial Weight Long/Short Simulation and Formula Results
*Source:* Morgan Stanley Research

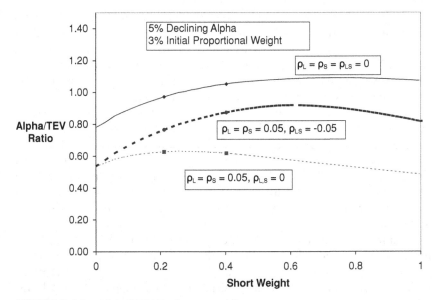

**EXHIBIT 9.14**　Alpha/TEV Ratio versus AE
*Source:* Morgan Stanley Research

**EXHIBIT 9.15** 20 and 40 Percent Extensions for 5 Percent Declining Alpha: Correlated Case ($\rho_L = \rho_S = 0.05$)

| Alpha Ranking Model | 5% Declining Alpha | | |
|---|---|---|---|
| Weighting Function | 2% Fixed | 3% Initial | 7.5% Initial |
| PORTFOLIO ALPHA | | | |
| Long-Only | 1.75 | 1.85 | 2.14 |
| 20% Short/Long | 2.91 | 3.02 | 3.11 |
| 40% Short/Long | 3.72 | 3.83 | 3.87 |
| *TEVs* | | | |
| Long-Only | 3.41 | 3.46 | 4.13 |
| 20% Short/Long | | | |
| $\rho_{LS} = 0$ | 4.80 | 4.86 | 5.68 |
| $\rho_{LS} = -.05$ | 3.96 | 4.02 | 4.97 |
| 40% Short/Long | | | |
| $\rho_{LS} = 0$ | 6.22 | 6.25 | 7.06 |
| $\rho_{LS} = -.05$ | 4.44 | 4.43 | 5.42 |
| *ALPHA/TEV* | | | |
| Long-Only | 0.51 | 0.53 | 0.52 |
| 20% Short/Long | | | |
| $\rho_{LS} = 0$ | 0.61 | 0.62 | 0.55 |
| $\rho_{LS} = -.05$ | 0.73 | 0.75 | 0.63 |
| 40% Short/Long | | | |
| $\rho_{LS} = 0$ | 0.60 | 0.61 | 0.55 |
| $\rho_{LS} = -.05$ | 0.84 | 0.86 | 0.71 |

*Source:* Morgan Stanley Research

completeness and because of its potential interest for more general forms of long/short portfolios.

## ALPHA-FOCUSED INVESTMENT

In practice, the alpha/TEV ratio may not always serve as a totally sufficient gauge of portfolio value. For typical asset allocations, the TE from any component portfolio is likely to have only a minimal impact on the overall fund volatility. Although the TE may be important for other reasons, including as an informational signal relating to risk discipline, consistency,

**EXHIBIT 9.16** 20 and 40 Percent Extensions for Flat and Concentrated Alpha: Correlated Case ($\rho_L = \rho_S = 0.05$)

| Alpha Ranking Model | 3.5% Flat Alpha | | | 13% Concentrated Alpha | | |
|---|---|---|---|---|---|---|
| Weighting Function | 2% Fixed | 3% Initial | 7.5% Initial | 2% Fixed | 3% Initial | 7.5% Initial |
| PORTFOLIO ALPHA | | | | | | |
| Long-Only | 1.75 | 1.75 | 1.75 | 1.75 | 2.20 | 3.65 |
| 20% Short/Long | 3.05 | 2.89 | 2.37 | 3.11 | 3.84 | 5.82 |
| 40% Short/Long | 4.35 | 3.80 | 2.98 | 3.31 | 4.18 | 6.94 |
| *TEVs* | | | | | | |
| Long-Only | 3.41 | 3.46 | 4.13 | 3.41 | 3.46 | 4.13 |
| 20% Short/Long | | | | | | |
| $\rho_{LS} = 0$ | 4.80 | 4.86 | 5.68 | 4.80 | 4.86 | 5.68 |
| $\rho_{LS} = -.05$ | 3.96 | 4.02 | 4.97 | 3.96 | 4.02 | 4.97 |
| 40% Short/Long | | | | | | |
| $\rho_{LS} = 0$ | 6.22 | 6.25 | 7.06 | 6.22 | 6.25 | 7.06 |
| $\rho_{LS} = -.05$ | 4.44 | 4.43 | 5.42 | 4.44 | 4.43 | 5.42 |
| *ALPHA/TEV* | | | | | | |
| Long-Only | 0.51 | 0.51 | 0.42 | 0.51 | 0.64 | 0.88 |
| 20% Short/Long | | | | | | |
| $\rho_{LS} = 0$ | 0.64 | 0.59 | 0.42 | 0.65 | 0.79 | 1.02 |
| $\rho_{LS} = -.05$ | 0.77 | 0.72 | 0.48 | 0.79 | 0.96 | 1.17 |
| 40% Short/Long | | | | | | |
| $\rho_{LS} = 0$ | 0.70 | 0.61 | 0.42 | 0.53 | 0.67 | 0.98 |
| $\rho_{LS} = -.05$ | 0.98 | 0.86 | 0.55 | 0.75 | 0.94 | 1.28 |

*Source:* Morgan Stanley Research

process reliability, and so on, there certainly are situations in which lower alpha/TEV ratios could be exchanged for higher returns as long as the TEV remained within some reasonable bound. As evident in Exhibit 9.17, in such situations, AEs can lead to significantly enhanced alphas.

## CONCLUSION

These results reinforce the earlier findings that AEs can be viewed as an extended form of traditional active equity management that has

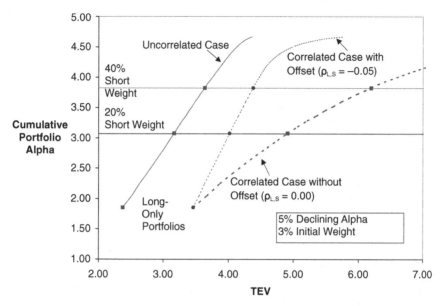

**EXHIBIT 9.17** Alpha/TEV Ratio versus AE
*Source:* Morgan Stanley Research

the potential to materially improve both portfolio alphas and alpha/TEV ratios by:

1. Creating access to a fresh crop of active underweight opportunities,
2. Reinvesting the short proceeds in productive new longs (even if they are of lower alpha rank), and
3. Providing offsets that reduce unproductive correlations and facilitate return-enhancing pairing opportunities.

The preconditions for realizing any of these benefits are managers who have a credible basis for producing positive alphas in both long and short portfolios, a high level of risk discipline, and an organizational ability to pursue AEs in a benchmark-centric, cost-efficient fashion.

Refer to Chapter 24 (Active 130/30 Extensions: Alpha Hunting at the Fund Level) for appendix details.

# CHAPTER 10

# Portfolio Concentration

**Anthony Bova**
Vice President
Morgan Stanley, Research

**Martin Leibowitz**
Managing Director
Morgan Stanley, Research

For securities with similar return/risk expectations, the theoretically optimal information ratio (IR) is obtained through a broad diversification with equal active weights.

In practice, actual portfolio weightings are rarely this "flat." For traditional funds and even most quantitative funds, the weightings typically follow some descending sequence. In a sample of mutual funds, 50 percent of the largest active weights ranged between 2.0 and 3.5 percent with weights decreasing in a generally exponential fashion. These weighting structures imply alpha expectations that also follow an exponential-like descent.

Most portfolio managers identify the maximum weight they are willing to assign to any single security. This number is often underutilized, especially given the valuable insights it can provide regarding a portfolio's risk characteristics.

This chapter moves forward from these observations to explore the portfolio characteristics obtained from applying various active weighting structures to different alpha patterns.

Assuming independent residuals, the optimal IR is reached with active weights proportional to the security alphas.

---

Originally published as part of the *Morgan Stanley Portfolio Notes*, July 17, 2007.

However, higher alphas and still near-optimal IRs can be derived from portfolios that are significantly more concentrated than those providing the optimal IR.

Most funds have significant unused capacity for active risk. Assuming that the gross weightings maintain the desired beta control, more concentrated active structures could enhance the alpha prospects while sustaining tolerable levels of tracking error (TE) and yet having near-optimal IRs.

Alpha ranking and position weighting models can be used to characterize the management process in active equity portfolios. In theory, with a constant residual volatility and zero correlation, the optimal weighting for each position should be proportional to its alpha ranking. With identical alpha expectations for all potential investments, this principle leads to a broadly diversified portfolio with equal weights. However, for other alpha situations and different correlation assumptions, portfolios that are more concentrated can also be optimal or at least near optimal.

Another key point is that optimal solutions are usually defined in terms of a maximum IR of alpha to TE. The IR ratio is an important metric, but it does not provide a totally comprehensive description of a portfolio's benefits. Given the role that TE plays at the sponsor level, it is also important to separately consider the two components of the IR. There may be situations where a sponsor is willing to accept a greater alpha at the expense of a higher TE and a lower IR.

## WEIGHTING MODELS AND MAXIMUM ACTIVE WEIGHTS

Most portfolios identify the maximum active weight (MW) that they would invest in any one position. When transformed into a maximum percentage weight for any active position, this number can provide valuable insights into the portfolio structure and its risk characteristics.

Exhibit 10.1 is a distribution of the MWs for a sample of 50 long-only mutual funds, ranging from $1 to $20 billion in total market value. Although a few outliers exist, the majority of MWs lie between 1 to 4 percent.

Exhibit 10.2 plots the median, 1st and 3rd quartile of the active weights through the first 50 positions of the sample portfolios. The median maximum active size is 2.7 percent with a decline to 1.0 percent by the 25th position, and 0.05 percent by the 50th position. These curves also show little activity after the 50th position. Thus, it becomes reasonable to focus on the first 50 positions.

By the nature of a long-only portfolio, all positive active weights must be funded by active underweights. However, in a typical long portfolio, all

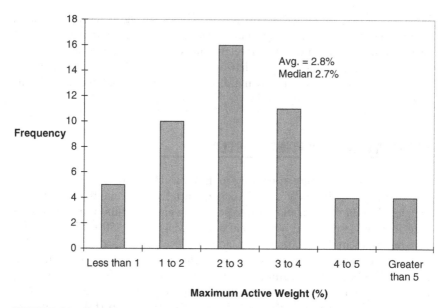

**EXHIBIT 10.1**  MWs for Sample Portfolios
*Source:* Morgan Stanley Research

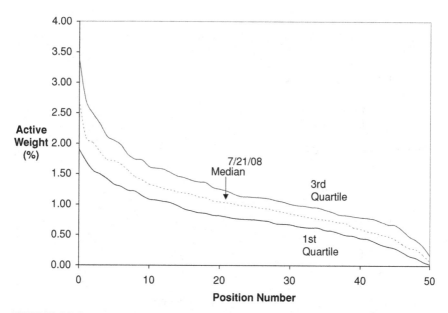

**EXHIBIT 10.2**  Active Weights for First 50 Positions for Sample Portfolios
*Source:* Morgan Stanley Research

but a few of the sizable active positions will be overweights with the funding underweights scattered across many smaller positions. For a number of reasons, these fragmented underweights have a relatively minor impact on the expected alphas or the TEs that are the focus of this chapter. Thus, in the interest of clarity, the following discussion will treat all active positions as if they were positive overweights.

## EXPONENTIAL WEIGHTING MODELS

The portfolio weighting functions in Exhibit 10.2 can be roughly modeled with an initial MW and an exponential decline in the subsequent weights. Exhibit 10.3 displays three possible weighting functions, each specified to provide the total 50 percent active weight over 50 positions. With this requirement for a 50 percent activity level, the starting weight MW then fully determines the exponential weight curves shown in Exhibit 10.3. Exhibit 10.4 shows the cumulative weight for the three functions, with all curves ending at the total active weight of 50 percent.

The middle curve in Exhibit 10.3 approximates the portfolio weightings for the sample funds in Exhibit 10.2. It begins at 2.7 percent, declines to

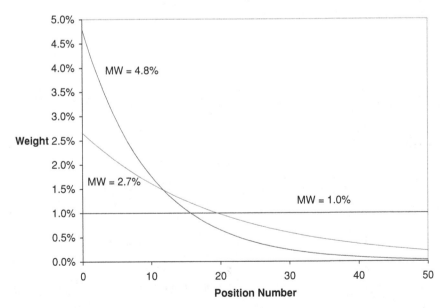

**EXHIBIT 10.3**  Exponential Weighting Models
*Source:* Morgan Stanley Research

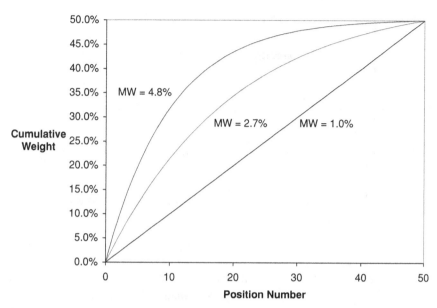

**EXHIBIT 10.4** Cumulative Portfolio Weights
*Source:* Morgan Stanley Research

0.8 percent by the 25th position, and then drops to 0.2 percent by the 50th position. The higher curve represents a more concentrated weighting scheme with a maximum weight of 4.8 percent that declines to 0.4 percent by the 25th position and then reaches 0.03 percent at the 50th position. The bottom flat line represents a fixed 1 percent weight.

## TRACKING ERRORS

Given a constant 20 percent TE for each position, we can determine the TE associated with a starting MW and its associated weighting function. The formula for this calculation is provided in the Appendix.

When each active position is assumed to be independent and uncorrelated, the TE calculation is quite simple. For MWs ranging from 1.0 to 4.8 percent, the TEs are shown on the lower curve in Exhibit 10.5. The lowest TE of 1.4 percent occurs with a MW of 1 percent, which is the most diversified portfolio with all 50 positions having the same 1 percent weight. With higher MWs, more of the total weight is concentrated in the earlier positions, leading to somewhat larger TEs. With a 4.8 percent MW, the uncorrelated TE reaches 2.25 percent.

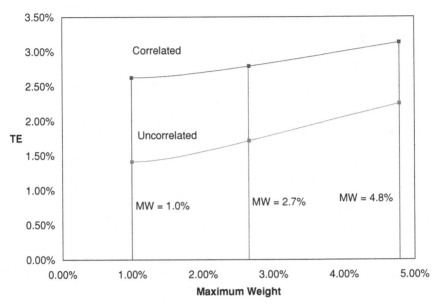

**EXHIBIT 10.5**   Correlated and Uncorrelated TE
*Source:* Morgan Stanley Research

There will be common factors that exist among the positions in most long-only portfolios. These effects can be modeled by assuming that a positive correlation exists between any two positions. In Exhibit 10.5, the top line depicts the TE for a pairwise correlation of 0.05.

For a MW of 1 percent, the correlated TE is 2.6 percent. The TE then increases with higher MWs, reaching 3.1 percent for the most concentrated portfolio with an MW of 4.8 percent. It is interesting to note that curve for the correlated case in Exhibit 10.5 is flatter than the uncorrelated case. This is because correlation in effect forces a certain concentration even across diversified weightings.

## ALPHA RANKING FUNCTIONS

Portfolio managers generally have some formal way (in the case of quantitative funds) or informal way (in the case of fundamental managers) for sequencing their active investments in terms of expected excess returns. The declining curve in Exhibit 10.6 is an example of an alpha ranking model that

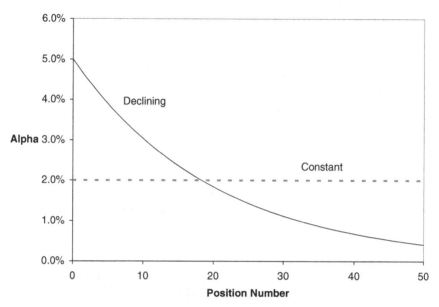

**EXHIBIT 10.6**   Alpha Ranking Models
*Source:* Morgan Stanley Research

follows the same rate of exponential decay (0.05) as the weighting function for an MW of 2.7 percent shown in Exhibit 10.3. As shown in Exhibit 10.6, the highest expected alpha is 5 percent, which then declines to 0.4 percent by the 50th position. Exhibit 10.6 also displays an alpha ranking model that is constant at 2 percent for each position.

Exhibit 10.7 depicts the cumulative portfolio alpha from combining the two alpha-ranking curves shown in Exhibit 10.6 with the exponential weighting functions for MWs ranging continuously from 1.0 to 4.8 percent. For the constant alpha case, the portfolio alpha is also constant because all weighing functions are designed to accumulate to the same 50 percent activity level.

For the case of the declining alphas, the higher MWs assign greater weights to the larger alphas. This greater concentration in the more alpha-rich positions generates portfolio alphas that rise with higher MWs, as shown by the curve in Exhibit 10.7. Comparing Exhibit 10.7 with Exhibit 10.5, we see that these higher portfolio alphas are associated with greater TEs. A standard approach for integrating these two measures is the IR composed of the portfolio alpha divided by the corresponding TE.

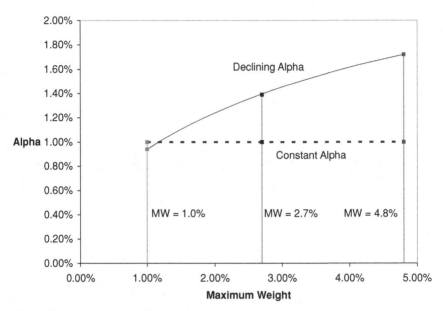

**EXHIBIT 10.7**   Portfolio Alphas
*Source:* Morgan Stanley Research

## THE INFORMATION RATIO FOR CONSTANT ALPHAS

Focusing on constant alpha case, with the numerator being constant across all MWs, the IR value varies only with the TE in the denominator. As evident in Exhibit 10.5, for both the correlated and the uncorrelated cases, the TE rises with higher MWs so the IR must always fall with higher MWs, as shown in Exhibit 10.8. Thus, for constant alphas, the most diversified portfolio—that is, the one with all weights equal to 1 percent—provides the best IR.

## THE INFORMATION RATIO FOR DECLINING ALPHAS

For the declining alpha case, the IR story becomes more complicated. In contrast to the constant alpha case, the portfolio alpha now rises with higher MWs (Exhibit 10.7). The IR curve, therefore, depends on the specific relationship between the increasing alpha in the numerator and the increasing TEs in the denominator. Exhibit 10.9 plots the resulting IR curves.

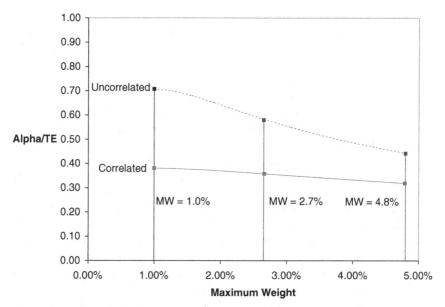

**EXHIBIT 10.8** IRs for Constant Alphas
*Source:* Morgan Stanley Research

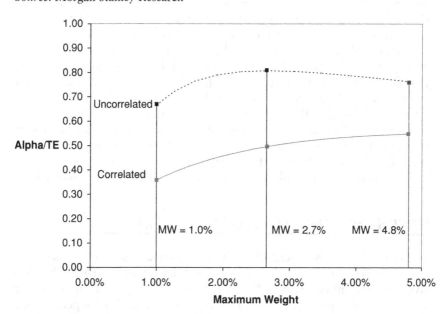

**EXHIBIT 10.9** IRs for Declining Alphas
*Source:* Morgan Stanley Research

For uncorrelated positions, the IRs rise with higher concentrations, reach a peak at an MW of 2.7 percent, and then decline slowly. Recall that declining alphas had the same (0.05) exponential rate of decay as the weighting function for a starting MW of 2.7 percent. This is, of course, no coincidence. With all positions being independent and having the same residual error, it can be shown that each position's optimal (IR-based) weight must be proportional to its alpha value. Thus, the maximum IR will be achieved with an exponential weighting having the same 0.05 decay rate as the alpha function. Therefore, it is no surprise that the optimized IR is attained for a decay-matching MW value of 2.7 percent.

At the same time, it is interesting to note that the IR curve is relatively flat, even beyond the 2.7 percent peak. This near-optimality of more concentrated weightings raises the question as to whether higher concentrations may be preferred under certain conditions. For example, some fund sponsors may be willing to tolerate somewhat greater TEs in exchange for materially higher alphas. The flat portion of the IR curve in Exhibit 10.9 suggests that such a trade-off could lead to more concentrated portfolios with significantly higher alphas (Exhibit 10.7), but only slightly below-optimal IRs.

This alpha-versus-TE tradeoff becomes more compelling at the sponsor level. At this overall fund level, the alpha adds to the return whereas the TE can be shown to be largely submerged by the dominating beta risk. Thus, although moving from the IR-optimal point incurs higher TE in a component portfolio, the risk at the overall fund level will not significantly change.

The correlated situation can lead us even further away from the diversified portfolio. Exhibit 10.5 showed that correlation increased the overall TEs while flattening the TE curve. With this flatter TE, the rising alpha curve becomes more dominant. As shown in the lower curve in Exhibit 10.9, the net result is that the IR actually increases continuously with higher MWs. From a pure IR perspective, the highest IR value is only attained with an MW of 4.8 percent (i.e., the most concentrated portfolio considered in our example). Given the shape of this correlated IR curve, it might be that some TE limit would take precedence over reaching for the highest possible IR.

## EFFICIENT FRONTIERS FOR DECLINING ALPHAS

In Exhibit 10.10, the uncorrelated and correlated cases for the declining alphas are depicted as efficient frontiers in alpha versus TE space. The most diversified weighting, with MW of 1 percent, provides both the lowest TE and the smallest portfolio alpha. Consequently, an MW of 1 percent corresponds to the beginning point of the frontier for both the correlated and uncorrelated frontiers. With increasing MWs, the alphas and the TEs both rise continually. However, the optimal IR corresponds to the frontier point

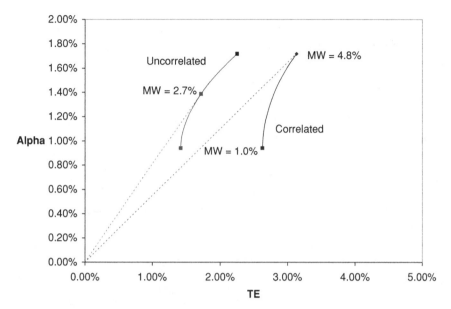

**EXHIBIT 10.10** Alpha versus TE: Uncorrelated and Correlated
*Source:* Morgan Stanley Research

having the greatest slope for the line drawn from the origin. As seen in Exhibit 10.8, this maximum slope for the uncorrelated case is reached at the midpoint with an MW of 2.7 percent. In contrast, for the correlated case, the higher IR is only reached at an MW of 4.8 percent.

## SIMPLE FIXED WEIGHTS

All weighting functions thus far have assumed an initial MW followed by an exponential decline. The preceding discussion indicated that there might be situations when portfolios that are more concentrated may be preferred. Exponential weightings with higher starting MWs were explored as a way to achieve greater concentrations on the higher alpha investments. However, another approach to intensified concentrations is achieved by simply keeping the weight fixed at the starting MW until the 50 percent activity budget is exhausted.

Exhibit 10.11 provides three examples of these fixed weightings using the same maximum weights as in Exhibit 10.3 for the exponential weighting function. A 4.8 percent fixed weight covers slightly more than 10 positions, whereas a 2.7 percent fixed weight spans roughly 19 positions. The fixed

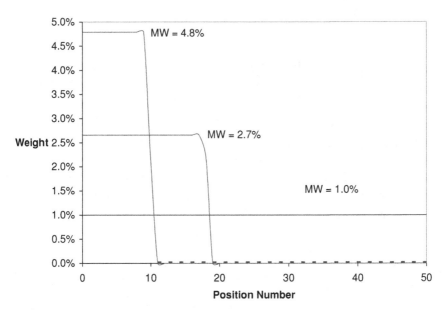

**EXHIBIT 10.11**  Fixed Weighting Function
*Source:* Morgan Stanley Research


1 percent weight case obviously corresponds to 50 positions each having the same 1 percent MW.

Exhibits 10.12 and 10.13 compare the exponential and the fixed weighting approaches for the two correlation assumptions. The exponential weighting curves are the solid lines; the fixed weighting curves are shown as dashed lines.

It is interesting to note that in the uncorrelated case, the exponential IR curve in Exhibit 10.12 appears to significantly dominate the fixed weighting. However, with the 0.05 pairwise correlation, the IR curves become virtually coincidental. In the efficient frontiers shown in Exhibit 10.13, the fixed weights provide significantly higher alphas with near-optimal IRs, especially in the correlated case.

Of course, a key problem is that the alpha function, even if known, rarely fits any simple functional pattern. However, in practice, the actual weights assigned to various positions within a given portfolio do provide some indication of the presumed alphas. To the extent that these estimates allow higher-conviction investments to be at least classified into tiers, similarly clustered fixed weightings might provide a robust approach to higher-alpha portfolios that remain near optimal in IR terms.

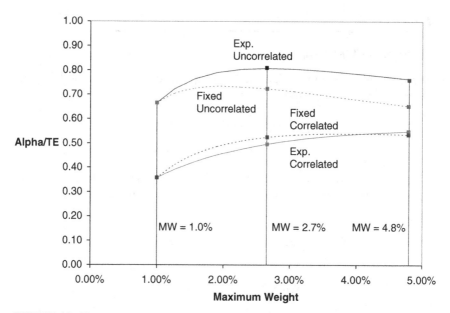

**EXHIBIT 10.12**  Alpha/TE: Four Weighting Scenarios
*Source:* Morgan Stanley Research

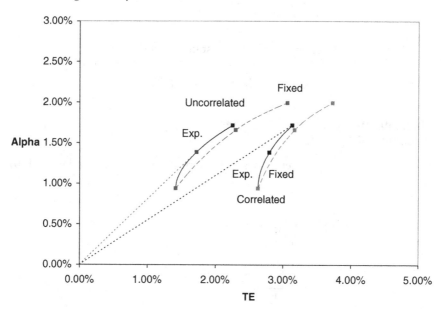

**EXHIBIT 10.13**  Alpha versus TE: Four Weighting Scenarios
*Source:* Morgan Stanley Research

## APPENDIX

### Exponential Weightings

For a starting maximum weight MW, an exponential weighting model would assign active weight $\omega_i$ to the ith position:

$$\omega_i = (MW)e^{-\lambda(i-1)} \qquad i = 1, N$$

where $\lambda$ is the decay rate.

In this chapter, the total active weight accumulates to a level W so that $\lambda$ can be determined as a function of MW from the implicit equation:

$$W = \sum_{1}^{N} \omega_i$$

$$= (MW) \sum_{1}^{N} e^{-\lambda(i-1)}$$

$$= (MW) \left[ \frac{\left(1 - e^{-\lambda N}\right)}{\left(1 - e^{-\lambda}\right)} \right] \qquad MW > 1\%$$

For MW = 1 percent, we have constant weightings:

$$\omega_i = (MW) \qquad i = 1, N$$

### Uncorrelated Tracking Error and Exponential Weights

With a uniform residual error $\sigma$ across all positions, the uncorrelated TE(0) is given by

$$TE^2(0) = \sum_{1}^{N} (\omega_i \sigma)^2$$

$$= \sigma^2 \sum_{1}^{N} (MW)^2 e^{-2\lambda(i-1)}$$

$$= (MW)^2 \sigma^2 \left( \frac{1 - e^{-2\lambda N}}{1 - e^{-2\lambda}} \right) \qquad MW > 1\%$$

For MW = 1 percent:

$$TE^2(0) = N(MW)^2\sigma^2$$

$$= N\left(\frac{W}{N}\right)^2 \sigma^2$$

$$= (W\sigma)^2 \left(\frac{1}{N}\right)$$

## Correlated Tracking Error and Exponential Weights

With a uniform pairwise correlation, the TE $(\rho)$ is given by

$$TE^2(\rho) = \sum_{i,j} \omega_i\omega_j\rho_{ij}\sigma^2$$

$$= \sigma^2 \left[ \sum_{i\neq j} \omega_i\omega_j\rho + \sum_{i=1}^{N} \omega_i^2 \right]$$

$$= \sigma^2 \left\{ \left[ \left(\sum_{i=1}^{N} \omega_i\right)^2 - \sum_{1}^{N} \omega_i^2 \right] \rho + \sum_{1}^{N} \omega_i^2 \right\}$$

$$= \left[ (W\sigma)^2 - TE^2(0) \right]\rho + TE^2(0)$$

For the special case when MW = 1 percent and $\omega_i$ = 1 percent:

$$TE^2(\rho) = \left[ (W\sigma)^2 - (W\sigma)^2 \left(\frac{1}{N}\right) \right]\rho + (W\sigma)^2 \left(\frac{1}{N}\right)$$

$$= (W\sigma)^2 \left\{ \left[ 1 - \frac{1}{N} \right]\rho + \frac{1}{N} \right\}$$

and because W = N(MW),

$$TE^2(\rho) = N^2(MW)^2\sigma^2 \left\{ \left[ 1 - \frac{1}{N} \right]\rho + \frac{1}{N} \right\}$$

$$= (MW)^2\sigma^2 \left\{ \left[ N^2 - N \right]\rho + N \right\}$$

## Alpha Function

An exponential alpha function with a starting alpha $\alpha_o$ and a decay rate $\mu$ will have position alphas

$$\alpha_j = \alpha_o e^{-\mu(j-1)} \qquad j = 1, N$$

The portfolio alpha $\alpha_p$ with exponential weighing then becomes

$$\alpha_p = \sum_1^N \omega_j \alpha_j$$

$$= (MW)\alpha_o \sum_{j=1}^N e^{-(\lambda+\mu)(j-1)}$$

$$= (MW)\alpha_o \left[ \frac{\left(1 - e^{-N(\lambda+\mu)}\right)}{\left(1 - e^{-(\lambda+\mu)}\right)} \right]$$

for MW > 1 percent and $\mu > 0$.

For MW = 1 percent and/or $\mu = 0$ (the flat alpha case), the formula must be adjusted as shown earlier.

## The Information Ratio

The IR is defined as

$$IR = \frac{\alpha_p}{TE\,(\rho)}$$

With exponential alpha ($\mu > 0$) and uncorrelated exponential weights ($\lambda > 0$), this ratio takes the form

$$IR = \frac{(MW)\alpha_o \left[ \frac{\left(1 - e^{-N(\lambda+\mu)}\right)}{\left(1 - e^{-(\lambda+\mu)}\right)} \right]}{(MW)\sigma \sqrt{\left[ \frac{\left(1 - e^{-2N\lambda}\right)}{\left(1 - e^{-2\lambda}\right)} \right]}}$$

When $\lambda = \mu$, this IR can be shown to reach a maximum value IR*:

$$IR^* = \frac{\alpha_0}{\sigma} \sqrt{\left[ \frac{\left(1 - e^{-2N\lambda}\right)}{\left(1 - e^{-2\lambda}\right)} \right]}$$

Thus, for the numerical values used in Exhibit 10.9, with MW = 2.7 percent, which implies an $\lambda = 0.05$, the optimal IR* is given by

$$IR^* = \frac{5}{20} \sqrt{\left[ \frac{\left(1 - e^{-2(50)(.05)}\right)}{\left(1 - e^{-2(.05)}\right)} \right]}$$

$$= 0.81$$

## Fixed Weights

For a given fixed weight (MW), the position weightings can be approximated by

$$\omega_i = \begin{cases} (MW) & i = 1, \dfrac{W}{(MW)} \\[3mm] 0 & i > \dfrac{W}{(MW)} \end{cases}$$

so that the uncorrelated TE simply becomes

$$TE^2(0) = \sigma^2 (MW)^2 \frac{W}{(MW)}$$

$$= \sigma^2 (MW) W$$

whereas the correlated TE is again given by

$$TE^2(\rho) = \left[ TE^2(1) - TE^2(0) \right] \rho + TE^2(0)$$

$$= \left[ (W\sigma)^2 - \sigma^2 (MW) W \right] \rho + \sigma^2 (MW) W$$

$$= \sigma^2 W \left\{ [W - (MW)] \rho + (MW) \right\}$$

The portfolio alpha under exponential weighting ($\lambda > 0$) is found from

$$
\alpha_{\mathrm{p}} \cong \sum_{i=1}^{\left(\frac{\mathrm{W}}{\mathrm{MW}}\right)} \omega_i \alpha_i
$$

$$
\cong \sum_{i=1}^{\left(\frac{\mathrm{W}}{\mathrm{MW}}\right)} (\mathrm{MW}) \alpha_o e^{-\mu(i-1)}
$$

$$
\cong (\mathrm{MW}) \alpha_o \left[ \frac{\left(1 - e^{-\mu\left(\frac{\mathrm{W}}{\mathrm{MW}}\right)}\right)}{(1 - e^{-\mu})} \right]
$$

# CHAPTER 11

# Generic Shorts in Active 130/30 Extensions

**Anthony Bova**
Vice President
Morgan Stanley, Research

**Martin Leibowitz**
Managing Director
Morgan Stanley, Research

Generic investments such as exchange-traded funds (ETFs) and index funds provide exposure to a specific sector or to a broad market index. Because generics have zero alpha relative to their respective benchmarks, they can be viewed as consuming or generating funds without disturbing the portfolio's active position structures.

In a long/short fund, generics can top off one side or the other to balance the portfolio to a desired net level of investment. Compared with balancing through the use of low alpha or marginal security-specific positions, generics have the advantage of being less research intensive, more liquid, and more readily sustained over time.

Active portfolios often embed factor exposures that are less than fully productive in alpha terms. An appropriate basket of generics can limit unwanted factor effects, lower tracking errors (TEs), and improve information ratios (IRs).

In active 130/30 extensions, it can sometimes be difficult to find a full complement of active short positions. This chapter presents a simplified model that illustrates how zero-alpha generics can provide funds needed for reinvestment, augment long alphas, and offset potential factor effects.

Originally published as part of the *Morgan Stanley Portfolio Notes*, November 14, 2007.

A generalization of the generic concept can be applied to any active portfolio by separating out an activity component containing all positions in which the primary purpose is alpha generation. The remaining positions then consist of basic market weights and fragmented overweights and underweights, as well as literal generic instruments. The percentage weight devoted to this activity component, usually well below 50 percent, plays an important role in assessing the portfolio's alpha-producing capability.

## THE SHORT GENERIC MODEL

The potential benefit from active extension (AE) is derived from:

- The opportunity to augment the active positions in the long portfolio,
- The use of the short positions to offset unproductive factor risks in the long positions, and
- The addition of fresh active short positions with positive alphas.

One possible method of AE construction can be Long Reinvestment Only (LRO). In this case, the short extension would be basically index-like with zero cost, zero alpha, and zero residual volatility. However, this short extension would generate proceeds that could be reinvested to augment the original alpha-producing long positions. This situation essentially represents a form of leverage that proportionally increases the existing long active positions with no alpha or offset impact from the short positions. The net result is a constant IR because any alpha increase is matched by a corresponding increase in TE.

The use of more customized generic shorts has the capability to offset factor effects in the long portfolio. These generics can be thought of as style/sector-specific instruments, such as ETFs or tailored baskets, that are tied to an existing factor in the long-only portfolio. Thus, the crux of this analysis is that although these generic shorts have zero alpha, they can still provide benefits in terms of providing reinvestable funds and correlation offsets.

In our basic model, the long-only portfolio has 25 positions with 2 percent active weights, leading to an initial active weight of 50 percent. An exponential alpha ranking curve is assumed, which begins at 5 percent and then declines to 1.5 percent by the 25th position. The residual volatility of each active position is 20 percent. Most portfolios will have multiple factors that represent exposures of the individual positions to common variables. These include factors that may be value-based (dividend yield, book/price, earnings/price), growth-based (earnings per share growth, long-term growth rate), or factors related to various industries and sectors. Our simple model for these unproductive factor effects is a $+0.05$ pairwise correlation across all long positions. The resulting long-only portfolio has an alpha of 1.46 percent, TE of 3.0 percent, and an IR of 0.49.

The characteristics of the generic short portfolio will be quite different. Due to management fees and tracking/trading transactions, there will be costs associated with using generic shorts even though they have a zero alpha expectation. To estimate the residual volatilities for the generic shorts, a sample of style-based ETF returns was taken that yielded an average residual volatility of 5 percent. For simplicity, the generic short portfolio is modeled as a single position on the short side having this 5 percent residual volatility. The correlation of this single generic short with each long portfolio was set at −0.25, a value that would enable the generics to fully offset the 0.05 correlation within a long portfolio of comparable size.

## EXTENSIONS WITH GENERIC OFFSETS

The LRO case treats the generic shorts as having no alpha or TE effects. However, there are opportunities to offset unproductive correlations (and better control TE) with more focused generic shorts. The trade-off is the costs associated with the generics that can erode the overall portfolio alpha.

Exhibit 11.1 compares the portfolio alpha for the LRO case along with two generic offset cases with shorting costs of 50 basis points (bps) and

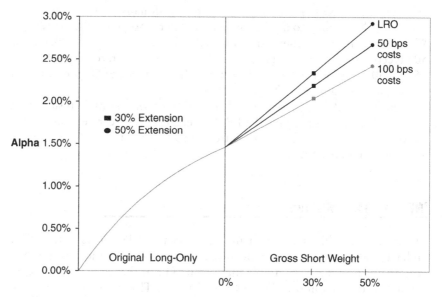

**EXHIBIT 11.1** Alpha versus Short Weight
*Source:* Morgan Stanley Research

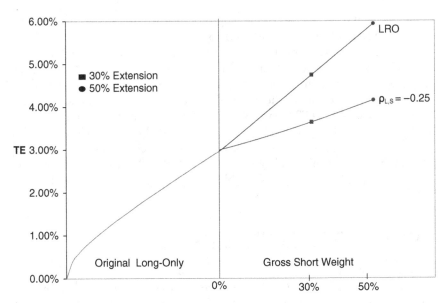

**EXHIBIT 11.2**  TE versus Short Weight
*Source:* Morgan Stanley Research

100 bps. The LRO portfolio alpha rises proportionally with the increasing active weight, leading to a 2.93 percent alpha at a 50 percent short weight. With 50 and 100 bps generic shorting alpha costs, the portfolio alpha at the 50 percent short weight declines to 2.68 and 2.43 percent, respectively. This 25 and 50 bps alpha reduction is simply a function of the 50 percent short weight multiplied by the 50 and 100 bps costs.

Exhibit 11.2 reflects the TE. The −0.25 offset situation results in a significant drop in TE versus the LRO case. At a 50 percent extension, the active weight in each position rises from 2 to 4 percent, and the associated TE grows to 4 percent.

## INFORMATION RATIOS

Exhibit 11.3 combines the alpha and TEs to generate IR curves based on the alpha/TE ratio. With LRO, the IR stays constant at 0.49 as the higher alphas are obtained with a comparable increase in TE. In the cases with a −0.25 offset, the IR rises into the 0.60 to 0.65 range. Thus, a 20 to 30 percent improvement in IR can be obtained with the use of generic shorts as offsets.

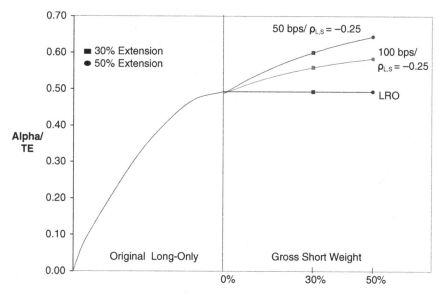

**EXHIBIT 11.3** Alpha/TE versus Short Weight
*Source:* Morgan Stanley Research

Exhibit 11.4 separates the alpha/TE ratio into its two components. The 30 and 50 percent points on each curve are marked by squares and dots, respectively. The alphas fall between 2.0 to 2.3 percent at a 30 percent short weight, and between 2.4 to 2.9 percent at a 50 percent short weight. The TEs have a much wider range—between 3.7 to 4.8 percent at 30 percent, and 4.2 to 5.9 percent at 50 percent.

For situations in which the binding constraint is a maximum TE, such as 5 percent, the LRO would not be viable for short weights above 30 percent. For the −0.25 offset cases, the TEs fall below 4 percent for all short weights, with alphas increasing to 2.4 to 2.9 percent.

## GENERIC COMPLETIONS

In practice, individual alpha-generating shorts would generally be used to the extent possible. However, when all such specific shorts have been put in place, there may still be opportunities for deploying additional funds on the long side. To generate these funds, the portfolio manager may turn to generic shorts to complete the extension.

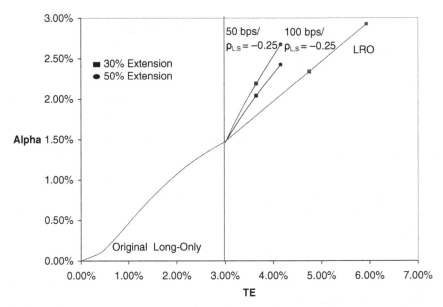

**EXHIBIT 11.4** Alpha versus TE
*Source:* Morgan Stanley Research

Exhibit 11.5 presents the alpha versus TE for three cases:

1. The offsetting all-generics with 50 bps costs (from Exhibits 11.1 through 11.4),
2. The all-active shorts, and
3. A mixed scenario when the first 20 percent short weight is actively invested while the remaining 30 percent of the extension is completed with generic shorts.

The fully active and 20 percent active/30 percent generic cases yield identical alphas and TEs for a 20 percent extension. At higher extensions, the generic shorts provide no alpha, and all the alpha benefits come from the reinvested longs. In terms of TE, the generic and the active shorts both act to offset the correlations within the long portfolio. However, the generic shorts have a lower overall volatility and, therefore, have a lower TE contribution.

Thus, the use of offsetting generics allows for higher extension percentages—and higher alphas—to be obtained while staying within more

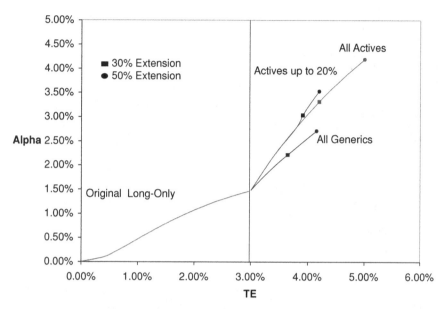

**EXHIBIT 11.5** Alpha versus TE: Generics and Active Shorts
*Source:* Morgan Stanley Research

clearly specified TE bounds. For example, with a 50 percent extension, the TE reaches 5 percent for all-active portfolios, but only 4.2 percent for the 20 percent active/30 percent generic case. At this 4.2 percent TE, the 20 percent active/30 percent generic case actually provides higher alphas than either the all-generic or even the all-active portfolio. Such generic completions would prove particularly valuable in a highly TE-sensitive situation.

The value of correlation offsets is underscored in Exhibit 11.6, where the results from offsetting generics are compared with generic completions that are simply independent of all long and short active positions. For a given extension level, the alphas will be close, but the portfolio TEs are seen to be much greater without the offsets.

In practice, it is not unusual for situations to arise where the potential investment in active longs exceeds that available in active shorts (or vice versa). Some form of generic completion will then be needed to take full advantage of the alpha potential, while still maintaining beta neutrality. To the extent that offsetting generics can be found, the fund's alpha potential can be realized while restraining its TE to fall within tolerable limits.

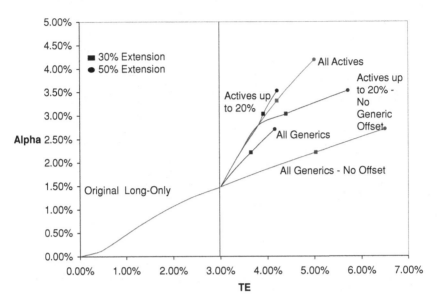

**EXHIBIT 11.6** Alpha versus TE: Generic Shorts with No Offset
*Source:* Morgan Stanley Research

## APPENDIX

### The Basic Tracking Error Model with Generics

In our previous chapter, the number of long positions $n_L$ and short positions $n_S$ were both fixed. The weight $\omega$ assigned to each position was then determined by the total active long and short weights $A_L$ and $A_S$:

$$\omega_L = \frac{A_L}{n_L}$$

$$\omega_S = \frac{A_S}{n_S}$$

Residual volatilities of $\sigma_L$ and $\sigma_S$ were assigned to both long and short positions, with pairwise correlations $\rho_L$ and $\rho_S$ *within* the longs and shorts, respectively, and $\rho_{LS}$ *between* the long and short positions.

The portfolio TE was then given by

$$(TE)^2 = n_L\omega_L^2\sigma_L^2 + n_S\omega_S^2\sigma_S^2 + n_L\,(n_L - 1)\,\omega_L^2\sigma_L^2\rho_L + n_S\,(n_S - 1)\,\omega_S^2\sigma_S^2\rho_S$$

$$+ 2n_L\omega_L\sigma_Ln_S\omega_S\sigma_S\rho_{LS}$$

When $n_L$ and $n_S$ are both reasonably large, the following approximation can be used:

$$(TE)^2 \cong n_L \omega_L^2 \sigma_L^2 + n_S \omega_S^2 \sigma_S^2 + (n_L \omega_L)^2 \sigma_L^2 \rho_L + (n_S \omega_S)^2 \sigma_S^2 \rho_S$$

$$+ 2 (n_L \omega_L) \sigma_L (n_S \omega_S) \sigma_S \rho_{LS}$$

$$= \frac{A_L^2}{n_L} \sigma_L^2 + \frac{A_S^2}{n_S} \sigma_S^2 + A_L^2 \sigma_L^2 \rho_L + A_S^2 \sigma_S^2 \rho_S + 2 A_L \sigma_L A_S \sigma_S \rho_{LS}$$

However, in this chapter with generic shorting, $n_S = 1$, $\rho_S$ becomes irrelevant and the $\rho_S$ term effectively disappears. The previous TE expression therefore becomes

$$(TE)^2 = n_L \omega_L^2 \sigma_L^2 + \omega_G^2 \sigma_G^2 + n_L (n_L - 1) \omega_L^2 \sigma_L^2 \rho_L + 2 n_L \omega_L \sigma_L \omega_G \sigma_G \rho_{LG}$$

where we have now substituted the subsequent G for S to clarify our reference to the generic shorts.

Because $\omega_G = A_G$, the approximation now takes on the form

$$(TE)^2 \cong \frac{A_L^2}{n_L} \sigma_L^2 + A_G^2 \sigma_G^2 + A_L^2 \sigma_L^2 \rho_L + 2 A_L \sigma_L A_G \sigma_G \rho_{LG}$$

## Tracking Error Model with Generic Completions

The model becomes somewhat more complex when the AE begins with specific short positions and is then completed with generic shorts.

Using the subscript S to refer to the specific shorts, the TE equation takes on the form

$$(TE)^2 = n_L \omega_L^2 \sigma_L^2 + n_S \omega_S^2 \sigma_S^2 + n_G \omega_G^2 \sigma_G^2 + n_L (n_L - 1) \omega_L^2 \sigma_L^2 \rho_L$$

$$+ n_S (n_S - 1) \omega_S^2 \sigma_S^2 \rho_S + n_G (n_G - 1) \omega_G^2 \sigma_G^2 \rho_G$$

$$+ 2 n_L \omega_L \sigma_L n_S \omega_S \sigma_S \rho_{LS} + 2 n_L \omega_L \sigma_L n_G \omega_G \sigma_G \rho_{LG} + 2 n_S \omega_S \sigma_S n_G \omega_G \sigma_G \rho_{SG}$$

As before, we assume that the generic is a single uniform position, so $n_G = 1$. For simplicity, we assume that $\sigma_S = \sigma_L$ and that $\rho_{SG} = 0$ (i.e., that the generic short addresses different factors). The TE approximation then takes on the form

$$\left(\frac{TE}{\sigma_L}\right)^2 = \frac{A_L^2}{n_L} + \frac{A_S^2}{n_S} + A_G^2 \left(\frac{\sigma_G}{\sigma_L}\right)^2 + \left(A_L^2 + A_S^2\right)\rho_L + 2A_L A_S \rho_{LS}$$

$$+ 2A_L A_G \left(\frac{\sigma_G}{\sigma_L}\right)\rho_{LG}$$

Finally, if E is the total percentage extension, the generic short acts as a completion piece:

$$A_G = E - A_S$$

and

$$A_L = A_{LO} + E$$

where $A_{LO}$ is the active percentage of the original long-only portfolio.

### Alpha Functions

The alpha function $\alpha_i$ depicts the ith long position's expected return relative to the specified benchmark. This function is assumed to have an exponential form with an initial alpha $\alpha_o$ and a position-by-position decay rate $\mu$:

$$\alpha_i = \alpha_o e^{-\mu(i-1)} \quad i = 1, n_L$$

In this paper, the long alpha function has the values $\alpha_o = 5\%$, $\mu = .05$, and $N_L = 25$.

In general, for active weights $\omega_i$, the expected alpha return for a long portfolio will be

$$\alpha_L(n_L) = \sum_1^{n_L} \omega_i \alpha_i$$

$$= \alpha_o \sum_1^{n_L} \omega_i e^{-\mu(i-1)}$$

In this chapter, the active weight $\omega_i$, in the long portfolio will be treated as uniform value $\omega_L$ across all 25 positions, so that

$$\alpha_L\left(n_L\right) = \alpha_0 \omega_L \left[ \frac{1 - e^{-\mu n_L}}{1 - e^{-\mu}} \right]$$

for the initial long portfolio with its 25 positions having 2 percent active weights.

In AE, the new shorts create proceeds E that are reinvested proportionally across the 25 long positions, so that the total alpha combination from the longs is

$$\alpha_L\left(n_L\right)\left[1 + E\right]$$

The active shorts are assumed to follow the same alpha pattern as the longs, less a shorting cost $c_S$. Thus, for $n_s$ short active positions:

$$\alpha_S\left(n_S\right) = \left(\alpha_0 - c_S\right) \sum_1^{n_s} \omega_i e^{-\mu(i-1)}$$

$$= \left(\alpha_0 - c_S\right) \omega_S \left[ \frac{1 - e^{-\mu n_S}}{1 - e^{-\mu}} \right]$$

The short generics provide no alpha, but they do incur a cost $c_G$. For an extension E with $n_L$ long positions and $n_S$ short actives, the portfolio alpha becomes

$$\alpha_P\left(E|n_L, n_S\right) = \alpha_L\left(n_L\right)\left[1 + E\right] + \alpha_S\left(n_S\right) - A_G c_G$$

$$= \alpha_L\left(n_L\right)\left[1 + E\right] + \alpha_S\left(n_S\right) - \left(E - n_S \omega_s\right) c_G$$

# CHAPTER 12

# Beta-Based Asset Allocation

**Anthony Bova**
Vice President
Morgan Stanley, Research

**Martin Leibowitz**
Managing Director
Morgan Stanley, Research

The primary risk factor in U.S. institutional portfolios is U.S. equities. The explicit beta exposure is an inadequate risk gauge for highly diversified funds having a low percentage weight directly allocated to equities. An assumed co-movement of an asset class with U.S. equities provides an implicit beta measure that can be used to help determine a fund's total beta.

Most U.S. institutional portfolios have betas and volatilities that fall within a narrow range. In actual practice, the funding source for a portfolio's diversification is some combination of both high-beta equity and low-beta bonds. This exchange of a mid-beta funding package for a new mid-beta asset results in a relatively unchanged portfolio beta. Moreover, the allocations to alternative assets tend to be fragmented, so that the total beta still dominates the fund's volatility.

When a beta value has been found for an asset class, the structural alphas can be determined. These alphas are passive in that there is no presumption of positive outcomes from direct active investment. They will always have a zero correlation with U.S. equity, but may incorporate other risk factors. Because of the fragmented allocation and weak cross correlations, the sum of these alpha volatilities will have a minimal impact at the portfolio level.

This beta-based approach highlights the role of alpha sources in determining expected portfolio returns. A policy portfolio represents the

Originally published as part of the *Morgan Stanley Portfolio Notes*, November 30, 2005.

sponsor's acceptance of a prescribed alpha core as a passive benchmark at a specific point in time. However, positive alphas should lead to significant net inflows, which can lead to erosion in these alpha returns over time. Thus, policy portfolios with broad-based alpha cores should be subject to more frequent review than traditional allocations.

## TOTAL PORTFOLIO BETAS

The motivation for this project began with an invitation to speak in 2003 before a group of large endowment funds. These funds had been at the forefront of the trend toward diversification into a broad range of asset classes. For the most part, this diversification turned out to be quite productive, helping to materially increase the size of their endowments. However, with this proliferation of asset classes, it became more difficult to have a clear insight into the fundamental risk characteristics of the increasingly complex policy portfolios.

In a search for such a risk measure, we examined a number of institutional-style allocations, from the traditional 60/40 equity/bond approach to more modern allocations, some having as many as 12 different asset classes and only a 15 to 20 percent explicit exposure to U.S. equity.

The first step was to identify a primary risk factor. The natural candidate was the exposure to U.S. equities. However, the *explicit* beta exposure was clearly an inadequate risk gauge for highly diversified funds having a low percentage weight directly allocated to equities. Some way was needed to capture the *implicit* beta effects contributed by the increasing allocation to alternative asset classes.

One path to these implied betas led us to the covariance matrix that funds (and/or their consultants) used to develop recommended allocations. In essence, these covariance matrices represented market models for the statistically anticipated co-movements among asset classes. Exhibit 12.1 presents a sample of the components that may comprise such a covariance matrix.

From the assumed co-movement of an asset class with U.S. equities, it was possible to calculate an implicit beta measure (Exhibit 12.2). Then, for a given allocation, all the weighted beta values—both implicit and explicit— would be rolled up to arrive at a *total* beta sensitivity for the fund as a whole.

## BETA AND VOLATILITY CLUSTERING

At this point, a number of surprises emerged.

The first surprise was when this beta-based analysis was applied to representative U.S. institutional portfolios, the total beta values all fell into a common range between 0.55 and 0.65 (Exhibit 12.3).

**EXHIBIT 12.1**  A Sample Return/Covariance Matrix

|  |  |  | Correlations | | | |
|---|---|---|---|---|---|---|
|  | Expected Return | Volatility | REITS | U.S. Equity | U.S. Bonds | Cash |
| REITS | 6.50 | 14.50 | 1.00 | 0.55 | 0.30 | 0.00 |
| U.S. Equity | 7.25 | 16.50 | 0.55 | 1.00 | 0.30 | 0.00 |
| U.S. Bonds | 3.75 | 7.50 | 0.30 | 0.30 | 1.00 | 0.00 |
| Cash | 1.50 | 0.00 | 0.00 | 0.00 | 0.00 | 1.00 |

*Source:* Morgan Stanley Research

The second surprise was that virtually every fund had a total volatility in the 10 to 11.50 percent range. Although most fund managers knew their own volatility level, they were quite surprised to find that other funds, some of which looked very different, also fell into this same narrow volatility band.

The third surprise was that roughly 90 percent or more of this total volatility was explained by portfolio betas. Thus, despite their diversification into multiple asset classes, most funds' volatility characteristics remain fundamentally unchanged.

The explanation for these three effects is quite straightforward. The natural tendency is to equate diversification with risk reduction. However, diversification can take many forms, with some lowering the fund's risk whereas other may actually raise it.

Exhibit 12.4 provides an illustration of three ways that a standard 60/40 portfolio can be diversified into an allocation incorporating 20 percent REITS. With 20 percent equities as the funding source, both the beta and the volatility are obviously reduced. However, funding with 20 percent bonds increases both the beta and the total volatility. The third case is more representative of the actual practice among institutional funds—the funding source is some combination of high-beta equity and low-beta bonds.

**EXHIBIT 12.2**  Beta: REITS

$$\text{Beta} = \text{Correlation with U.S. Equity} \left[ \frac{\text{Volatility of REITS}}{\text{Volatility of U.S. Equity}} \right]$$
$$= .55 \left[ \frac{14.5}{16.5} \right]$$
$$= .48$$

*Source:* Morgan Stanley Research

**EXHIBIT 12.3**  Model Portfolios with Clustered Betas and Volatilities

|  | A | B | S | C |
|---|---|---|---|---|
| Swing Assets |  |  |  |  |
| U.S. Equity | 60% | 60% | 45% | 20% |
| U.S. Bonds |  | 40% | 35% | 20% |
| Cash | 40% |  |  |  |
| Total Swing Assets | 100% | 100% | 80% | 40% |
| Alpha Core |  |  |  |  |
| International Equity |  |  | 20% | 15% |
| Emerging Mkt. Equity |  |  |  | 5% |
| Absolute Return |  |  |  | 10% |
| Venture Capital |  |  |  | 10% |
| Private Equity |  |  |  | 10% |
| Real Estate |  |  |  | 10% |
| Alpha Core % | 0% | 0% | 20% | 60% |
| Total Beta | 0.60 | 0.65 | 0.65 | 0.57 |
| Expected Return | 4.95 | 5.85 | 6.03 | 7.08 |
| Total Volatility | 9.90 | 11.17 | 11.43 | 10.45 |
| Beta % Equity Volatility | 9.90 | 10.80 | 10.75 | 9.45 |
| % Volatility from Beta | 100.0% | 96.7% | 94.1% | 90.4% |

*Source:* Morgan Stanley Research

**EXHIBIT 12.4**  Diversification and Total Volatility

|  | Portfolio Allocation | | | Risk/Return Characteristics | | | |
|---|---|---|---|---|---|---|---|
|  | Equity 60% | Bonds 40% | REITS 0% | Total Beta 0.65 | Total Volatility 11.17 | Total Return 5.85 | % Vol from Beta 96.7% |
| Diversifying Move into 20% REITS Funded with |  |  |  |  |  |  |  |
| 20% Equity | 40% | 40% | 20% | 0.55 | 9.82 | 5.70 | 92.4% |
| 20% Bonds | 60% | 20% | 20% | 0.72 | 12.26 | 6.40 | 97.3% |
| 10% Bonds⎤ 10% Equity⎦ | 50% | 30% | 20% | 0.64 | 10.99 | 6.05 | 95.6% |

*Source:* Morgan Stanley Research

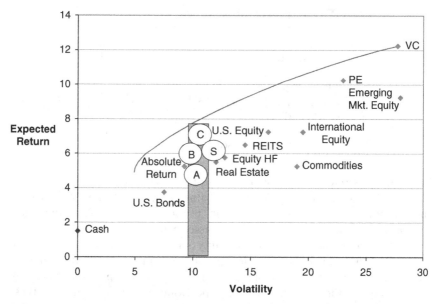

**EXHIBIT 12.5** Unconstrained Efficient Frontier with Model Portfolios
*Source:* Morgan Stanley Research

This exchange of a mid-beta funding package for a new mid-beta asset results in a relatively unchanged portfolio beta. Moreover, the allocations to alternatives tend to be fragmented, so that it is the total beta that dominates the fund's volatility.

This early work on the total beta concept was presented in two articles in the *Journal of Portfolio Management* and the *Financial Analyst Journal.*

Exhibit 12.5 displays a computer-generated efficient frontier based on a return/covariance matrix. This graph visibly confirms the narrow range of volatilities, even though the four model portfolios represent very different levels of diversification. Thus, contrary to conventional wisdom, diversification, as typically pursued, has a relatively minor impact on fund volatility.

## PASSIVE ALPHAS

In mid-2004, we began a research effort to further explore the ramifications of this beta-based approach.

After a beta value has been found for an asset class, some component of its expected return premium can be ascribed to its co-movement with U.S. equities (Exhibit 12.6). These residual returns can be viewed as alpha-like,

**EXHIBIT 12.6**  Passive Alpha: REITS

| | |
|---|---|
| Total Return | 6.50 |
| Less Risk-Tree Rate | (1.50) |
| REIT Risk Premium | 5.00 |
| Less $\left(\begin{array}{c}\text{REIT Beta .48}\\ \text{*Equity RiskPremium 5.75}\end{array}\right)$ | $=\dfrac{(2.78)}{2.22}$ |
| Passive REIT Alpha | |

*Source:* Morgan Stanley Research

and variously referred to as structural alphas, diversification alphas, allocation alphas, or embedded alphas. These alphas are passive in that there is no presumption of positive outcomes from the selection of superior managers or from direct active investment by an asset manager. Passive alphas derive from market inefficiencies, the volatility structure of typical institutional portfolios, and our deliberate selection of U.S. equities as the fundamental risk factor (rather than a global market index or a policy portfolio baseline).

All alphas add directly to the total portfolio return. By definition, these passive alphas will always have a zero correlation with U.S. equity. However, they may incorporate a variety of other risk factors such as currencies, interest rates, liquidity concerns, and so on. These non-equity-related risks may be quite large. However, because of the generally fragmented allocation and weak cross correlations, the sum total of these alpha volatilities will typically have a minimal impact at the portfolio level. Hence, the benefit from multi-asset diversification is to be found not in reduced volatilities, but rather in enhanced fund returns.

## ALPHA CONSTRAINTS AND DRAGON RISKS

This analysis suggests that, at the fund level, positive alpha assets can provide a higher expected return with little impact on total volatility. This raises the question as to why this apparently "free lunch" should not be pursued more vigorously. A related question is why not concentrate the alternative allocation on the single highest-alpha source, rather than having the weight spread over multiple alpha assets.

In practice, the allowable allocation into any alternative asset is always subject to constraints. These position limits may be based on a variety of factors that include:

- Underdeveloped financial markets,
- Liquidity concerns,

- Limited access to acceptable investment vehicles or first-class managers
- Problematic fee structures,
- Regulatory or organizational strictures,
- Peer-based standards,
- Headline risk,
- Insufficient or unreliable historical data.

We have coined the term *dragon risks* to capture the cornucopia of concerns that lead to these constraints. Regardless of any optimization results based on a given return/covariance matrix, it is these beyond-model dragon risks that determine the percentage weight ultimately assigned to the various alpha sources.

## THE ALPHA CORE

The term *alpha core* refers to the subportfolio of alternative assets. As noted earlier, the beta risk in most institutional portfolios tends to overwhelm any volatility impact from an alpha core. This effect is clearly evident in Portfolio C (Exhibit 12.3), in which the incremental return of 1.23 percent relative to Portfolio B is accompanied by a slight decline in portfolio risk. Thus, rather than the often-cited diversification argument, the alpha core's real benefit is return enhancement.

The traditional assets—U.S. equity, U.S. bonds, and cash—are generally less constrained and hence can be viewed as swing assets. The allocation process has historically proceeded from a basic equity/fixed income allocation and then evolved step by step toward some alternative assets.

However, the central role of the alpha core in determining the fund's expected return argues for a three-step process that reverses this conventional approach:

1. Determine maximum acceptable limits for the "non-traditional" asset classes,
2. Combine these alternative assets into an optimal alpha core, and
3. Adjust the composition of the swing assets to achieve the desired risk level for the overall fund.

For most long-term institutional funds, the total beta lies between 0.55 and 0.65, and it is this total beta that basically determines the total fund volatility. For example, with Portfolio C (Exhibit 12.7), the alpha core provides an implied beta of 0.35. To achieve Portfolio C's presumed target beta of 0.57, the swing assets would have to consist of a 20/20 mixture of bonds and U.S. equity.

**EXHIBIT 12.7** Portfolio C Decomposition into Alpha Core and Swing Assets

| | Alpha Core %<br>60% | Swing Assets %<br>40% | Total Portfolio %<br>100% |
|---|---|---|---|
| International Equity | 15.00 | | |
| Emerging Mkt. Equity | 5.00 | | |
| Absolute Return | 10.00 | | |
| Venture Capital | 10.00 | | |
| Private Equity | 10.00 | | |
| Real Estate | 10.00 | | |
| U.S. Equity | | 20.00 | |
| U.S. Bonds | | 20.00 | |
| Cash | | 0.00 | |
| Expected Return Contribution | 3.98 | 1.60 | 5.58 |
| Risk-Free Rate | 0.90 | 0.60 | 1.50 |
| Total Return Contribution | 4.88 | 2.20 | 7.08 |
| Beta Contribution | 0.35 | 0.23 | 0.57 |
| Volatility | 7.10 | 4.01 | 10.45 |

*Source:* Morgan Stanley Research

## LIMITS ON THE ALPHA CORE

One of the key determinants of portfolio return is the maximum percentage that can be allocated to the alpha core (i.e., the aggregate weight limit for all alternative assets). With this core limit, the individual alpha returns and constraints can be used to construct an alternative subportfolio having the best possible alpha return.

Generally speaking, the higher-returning alpha sources will be filled up first, followed by the next highest alpha source, and so on until the core's capacity limit is reached. Thus, the core's marginal alpha returns will decrease as more weight is pushed down into lower-returning alpha sources. Because the alpha volatilities have minimal effect in beta-dominated portfolios, it is the alpha returns (and the respective constraints) that will determine the best composition of the alpha core. It follows that standard return/risk ratios, such as the Sharpe ratio, will tend to be of little relevance in constructing alpha cores for such funds.

In theory, any overall cash limit on the alpha core could be overcome by allowing for leverage. However, if the individual asset constraints remain in force, the benefit generated from any leveraged expansion of the alpha core will still be subject to the decreasing marginal returns.

In cases in which the alpha core can be expanded beyond the usual boundaries, the alpha volatility may begin to challenge the fund's beta dominance. When this point is reached, the core's benefit will be moderated by diminishing alpha returns as well as a more significant volatility impact.

## THE FIXED CORE FRONTIER

The partition into an alpha core and swing assets leads to a simplified three-part version of the efficient frontier:

1. A basic fixed core segment consisting of the core at its maximum weight, with varying mixtures of bonds and equity,
2. A lower-risk cash line segment with varying amounts of cash, and
3. A higher volatility equity extension segment that trades off the alpha core for greater equity exposure.

Exhibit 12.8 displays this three-segment fixed core frontier along with the unconstrained frontier, and shows the placement of the four model portfolios. The three-segment frontier covers a more limited volatility range,

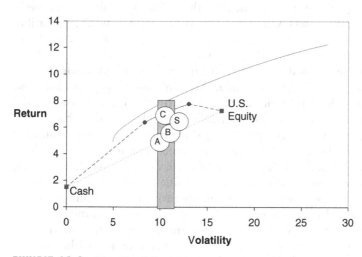

**EXHIBIT 12.8** The Fixed Core Frontier
*Source:* Morgan Stanley Research

and has expected returns that naturally lie below the unconstrained frontier. However, the unconstrained frontier will contain portfolios that fall well outside the viable boundary for most U.S. portfolios (e.g., 30% private equity, 40% emerging markets, 30% real estate).

The four model portfolios fall within the middle segment of the fixed alpha core segment, in which the maximum core is mixed with equal proportions of bonds and equity. There appears to be an incentive for long-term funds to move beyond the cash line, and also a strong basis for not pursuing the equity extension. These boundaries establish the fixed core segment as a sweet spot on the efficient frontier, in which most allocations in fact tend to cluster. This clustering raises some interesting questions as to whether the efficient frontier itself really has meaning as a range of truly viable options, or whether the alpha core and the target beta essentially determine the fund's total volatility and expected return. This observation again argues for reversing the standard procedure and directly addressing the alpha core structure at the outset, rather than developing it incrementally after the fixed income and equity positions have been established.

## THE VOLATILITY BARRIER AND THE POLICY BOX

Given that most allocations are nestled near a common volatility barrier, it is interesting to speculate what return/risk considerations lead funds to this particular position. There appears to be a standard volatility limit that funds are not likely to go beyond, even those that are quite aggressive in terms of alternative assets. One conjecture is that funds limit their volatility to minimize the probability of an adverse event so severe that it would lead to reconsideration of the established policy portfolio. At the same time, funds often have a stated minimum return that is required to satisfy their organizational goals. When combined, this minimum return threshold and the maximum volatility barrier demark a relatively narrow box along the efficient frontier in which a policy portfolio can be located (Exhibit 12.9).

In theory, the policy benchmark may shift from one position to another within this policy box, given changes in the fund's risk tolerance or realignments among the market risk premiums for the various asset classes. Thus, a required return/risk trade-off could determine whether a fund elects for the lower-risk policy portfolio L that simply provides the minimum return or pushes forward to the portfolio H at the maximum volatility barrier. However, the clustering of funds would seem to suggest that most funds press for the higher returns available at the maximum volatility barrier without consideration of more refined return/risk trade-offs.

The main difference among funds is the extent to which they climb up the volatility barrier by expanding their alpha core and incorporating a

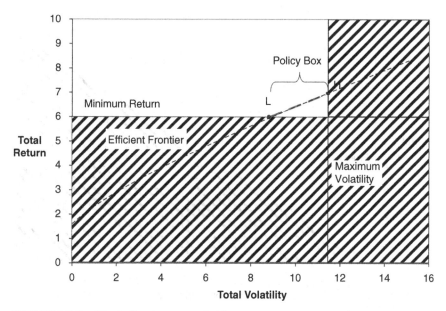

**EXHIBIT 12.9** The Policy Box Bounded by Minimum Return and Maximum Volatility Barriers
*Source:* Morgan Stanley Research

wider range of alpha sources. The larger alpha core would provide higher expected returns with roughly the same volatility, but would require greater acceptance of the associated dragon risks.

## CONVERGENCE OF SHORTFALL RISKS

The concept of shortfall risk—the probability of falling below some specified minimum asset level—may provide a somewhat deeper explanation for the volatility clustering of policy portfolios.

Institutions often have some minimum asset level that they would be loathe to fall below. This critical threshold may be articulated as an annualized return over a specific benchmark such as cash, bonds, inflation, and so on. A shortfall measure bifurcates the risk/return space into one region in which the return/risk combinations satisfy the shortfall constraint, and a second region in which they fall short. Because the expected return grows linearly, whereas the volatility risk grows as the square root of time, the region of acceptability expands as the time horizon lengthens (Exhibit 12.10).

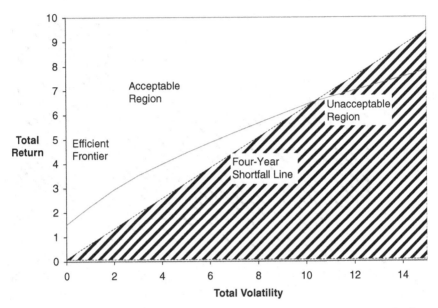

**EXHIBIT 12.10** Frontier Bounded by Minimum Return and Maximum Volatility Barriers
*Source:* Morgan Stanley Research

Given the magic 10 to 11.5 percent volatility band, the typical institutional portfolio has a 25 percent probability of realizing a negative return over a one-year period. However, by the end of a more reasonable four-year investment horizon, this probability of a negative return decreases to about 10 percent.

There are intraperiod measures of risk that may also be relevant to the setting of volatility limits. For example, a −10 percent return *at any point within* a four-year investment horizon could be considered a shortfall event. For the standard fund, this intraperiod shortfall of −10 percent would also have a probability of 10 percent.

Another risk criteria is a certain percentage decline (e.g., −15%) from the highest value achieved. Over a three- to five-year horizon, each of these shortfall criteria—an end-of-period prospect of negative returns, a within-period of a possible −10 percent decline from the starting asset level, and a −15 percent drop from the high water mark—all coincide in having a 10 percent shortfall probability. Such shortfall criteria could play some implicit role in how institutions set targets for their funds' volatility.

The shortfall risk criteria can also be used to develop a dynamic rebalancing strategy in which the portfolio beta, as the primary risk factor, is adjusted annually to obtain a given probability of meeting some prescribed shortfall threshold.


## INTEGRATING ACTIVE AND PASSIVE ALPHAS

Allocation alphas arise from passive investments in generic asset classes that are less than fully correlated with U.S. equity movements. They are available to any given investor without taking away opportunities from other investors. As such, these passive alphas are quite distinct from the more zero-sum alphas associated with active management.

For our purposes, it is useful to classify active alphas as either freely portable or bound to their home-asset class. By their very nature, portable alphas can be layered onto any policy portfolio, and, therefore, need not affect the structuring of the policy benchmark. However, if a fund believes there are positive active alphas that require a literal investment in the relevant asset class, these bound active alphas should be incorporated in evaluating that asset's potential role within the alpha core.

This dual alpha approach would suggest that the basic return/covariance model should be extended to incorporate the potential for active bound alphas. However, the estimation of active alpha entails fundamentally different levels of judgment and confidence than the market models for passive investments in generic asset classes.

Active alpha assumptions are highly fund-specific, reflecting an individual fund's structural advantages and presumed ability to extract positive incremental returns from active management. Consequently, considerable caution should be exercised when combining these very different inputs into a cohesive dual alpha model. (The nature and sustainability of active alphas is discussed in the 2005 *Financial Analysts Journal* article, "Alpha Hunters and Beta Grazers.")


## EQUITY DURATION AND INTEREST RATE EFFECTS

The fixed-income markets impact asset allocation in a number of both direct and indirect ways.

First, given that a policy portfolio should focus on longer-term investment horizons, it can be argued that the risk-free baseline should be some bond yield rather than a money market rate. Indeed, it is not uncommon for equity risk premiums to be defined relative to the 10-year treasury bond or some comparable corporate benchmark. As may be expected, with a positive yield curve, this rebasing can lead to a significantly revised covariance matrix and a flatter efficient frontier.

Next, the movement of interest rates will certainly have an impact on equity prices. Over short-term periods, the correlation between bonds and equities tends to be rather weak as well as unstable, with only a modest percentage of equity volatility being derived from movements in nominal rates. Thus, historical data are not supportive of a reliable equity duration for short-term rate movements.

However, there is a common belief that sustained major upswings in nominal rates can have a profound adverse effect on equity valuations. In exploring these level effects in terms of real rates, we have found some evidence that allows for the rather intriguing conjecture that equity valuations may decline under both significantly lower as well as significantly higher real rates. In essence, this response pattern for price/earnings (P/E) ratios relative to real rates would then resemble a flat-top tent that angles downward at both ends (Exhibit 12.11).

Finally, the co-movement behavior of equities and interest rates has major implications for asset/liability situations, especially where the liability

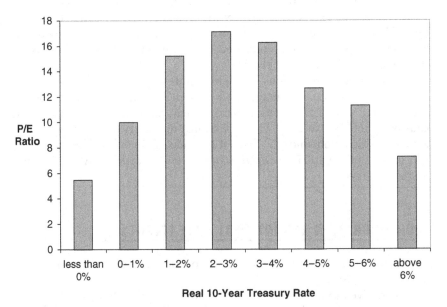

**EXHIBIT 12.11**　Histogram of Price/Earnings Ratios versus Real Interest Rate Levels (1978–2004)
*Source:* Morgan Stanley Research, BARRA, Thomson Financial, Standard & Poor's, Federal Reserve, IBES, First Call

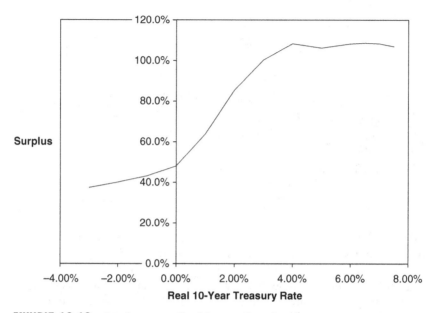

**EXHIBIT 12.12** Surplus versus Real Interest Rate Levels
*Source:* Morgan Stanley Research, BARRA, Thomson Financial, Standard &
Poor's, Federal Reserve, IBES, First Call

value is highly dependent on interest rate levels. In situations with very-
long-duration liabilities, the surplus measure will be directly sensitive to rate
movements, and any asset correlation with interest rates must be incorporated into the allocation. In particular, long-duration liabilities can lever a
modest equity/bond correlation into a significant beta factor. On one hand,
when the liability is nominal in character, these beta effects can be partially
offsetting, resulting in a more stable surplus function. On the other hand,
when the liability is defined in real terms, the lower real rate region of the
tent combines a decline in equity valuation with a surging liability cost. The
net result can be a cliff-like fall-off for the surplus function from the more
stable level achieved at higher real rates (Exhibit 12.12).

## RELATIVE RETURN ANALYSIS

When a policy benchmark has been established, opportunistic departures
may be pursued in the hope of generating incremental returns. These departures may take the form of three distinct types of active management

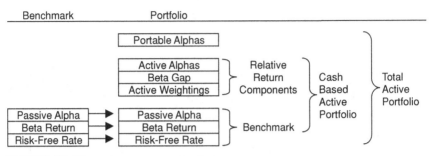

**EXHIBIT 12.13**   Relative Return Analysis
*Source:* Morgan Stanley Research

(Exhibit 12.13). First, a decision may be made to overweight or under-weight each asset class relative to its weight in the fund's benchmark, possibly including the funding of some entirely new asset classes. These active weighting decisions will hopefully provide additional passive alpha return, but they may also create a beta gap relative to the benchmark portfolio. A second initiative could take the form of an explicit beta adjustment either to reverse this reweighting-induced beta gap, or to deliberately achieve a differentiated beta exposure. Finally, active management within asset classes may constitute a third type of departure from a purely passive investment in the policy allocation.

A key measure of performance then becomes the portfolio's return relative to its policy benchmark. Because of the high volatility of U.S. equity, an unintentional beta gap can seriously confound the interpretation of realized returns. Extracting the beta-gap effects allows for a more insightful analysis of the respective contributions from active weighting decisions *across* asset classes versus active management *within* asset classes.

## GREATER FLUIDITY IN POLICY PORTFOLIO

The overall outline of this alpha/beta framework is schematically presented in the flow chart in Exhibit 12.14.

This beta-based approach highlights the role of the alpha sources in determining expected portfolio returns. A given policy portfolio represents the sponsor's acceptance of a prescribed alpha core as a passive benchmark at a specific point in time. If a fund becomes better able to deal with the associated dragon risks, the various alpha sources may become a larger contributor to the benchmark return. A fund's move into an enhanced

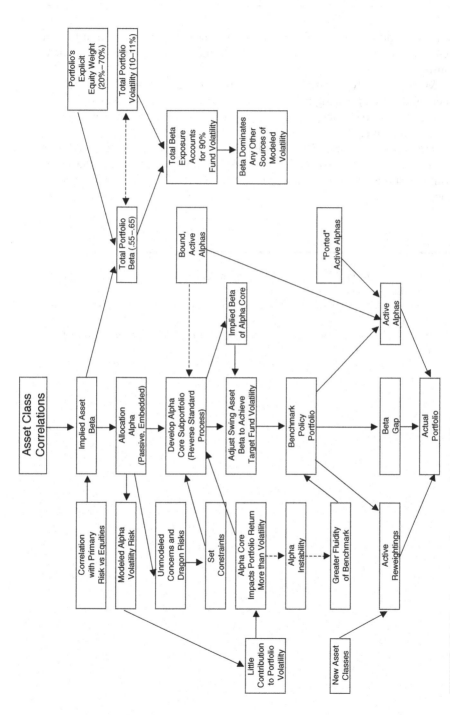

**EXHIBIT 12.14** Overview of Beta-Based Asset Allocation
*Source:* Morgan Stanley Research

alpha core could then be interpreted as tantamount to a progression from a pre-established policy portfolio toward a point on a newly revised efficient frontier.

More generally, positive alphas should act as a powerful magnet for other funds. As a growing number of institutions achieve the flexibility and confidence to pursue these alphas, it would be natural to expect some return erosion over time.

This intrinsic instability in alpha would seem to argue that, relative to traditional allocations, policy portfolios with broad-based alpha cores should be subject to more frequent review and a more fluid decision-making process.

## REFERENCES

Leibowitz, M. L. 2004. "The $\beta$-Plus Measure in Asset Allocation." *Journal of Portfolio Management*. Spring.

Leibowitz, M. L., and A. Bova. 2005. "Allocation Betas." *Financial Analysts Journal*. July/August.

Leibowitz, M. L. 2005. "Alpha Hunters and Beta Grazers." *Financial Analysts Journal*. September/October.

# CHAPTER 13

# Beta Targeting: Tapping into the Appeal of Active 130/30 Extensions

**Anthony Bova**
Vice President
Morgan Stanley, Research

**Martin Leibowitz**
Managing Director
Morgan Stanley, Research

**H**aving a well-defined beta with a sufficiently low beta volatility, even if different from the beta-1 standard, can provide 130/30 extension-like characteristics.

Without a clear beta target, market movements can confound any estimate of a fund's alpha, tracking error (TE), and/or information ratio (IR). By making use of a formula that explicitly incorporates beta volatility, this chapter explores the precision limits needed for a beta target to maintain its functional integrity.

The target beta should conform to the portfolio's management style, rather than being forced to match the beta value ultimately required by the sponsor. With currently available overlay techniques, any target beta can be efficiently stretched (or compressed) to match the sponsor's desired beta value.

The beta factor accounts for over 90 percent of the standard volatility of most U.S. institutional funds, even those that are highly diversified. To control this volatility risk, sponsors must have some coherent beta estimates

Originally published as part of the *Morgan Stanley Portfolio Notes*, April 20, 2007.

for their component portfolios. Beta targeting, especially within the more significant allocations, can greatly facilitate management of this critical risk control factor.

Varying degrees of beta volatility can be acceptable, allowing some (often needed) flexibility in the management process. For tightly controlled enhanced index portfolios, the beta volatility must be close to zero. For more intense forms of active management, the IRs can retain validity even with more sizable beta volatilities. However, beta targeting still remains the key to maintaining risk control even with more aggressive forms of alpha hunting.

## BENEFITS OF BETA TARGETING

In a typical 130/30 active extension (AE), a long-only manager obtains an authorization to take short positions amounting to 30 percent of the original asset base, subject to full reinvestment of the proceeds into an additional 30 percent in long positions. The basic constraints on AE funds are a beta of 1, TEs maintained within reasonable bounds, and full reinvestment of the short proceeds to maintain the net long exposure of 100 percent. This structure inherently allows for more reliably measurable alphas, TEs, and IRs.

Thus far, the majority of AE funds have been launched with a target beta of 1 relative to the Standard and Poor's (S&P) 500 or Russell 1000 and TEs of 2 to 6 percent. With such constraints in place, these strategies can be viewed as a literal extension of the basic equity allocation rather than as excursions into the realm of alternatives.

The target beta of 1 helps ensure that AEs maintain risk characteristics that are similar to the initial long-only portfolios. This risk-similarity and the consequent inclusion within the basic equity allocation have been central to the surge in interest in 130/30-type funds. The question naturally arises as to whether other active equity strategies can be designed to draw upon this powerful extension-like appeal of 130/30 funds.

This chapter makes use of a formula that incorporates a beta volatility concept to explore the multiple benefits of having a well-defined target beta combined with sufficiently low beta volatility.

One immediate benefit that beta targeting shares with 130/30 extensions is the direct evidence of a tight risk-control process. Well-defined beta targets sharpen the measurement of skill-based active alphas as well as the associated TE. As these two metrics become more reliably measurable, their ratio (sometimes referred to as the IR) can help assess the statistical reliability of positive skill in the management process.

A second benefit from beta targeting is that it loosens the beta-1 constraint and allows a much broader range of active equity strategies to be brought under the extension umbrella. Many long/short managers as well as long-only managers are more comfortable having portfolios with average betas other than 1. By embracing a beta-targeting approach, they can retain their basic management process while attaining a sharper focus to their alpha generation and underlying TE. A beta-targeting approach would be particularly beneficial for currently long-only funds considering migration to a long/short format.

Another benefit from beta targeting relates to the risk structure of sponsor funds. A series of studies on asset allocation have shown that the total beta (in terms of U.S. equity exposure) accounts for over 90 percent of the overall volatility of most U.S. institutional portfolios. This high level of beta domination is common not only for the traditional 60 percent equity/40 percent bond portfolio, but also for highly diversified endowment-like funds with as little as 15 to 20 percent in U.S. equity. This surprising result is due to the buildup of the implicit betas from the nonequity asset classes that have some level of statistical correlation with equity movements.

A well-defined beta target can play a key role in enabling sponsors to control this total beta risk. With a prescribed beta for a given fund component, the desired total fund volatility can be achieved by either adjusting the mixture of other fund assets, or by applying a beta overlay at the fund level. (However, there may be cases in which a sponsor prefers that the equity manager provide the overlay function needed to achieve the desired beta.)

With the total beta forming the dominant source of total fund volatility, other sources of volatility tend to be diversified away so that they have a relatively minor impact on total risk. Beta-targeted strategies help to more clearly identify the TEs that are reliably uncorrelated with the beta risk. By helping to minimize sponsor-level impact of such TEs, beta targeting can more readily accommodate aggressive alpha seeking that tends to incur high TEs.

Thus, in addition to enlarging the boundaries for extension-like status, beta targeting can provide a number of valuable benefits for both managers and sponsors.

## RELATIVE VOLATILITY AND INTRINSIC TRACKING ERROR

A fund's relative return is the difference between its total return and that of a prescribed benchmark. We will use the term *relative volatility* to refer to the standard deviation of these relative returns.

Consider a portfolio process with returns that are assumed to vary around some average beta that may or may not coincide with the benchmark. Then, apart from any alpha-based excess return, there are three sources of relative volatility that can be identified:

1. The beta gap between the fund's average beta value and the benchmark,
2. The beta volatility of the fund's actual beta at different points in time, and
3. An intrinsic TE that characterizes the fund's deviation from its beta-based returns.

The intrinsic TE can be viewed as the fund's active risk in the absence of any beta gap or beta volatility. However, any active strategy will have some discrepancy between the realized beta at a given point in time and the benchmark beta. Consequently, it will be the relative volatility that is perceived as the deviation from the benchmark, rather than the underlying intrinsic TE.

An explicit formula for the relative volatility can be derived for this three-component model (see Appendix). The beta gap and the intrinsic TE components are quite straightforward. However, the beta volatility term depends on both the volatility and the average return of the reference market. The explicit formula can help when exploring the interaction of these multiple sources of relative volatility. The ultimate objective is to identify the beta-targeting conditions that can enable the relative volatility to act as a reasonable representation for the fund's intrinsic TE.

## AN EMPIRICAL EXAMPLE

The three-component analysis of fund volatility can be illustrated by using a sample of 50 long/short (L/S) funds from the Morgan Stanley Capital International (MSCI) database. Many L/S hedge fund managers do not structure themselves around a set beta target. Given their ability to change their gross and net exposures, the range of beta volatilities can be quite high. This can be seen in Exhibit 13.1, which shows a scatter plot of the average beta and beta volatility for this sample from 1999 to 2006.

Exhibit 13.2 plots the total volatility versus the beta volatility for the sample funds. There is a clear upward trend between the beta volatility and the absolute level of volatility. The higher average beta is associated with the larger beta volatilities, and this combination naturally results in higher total volatilities.

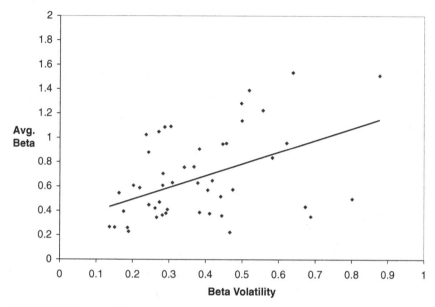

**EXHIBIT 13.1**  Average Beta versus Beta Volatility for Sample L/S Funds
*Source:* Morgan Stanley Research. MSCI

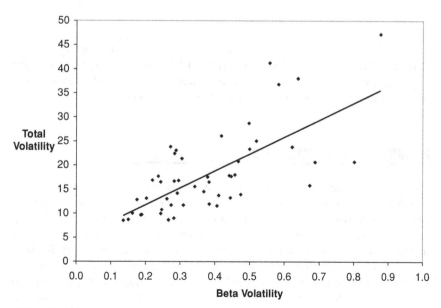

**EXHIBIT 13.2**  Total Volatility versus Beta Volatility for Sample L/S Funds
*Source:* Morgan Stanley Research. MSCI

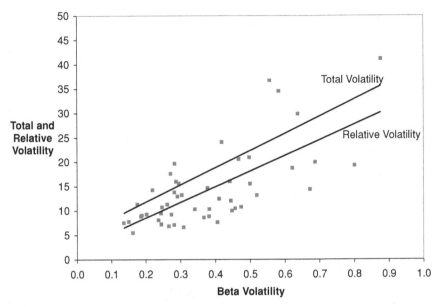

**EXHIBIT 13.3** Relative Volatility for L/S Funds
*Source:* Morgan Stanley Research, MSCI

Exhibit 13.3 now removes the average beta effect to uncover the relative volatility. The total volatility from Exhibit 13.2 is also displayed here as the higher regression line. The difference between the total volatility and the relative volatility is evident in the two regression lines.

## A MONTE CARLO SIMULATION

The previous empirical results point in the right direction, but they are clouded by autocorrelations and various problems inherent in estimating contemporaneous beta values. A Monte Carlo simulation that more directly reflects the dynamics of the three-component volatility model is depicted in the flow chart in Exhibit 13.4. For each run, a realized portfolio beta is first drawn from a beta distribution with a fixed mean value and a beta volatility. This realized beta is combined with a random market return to form the portfolio's beta-based return. A tracking deviation is then drawn from a distribution with a mean of zero and volatility equal to the intrinsic TE. (For simplicity, the alpha term is neglected because it does not play a

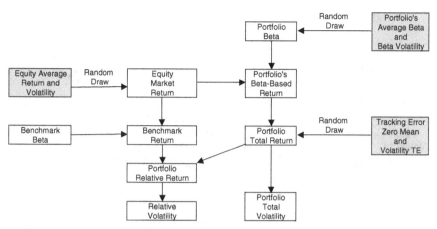

**EXHIBIT 13.4** Monte Carlo Simulation
*Source:* Morgan Stanley Research

role in the volatility calculation.) The realized portfolio return is then found by adding the realized deviation to this beta-based return.

This process is repeated with fresh random draws, and the total portfolio volatility is defined to be the annualized standard deviation of the return series. The relative return is just the portfolio return less the product of the benchmark beta and the market return. The standard deviation of these returns is then referred to as the relative volatility.

Exhibit 13.5 presents the simulation results for total portfolio volatility based on 1,000 random draws from the following three distributions:

1. A portfolio beta with an average value of 0.6 and with beta volatilities ranging from 0 to 1,
2. An equity market return with an annual average value of 7 and a 15 percent volatility,
3. An intrinsic TE with a mean of zero and 4 percent volatility.

The solid line in Exhibit 13.5 is the expected result based on the three-component formula developed in the Appendix. It is interesting to see how the Monte Carlo results are tightly clustered around the formula line when the beta volatility is low. At higher beta volatilities, the scatter widens considerably.

The relative volatility of a fund depends on the benchmark. The top curve in Exhibit 13.6 represents the absolute level of volatility. The middle scatter is the relative volatility for a target beta that coincides with the

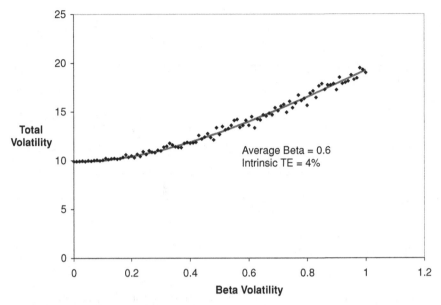

**EXHIBIT 13.5** Total Volatility Simulations
*Source:* Morgan Stanley Research

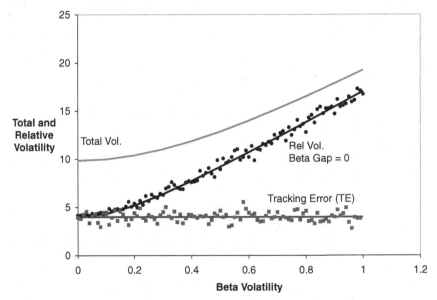

**EXHIBIT 13.6** Three Volatility Components
*Source:* Morgan Stanley Research

portfolio's average 0.6 beta (i.e., a beta gap of 0). The lowest scatter line reflects the 4 percent intrinsic TE. The distance between these two lower lines gives a sense of how the beta volatility contributes to the relative volatility.

Exhibit 13.6 illustrates the benefit of having reasonable bounds on the beta volatility. With modest beta volatility, the relative volatility is close to the 4 percent TE. As the beta volatility moves toward higher levels, the relative volatility rises well above the 4 percent TE.

## THE BETA VOLATILITY FORMULA

The Monte Carlo results in Exhibits 13.5 and 13.6 demonstrate that the three-component formula in the Appendix can serve as a satisfactory tool for exploring the interactions of the three volatility components.

In virtually any active strategy, there is almost sure to be some slippage between the intended beta target and the benchmark beta. Over any specific investment horizon, this slippage will result from the combination of the basic beta volatility and some (possibly unintentional) gap between the average beta and the benchmark beta. This slippage will lead to a relative volatility that exceeds the portfolio's intrinsic TE. This relative volatility then appears as the measure of the fund's active risk. Therefore, a key question is to what extent this relative volatility is a reasonably close proxy for the underlying TE. In other words, what are the allowable combinations of beta gap, beta volatility, and TE that keep the relative volatility sufficiently close to the TE? In the following section, we make use of the beta volatility formula to investigate a wide range of such combinations.

In the following series of exhibits, the formula values for the relative volatility are plotted against a range of benchmark betas. In all cases, the portfolio is assumed to have an average beta value of 0.6, so that the difference between the benchmark beta and 0.6 represents the beta gap. The three curves correspond to beta volatilities of 0, 0.1, and 0.2, and each exhibit is based on different TE levels. The purpose of these graphs is to visualize how the different combinations of beta gap and beta volatility affect the proximity of the relative volatility to the underlying intrinsic TE.

In Exhibit 13.7, the intrinsic TE is set at 0 percent, essentially reflecting a fund composed of a 60 percent pure index fund and the remaining 40 percent in cash. As may be expected, virtually any level of beta gap or beta volatility would lead to unacceptable deviations from the index fund's objective.

Exhibits 13.8, 13.9, and 13.10 show the comparable relative volatility curves for TEs of 2, 4, and 8 percent, respectively. For the 2 and 4 percent TE, a proxy function could tolerate beta gaps of ± 0.1 or beta volatilities

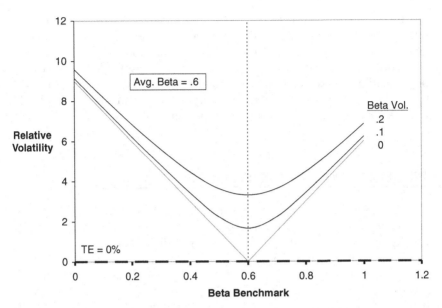

**EXHIBIT 13.7** Relative Volatility versus Benchmark Betas with TE = 0 percent
*Source:* Morgan Stanley Research

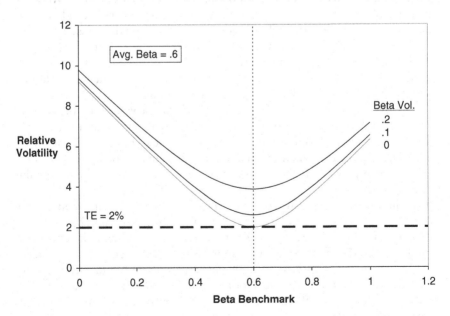

**EXHIBIT 13.8** Relative Volatility versus Benchmark Betas with TE = 2 percent
*Source:* Morgan Stanley Research

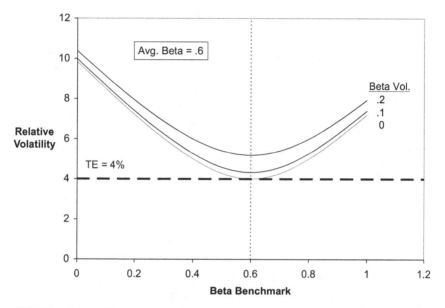

**EXHIBIT 13.9** Relative Volatility versus Benchmark Betas with TE = 4 percent
*Source:* Morgan Stanley Research

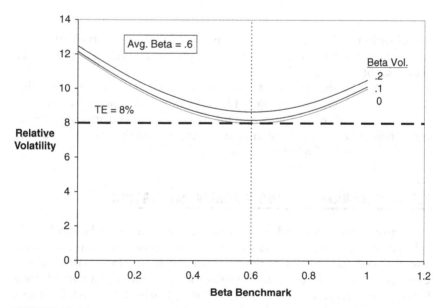

**EXHIBIT 13.10** Relative Volatility versus Benchmark Betas with TE = 8 percent
*Source:* Morgan Stanley Research

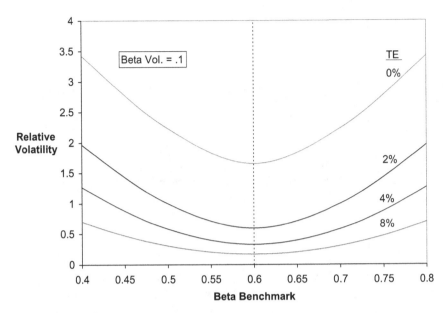

**EXHIBIT 13.11**   Relative Volatility versus Benchmark Betas
*Source:* Morgan Stanley Research

of 0.1 or lower. However, with an 8 percent TE, the TE curve flattens out considerably so that a beta gap of ± 0.2 may be acceptable, as long as the beta volatility remains below 0.2.

By enlarging the scale and focusing specifically on the 0.1 beta volatility curves from Exhibits 13.7 through 13.10, Exhibit 13.11 shows the deviation between the relative volatilities and the intrinsic TE. The flattening of these curves reflects the increasing dominance of the TE and the consequent ability to accept somewhat higher beta gaps.

## ALPHA MEASUREMENT AND INFORMATION RATIOS

The active alpha is usually defined as an average return over the benchmark. When there is a significant beta gap, this average relative return will include a term that is the product of the beta gap and the average market return. Consequently, the clearest possible basis for measuring alpha will call for a beta gap of 0 (zero). In turn, this will call for a reasonably well-defined beta target that is centered on the benchmark.

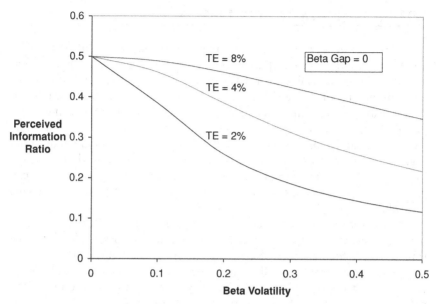

**EXHIBIT 13.12** Beta Volatility Impact on IR
*Source:* Morgan Stanley Research

Even with a zero beta gap, beta volatilities will enlarge the perceived TE, resulting in distortion of the IR. Exhibit 13.12 provides a graphic illustration. In this exhibit, the true IR—the ratio of the expected active alpha to the intrinsic TE—is fixed at 0.5. For each TE curve, the alpha is presumed to be at a level that would yield this 0.5 IR (e.g., for the 4% TE curve, the assumed alpha value is 2%). With a beta gap taken to be 0 (zero), the perceived IR is based on using the relative volatility in the denominator. As the beta volatility increases, it becomes evident how quickly the perceived IR falls below the true value of 0.5, especially for the lower TEs.

The IR serves as an important gauge of the statistical reliability of the fund's ability to generate positive alphas over time. With rising beta volatilities, Exhibit 13.12 shows how quickly any evidence of positive skill is severely eroded. By establishing beta targets centered on a benchmark beta, and by endowing that target with integrity through a beta volatility that is appropriately constrained, the portfolio manager (and the sponsor) will have more assurance that the true alpha-hunting skills are being revealed.

## SETTING COMFORTABLE BETA TARGETS

It is worth noting that for the 2 to 4 percent TE range, a minimal level of beta volatility is still tolerable as long as the beta gap is kept small. This suggests that there is some flexibility in the beta targeting, even at these modest TE levels. In other words, the risk control procedures need not be so limiting as to seriously hamper a manager's basic approach to active management.

This flexibility also extends to the manager's choice of the beta target itself. Many active managers have a style that centers on beta values other than 1. This natural beta can be set as the target beta. With sufficiently low beta volatility to maintain this target's integrity, the resulting IR calculation would be a reasonable yardstick for the fund's alpha-producing reliability.

Moreover, a target beta set at some comfortable but nonstandard level need not restrict the fund's or the sponsor's ability to stretch to a more standard beta for purposes of asset allocation or peer comparability. With overlays and/or portfolio reallocations, a given target beta can be efficiently transformed to virtually any value. The key to this transformation is having a beta target that has sufficiently low beta volatility.

There are certainly many established portfolios without explicitly named beta targets. On one hand, some of these untargeted portfolios have beta values that are consistently centered on some average value. For such portfolios, it may be a small step to explicitly target an average beta value. The necessary risk control discipline for beta targeting can often be put in place without overly cramping the existing management style.

On the other hand, there are also situations in which the beta targeting may prove quite counterproductive. One obvious example is managers that utilize broad-based tactical beta shifts as their basic return-seeking process. Another broad class consists of those managers, both long-only and long/short, that require as part of their competitive advantage the unconstrained pursuit of returns wherever they can be found.

The generation of positive excess returns, whether absolute or relative, is the paramount goal of all active management. Any new risk control discipline, including beta targeting, makes sense only to the extent that it fundamentally furthers this basic objective.

## BETA TARGETING AND TOTAL FUND RISK

The preceding section was concerned with how beta targeting can improve the portfolio's IR. However, the concept of a beta target can be beneficial in a number of other ways.

A well-defined target beta allows sponsors to better integrate specific portfolios within their risk budgets. In virtually all U.S. institutional portfolios, the expected total volatility is overwhelmingly dependent on the fund's co-movement with the equity market. This equity co-movement will typically account for 90 percent or more of the fund's volatility. This surprisingly high level of correlation is derived from the explicit equity percentage together with the accumulated implicit correlation from nonequity allocations. Thus, even highly diversified funds—those with as little as 15 to 20 percent allocated to domestic equity—will have expected levels of equity co-movement that are comparable to traditional 60/40 portfolios.

This equity dominance can be quantified through the concept of an implicit beta based on the asset's expected correlation with equity movements. These implicit betas add to the explicit betas to form a fund's total beta, as shown in Exhibit 13.13. For most institutional funds, the total beta values are quite similar, falling between 0.55 and 0.65. Indeed, this similarity in the total beta values explains why most funds also have total volatilities in the 10 to 11 percent range.

For funds with multiple allocations to active equity and equity-related strategies, the diversification effects will be different for the three volatility components. To the extent that active alpha seeking is independently pursued, the TEs will have minimal impact on the total fund volatility.

**EXHIBIT 13.13** Typical Diversification Does Not Materially Change Fund Volatility: 90 Percent-plus Comes from Equity

| | Correlation-Based Implicit Beta | B | C |
|---|---|---|---|
| Cash U.S. Equity | 1.00 | 60% | 20% |
| Cash U.S. Bonds | 0.14 | 40% | 20% |
| International Equity | 0.77 | | 15% |
| Emerging Mkt. Equity | 0.76 | | 5% |
| Absolute Return | 0.28 | | 10% |
| Venture Capital | 0.59 | | 10% |
| Private Equity | 0.98 | | 10% |
| Real Estate | 0.07 | | 10% |
| Total | | 100% | 100% |
| Total Volatility | | 11.17 | 10.45 |
| Total Beta | | 0.65 | 0.57 |
| % Volatility from Beta | | 96.7% | 90.4% |

*Source:* Morgan Stanley Research

Similarly, if the beta volatilities of the various portfolios are uncorrelated, these volatility effects will also be diversified and, hence, have only a modest effect at the total fund level. However, the individual portfolio betas will add to the fund's total beta, so their effect cannot be diversified away. Because this total beta is the dominant source of fund volatility, each incremental beta contributes to a corresponding increase in total fund volatility.

Without beta targets, the sponsor will have little guidance on how to incorporate equity-related portfolios into a beta-based risk control format. Thus, having beta targets with some integrity serves a very concrete purpose.

Beta targeting can also be viewed as a way of translating an implicit beta based on a correlation model into a more explicit beta value. One may be tempted to argue that the standard covariance models are all that are needed. However, to the extent that the betas are uncertain, the covariance estimates themselves will also be ambiguous. Moreover, the key risk scenarios for beta-dominated funds tend to be associated with significant adverse movements in equities. The standard covariance analysis reflects asset behavior across a full range of scenarios, with a greater emphasis on the more frequent movements of modest magnitude. Consequently, standard covariance analysis cannot address the special contingencies that create stress situations in practice. The total beta approach provides a much more direct (if still imperfect) gauge of a fund's vulnerability under such adverse conditions.

With the total beta playing such a dominant role in determining the fund's risk profile, a sponsor will want to have the best possible estimate of the beta contribution from each component portfolio. This would be especially true for funds with sizable allocations to equity-related portfolio strategies. The key to having these well-defined betas is, first, to have prescribed targets, and then to maintain a reasonable beta volatility around them.

## THE ALPHA/BETA MATRIX

The term *alpha/beta barbell* generally refers to the spectrum of equity-related strategies that range from passive indexing on the far left to portable alpha formats on the far right. The alpha/beta matrix (Exhibit 13.14) is an attempt to place beta-targeted equity funds in a somewhat broader context that also incorporates non-equity asset classes.

*Beta grazers* are passive index funds that are content to access the risk premium in the most cost-efficient possible way.

*Alpha hunters* refer to those benchmark-centric strategies that seek active alpha returns, but do so in a risk-controlled fashion. Beta-targeted equity

**EXHIBIT 13.14** The Alpha/Beta Matrix

| Metaphor | Betas | Management Styles | Nature of Alphas | Fund Level Effects | | |
|---|---|---|---|---|---|---|
| | | | | Volatility | Model Risk | TE vs. Policy |
| Beta Grazing | Stapled | Passive Investing in Broad Equity/Fixed Income Markets | Risk Premium | Fundamental Source | Very Low | Zero |
| Alpha Hunting | Beta-Targeted | Risk-Controlled Active Equity Market Neutral Active Extension Some Hedge Funds | Active Management | Low | Low | Low |
| Alpha Gathering | Correlation-Based | Diversification into New Asset Classes | Implicit Correlation-Based Passive Alphas | Low | High | Low |
| Alpha/Beta Foraging | "Free Range" | Beta-Agnostic Opportunistic Investment Some Hedge Funds Macro Funds Some Concentrated Long-Only | Intense to Hyper Active | High | High | High |

*Source:* Morgan Stanley Research

strategies would fall into this category. With beta targeting, the TE should be definitively uncorrelated with the beta factor, and consequently have little impact on the fund volatility. Thus, a beta-targeted equity strategy should incur relatively little model risk; that is, in which the return behavior deviates significantly from the modeled assumptions.

The next category is the *alpha gatherers*, which includes new asset classes with return/covariance models that are typically derived from some modification of historical statistics. The correlations with equity that are embedded in these models can be used to derive implicit beta values. In turn, these implicit betas suggest implicit alphas that represent the asset's expected return beyond that associated with its correlation-based beta. These implicit alphas represent incremental expected returns for a beta-dominated fund making a new investment in the asset class.

However, there is always a question of past performance being a predictor of future returns, and the same question exists with respect to past correlations. These ambiguities become even more serious when the asset class is undergoing structural change and/or becoming more or less fashionable. The net result is that these implicit betas and alphas can be more vulnerable to model risk than beta-targeted equity strategies.

Finally, there are alpha/beta *foragers* who venture forth and opportunistically seek returns wherever they can be found. Even where return/covariance models do exist for this behavior, they will inspire little confidence. Consequently, it will always be difficult to estimate their effect on total fund risk, unless the allocations are kept small and very highly diversified.

All these return-seeking pursuits are often present in any given fund, and each can prove valuable if successfully pursued. However, they do differ materially in the character of the risks entailed—and nature of their fund-level effects.

Beta-targeted alpha hunting appears to occupy a special and perhaps uniquely valuable niche. It provides identifiable beta values that can be incorporated into the sponsor's risk budget. The residual TE risk should be inherently uncorrelated with the beta factor and hence mostly diversifiable at the fund level. Finally, there is relatively little model risk clouding the projected behavior of such strategies. The key assumption, as always, is that the strategies can generate positive alpha returns, at least over sufficiently long horizons.

## CONCLUSION

Beta targeting allows for clearer separation of the excess alpha return from the beta-based return. The manager's performance, whether on a pure alpha or IR basis, surely becomes easier to measure when a beta target has been established.

For the sponsor, beta targeting also enables better control of the overall volatility risk. A desired level of portfolio volatility can be achieved by combining the individual portfolio betas with appropriate reallocations and/or beta overlays.

Many long-only as well as L/S funds intensively pursue alphas with a process that revolves around some average beta value but without specifying a formal beta target. The question naturally arises as to whether such funds, especially those with good records of alpha generation, can develop a closely related process that can tap into the evident interest in 130/30 AE strategies.

In particular, can such funds maintain their comfortable and presumably successful style while migrating from a somewhat ill-defined average beta to a more clearly specified beta target? Does such a beta target in itself capture the most desirable features of AE? Finally, even with beta targets that fall below the AE's standard beta of 1, can institutional sponsors bring themselves to include such funds within their active equity allocation?

Subject to certain conditions, we believe that all the preceding questions can be answered affirmatively. The key conditions are:

1. That a beta target be specified,
2. That the drift around this beta target be contained within some reasonably modest level,
3. That the TE be reliably uncorrelated with the fund's total risk, and
4. Most importantly, that the alpha generating capability be sufficiently robust and positive so as to attest to the presence of positive management skill.

## APPENDIX

One standard formulation for an equity portfolio's return $\tilde{r}_P$ is

$$\tilde{r}_P = \alpha + \tilde{\beta}_P \tilde{r}_e + \tilde{\varepsilon}$$

where $\tilde{\beta}_P$ is the portfolio's beta, $\tilde{r}_e$ is the return of the relevant equity market, $\tilde{\varepsilon}$ is the TE variable, and $\alpha$ is the excess return. The standard random variables on the righthand side of this expression are $\tilde{r}_e$ and $\tilde{\varepsilon}$, with the latter usually assumed to have zero mean. For the analysis in this paper, this standard formulation must be slightly extended to allow the portfolio's beta $\tilde{\beta}_P$

to also become a random variable with mean $\bar{\beta}_P$ and standard deviation $\sigma_\beta$. (A 2003 Lehmann and Modest NBER paper provides a highly generalized treatment of the much broader question of factor errors.)

In the following analysis, the random variables $\tilde{r}_e$, $\tilde{\varepsilon}$, and now $\tilde{\beta}_P$, are treated in a nonparametric fashion (i.e., without any requirements on their distribution functions other than the existence of means and variances). All three are also assumed to be independent of one another. (However, although this independence assumption is certainly quite common, it should be pointed out that, in practice, extreme market movements are likely to create higher stress betas.)

Under these conditions, the expected portfolio return $\bar{r}_P$ remains the same as under the standard model

$$\bar{r}_P = \alpha + E\{\tilde{\beta}_P\tilde{r}_e\} + E\{\tilde{\varepsilon}\}$$
$$= \alpha + E\{\tilde{\beta}_P\}E\{\tilde{r}_e\} + 0$$
$$= \alpha + \bar{\beta}_P\bar{r}_e$$

However, the variance $\sigma_{r_p}^2$ does become somewhat more complex. As a first step, we derive

$$E\{\tilde{r}_p^2\} = E\{[\alpha + \tilde{\beta}_P\tilde{r}_e + \tilde{\varepsilon}]^2\}$$
$$= \alpha E\{\alpha + \tilde{\beta}_P\tilde{r}_e + \tilde{\varepsilon}\} + E\{\tilde{\beta}_P\tilde{r}_e[\alpha + \tilde{\beta}_P\tilde{r}_e + \tilde{\varepsilon}]\} + E\{\tilde{\varepsilon}[\alpha + \tilde{\beta}_P\tilde{r}_e + \tilde{\varepsilon}]\}$$
$$= \alpha\bar{r}_p + [\alpha\bar{\beta}_p\bar{r}_e + E\{(\tilde{\beta}_P\tilde{r}_e)^2\} + \bar{\beta}_P\bar{r}_e E\{\tilde{\varepsilon}\} + [0 + E\{\tilde{\varepsilon}\tilde{\beta}_P\tilde{r}_e\} + E\{\tilde{\varepsilon}^2\}]$$
$$= \alpha\bar{r}_p + [\alpha\bar{\beta}_p\bar{r}_e + E\{\tilde{\beta}_P^2\}E\{\tilde{r}_e^2\} + 0] + [0 + 0 + E\{\tilde{\varepsilon}^2\}]$$
$$= \alpha\bar{r}_p + \alpha\bar{\beta}_p\bar{r}_e + E\{\tilde{\beta}_P^2\}E\{\tilde{r}_e^2\} + E\{\tilde{\varepsilon}^2\}$$

The variance $\sigma_{r_p}^2$ can then be written as

$$\sigma_{r_p}^2 = E\{\tilde{r}_p^2\} - \bar{r}_p^2$$
$$= E\{\tilde{r}_p^2\} - [\alpha + \bar{\beta}_p\bar{r}_e]^2$$
$$= \alpha[\alpha + \bar{\beta}_p\bar{r}_e] + \alpha\bar{\beta}_p\bar{r}_e + E\{\tilde{\beta}_P^2\}E\{\tilde{r}_e^2\} + E\{\tilde{\varepsilon}^2\} - [\alpha^2 + 2\alpha\bar{\beta}_p\bar{r}_e + (\bar{\beta}_p\bar{r}_e)^2]$$
$$= E\{\tilde{\beta}_P^2\}E\{\tilde{r}_e^2\} + E\{\tilde{\varepsilon}^2\} - (\bar{\beta}_p\bar{r}_e)^2$$
$$= [\sigma_\beta^2 + \bar{\beta}_p^2][\sigma_e^2 + \bar{r}_e^2] + [\sigma_\varepsilon^2 + 0] - (\bar{\beta}_p\bar{r}_e)^2$$

Thus, the formula for the total portfolio variance given random betas becomes

$$\sigma_{r_p}^2 = \sigma_\beta^2 [\sigma_e^2 + \bar{r}_e^2] + \bar{\beta}_p^2 \sigma_e^2 + TE^2$$

where $\sigma_\beta^2$, $\sigma_e^2$, and $TE^2$ are the variances of $\tilde{\beta}_P$, $\tilde{r}_e$, and $\tilde{\varepsilon}$, respectively.

This expression differs from the variance for the standard formulation

$$\beta_p^2 \sigma_e^2 + TE^2$$

in the first term that depends on $\sigma_\beta^2$,

$$\sigma_\beta^2 [\sigma_e^2 + \bar{r}_e^2]$$

With $\sigma_\beta = 0$, the two results coincide.

A second result needed in this development is the concept of the portfolio's return R relative to some benchmark target. The simplest characterization of this benchmark is through a fixed beta $\beta_B$ that applies to the same reference market $\tilde{r}_e$. The relative return R then becomes

$$\tilde{R} = \tilde{r}_p - \tilde{\beta}_B \tilde{r}_e$$
$$= \alpha + (\tilde{\beta}_P - \beta_B)\tilde{r}_e + \tilde{\varepsilon}$$

The expected relative return is just

$$\bar{R} = \alpha + (\bar{\beta}_P - \beta_B)\bar{r}_e$$
$$= \alpha + (\Delta\beta)\bar{r}_e$$

where the expected difference between the two betas can be referred to as the beta gap, $\Delta\beta$.

The expression for the relative return has the same form as the portfolio return when the beta difference is substituted for the portfolio beta. Thus, because $\sigma_{\Delta\beta}^2 = \sigma_\beta^2$, the variance of relative returns can be immediately expressed as

$$\sigma_R^2 = \sigma_\beta^2 [\sigma_e^2 + \bar{r}_e^2] + (\Delta\beta)^2 \sigma_e^2 + TE^2$$

The relative volatility $\sigma_R$ is a measure of the deviation of the portfolio returns from the benchmark target. As such, it may be taken as a perceived TE, especially when there is a lack of visibility regarding the beta gap $\Delta\beta$

and/or the beta volatility $\sigma_\beta$. The perceived TE should be distinguished from the intrinsic TE that would remain even if the $\Delta\beta$ and $\sigma_\beta$ effects could be removed either through more visible decomposition or by risk control revisions.

By incorporating a market effect, a beta gap will also affect the *ex post* estimation of the portfolio's excess return. Thus, with these distortions in both the numerator and the denominator, the ratio

$$\left(\frac{R}{\sigma_R}\right)$$

can become a seriously degraded form of the intrinsic IR:

$$\left(\frac{\alpha}{TE}\right)$$

## REFERENCES

Lehmann, B. N., and D. M. Modest. 2003. "Diversification and the Optimal Construction of Basis Portfolios." *National Bureau of Economic Research.* January.

# CHAPTER 14

# Activity Ratios: Alpha Drivers in Long/Short Funds

**Anthony Bova**
Vice President
Morgan Stanley, Research

**Martin Leibowitz**
Managing Director
Morgan Stanley, Research

Long/short (L/S) funds are typically described in terms of their long, short, and net exposures expressed as a percent of invested assets. The net beta value is also sometimes provided as an indication of the fund's probable response to broad market movements. However, the long and short side can include both generic (non-alpha) investments as well as truly active positions. Therefore, the standard exposure and beta measures may shed little light on the fund's alpha potential, tracking error (TE), or information ratio (IR).

One key to alpha potential will be found in the fund's activity level (AL)—the aggregate weight of all meaningfully sized active long and short positions. For a given fund structure, the activity level determines the fund's basic alpha characteristics.

It turns out that the IR depends largely on the activity ratio (AR)—the short activity divided by the long activity. With a given AR, the expected alpha and TE both increase (or contract) proportionally with the long activity level acting as a scaling factor. Thus, funds with the same AR can be viewed as simply rescaled versions of one another with respect to their intrinsic alpha-producing potential.

---

Originally published as part of the *Morgan Stanley Portfolio Notes*, October 12, 2007.

Many L/S funds—even those that consider themselves beta-agnostic—have investment styles that circle around some average beta value. A modest degree of beta variability does not preclude such funds from being beta-stretched to fit specified target levels.

By moving from active to generic positions or vice versa, a fund can adjust its activity levels to achieve a given AR and activity scale. With beta and AR flexibility, some L/S funds can be reshaped to serve as more generalized versions of a 130/30 or 150/50 active extension (AE).

## STRUCTURE OF LONG/SHORT FUNDS

The majority of long/short portfolio analysis studies focus on the gross weights of the portfolio. The exposures are usually quoted in gross terms, whether they are a L/S hedge fund (e.g., 130% long/70% short), a market-neutral (MN) fund (e.g., 100% long/100% short), or an AE fund (e.g., 130% long/30% short). However, these gross exposures can be composed of varying proportions of truly active positions and generic (non-alpha) investments.

The sensitivity to broad market movements is always a paramount consideration, and in this regard, the beta value is a critical parameter. However, for those funds in which some average beta can be identified, the analysis naturally next turns to the issues of alpha generation, TE, and the associated IR. Here, the most important variable becomes the activity level; that is, the aggregate weights of significant active positions on the long and the short sides. In fact, for a given fund, it can be shown that the IR is determined in large part by the AR—the short activity divided by the long activity level.

The key to bringing different long/short combinations within a given set of beta constraints is the ability to specify some average beta target and a reasonable degree of beta volatility. Many L/S managers have beta-agnostic investment styles, but their betas tend to circle around some average value. An L/S fund with an average beta of 0.6 may have a beta volatility of ±0.1 or ±0.2. It turns out that such levels of beta volatility will not have an overriding impact on either the fund's benchmark TE or its total volatility. Thus, a modest change in activity structure, accompanied by a shift from the average beta value, can be used to transform an L/S fund so it falls within a specified set of constraints.

## GROSS, MARKET, AND ACTIVE EXPOSURES

Exhibit 14.1 shows how a typical L/S fund—Fund A—could be described in terms of three different types of yardsticks. The first set of columns is

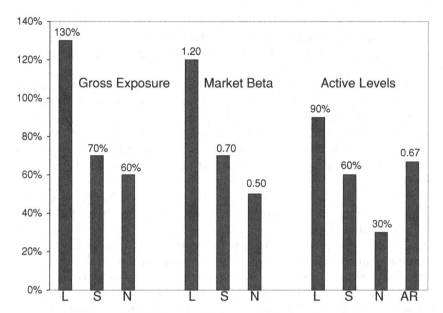

**EXHIBIT 14.1** Gross, Market, and Active Exposures for L/S Fund A
*Source:* Morgan Stanley Research

the gross weights of the portfolio 130 percent long, 70 percent short, and 60 percent net. The second set represents the beta exposures of the fund, which may not always correspond with the gross exposures. In this example, the long portfolio has a beta of 1.20 (i.e., somewhat lower than the 130% gross long exposure). In contrast, the short portfolio beta of 0.70 is a direct outcome of the 70 percent gross exposure. The net beta is thus 0.5, somewhat lower than the net portfolio exposure of 60 percent.

## ACTIVITY LEVELS AND ACTIVITY RATIOS

The third set of columns represents the activity levels. To appreciate the significance of the activity level concept, first consider a long-only equity portfolio. The gross (and net) exposure of 100 percent may translate into an effective active weight of 60 percent (or less). Typically, these effective active weights are concentrated on the overweight side, with the funding underweights being so widely fragmented and dispersed as to contribute negligibly to portfolio alpha and TE. However, because the beta effects are additive, these underweights will accumulate in beta terms and affect the portfolio's market risk.

For L/S funds, the long activity level may also fall well below the gross long exposure. For Fund A depicted in Exhibit 14.1, this situation is evident in having a long activity level of 90 percent compared with a gross level of 130 percent.

Turning to the 70 percent shorts in Exhibit 14.1, these investments can also be separated into the active and non-active categories. However, in practice, the non-active component is more likely to consist of generic investments (or derivatives) that help control the beta and factor risks, but are not primarily intended to be alpha-seeking. In Exhibit 14.1, of the fund's 70 percent shorts, 60 percent are allocated to active positions, and 10 percent to generics.

Thus, the fund's activity level consists of 90 percent longs and 60 percent shorts, which is quite distinct from its respective gross exposures of 130 percent and 70 percent. It should be emphasized that the activity levels are also quite different from the beta values that affect the fund's response to broad market movements. In contrast, these activity levels are strictly related to the fund's active alpha expectations and the associated TE.

These long and short activity levels can be usefully compressed into a single value, such as the net activity level of 30 percent shown in Exhibit 14.1. However, for reasons that will be clear later in the discussion, it turns out that a more useful measure is the AR composed of the short activity level divided by the long activity level.

## EVOLUTION OF THE IR

Exhibit 14.2 is a schematic of the IR improvement in an active 130/30 extension as the gross exposure expands due to an increasing level of shorting together with the reinvestment of the short proceeds back into the long portfolio. To achieve significant IR improvement when moving from a long-only portfolio, shorts must be found that can serve both as positive alpha sources and as offsets to any unproductive correlations within the long portfolio. This combination of new alpha-generating positions and offsets accounts for the rise in the IR from the initial phase of shorting.

In the next phase, the opportunity for new active positions has been exhausted, and any incremental funds are simply deployed in the existing long and short active positions. This proportional amplification of the pre-existing actives leads to a flat IR because it is tantamount to simple alpha leverage. In the last phase, the expansion encounters constraints such as size limits on the active positions. In this phase, the portfolio alpha may continue to grow whereas the IR departs from its flat path. In general, the constraints will force the IR to turn down, but there are circumstances in which the offset effect becomes more powerful and the IR actually rises.

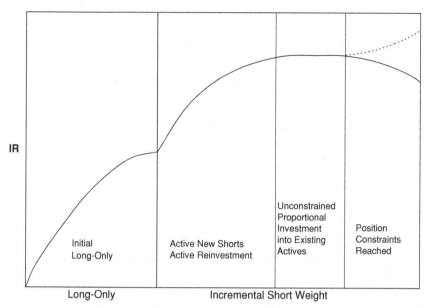

**EXHIBIT 14.2** IR Evolution as the Activity Level Expands
*Source:* Morgan Stanley Research

Exhibit 14.3 now focuses specifically on Fund A, shown in Exhibit 14.1, with its fixed 90 percent long activity level. Using the basic model described in the Appendix, Exhibit 14.3 depicts the alpha, TE, and IR as the activity level of the short side is varied from 0 percent to 100 percent. With increasing alpha-generating shorts, the portfolio alpha rises linearly from its long-only value. In contrast, the TE at first begins to decrease from the offset effect, but then rises as the growing short weight becomes overriding. The IR curve displays roughly the same ascending and saturation shape as depicted in Exhibit 14.2.

In general, there will be some point at which a maximum IR is reached and sustained. As noted earlier in this chapter, a flat IR does not necessarily reflect the optimal design point. Even when the IR is constant, the portfolio continues to gain alpha with proportional increases in TE. If the fund has unused capacity for higher TEs, there may be good reason for pressing for the higher alphas even in the face of a flat IR.

Exhibit 14.4 introduces Fund B, a second L/S fund that has the same active position structure as Fund A, but differs along several dimensions. In particular, Fund B has active longs of 120 percent versus Fund A's 90 percent. Consequently, Fund B has a higher alpha and higher TE than Fund A.

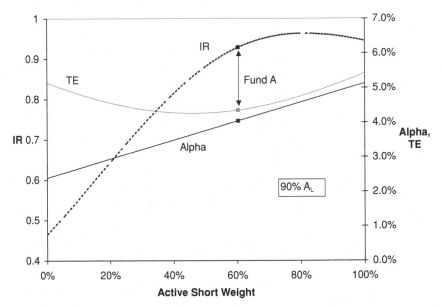

**EXHIBIT 14.3** Alpha, TE, and IR at Varying Short Active Weights
*Source:* Morgan Stanley Research

**EXHIBIT 14.4** IR Determined by Activity Ratio

|  | L/S A | L/S B |
| --- | --- | --- |
| Gross Exposure |  |  |
| Long | 130% | 160% |
| Short | 70% | 110% |
| Net | 60% | 50% |
| Long | 1.2 | 1.3 |
| Short | 0.7 | 0.7 |
| Net Beta | 0.5 | 0.6 |
| Activity Levels |  |  |
| Long ($A_L$) | 90% | 120% |
| Short | 60% | 80% |
| Net | 30% | 40% |
| AR | 0.67 | 0.67 |
| Alpha | 4.04 | 5.39 |
| TE | 4.35 | 5.80 |
| IR | 0.93 | 0.93 |

*Source:* Morgan Stanley Research

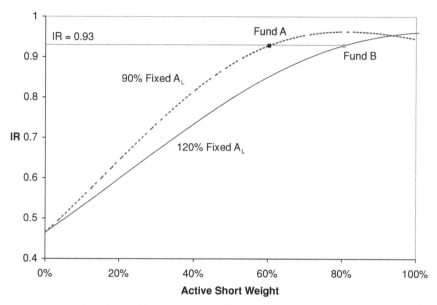

**EXHIBIT 14.5** Fund A and Fund B: IR versus Active Short Weights
*Source:* Morgan Stanley Research

Exhibit 14.5 plots the IR curves for various active short weights for funds with fixed long activity weights of 90 percent and 120 percent. We can see that Fund A and Fund B both generate the same 0.93 IR.

## MOVING TO THE ACTIVITY RATIO

The preceding graphs followed the more standard procedure of using the active short weights as the horizontal axis. An alternative approach is to make use of the AR to reflect the shorts as a percentage of the total longs. Exhibit 14.6 shows how the varying active short weights translate into ARs. It can be seen that Funds A and B share the same AR value of 0.67.

The benefit of using the AR becomes evident in Exhibit 14.7. Similar to Exhibit 14.3, the AR plots alpha, TE, and IR for a fixed 90 percent long weight, under varying short weights, but now with the AR as the horizontal axis. Fund A with its 60/90 ratio and Fund B with its 80/120 ratio both have the same AR ratio. The specified values for Fund A fall on the designated points on their respective curves. The corresponding values for Fund B are also plotted and can be seen to all lie on the same vertical line, although

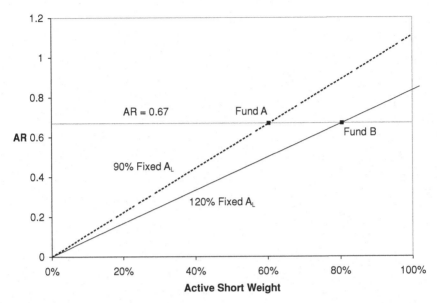

**EXHIBIT 14.6**   AR as Function of Active Short Weight
*Source:* Morgan Stanley Research

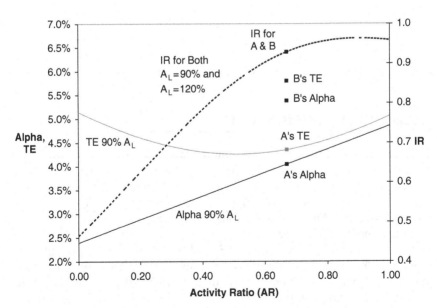

**EXHIBIT 14.7**   Coincidence of IR Curves
*Source:* Morgan Stanley Research

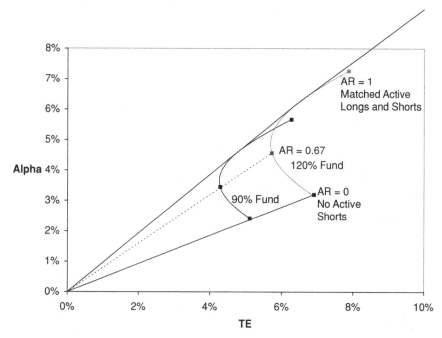

**EXHIBIT 14.8**   Alpha versus TE for 90 Percent and 120 Percent Active Long Funds
*Source:* Morgan Stanley Research

Fund B's alpha and TE are positioned above Fund A's values. However, the IR point for Fund B coincides exactly with Fund B's IR. If we were to trace the corresponding curves for Fund B, we would find that, although the alpha and TE curves were quite distinct, the two IR curves would be identical.

Any combination of long and short activity levels that results in the same AR value will lead to the same IR. More generally, any funds that have the same structure, regardless of their long activity level, will have the same IR curve.

## AR-BASED EFFICIENT FRONTIERS

Exhibit 14.8 places the curves for the two funds in alpha versus TE space. For each fund, the curve here represents the alpha and TE values as the AR moves from 0 to 1.0. All points falling on a straight line from the origin will have the same IR and the same AR. Thus, even though these funds have very different alphas and TEs, they have the same IR. As a result, the increase in

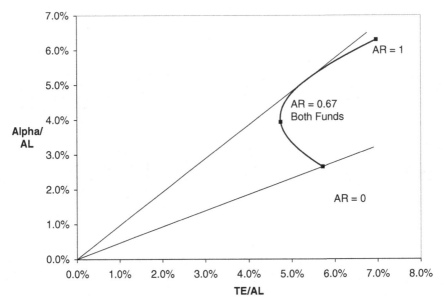

**EXHIBIT 14.9**   Normalized Alpha versus TE Curves
*Source:* Morgan Stanley Research

the active long weight from 90 to 120 percent can be seen as a scaling effect as higher alphas are accompanied by higher TEs.

The results from Exhibit 14.8 can be normalized by dividing both the alpha and TE by their active long weights. This leads to a single curve for both the 90 and 120 percent cases as shown in Exhibit 14.9. Basically, all L/S funds having the same structure are described by this single curve in normalized alpha versus normalized TE space.

## CORRELATION, POSITION COUNT, AND ALPHA RANKING EFFECTS

To this point, the funds have been assumed to have a common structure in terms of the number of active long and short positions, the correlations within and between the long and short portfolios, as well as the alpha ranking functions. Basically, the different activity levels have served to determine the magnitude of the average weight for the long and the short active positions. In this section, we begin to explore how changes in the fund structure affect the IR curves.

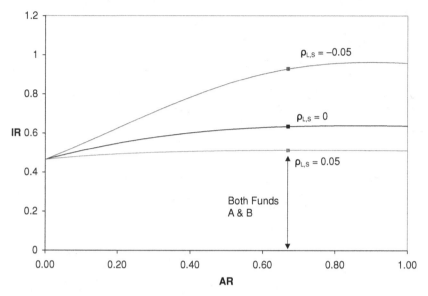

**EXHIBIT 14.10** IR with Different Correlations
*Source:* Morgan Stanley Research

Exhibit 14.10 shows the effect of different correlation assumptions between the long and short positions. The base case used in the preceding discussion assumed a −0.05 correlation between the longs and shorts. This offset correlation played an important role in raising the IR to 0.93. With zero correlation, the IR at the 0.67 AR declines to 0.63, whereas with a positive correlation (reinforcing common factor risks), the IR drops to 0.51.

The previous examples assumed active structures composed of 30 long positions and 20 short positions. Exhibit 14.11 displays the IRs for three different position structures, each with equal position counts on both the long and short side. Because the same declining alpha function is applied, greater diversification lowers the portfolio alpha to a greater extent than it reduces the TE. This effect is evident in the IR for the 100L/100S portfolio falling significantly below the IR for the more concentrated 25L/25S portfolios.

The results from Exhibit 14.11 should not be too surprising, given the nature of the declining alpha ranking curve used. In these examples, the highest expected alpha is 5 percent, which then declines to 0.4 percent by the 50th position. With a flat alpha ranking curve (here assumed to be at a constant 1.5%), the results are quite different, as shown in Exhibit 14.12. The more diversified portfolio of 100L/100S provides a higher IR than in the 25L/25S case.

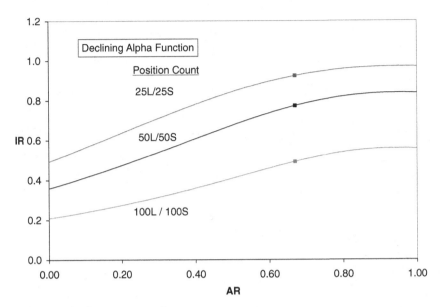

**EXHIBIT 14.11** IR with Different Position Counts
*Source:* Morgan Stanley Research

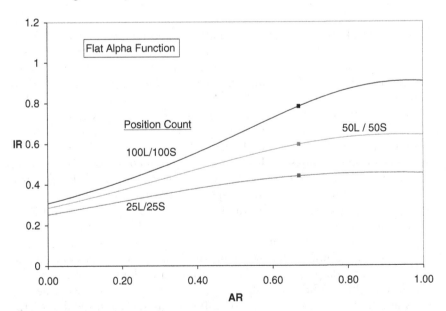

**EXHIBIT 14.12** IR with Flat Alpha Rankings
*Source:* Morgan Stanley Research

## IR CURVES FOR DIFFERENT FUND TYPES

We can also compare fund strategies that have different combinations of position structures and assumed alpha functions. Exhibit 14.13 displays the IR curves for long/short strategies having the same structure as Funds A and B, as well as for representative examples of AE and MN strategies. The AE strategy tends to be more diversified than an L/S fund, so the structure assumed here consists of 40 long positions and 30 short positions. With its quantitative investment approach, the market-neutral portfolio becomes even more diversified with 90 longs and 70 shorts. Both the L/S and AE portfolios use the declining alpha ranking function, whereas the MN assumes flat alpha ranking.

The AE portfolio depicted represents gross levels of 150/50, but 110/50 in activity terms.

Exhibit 14.14 displays the three portfolio strategies in alpha/TE space. Notice that points from Exhibit 14.13 all lay close to the dotted line representing an IR near 0.80. Given this opportunity for moving to different beta values, an L/S fund may also be able to adjust its long and short exposures to fit within more constrained frameworks. In this sense, an L/S fund could be transformed into a generalized version of an AE fund.

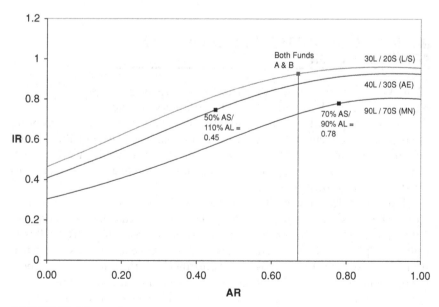

**EXHIBIT 14.13** IR for L/S, AE, and MN
*Source:* Morgan Stanley Research

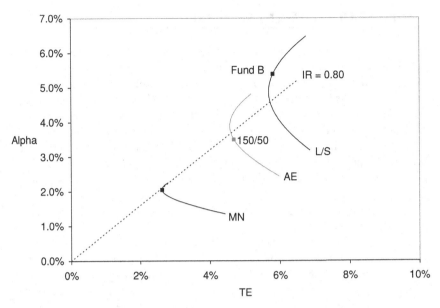

**EXHIBIT 14.14**   Alpha versus TE for L/S, AE, and MN
*Source:* Morgan Stanley Research

## MOVING A LONG/SHORT INTO A GENERALIZED ACTIVE EXTENSION

Many L/S funds—even those that view themselves as beta agnostic—tend to have some average beta value. The beta variability around this average value can often be kept within some reasonable bounds without overly disrupting the basic management style. Moderate beta variability may contribute a surprisingly small incremental TE around a specified average beta value. Such funds could then have their effective beta values stretched (or contracted) to satisfy a specified beta constraint.

Exhibit 14.15 explores how Fund A could be moved into an AE framework. The gross exposures on the long side are increased from 130 percent to 150 percent, whereas the gross short exposures are contracted from 70 percent to 50 percent. The revised fund would now have a 150/50 structure in terms of gross long/short exposures. Adjustments to the long and short beta (or to the net beta) could bring the fund to the required beta-1 status.

In an effort to maintain as much as possible of the basic management style, it may be desirable to minimize the adjustment of the activity level. For example, the long activity levels could be kept at 90 percent, whereas the

**EXHIBIT 14.15**  L/S Contraction into an AE Framework

|  | Fund A | Contracted A | Standard AE |
|---|---|---|---|
| Gross Exposure |  |  |  |
| Long | 130% | 150% | 150% |
| Short | 70% | 50% | 50% |
| Net | 60% | 100% | 100% |
| Long | 1.2 | 1.5 | 1.5 |
| Short | 0.7 | 0.5 | 0.5 |
| Net Beta | 0.5 | 1.0 | 1.0 |
| Activity Levels |  |  |  |
| Long ($A_L$) | 90% | 90% | 110% |
| Short | 60% | 40% | 50% |
| Net | 30% | 50% | 60% |
| AR | 0.67 | 0.45 | 0.45 |
| Alpha | 4.04 | 3.50 | 3.50 |
| TE | 4.35 | 4.28 | 4.68 |
| IR | 0.93 | 0.82 | 0.75 |

*Source:* Morgan Stanley Research

shorts could be reduced from 60 percent to 40 percent. The resulting ARs would then be 0.45 (i.e., the same AR as for the illustrative 150/50 AE fund).

In Exhibit 14.16, the arrow shows the movement along the IR curve from the L/S fund into an AE format. The contraction process lowers Fund A's IR from 0.93 to 0.82, but it still remains higher than the standard AE's 0.75 IR.

The same results are displayed in alpha versus TE space in Exhibit 14.17. The original L/S Fund A had an alpha of 4.0 percent with a 4.4 percent TE, whereas the contracted L/S A had an alpha of 3.5 percent and TE of 4.3 percent. By comparison, the standard AE has an alpha of 3.5 percent and TE of 4.7 percent.

# CONCLUSION

The key point is that a fund's long and short weight may cover many different combinations of investments that can be either generic (nonalpha) or actively alpha-generating. Consequently, the standard exposure yardsticks may provide little insight about a fund's alpha potential. The ultimate source

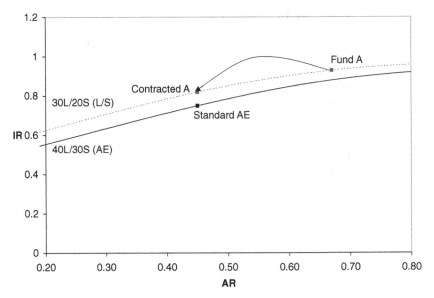

**EXHIBIT 14.16**   L/S Contraction along the IR Curve
*Source:* Morgan Stanley Research

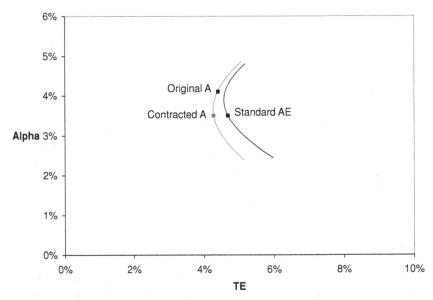

**EXHIBIT 14.17**   Alpha versus TE–L/S Contraction into AE
*Source:* Morgan Stanley Research

of alphas resides in the meaningfully sized active positions (on both the long and the short side). The cumulative effective weight of these active positions constitutes what we have termed the fund's activity level. Together with the position structure, the activity levels determine a fund's alpha potential, the associated TE, and hence the prospective IR.

Moreover, within the context of the basic model described in the chapter, the most compact characterization of the fund's alpha potential is given by its AR (i.e., the ratio of the short to the long activity levels). For funds with similar position structures, it is this AR that determines the IR. All such funds with the same AR will have the same IR.

## APPENDIX

In our basic model, the number of long positions $n_L$ and short positions $n_S$ are both fixed. The uniform weight $\omega$ assigned to each position is then determined by the total active weights $A_L$ and $A_S$ assigned for the longs and the shorts:

$$\omega_L = \frac{A_L}{n_L}$$

$$\omega_S = \frac{A_S}{n_S}$$

In the basic model, a fixed residual volatility $\sigma$ is assigned for all positions, with pairwise correlations $\rho_L$ and $\rho_S$ within the longs and shorts, respectively, and $\rho_{LS}$ between the long and short positions.

The portfolio TE is then approximated by

$$
\begin{aligned}
\left(\frac{TE}{\sigma}\right)^2 &= n_L\omega_L^2 + n_S\omega_S^2 + n_L\,(n_L - 1)\,\omega_L^2\rho_L + n_S\,(n_S - 1)\,\omega_S^2\rho_S \\
&\quad + 2n_L\omega_L n_S\omega_S\rho_{LS} \\
&\cong n_L\omega_L^2 + n_S\omega_S^2 + (n_L\omega_L)^2\,\rho_L + (n_S\omega_S)^2\,\rho_S + 2\,(n_L\omega_L)\,(n_S\omega_S)\,\rho_{LS} \\
&= \frac{A_L^2}{n_L} + \frac{A_S^2}{n_S} + A_L^2\rho_L + A_S^2\rho_S + 2A_LA_S\rho_{LS} \\
&= A_L^2\left\{\frac{1}{n_L} + \frac{AR^2}{n_S} + \rho_L + AR^2\rho_S + 2AR\rho_{LS}\right\}
\end{aligned}
$$

where AR measures the short activity as a fraction of the long activity,

$$AR = \frac{A_S}{A_L}$$

This expression simplifies if $\rho_L = \rho_S = \rho$,

$$\left(\frac{TE}{\sigma}\right)^2 = A_L^2 \left\{ \frac{1}{n_L} + \frac{AR^2}{n_S} + \left(1 + AR^2\right)\rho + 2AR\rho_{LS} \right\}$$

For the two extreme cases of $AR = 0$ (the long-only portfolio) and $AR = 1$ (matched levels of short and long activity), one obtains

$$\left(\frac{TE}{A_L\sigma}\right)^2 = \begin{cases} \dfrac{1}{n_L} + \rho & AR = 0 \\[2ex] \dfrac{1}{n_L} + \dfrac{1}{n_S} + 2\left(\rho + \rho_{LS}\right) & AR = 1 \end{cases}$$

and for the pure offset case where $\rho_{LS} = -\rho$,

$$\left(\frac{TE}{A_L\sigma}\right)^2 = \begin{cases} \dfrac{1}{n_L} + \rho & AR = 0 \\[2ex] \dfrac{1}{n_L} + \dfrac{1}{n_S} & AR = 1 \end{cases}$$

It is interesting to note that the TE may actually be lower for the matched case ($AR = 1$) when $\rho > 1/n_S$.

For the portfolio alpha, with average alphas $\bar{\alpha}_L$ and $\bar{\alpha}_S$ for the long and short positions, respectively,

$$\alpha_P = \omega_L n_L \bar{\alpha}_L + \omega_S n_S \bar{\alpha}_S$$

And, where the alpha $\bar{\alpha}_S$ simply is a constant c lower than $\bar{\alpha}_L$ (usually based on shorting costs):

$$\bar{\alpha}_S = \bar{\alpha}_L - c$$

then,

$$\begin{aligned} \alpha_P &= \omega_L n_L \bar{\alpha}_L + \omega_S n_S \left(\bar{\alpha}_L - c\right) \\ &= \left(A_L + A_S\right)\bar{\alpha}_L - A_S c \\ &= A_L \left\{ [1 + (AR)]\,\bar{\alpha}_L - (AR)\,c \right\} \end{aligned}$$

This expression underscores the general form of the alpha-generating structure.

Note that both $\alpha_p$ and TE have $A_L$ as a common factor so that the IR does not depend on $A_L$. Thus, $A_L$ can be viewed as scaling the level of long activity relative to the original invested amount.

If the TE is then expressed as

$$TE = A_L \sigma \, (te)$$

where

$$(te)^2 = \frac{1}{n_L} + \frac{AR}{n_S} + \rho_L + AR^2 \rho_S + 2AR\rho_{LS},$$

the portfolio IR then becomes

$$
\begin{aligned}
IR &= \frac{\alpha_p}{TE} \\
&= \frac{\{[1 + (AR)]\bar{\alpha}_L - (AR)c\}}{\sigma(te)} \\
&= \left[\frac{1 + (AR)}{(te)}\right] IR_L - \frac{(AR)c}{\sigma(te)}
\end{aligned}
$$

where

$$IR_L = \left(\frac{\bar{\alpha}_L}{\sigma}\right)$$

When $\frac{c}{\sigma(te)}$ is small, the long/short structure can be viewed as an amplification of IR:

$$IR \cong \left[\frac{1 + AR}{(te)}\right] IR_L$$

In Funds A and B used in this chapter, the portfolio alphas are based on an exponential alpha function. Both the longs and the shorts begin with initial $\alpha_o$ for the first-ranked position, followed by a decay at a rate $\mu$, with a cost c deducted for each short position:

$$
\begin{aligned}
\alpha_p &= \omega_L \sum_{j=1}^{n_L} \alpha_o e^{-\mu(j-1)} + \omega_S \sum_{j=1}^{n_S} \left[\alpha_o e^{-\mu(j-1)} - c\right] \\
&= \omega_L \alpha_o \left[\frac{1 - e^{-\mu n_L}}{1 - e^{-\mu}}\right] + \omega_S \alpha_o \left[\frac{1 - e^{-\mu n_S}}{1 - e^{-\mu}}\right] - \omega_S n_S c
\end{aligned}
$$

$$= \left(\frac{A_L}{n_L}\right)\alpha_o\left[\frac{1-e^{-\mu n_L}}{1-e^{-\mu}}\right] + \left(\frac{A_S}{n_S}\right)\alpha_o\left[\frac{1-e^{-\mu n_S}}{1-e^{-\mu}}\right] - A_S c$$

$$= A_L\left\{\frac{\alpha_o}{n_L}\left[\frac{1-e^{-\mu n_L}}{1-e^{-\mu}}\right] + \left(\frac{AR}{n_S}\right)\alpha_o\left[\frac{1-e^{-\mu n_S}}{1-e^{-\mu}}\right] - cAR\right\}$$

and for the extreme points

$$\frac{\alpha_p}{A_L} = \begin{cases} \dfrac{\alpha_o}{n_L}\left[\dfrac{1-e^{-\mu n_L}}{1-e^{-\mu}}\right] & AR = 0 \\[3ex] \dfrac{\alpha_o}{n_L}\left[\dfrac{1-e^{-\mu n_L}}{1-e^{-\mu}}\right] + \dfrac{\alpha_o}{n_S}\left[\dfrac{1-e^{-\mu n_S}}{1-e^{-\mu}}\right] - c & AR = 1 \end{cases}$$

For these two extreme points, when $\rho_{LS} = -\rho$

$$IR = \begin{cases} \dfrac{\left(\frac{\alpha_o}{n_L}\right)\left[\frac{1-e^{-\mu n_L}}{1-e^{-\mu}}\right]}{\sigma\sqrt{\frac{1}{n_L}+\rho}} & AR = 0 \\[4ex] \dfrac{\frac{\alpha_o}{n_L}\left[\frac{1-e^{-\mu n_L}}{1-e^{-\mu}}\right] + \frac{\alpha_o}{n_S}\left[\frac{1-e^{-\mu n_S}}{1-e^{-\mu}}\right] - c}{\sigma\sqrt{\frac{1}{n_L}+\frac{1}{n_S}}} & AR = 1 \end{cases}$$

In our examples, where $n_L = n_S = n$

$$IR = \begin{cases} \dfrac{\frac{\alpha_o}{n\sigma}\left[\frac{1-e^{-\mu n}}{1-e^{-\mu}}\right]}{\sqrt{\frac{1}{n}+\rho}} & AR = 0 \\[4ex] \dfrac{\frac{\alpha_o}{\sigma}\left(\frac{2}{n}\right)\left[\frac{1-e^{-\mu n}}{1-e^{-\mu}}\right] - \left(\frac{c}{\sigma}\right)}{\sqrt{\frac{2}{n}}} & AR = 1 \end{cases}$$

$$= \begin{cases} IR_o\dfrac{\frac{1}{\sqrt{n}}\left[\frac{1-e^{-\mu n}}{1-e^{-\mu}}\right]}{\sqrt{1+(n\rho)}} & AR = 0 \\[4ex] IR_o\sqrt{\frac{2}{n}}\left[\frac{1-e^{-\mu n}}{1-e^{-\mu}}\right] - \sqrt{\frac{n}{2}}\left(\frac{c}{\sigma}\right) & AR = 1 \end{cases}$$

where

$$IR_o = \frac{\alpha_o}{\sigma}$$

# CHAPTER 15

# Generalizations of the Active 130/30 Extension Concept

**Anthony Bova**
Vice President
Morgan Stanley, Research

**Martin Leibowitz**
Managing Director
Morgan Stanley, Research

The motivation behind moving into 130/30 active extensions (AEs) is to extract higher alpha returns from the basic equity allocation. This same alpha-seeking motivation applies to taking one step further toward generalized AEs that offer more intensively active, risk-controlled equity management. These generalized AE-Plus strategies may not necessarily have a 100 percent net exposure or beta target of 1. The key to this broader extension umbrella is to establish a well-defined beta target, which may be smaller than beta-1, and a stable net investment basis (although that need not be 100%). It is the clear-cut distinction between beta and alpha risk that represents the hallmark of such generalized AE-Plus funds.

Beta-targeted generalizations of the AE concept can encompass a far wider range of long/short strategies with more intensively active management styles. The main objective is to generate positive alphas with a beta value that can be properly accommodated in a fund's overall risk framework. With the generalized AE-Plus fund's stable beta target, the actual level of the target should play a relatively minor role. In the two examples in this report, the portfolio beta is 0.7 with different levels of active and net exposures. Investors who choose AE-Plus funds with such low betas will do

---

Originally published as part of the *Morgan Stanley Portfolio Notes*, April 29, 2008.

so either because the lower beta is desirable or because the total beta can be remediated to the desired level within the overall fund.

As long as the mandates are reasonably diversified across management styles, an institutional fund's total volatility generally has capacity for accommodating greater active risks. The suppressive effect of a fund's dominant beta risk continues to hold for tracking errors (TEs) considerably greater than the 3 to 4 percent associated with standard 130/30 AEs. Although higher TEs from generalized AE-Plus funds add to the variability of relative returns, the total volatility of the fund's asset value may be only minimally affected.

## CHARACTERISTICS OF ACTIVE-EXTENSION-PLUS STRATEGIES

With the growth in AE funds over the last few years, the lines between traditional equity and what is considered alternative equity have been blurred. The argument as to why alternative equity is viewed separately from long-only equity has to do with the perception that long/short (L/S) funds have great freedom to vary their long, short, and net exposures. An L/S fund with this type of variability in exposures will subsequently have significant variability in its beta value.

With its beta-1 equity risk, its 100 percent net long base, and its clearly delineated alphas, AE can be viewed as an incremental expansion of standard long-only active equity. Indeed, it is these familiar and comfortable features that enable AE strategies to be kept within the basic equity allocation rather than being thrust into the generally smaller allocation dedicated to alternatives.

The basic motivation behind the AE initiative has been the desire for more alpha return without taking on directional leverage or moving too far afield from standard equity management. To pursue higher alphas usually entails accepting higher TEs. However, as long as the mandates are reasonably diversified across management styles, the suppressive effect of the dominant beta can continue to hold for TEs considerably greater than the 3 to 4 percent associated with the typical 130/30 AE. This raises the question as to whether more intensively active benchmark-centric strategies can still be accommodated within the general AE guidelines. It turns out that there are a number of generalizations of the basic AE format that offer the promise of higher alphas while still retaining the AE's essential structural features and risk characteristics.

These generalized AE-Plus strategies may not necessarily have a 100 percent net exposure or beta target of 1. The key to this broader extension umbrella is to establish a well-defined beta target, which may be smaller or larger than beta-1, and a stable net investment basis that need not be 100 percent.

Rather than being a rigidly fixed value, the beta target can be more of design objective that may vary from period to period. As long as the average realized beta matches the target value, it can be shown that the fund volatility will closely approximate the estimated level over time. Thus, as long as the beta target remains fundamentally stable, an AE-Plus strategy can be viewed as benchmark-centric with well-defined risk characteristics and clearly delineated alphas. Clarity of the beta risk level and the clear-cut distinction between beta and alpha risk represent the hallmarks of a generalized AE-Plus fund.

Many long/short managers as well as long-only managers have portfolio styles that are not pinned to specific beta values. However, their strategies often rotate around some average beta value. Such funds could be brought within the generalized AE framework by simply formalizing this pre-existing average as a beta target. This beta target need not be rigidly realized in every period, as long as it can be construed as a reasonable average value. With this flexibility, the managers can retain their basic investment style and have a basis to access the evident appeal of the AE framework.

In the course of time, one may expect to see convergence between the various types of long/short equity strategies. Benchmark-centric, alpha-hunting strategies may come to encompass a wider range of long-only and long/short strategies. In addition to fitting within a fund's dominant beta risk, well-defined beta targets sharpen the measurement of both skill-based active alphas and the associated TEs. The resulting better delineation of alphas can facilitate the earlier and more reliable identification of the true level of skill embedded in a given performance history.

## GENERALIZED ACTIVE-EXTENSION-PLUS EXAMPLES

Exhibit 15.1 presents an illustrative alpha ranking for long and short positions with various position counts. The original long-only portfolio (100/0) is assumed to have a total active weight of 50 percent, composed of 25 active positions, each with 2 percent weight. These weights applied to the alpha ranking lead to an expected alpha of 1.46 percent. Moving into an AE (130/30) with 30 percent shorts, the position size is kept fixed at 2 percent. The 30 percent short proceeds are then reinvested proportionally back into the 25 original long positions, raising their position weight to 3.2 percent.

The motivation behind moving into generalized AE-Plus funds would be to seek more aggressive active forms of equity management in a risk-controlled manner, with the ultimate goal of achieving higher alphas. Exhibit 15.2 illustrates two very different examples of such higher alpha

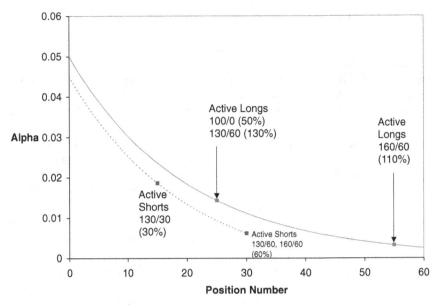

**EXHIBIT 15.1**  Alpha Ranking Models
*Source:* Morgan Stanley Research

strategies that are consistent with a generalized AE format, labeled AE-Plus (1) and AE-Plus (2).

These two AE-Plus portfolios are envisioned to be true L/S funds in the sense that they were not created by extending an original long-only fund. In contrast to the standard 130/30 AE fund, these funds were designed at the outset to be more intensively active, so that their gross long portfolios could have a significantly greater active density. Exhibit 15.2 summarizes the fund characteristics.

## ACTIVE-EXTENSION-PLUS ALPHAS

The first generalized fund, AE-Plus (1), is a 160/60 fund with gross footings of 160 percent long and 60 percent short. In all instances, the shorts will be presumed to be fully active with a fixed 2 percent weight for each position. With the alpha ranking curve depicted in Exhibit 15.1, the 30 short positions of 2 percent each generate an alpha of 1.29 percent. However, in this example, the long side is (arbitrarily) assumed to have an active weight of 110 percent. With the 130/30 AE reinvestment of the 30 percent short proceeds, the AE's active position weight rises to 3.2 percent. We have assumed this 3.2 percent position size remains the maximum limit in the AE-Plus (1). This results in 55 positions, 30 more than the original LO and 130/30 AE.

**EXHIBIT 15.2** AE-Plus versus AE and LO Summary

|  | Long-Only 100/0 | AE 130/30 | AE+ (1) 160/60 | AE+ (2) 130/60 |
|---|---|---|---|---|
| Original Long Investment | 100% | 100% | — | — |
| New Longs | 0% | 30% | — | — |
| Total Longs | 0% | 130% | 160% | 130% |
| Total Shorts | 0% | 30% | 60% | 60% |
| Net Long | 100% | 100% | 100% | 70% |
| Significant Active Weights |  |  |  |  |
| Long-Only | 50% | 50% | — | — |
| New Longs | 0% | 30% | — | — |
| Total Longs | 50% | 80% | 110% | 130% |
| Total Shorts | 0% | 30% | 60% | 60% |
| Total Significant Actives | 50% | 110% | 170% | 190% |
| Beta Target | 1.0 | 1.0 | 0.7± | 0.7± |
| Alpha |  |  |  |  |
| Original Longs | 1.46% | 1.46% | — | — |
| Shorts | — | 0.93% | 1.29% | 1.29% |
| Total Longs | — | 2.34% | 2.68% | 3.80% |
| Total Alpha | 1.46% | 3.27% | 3.97% | 5.09% |
| Tracking Error from Shorts | — | 2.62% | 2.93% | 2.93% |
| Tracking Error from Longs | — | 4.75% | 6.13% | 7.71% |
| Total Tracking Error | 2.97% | 4.12% | 4.79% | 6.33% |
| Alpha/TE Ratio | 0.49 | 0.79 | 0.83 | 0.80 |
| Total Return | 8.71% | 10.52% | 9.50% | 10.62% |
| Total Volatility | 16.77% | 17.01% | 12.50% | 13.17% |
| Return/Volatility Ratio | 0.52 | 0.62 | 0.76 | 0.81 |
|  | 1 | 1 | 0.7 | 0.7 |

*Source:* Morgan Stanley Research

However, to keep the position size at 3.2 percent, the additional positions had to be invested in the lower tail of the ranking curve in Exhibit 15.1, so that the additional alpha only amounts to 1.22 percent. The net result is that AE-Plus (1)'s higher active weight generates a total alpha of only 3.97 percent.

It should be noted that the AE-Plus (1) has a net long base of 100 percent, but its beta is only assumed to be 0.7. This lower beta may have been achieved through either focusing on a universe of lower-beta stocks, by shorting higher-beta stocks, or by the use of derivatives or overlays. (In the first two cases, there is likely to be a definite style bias relative to a broad-based equity benchmark.)

In the second generalized example, AE-Plus (2), the fund has gross longs of 130 percent, gross shorts of 60 percent, for a net long position of 70 percent. In this case, the beta target of 0.70 is more coincident with the 70 percent net long position. As before, the 60 percent short side is assumed to be all active, with 30 positions, each with 2 percent fixed weights. On the long side, however, all 130 percent is presumed to be active, with the cash proceeds from the shorts reinvested proportionally into the initial 25 long positions. This 130 percent long active weight results in a highly concentrated long portfolio with position sizes of 5.2 percent. With this high level of concentration in the higher-alpha positions, the AE-Plus (2) is able to generate a significantly greater alpha of 5.09 percent.

## ACTIVE-EXTENSION-PLUS TRACKING ERRORS AND INFORMATION RATIOS

The lower sections of Exhibit 15.2 show the TE and total volatility characteristics for the four different portfolios. All individual positions have a TE of 20 percent with a 0.05 correlation *within* the long and *within* the short portfolios, and a −0.05 offset correlation *between* the longs and shorts. This ability of the shorts to offset unproductive correlations is an important benefit in any long/short format. As shown in Exhibit 15.2, the longs account for a much greater TE than the shorts, but the offsets reduce the TEs to the indicated total values.

Not surprisingly, the TEs generally increase with the active weight. However, the alpha/TE information ratios are surprisingly close across the three very different long/short strategies.

The alpha/TE ratio is a valuable metric, but it cannot fully describe the benefits from moving into these types of long/short strategies. In a portfolio situation in which exogenous leverage is freely available, the return/risk ratio may be the ultimate yardstick. However, by their very nature, AE strategies are intended to stand on their own without access to exogenous leverage.

The implicit investment objective is to generate higher alphas within the confines of an acceptable risk structure that depends on the asset format, the beta value stability, and the TE. Thus, an institution that could only tolerate a 5 percent TE may find AE-Plus (1) with its 4.79 percent TE acceptable.

The AE-Plus (2) strategy generates the highest TE of 6.33 percent, but has results in the highest alpha as well. Sponsors that can tolerate this TE will look to reap the reward of the 5.09 percent alpha. Although AE-Plus (2)'s alpha/TE ratio of 0.80 is slightly lower than AE-Plus (1)'s 0.83, an investor who can accept the higher TE would likely prefer AE-Plus (2)'s greater alpha. Moreover, it should be noted that the TEs from AEs and generalized AE-Plus funds are intended to be largely uncorrelated. Such uncorrelated TEs will tend to have only a modest impact on fund level volatility risk. (Although the expected volatility—the standard gauge of a fund's long-term risk—is little affected, remember that there could still be significant period-by-period TE relative to the fund's benchmark return.)

## ALPHA AND BETA RETURNS

The return differences are due to both the alpha and beta components of the portfolios. The two AE-Plus examples have a lower beta of 0.7, and this lower beta exposure naturally reduces both their total return and volatility. However, as shown in Exhibit 15.2, the higher alphas in the generalized AE-Plus funds compensate somewhat for the lower beta returns. At the same time, the AE-Plus funds' lower beta reduces their total volatility, so that the total return/volatility ratios far exceed those of the long-only and the standard AE.

However, to a large extent, these total returns and total volatilities are beside the point. Any investor who chooses the generalized AE-Plus funds will do so either because the lower beta is desirable, or because the beta can be remediated to the desired level within the overall fund. Thus, with the stable beta target that is a key design feature of the AE-Plus, the actual level of the beta target should play a relatively minor role. The main objective is to generate good positive alpha within a stable beta framework that can be properly accommodated within a fund's overall risk framework.

Most institutional funds have low levels of active risk, and TEs that are reliably orthogonal to the dominating beta risk will have a minimal impact on the overall fund volatility. Beta-targeted generalizations of the AE concept can encompass a far wider range of long/short strategies with more intensively active management styles, and thereby offer the prospect pf more significant alpha returns within a moderate extension of the AE risk framework.

## THE FUND LEVEL CONTEXT

Generalized AE-Plus funds with higher TEs could have a significant effect on fund-level relative returns, but a minimal impact on the overall fund volatility. Exhibits 15.3 and 15.4 summarize the results from adding five active equity mandates with 3 percent weight each to a diversified fund with a volatility of 10.45 percent. The beta level is assumed to have been maintained at the desired level so that the only incremental risk comes from

**EXHIBIT 15.3** Fund-Level TE Effect

| | Initial Fund Volatility 10.45% | | | |
| | Adding Five 3% AE Mandates | | | |
| | Correlation among Mandates | | | |
| TE | 1 | 0.5 | 0.25 | 0 |
|---|---|---|---|---|
| 3 | 0.01% | 0.01% | 0.00% | 0.00% |
| 5 | 0.03% | 0.02% | 0.01% | 0.01% |
| 7 | 0.05% | 0.03% | 0.02% | 0.01% |

*Source:* Morgan Stanley Research

the active manager TEs, which range from 3 to 7 percent, and from varying degrees of correlation among the managers.

Exhibit 15.3 shows the standard deviation of relative returns versus the policy portfolio. As long as correlations among the managers remain low, only about 40 to 60 percent of the weighted TE will be projected to the fund level. For example, at 0.25 correlation across the five managers, each with a 7 percent TE, the fund-level TE would amount to 0.66 percent. This fund-level TE reflects the variability of the overall return relative to the policy portfolio.

In contrast, Exhibit 15.4 displays the total fund-level volatility risk. For the same 0.25 correlation across the 7 percent TE managers, the total volatility of the fund's asset value rises from 10.45 to 10.47 percent, an increase of only 0.02 percent. It is this total volatility that enters into estimating the

**EXHIBIT 15.4** Fund-Level Total Volatility

| | Total Fund Volatility 10.45% | | | |
| | Adding Five 3% AE Mandates | | | |
| | Correlation among Mandates | | | |
| TE | 1 | 0.5 | 0.25 | 0 |
|---|---|---|---|---|
| 3 | 0.45% | 0.35% | 0.28% | 0.20% |
| 5 | 0.75% | 0.58% | 0.47% | 0.34% |
| 7 | 1.05% | 0.81% | 0.66% | 0.47% |

*Source:* Morgan Stanley Research

probability for a given loss or for any other shortfall threshold that may be chosen as a measure of overall fund risk.

In terms of the total volatility of their asset values, most institutional funds have an underutilized capacity for accommodating additional productive active risk. Active management with TEs that are reliably orthogonal to the dominating beta risk will have a minimal impact on the overall fund volatility. For some sponsors, a generalized AE-Plus fund's greater return prospects may be considered sufficient compensation for a slightly larger total volatility, and even for a more substantial increase in the variability of relative returns versus the policy portfolios.

# Key Journal Articles

# On the Optimality of Long/Short Strategies

**Bruce I. Jacobs**
Principal
Jacobs Levy Equity Management

**Kenneth N. Levy**
Principal
Jacobs Levy Equity Management

**David Starer**
Senior Quantitative Analyst
Jacobs Levy Equity Management

*We consider the optimality of portfolios not subject to short-selling constraints and derive conditions that a universe of securities must satisfy for an optimal active portfolio to be dollar neutral or beta neutral. We find that following the common practice of constraining long/short portfolios to have zero net holdings or zero betas is generally suboptimal. Only under specific unlikely conditions will such constrained portfolios optimize an investor's utility function. We also derive precise formulas for optimally equitizing an active long/short portfolio using exposure to a benchmark security. The relative sizes of the active and benchmark exposures depend on the investor's desired residual risk relative to the residual risk of a typical portfolio and on the expected risk-adjusted excess return of a minimum-variance active portfolio. We demonstrate that optimal portfolios demand the use of integrated optimizations.*

The construction and management of long/short portfolios are complicated tasks involving assumptions and actions that may seem counterintuitive to the investor unfamiliar with shorting. Despite attempts by Jacobs and Levy (1996b, 1997) to clarify the issues, many practitioners—even some of the most experienced—have been beguiled by an assemblage of myths and misconceptions. With long/short strategy becoming an increasingly important component of institutional portfolios,[1] some of the more egregious misunderstandings must be purged from the collective psyche of the investment community.

One myth that many practitioners evidently believe (see, e.g., Michaud, 1993, and Arnott and Leinweber, 1994) is that an optimal long/short portfolio can be constructed by blending a short-only portfolio with an independently generated long-only portfolio.[2] Adherents to this belief tend to characterize the overall portfolio in terms of the excess returns of, and correlation between, the two constituent portfolios. One of the reasons such an approach is suboptimal (see Jacobs and Levy, 1995) is that it fails to use the correlations between the *individual* (long and short) securities to achieve an overall reduction in variance.

Another myth is that a long/short portfolio represents a separate asset class. This misconception is common. For example, Brush (1997) described a technique for optimally blending a long/short portfolio with a long-only portfolio to achieve an overall portfolio that has a greater Sharpe ratio than either of its constituent portfolios. In so doing, Brush implicitly assigned long/short and long-only portfolios to different asset classes. Although this blending approach appears to acknowledge the benefits of long/short investment, it misses the points that a long/short portfolio does not belong to a separate asset class and that combining a long/short portfolio with a long-only portfolio produces (in the aggregate) only a single portfolio! The optimal weights of that single portfolio should be obtained from an integrated optimization. The important question is not how one should allocate capital between a long-only portfolio and a long/short portfolio but, rather, how one should blend active positions (long and short) with a benchmark security in an integrated optimization.

In addition to falling victim to such myths, some practitioners have followed common practices that may not be optimal. For example, they often seek to constrain their portfolios to be neutral with respect to some factor (i.e., to be independent of, or insensitive to, that factor).[3] In particular, they often constrain their portfolios to be dollar neutral by committing the same amount of capital to their long holdings as they commit to their short holdings. In so doing, in a naive sense, they set their net market exposure to zero. Another constraint often imposed is that of beta neutrality, in which the manager constrains the portfolio to have a beta of zero. Such a beta-neutral portfolio is theoretically insensitive to market movements.

The manager may apply neutrality constraints voluntarily or because the client requires them. But although valid taxation, accounting, or behavioral reasons may exist for imposing such constraints, there are generally no pressing financial reasons for doing so.[4] On the contrary, imposing them may actually prevent managers from fully using their insights to produce optimal portfolios. A general principle of optimization is that constrained solutions do not offer the same level of utility as unconstrained solutions unless, by some fortunate coincidence, the optimum lies within the feasible region dictated by the constraints. Given that neutrality is often imposed, we consider here the conditions under which this coincidence can occur. That is, we set out to find the conditions under which dollar-neutral or beta-neutral portfolios are optimal.

When Treynor and Black (1973) discussed similar issues in a classic paper, they posed the question: "Where practical is it desirable to so balance a portfolio between long positions in securities considered underpriced and short positions in securities considered overpriced that market risk is completely eliminated?" (p. 66). This article tackles Treynor and Black's question and extends the analysis to the following:

1. Under what conditions will a net holding of zero (i.e., dollar neutrality) be optimal for a long/short portfolio?
2. Under what conditions will the combined optimal holdings in a long/short portfolio be beta neutral?
3. How should one optimally equitize a long/short portfolio? In particular, under what conditions will dollar neutrality or beta neutrality be optimal for the active portion of an equitized long/short portfolio?

This article is essentially divided into two parts. The first part considers an active portfolio (which we define as one that has no explicit benchmark holding), and the second part considers an equitized active portfolio (which we define as one that consists of the active portfolio combined with an explicit exposure to the benchmark security). The first part is concerned mainly with risk and return in an absolute sense, and the second part is concerned mainly with risk and return in a relative sense.

Within this framework, we first consider the optimality of dollar and beta neutrality in active long/short portfolios. We then reconsider dollar neutrality and beta neutrality in portfolios designed to minimize residual risk and in portfolios designed to maximize return subject to a constraint on residual risk. Finally, we extend the analysis to consider equitized portfolios.

We examine the optimality of dollar neutrality and beta neutrality for the active portion of an equitized long/short portfolio, and we show how optimal exposure to the benchmark security should be computed.

## PORTFOLIO CONSTRUCTION AND PROBLEM FORMULATION

In answering the first two questions posed in the introduction, we assume that the investor has solved the usual expected utility maximization problem and that the solution permits shorting. We determine what properties the universe of investment opportunities should possess for the portfolio resulting from the maximization problem to be dollar neutral or beta neutral. To answer the third question, we set up an integrated criterion function and examine its properties.

We will be concerned mainly with variations of the utility function favored by Markowitz (1952) and Sharpe (1991):

$$U = r_P - \frac{1}{2\tau}\sigma_P^2 \qquad (16.1)$$

where $r_p$ is the expected return on the investor's portfolio, $\sigma_P^2$ is the variance of the return, and $\tau$ is the investor's risk tolerance. For mathematical convenience, we have included a factor of one-half in the utility function. This utility function can be considered an approximation to the investor's expected utility in the sense of von Neumann and Morgenstern (1944). As Sharpe (1991) pointed out, if the investor has a negative exponential utility function over wealth and if returns are jointly normally distributed, then the approximation will be exact. Moreover, Levy and Markowitz (1979) showed that the approximation is good even if the investor has a more general utility function, or if returns are not jointly normally distributed or both.

Assume that, in seeking to maximize the utility function in Equation 16.1, the investor has an available capital of $K$ dollars and has acquired $n_i$ shares of security $i \in \{1, 2, \ldots, N\}$. A long holding is represented by a positive number of shares, and a short holding is represented by a negative number.[5] The holding $h_i$ in security $i$ is the ratio of the amount invested in that security to the investor's total capital. Thus, if security $i$ has price $p_i$, then $h_i = n_i p_i / K$.

In addition to the $N$ securities, assume also that the investor may have an exposure of $K_B$ dollars to a benchmark security. We are intentionally vague about the nature of the benchmark security to emphasize that long/short portfolios are neutral and can be transported to any asset class by use of appropriate overlays. Thus, the benchmark security may be an equity index, a debt index, or any other instrument that the investor cares to specify. The holding of the benchmark security is $h_B = K_B/K$.[6] The investor seeks to maximize the utility function given in Equation 16.1 by choosing appropriate values for security holdings $h_i$.

Unlike the typical optimization problem for a fully invested portfolio, our utility function is not augmented with a constraint to ensure that the total holdings sum to unity. Instead, the long/short portfolio is constrained only by U.S. Federal Reserve Board Regulation T, which states that the total value of the investment should not exceed twice the investor's capital.[7] To express this constraint mathematically, we define a long set, $L$, and a short set, $S$, such that

$$L = \{i : n_i > 0\} \text{ and } S = \{i : n_i < 0\}$$

Regulation T states that each investor must satisfy the following inequality:

$$\sum_{i \in L} n_i p_i - \sum_{i \in S} n_i p_i \leq 2K$$

This inequality need not be included explicitly in the optimization because the relative sizes of holdings are unaffected by it and all holdings can simply be scaled up or down so that it is satisfied.

## OPTIMAL LONG/SHORT PORTFOLIOS

As discussed, many long/short investment approaches create suboptimal portfolios because they prepartition the problem. That is, they combine a long portfolio with an independently generated short portfolio, and they characterize the long/short portfolio in terms of the correlation between the two constituent portfolios. In contrast, our approach treats the portfolio as a single entity. Unlike Michaud and Arnott and Leinweber, we exploit the correlations among all of the individual securities (whether they are held long or sold short) in a single integrated optimization.

Consider first portfolios that have no explicit position in the benchmark security. Let $r_i$ be the expected return on security $i$. Using matrix notation, the absolute return on the active portfolio is then

$$r_P = h^T r \tag{16.2}$$

where $h = [h_1, h_2, \ldots, h_N]^T$ is a vector of holdings, $r = [r_1, r_2, \ldots, r_N]^T$ is a vector of returns, and the superscript $T$ denotes matrix or vector transposition.

In this analysis, we ignore risk-free holdings. If we were to consider them, however, they would simply result in the addition of the term $h_F r_F$ to the expression for the portfolio return.

The variance of the portfolio's absolute return is

$$\sigma_P^2 = h^T Q h \qquad (16.3)$$

where $Q = \operatorname{cov}(r, r^T)$ is the covariance matrix of the individual securities and is assumed to be known.

Substituting Equation 16.2 for the portfolio return and Equation 16.3 for the variance into the utility function (Equation 16.1), differentiating the utility with respect to holding vector $h$ (see, e.g., Magnus and Neudecker 1988), setting this derivative equal to zero, and solving for $h$ produces the optimal weight vector

$$h = \tau Q^{-1} r \qquad (16.4)$$

This form is typical for the expression for an optimal portfolio, and it shows that the best mix of risky assets in an investor's portfolio depends only on the expected returns and their covariances. The investor's wealth and preferences affect only his or her demand for risky assets through a *scalar τ* that is the same for all risky assets.

As with the portfolio given by Equation 16.4, optimal security weights in many portfolio problems turn out to be proportional to the securities' expected returns and inversely proportional to the covariance of the returns. In addition to maximizing the utility function of Equation 16.1, appropriately scaled versions of Equation 16.4 also give the optimal portfolio weights for such problems as maximizing the Sharpe ratio (Sharpe, 1994), minimizing portfolio variance while holding portfolio expected return fixed (Treynor and Black), and maximizing expected return subject to a constraint on variance.

We will find it useful to define the portfolio of Equation 16.4 with $\tau = 1$ as the unit-risk-tolerance active (URA) portfolio, $\phi$. That is,

$$\phi \equiv Q^{-1} r$$

The expected absolute return of this portfolio is

$$r_{URA} = r^T Q^{-1} r$$

and the variance of this portfolio's absolute return is

$$\sigma^2_{URA} = r^T Q^{-1} r$$

## Optimality of Dollar Neutrality

Consider now the conditions under which a portfolio would be dollar neutral. The net holding $H$ is the sum of all the individual holdings:

$$H = \sum_{i=1}^{N} h_i = 1_N^T h \tag{16.5}$$

where $1_N$ represents an $N \times 1$ vector of ones. Substituting Equation 16.4 into Equation 16.5 leads to the following expression for the net holding:

$$H = \tau 1_N^T Q^{-1} r \tag{16.6}$$

For the portfolio to be dollar neutral, the value of the long holdings must equal the negative of the value of the short holdings. By using the definitions of the long and short sets, this equality is expressed mathematically as

$$\sum_{i \in L} h_i = -\sum_{i \in S} h_i$$

Equivalently, because $L$ and $S$ are exhaustive, the sum of the weights must be zero and the general condition for dollar neutrality is

$$H = 0 \tag{16.7}$$

The logical argument attached to Equation 16.7 must be kept clearly in mind. The condition expressed in the equation is necessary but not sufficient for an optimal portfolio to be dollar neutral. Thus, if the condition holds, the optimal portfolio must be dollar neutral. One can, however, construct a portfolio that is dollar neutral (and thus satisfies Equation 16.7) but not optimal.

For the specific portfolio under consideration, substituting Equation 16.6 into Equation 16.7 gives the following condition for optimal dollar neutrality:

$$\tau 1_N^T Q^{-1} r = 0 \qquad (16.8)$$

This general condition for dollar neutrality can be simplified by making various assumptions about the structure of covariance matrix $Q$. For example, one special case arises if one subscribes to the assumptions of the constant correlation model of Elton, Gruber, and Padberg (1976), under which the elements of the covariance matrix are given by

$$q_{ij} = \begin{cases} \rho\sigma_i\sigma_j, & i \neq j \\ \sigma_i^2, & i = j \end{cases}$$

where $\sigma_i$ is the standard deviation of the return of the $i$th security and $\rho$ is a constant correlation factor. Equivalently, in the Elton, Gruber, and Padberg model, the covariance matrix can be written in matrix notation as

$$Q = (1 - \rho)D_\sigma + \sigma\rho\sigma^T \qquad (16.9)$$

where $D_\sigma$ is a diagonal matrix having the variances $\sigma_i^2$; $i = 1, \ldots, N$ along its diagonal and $\sigma$ is a vector of standard deviations: $\sigma = [\sigma_1, \sigma_2, \ldots, \sigma_N]^T$. The covariance matrix as written in Equation 16.9 is in a convenient form for application of the *matrix inversion lemma.*

The matrix inversion lemma (see, e.g., Kailath, 1980) states that for compatibly dimensioned matrixes $W$, $X$, $Y$, and $Z$,

$$[W + XYZ]^{-1} = W^{-1} - W^{-1}X$$
$$\times [Y^{-1} + ZW^{-1}X]^{-1} ZW^{-1} \qquad (16.10)$$

Using this lemma to invert the covariance matrix in Equation 16.9 and substituting the result into Equation 16.6 for the net holding produces

$$H = \frac{\tau}{1 - \rho}\left[ 1_N^T D_\sigma^{-1} r - \frac{\rho}{1 - \rho + \rho\sigma^T D_\sigma^{-1}\sigma} \times \left( 1_N^T D_\sigma^{-1}\sigma\right)\left(\sigma^T D_\sigma^{-1} r\right) \right]$$
$$(16.11)$$

One can easily verify the following identities:

$$1_N^T D_\sigma^{-1} r = \sum_{i=1}^N (r_i/\sigma_i^2)$$

$$1_N^T D_\sigma^{-1} \sigma = \sum_{i=1}^N (1/\sigma_i)$$

$$\sigma^T D_\sigma^{-1} r = \sum_{i=1}^N (r_i/\sigma_i)$$

$$\sigma^T D_\sigma^{-1} \sigma = \sum_{i=1}^N (\sigma_i^2/\sigma_i^2) = N$$

Thus, Equation 16.11 reduces to

$$H = \frac{\tau}{1-\rho} \left[ \sum_{i=1}^N \frac{r_i}{\sigma_i^2} - a \sum_{i=1}^N \frac{r_i}{\sigma_i} \right] \qquad (16.12)$$

where

$$a = \frac{\rho}{1 + N\rho - \rho} \sum_{i=1}^N \frac{1}{\sigma_i}$$

Intuition concerning Equation 16.12 can be obtained by defining a measure of return stability, $\xi_i$, as the inverse of the standard deviation of the return of security $i$. Then, for portfolios with many securities (i.e., those with large $N$), the constant $a$ is approximately equal to the average return stability. That is,

$$a = \frac{\rho}{1 + N\rho - \rho} \sum_{i=1}^N \frac{1}{\sigma_i} \approx \frac{1}{N} \sum_{i=1}^N \xi_i = \xi$$

Using this approximation in Equation 16.12 makes the net holding

$$H = \frac{\tau}{1-\rho} \sum_{i=1}^N (\xi_i - \xi) \frac{r_i}{\sigma_i} \qquad (16.13)$$

Thus, if the net risk-adjusted return of all securities weighted by the deviation of their stability from average is positive, the net holding should be long. Conversely, if this quantity is negative, the net holding should be short. Only under the special condition in which $H$ in Equation 16.12 is equal to zero will the optimal portfolio be dollar neutral. Constraining the holding to be zero when this condition is not satisfied will produce a suboptimal portfolio.[8]

Equation 16.13 formalizes the simple intuitive notion that you should be net long if you expect the market as a whole to go up and net short if you expect it to go down! Importantly, however, it tells you how long or how short your net exposure should be based on your risk tolerance, your predictions of security returns and standard deviations, and your estimate of the correlation between security returns.

Equation 16.13 and the requirement that $H = 0$ can also be used in a normative sense. For example, because Equation 16.13 is independent of the individual holdings, an investor could select a universe of securities such that, based only on their expected risk-adjusted returns and return stability, the net holding of the universe as computed with Equation 16.13 is zero. The investor could then be confident that the portfolio formed from this universe that maximizes the utility function (Equation 16.1) will be dollar neutral.

More precise conditions that an optimal portfolio must satisfy to be dollar neutral can be obtained by making further assumptions about Equation 16.12. For example, assuming that $\rho \neq 1$ and $\tau \neq 0$ gives

$$\sum_{i=1}^{N} \frac{r_i}{\sigma_i^2} = a \sum_{i=1}^{N} \frac{r_i}{\sigma_i} \tag{16.14}$$

A sufficient (but not necessary) condition for Equation 16.14 to hold is that both sums in the equation be zero simultaneously. Each of these sums can be regarded as a form of net risk-adjusted return that, if equal to zero, results in zero net holding being optimal. Alternatively, in the (admittedly unlikely) circumstance that all variances are equal, Equation 16.14 for optimal dollar neutrality is satisfied if the sum of the returns is zero. Roughly, in this case, the portfolio should have zero net holding if the average return is zero.

## Optimality of Beta Neutrality

In an exactly analogous manner to the preceding analysis, we consider in this section the conditions under which an unconstrained portfolio would optimally have a beta of zero. Because we are dealing here with beta sensitivity, it is appropriate to use Sharpe's diagonal model, which gives the expected return of the $i$th security, $r_i$, in terms of the alpha of that security, $\alpha_i$, and beta of that security, $\beta_i$, and the expected return of the benchmark security, $r_B$':

$$r_i = \alpha_i + \beta_i r_B$$

When this model is used, the beta of the portfolio is

$$\beta_P \sum_{i=1}^{N} h_i \beta_i = \beta^T h \qquad (16.15)$$

where $\beta = [\beta_1, \beta_2, \ldots, \beta_N]^T$. The covariance matrix of the security returns is

$$Q = D_\omega + \beta \sigma_B^2 \beta^T$$

where $D_\omega$ is a diagonal matrix whose $i$th diagonal entry is $\omega_i^2 = \text{var}(\alpha_i)$, and $\sigma_B^2 = \text{var}(r_B)$. The diagonal form of this matrix is consistent with the model's assumption that the correlation between any pair of stock return residuals is zero. Using the matrix inversion lemma (Equation 16.10), the inverse of the covariance matrix is

$$Q^{-1} = D_\omega^{-1} - \frac{D_\omega^{-1} \beta \beta^T D_\omega^{-1}}{\sigma_B^{-1} + \beta^T D_\omega^{-1} \beta} \qquad (16.16)$$

Using Equation 16.4 in Equation 16.15 and setting the portfolio beta equal to zero gives the following general condition for optimality of beta neutrality:

$$\beta^T Q^{-1} r = 0 \qquad (16.17)$$

Then, if Equation 16.16 is used, the condition shown in Equation 16.17 becomes

$$\left(\sigma_B^{-1} + \beta^T D_\omega^{-1} \beta\right)\left(\beta^T D_\omega^{-1} r\right) = \left(\beta^T D_\omega^{-1} \beta\right)\left(\beta^T D_\omega^{-1} r\right) \qquad (16.18)$$

The two conditions under which Equation 16.18 is satisfied are the following: Either

$$\sigma_B^{-2} + \beta^T D_\omega^{-1} \beta = \beta^T D_\omega^{-1} \beta$$

which would require $\sigma_{\bar{B}}^2 = \infty$, and is thus untenable, or

$$\beta^T D_\omega^{-1} r = 0$$

This second condition, rewritten as a summation, implies that the condition under which an optimal portfolio has zero beta is

$$\sum_{i=1}^N \frac{\beta_i r_i}{\omega_i^2} = 0 \qquad (16.19)$$

The lefthand side of Equation 16.19 can be interpreted as a beta-weighted, risk-adjusted net return. If this quantity is positive, then the optimal portfolio will have a positive beta. Conversely, if this quantity is negative, the optimal portfolio will have a negative beta. Constraining the portfolio beta to be zero when Equation 16.19 is not satisfied will result in suboptimal portfolio construction.

If one uses the Elton, Gruber, and Padberg approximation for the covariance matrix, one can show that an alternative condition for beta neutrality to be optimal is

$$\beta_p = \frac{\tau}{1 - \rho} \sum_{i=1}^N (\beta_i - \bar{\beta}) \frac{r_i}{\sigma_i} = 0$$

where beta is a volatility-weighted average beta,

$$\bar{\beta} = \frac{1}{N} \sum_{i=1}^N \frac{\beta_i}{\sigma_i}$$

This expression is analogous to Equation 16.13 and shows that the portfolio beta is optimally zero when the net risk-adjusted return of all securities weighted by the deviation of their betas from the average is zero.

We have dealt thus far only with absolute return and absolute variance. Most plan sponsors and investment managers, however, are concerned with relative measures rather than absolute measures. In particular, they are interested in maximizing return in excess of a benchmark return while simultaneously minimizing residual risk. In the next section, we extend the previous results to portfolios formed by optimizing such relative measures.

## Optimal Long/Short Portfolio with Minimum Residual Risk

The excess return of a portfolio, $r_E$, is simply $r_A - r_B$, the portfolio's absolute return minus the benchmark return.[9] The residual risk is the variance of the excess return, and can be shown to be

$$\sigma_E^2 = h^T Q h - 2h^T q + \sigma_B^2$$

where $q = \text{cov}(r, r_B)$ is a column vector of covariances between the individual security returns and the benchmark return. The active portfolio that minimizes the residual risk can be shown to be $h = Q^{-1}q$. Defining this portfolio as the minimum-residual-risk (MRR) portfolio, $\psi$, will be useful; that is,

$$\psi = Q^{-1}q$$

This portfolio's absolute return is

$$r_{MRR} = q^T Q^{-1} r$$

and its residual risk, the minimum attainable with an unequitized portfolio, is

$$\sigma_{MRR}^2 = \sigma_B^2 - q^T Q^{-1} q$$

Using the same type of analysis as in the previous section, we can state the condition for such a portfolio to be dollar neutral optimally as

$$H \approx \frac{1}{1-\rho} \sum_{i=1}^{N} (\xi_i - \xi)\frac{q_i}{\sigma_i} = 0$$

or

$$\sum_{i=1}^{N} \frac{q_i}{\sigma_i^2} = a \sum_{i=1}^{N} \frac{q_i}{\sigma_i}$$

Thus, the MRR (or minimum-tracking-error) portfolio will optimally be dollar neutral if the net risk-adjusted covariance of the securities' returns with the benchmark return, weighted by the deviations of the returns' stability from the average, is zero.

To find the condition for the optimality of beta neutrality, observe that

$$q = \text{cov}(r, r_B)$$
$$= \beta \sigma_B^2$$

so

$$\psi = Q^{-1} q$$
$$= \sigma_B^2 Q^{-1} \beta$$

and the beta of the portfolio is

$$\beta_P = \psi^T \beta$$
$$= \sigma_B^2 \beta^T Q^{-1} \beta$$

Because $Q$ is positive definite, so too is $Q^{-1}$. Thus, $\beta_p$ cannot be zero for any nonzero $\beta$.

For the specific case using the Sharpe diagonal model, the preceding expressions can be used to find that the condition for a minimum-excess-variance portfolio to be optimally beta neutral is

$$\sum_{i=1}^{N} \frac{\beta_i^2}{\omega_i^2} = 0$$

but this equation cannot be satisfied by any portfolio that contains even one security with a nonzero beta. Thus, we reach the conclusion that no practical active portfolio that minimizes residual risk can optimally be beta neutral. This conclusion accords with intuition: A portfolio that minimizes residual risk should have a beta that approaches 1, not zero.

## Optimal Long/Short Portfolio with Specified Residual Risk

Typically, a plan sponsor gives a manager a mandate to maximize return on a portfolio and simultaneously demands that the standard deviation or variance of that return equal some specified level.[10] For the manager, this task amounts to choosing, at each investment period, a portfolio that optimizes the Lagrangian

$$l = r_E - \lambda(\sigma_E^2 - \sigma_D^2)$$

where $\sigma_D^2$ is the desired excess variance (i.e., residual risk) and $\lambda$ is a Lagrange multiplier.

Although this approach differs slightly from the more traditional approach of Black (1972), which seeks to minimize variance subject to a constraint on excess return, we believe that the problem posed as return maximization subject to a constrained risk level is a more accurate reflection of the thought processes of plan sponsors and investment managers.

The portfolio that optimizes this Lagrangian can be shown to be

$$h = k\phi + \psi$$

where $\phi$ is the URA portfolio, $\psi$ is the MRR portfolio, and

$$k = \sqrt{\frac{\sigma_D^2 - \sigma_{MRR}^2}{\sigma_{URA}^2}}$$

The optimal portfolio in this case is the sum of the MRR portfolio and a scaled version of the URA portfolio. The scaling factor depends on the desired residual risk, the minimum attainable residual risk, and the variance of the URA portfolio. If the desired residual risk is less than the minimum attainable residual risk, then $\sigma_D^2 \sigma_{MRR}^2 < 0$, and no portfolio can be constructed. If the desired residual risk is equal to the minimum attainable residual risk, then $\sigma_D^2 - \sigma_{MRR}^2 = 0$, and the optimal portfolio will be simply $h = \psi$, the MRR portfolio. As the desired residual risk increases, the portfolio becomes more like a scaled version of $\phi$ (the URA portfolio) and $k$ tends asymptotically to the investor's risk tolerance, $\tau$.

The condition under which this portfolio is optimally dollar neutral again has the familiar form:

$$H \approx \frac{1}{1-\rho} \sum_{i=1}^{N} (\xi_i - \xi) \frac{kr_i + q_i}{\sigma_i} = 0 \tag{16.20}$$

or

$$\sum_{i=1}^{N} \frac{kr_i + q_i}{\sigma_i^2} = a \sum_{i=1}^{N} \frac{kr_i + q_i}{\sigma_i}$$

indicating that this portfolio is optimally dollar neutral if a net risk-adjusted linear combination of the securities' returns and covariances, weighted by deviation of return stability from average, is zero. The interpretation of Equation 16.20 is similar to that of Equation 16.13, where the term $kr_i + q_i$ now replaces $r_i$ and the presence of $k$ and $q_i$ reflects the investor's concerns about residual risk.

Similarly, the condition under which this portfolio will optimally be beta neutral is

$$\sum_{i=1}^{N} \frac{\beta_i}{\omega_i^2}(kr_i + q_i) = 0$$

equivalently, because $r_i = \alpha + \beta_i r_B$ and $q_i = \beta_i \sigma_B^2$,

$$k \sum_{i=1}^{N} \frac{\alpha_i \beta_i}{\omega_i^2} + (\sigma_B^2 + kr_B) \sum_{i=1}^{N} \frac{\beta_i^2}{\omega_i^2} = 0$$

## OPTIMAL EQUITIZED LONG/SHORT PORTFOLIO

We now address the third question posed in the introduction, namely: How should one optimally equitize a long/short portfolio? In this case, in addition to the long/short portfolio, the manager has an explicit benchmark exposure, either through ownership of a physical benchmark security or through a derivative overlay. We determine the optimal portfolio weights and the optimal benchmark exposure in a single integrated step. This approach differs from the approach used by Brush (1997), in which security weights were predetermined for two distinct portfolios—a long/short portfolio and a long-only portfolio—and then capital was allocated between these two existing portfolios. In Brush, the long-only portfolio served to provide both security and benchmark exposure whereas the long/short portfolio provided security but not benchmark exposure.

Treynor and Black showed that, under the assumptions of the diagonal model, an equitized long/short portfolio can be viewed *conceptually* as the outcome of the following separate decisions: selecting an active portfolio to maximize an appraisal ratio, blending the active portfolio with a suitable replica of the market portfolio to maximize the Sharpe ratio, and scaling the positions in the combined portfolio through lending or borrowing while preserving their proportions. These separate decisions are of a different nature from those of Brush. Treynor and Black arrived at the conceptual separability only after performing an explicit integrated optimization in which security positions (long and short) and benchmark exposure were determined jointly.

Treynor and Black showed, among other things, that a security may play two roles simultaneously: (1) a position based entirely on the security's expected independent return (appraisal premium) and (2) a position based solely on the security's role as part of the market portfolio. These two roles must be considered when blending individual security positions with a benchmark exposure. In this section, we derive expressions for the optimal benchmark holding that implicitly account for this dual nature of securities.

The absolute return on the equitized portfolio now includes a contribution from the return on the benchmark security and is, therefore, given by

$$r_P = h^T r + h_B r_B$$

The excess return on the equitized portfolio is

$$r_E = h^T r + h_B r_B - r_B = \mathbf{h}^T \mathbf{r}$$

where the augmented holding vector, $\mathbf{h}$, and the augmented return vector, $\mathbf{r}$, for the equitized portfolio are defined as

$$\mathbf{h} = \begin{bmatrix} h \\ \hbar_B \end{bmatrix}; \quad \mathbf{r} = \begin{bmatrix} r \\ r_B \end{bmatrix}$$

with $\hbar_B = h_B - 1$. Note that the augmented vectors (which are distinguished from the active portfolio vectors by the use of bold font) incorporate the corresponding active portfolio holding and return vectors.

The variance of the excess return of the equitized portfolio, $\sigma_E^2$, is

$$\sigma_E^2 = \mathbf{var}(r_E)$$
$$= \mathbf{h}^T \mathbf{Q} \mathbf{h}$$

where $\mathbf{Q}$ is the covariance matrix of the augmented return vector $\mathbf{r}$.[11] Noting that $\mathbf{r}$ is a partitioned vector, we can also write $\mathbf{Q}$ in the following partitioned form:

$$\mathbf{Q} = \begin{bmatrix} Q & q \\ q^T & \sigma_B^2 \end{bmatrix}$$

## Optimality of Dollar Neutrality with Equitization

In this section, we consider the active portion of the equitized long/short portfolio and determine the conditions under which that portion is optimally dollar neutral. As before, we consider an unconstrained portfolio designed to maximize the investor's utility. In the presence of equitization, the utility of interest is the portfolio's excess return tempered by the variance of its excess return. Specifically, the objective function to be maximized is

$$J = \mathbf{h}^T \mathbf{r} = \frac{1}{2\tau} \mathbf{h}^T Q \mathbf{h}$$

where, as before, $\tau$ is the risk tolerance of the investor.

By differentiating this objective function with respect to $\mathbf{h}$ and setting the derivative equal to zero, the benchmark and active portfolio weights are found to be

$$\hbar_B = -\tau m \quad \text{or} \quad h_B = 1 - \tau m$$

and

$$h = \tau Q^{-1}(r + mq)$$
$$= (\phi + m\psi)\tau$$

The scalar $m$ is given by

$$m = \frac{r_{MRR} - r_B}{\sigma_{MRR}^2}$$

The net holding in the active part of the portfolio is obtained by summing the components of $h$ to give

$$H = \mathbf{1}^T h$$
$$= \tau \mathbf{1}^T Q^{-1}(r + mq)$$

This quantity will be zero if dollar neutrality is optimal.

Using the constant correlation model discussed previously to provide more specific results for the inverse covariance matrix, we find the net holding to be

$$H \approx \frac{\tau}{1-\rho} \sum_{i=1}^{N} (\xi_i - \xi) \frac{r_i + mq_i}{\sigma_i}$$

This holding is exactly analogous to the holdings given in Equations 16.13 and 16.20. As in those equations, the net holding will be zero when the weighted average of a particular set of risk-adjusted returns is zero. As before, the weighting is the deviation of the stability of each security's return from the average stability. In this case, however, the particular risk-adjusted return includes one part equal to the security's return and a second part equal to a scaled version of the security's correlation with the benchmark security. The scaling, $m$, depends on the return and variance of the MRR portfolio relative to the return and variance of the benchmark security.

### Optimality of Beta Neutrality with Equitization

Following the method discussed in the section on beta neutrality, and using the expressions derived previously, we find that the condition for the active portion of an equitized long/short portfolio to be optimally beta neutral is

$$\sum_{i=1}^{N} \frac{\beta_i}{\omega_i^2} (r_i + mq_i) = 0$$

Equivalently, because $q_i = \beta_i \sigma_B^2$ and $r_i = \alpha_i + \beta_i r_B$, the condition for the active portion of an equitized long/short portfolio to be optimally beta neutral is

$$\sum_{i=1}^{N} \frac{\beta_i}{\omega_i^2} \left[\alpha_i + \beta_i \left(r_B + m\sigma_B^2\right)\right] = 0$$

### Optimal Equitized Long/Short Portfolio with Specified Residual Risk

For this problem, we define an optimal portfolio to be one that maximizes expected excess return while keeping the variance of the excess return (i.e., the residual risk) equal to some specified or desired level. To find the portfolio, we form the following Lagrangian:

$$l = r_E - \frac{1}{2}\lambda\left(\sigma_E^2 - \sigma_D^2\right)$$

$$= h^T r - \frac{1}{2}\lambda\left(\mathbf{h}^T\mathbf{Q}\mathbf{h} - \sigma_D^2\right)$$

Differentiating the Lagrangian with respect to **h** and $\lambda$ and setting these derivatives equal to zero yields

$$\mathbf{r} = \lambda\mathbf{Q}\mathbf{h} \tag{16.21}$$

and

$$\mathbf{h}^T\mathbf{Q}\mathbf{h} = \sigma_D^2 \tag{16.22}$$

By solving Equation 16.21 for **h**, substituting this solution into Equation 16.22, and noting that **Q** is Hermitian,[12] we arrive at the following solution for the optimal equitized portfolio:

$$\mathbf{h} = \frac{1}{\lambda}\mathbf{Q}^{-1}\mathbf{r} \tag{16.23}$$

where

$$\frac{1}{\lambda} = \frac{\sigma_D}{\sqrt{\mathbf{r}^T\mathbf{Q}^{-1}\mathbf{r}}} \tag{16.24}$$

Although Equation 16.23 enables one to compute the optimal holdings, it does not provide much intuition about the benchmark holding.

We now derive an explicit expression for the optimal benchmark exposure from which we can draw insight. First, use the definitions of **r**, **h**, and **Q** to rewrite Equation 16.21 as the following set of equations:

$$Qh + q\hbar_B = \frac{1}{\lambda}r \tag{16.25}$$

and

$$q^T h + \sigma_B^2 \hbar_B = \frac{1}{\lambda}r_B \tag{16.26}$$

Then, solving for $h$ from Equation 16.25, substituting this solution into Equation 16.26, and rearranging gives the optimal benchmark holding as

$$h_B = 1 + \hbar_B$$

$$= 1 - \frac{\sigma_D}{\sqrt{\mathbf{r}^T \mathbf{Q}^{-1} \mathbf{r}}} \left( \frac{q^T Q^{-1} r - r_B}{\sigma_B^2 - q^T Q^{-1} q} \right) \tag{16.27}$$

To attach intuition to Equation 16.27, it is convenient to state a number of definitions and associations. Define $\theta$ to be the unit-risk-tolerance equitized (URE) portfolio that optimizes the unconstrained mean–variance criterion function $J = \mathbf{h}^T \mathbf{r} - \frac{1}{2} \mathbf{h}^T \mathbf{Q} \mathbf{h}$. This portfolio is

$$\theta = \mathbf{Q}^{-1} \mathbf{r}$$

Its expected excess return and the variance of that return are

$$r_{URE} = \mathbf{r}^T \mathbf{Q}^{-1} \mathbf{r}$$

$$= \mathbf{r}^T \mathbf{Q}^{-1} \mathbf{Q} \mathbf{Q}^{-1} \mathbf{r}$$

$$= \theta^T \mathbf{Q} \theta$$

$$= \sigma_{URE}^2 \tag{16.28}$$

This variance is the term under the radical in the denominator of Equation 16.27.

Using the definitions of $\sigma_{URE}^2$, $\sigma_{MRR}^2$, and $r_{MRR}$ in Equation 16.27 gives the following equation:

$$h_B = 1 - \frac{\sigma_D}{\sigma_{URE}} \left( \frac{r_{MRR} - r_B}{\sigma_{MRR}^2} \right) \tag{16.29}$$

from which we can make the following qualitative inferences:

- The quantity in parentheses can be regarded as the risk-adjusted excess return of the MRR portfolio, and the benchmark holding should clearly decrease as this quantity increases. The following specific comments apply:

1. Generally, $r_{MRR} > r_B$, so the expression in parentheses in Equation 16.29 is positive.

2. As the return of the MRR portfolio, $r_{MRR}$, increases or the return of the benchmark security, $r_B$, decreases, the holding in the benchmark security should decrease.

3. As the MRR, $\sigma_{MRR}^2$ increases, the holding of the benchmark should increase.

▪ The weight in the benchmark security is generally negatively related to the desired residual risk; that is, as the desired residual risk, $\sigma_D$, increases, the holding in the benchmark should decrease. If no excess variance can be tolerated, $\sigma_D = 0$ and $h_B = 1$, so the portfolio should be fully invested in the benchmark. If the investor desires a large residual risk in pursuit of high returns, the benchmark portfolio weight can decrease to less than zero and the investor should sell the benchmark security short.

▪ The ratio $\sigma_D/\sigma_{URE}$ is an important determinant of the relative size of the benchmark holding. It is the ratio of the investor's desired residual risk to the residual risk of a portfolio that a unit-risk-tolerant investor would choose. As the ratio increases, the optimal benchmark holding generally decreases.

Regarding the active portfolio, $h$, note that the preceding definitions substituted into Equation 16.25 lead to

$$h = \frac{\sigma_D}{\sigma_{URE}}(\phi + m\psi)$$

As before, the optimal active holding is a function of the URA portfolio and the MRR portfolio. As $\sigma_D/\sigma_{URE}$ approaches zero, the optimal holdings in the active portfolio tend to zero. As before, with a requirement for zero excess variance, the optimal holding is a full exposure to the benchmark.

## Optimal Equitized Long/Short Portfolio with Constrained Beta

In addition to being required to produce portfolios that maximize return while keeping residual risk at a prescribed level, managers are typically expected to keep the betas of their portfolios very close to 1. If a portfolio beta differs significantly from 1, the manager may be viewed as taking undue risk or attempting to time the market.

These requirements are captured in the following Lagrangian:

$$l = r_E + \lambda_1\left(\sigma_E^2 - \sigma_D^2\right) + \lambda_2(\beta_P - \beta_D)$$

where the λs are Lagrange multipliers and $\beta_D$ is the desired portfolio beta (usually equal to 1). This Lagrangian can be optimized with respect to the unknown parameters, but the resulting solution is algebraically untidy and does not provide much insight. Instead, an intuitive result can be achieved by examining the constraint on the portfolio's beta. Specifically, the beta of the portfolio is

$$\beta_P = \sum_{i=1}^{N} h_i \beta_i + h_B$$

and substituting this expression into the constraint on the portfolio beta gives

$$h_B = \beta_D - \sum_{i=1}^{N} h_i \beta_i = \beta_D - \beta_A \qquad (16.30)$$

where $\beta_A$ is the beta of the active portfolio.

An intuitive explanation of Equation 16.30 is that with a constraint on the portfolio's beta, the benchmark holding is simply the difference between the desired beta and the beta of the active portfolio. One extreme case corresponds to a desired portfolio beta of 1 and an active portfolio beta of zero; under these conditions, the benchmark holding must be 1. That is, the manager should be exposed to the benchmark to the full value of the capital under management.

## CONCLUSION

We derived conditions that a universe of securities must satisfy for an optimal portfolio constructed from that universe to be dollar neutral or beta neutral. Using criterion functions that are most often used in practical investment management, we found conditions under which optimal portfolios become dollar or beta neutral. Only in fairly restrictive cases will optimal portfolios satisfy these conditions. Generally, an optimal long/short portfolio will be dollar neutral if the risk-adjusted returns of its constituent securities, weighted by the deviation of those securities' returns from average, sum to zero. This condition can be used to select a universe of securities that will naturally form a dollar-neutral optimal portfolio. Analogous conditions must hold for a long/short portfolio to be beta neutral.

We next considered optimal equitized portfolios and derived conditions under which the active portion of such portfolios will be dollar neutral or beta neutral. We derived an expression for the holding of a benchmark security that sets the residual risk of an equitized long/short portfolio equal to a desired value while simultaneously maximizing the portfolio's return. We showed that the optimal holding of the benchmark security depends on such parameters as the ratio of the desired residual risk level to the residual risk level of a portfolio that a unit-risk-tolerant investor would choose and the risk-adjusted excess return of the minimum-variance active portfolio over the benchmark return. The benchmark holding should decrease in the following circumstances: when the investor's appetite for residual risk increases, when the expected return of the minimum-variance active portfolio increases, when the variance of the minimum-variance active portfolio decreases, or when the expected return of the benchmark portfolio decreases. The portfolio should be fully equitized when the investor has no appetite for residual risk or when the active portfolio has a 0 beta and the equitized portfolio is to be constrained to have a beta of 1.

Optimal portfolios demand the use of integrated optimization. In the case of active long/short portfolios, the optimization must consider all individual securities (both long and short) simultaneously, and in the case of equitized long/short portfolios, this consideration must also encompass the benchmark security.

## NOTES

1. Recent tax rulings have made long/short investing more attractive to certain classes of investors than in the past. For example, borrowing *cash* to purchase stock (i.e., debt financing through margin purchases) can give rise to a tax liability for tax-exempt investors. However, according to a January 1995 Internal Revenue Service ruling (IRS Ruling 95–8), borrowing *stocks* to initiate short sales does not constitute debt financing, so profits realized when short sales are closed out are not considered unrelated business taxable income (UBTI). Furthermore, the August 1997 rescission of the short–short rule has enabled mutual funds to implement long/short investing. Under IRS Code sec. 851(b)(3), the short–short rule had required that in order to qualify for tax pass-throughs, a mutual fund must have derived less than 30 percent of its gross income from positions held less than three months. This rule severely restricted funds' ability to sell short because profits from closing short positions were considered to be short-term gains and thus included in this provision.

2. The practice of blending separate long and short portfolios may have arisen from investors with traditional long-only managers adding a dedicated short seller either to neutralize market risk or to enhance overall portfolio return.

3. Portfolios can be constrained to be neutral with respect to any particular factor, such as interest rates. Furthermore, portfolios can be constrained to be insensitive to several factors simultaneously. We focus on dollar neutrality and beta neutrality because they appear to be of greatest interest to investors. Application of our results to other cases is straightforward.

4. As discussed in Note 1, from a taxation perspective, interest indebtedness generates UBTI for tax-exempt investors. For instance, a 200 percent long position would give rise to margin debt in the amount of 100 percent of capital, which would generate UBTI. But investing capital both 100 percent long and 100 percent short incurs no interest indebtedness while providing the maximum amount of leverage under U.S. Federal Reserve Board Regulation T. From an accounting perspective, balanced long and short positions can easily be monitored. Because true parameter values are unknown and can be estimated only with uncertainty, market neutrality is problematic. Thus, investors may be more comfortable with the accounting certainty of dollar balance. From a behavioral and mental accounting perspective, investors can easily categorize all beta-neutral long/short portfolios as market neutral and may prefer knowing that certain pockets of assets are neutralized from market movements—especially when the investor wants to separate the security selection decision and the derivative overlay decision.

5. As described by Sharpe (1991), "A 'short position' is achieved by borrowing an asset such as a share of stock, with a promise to repay in kind, typically on demand. The borrowed asset is then sold, generating a cash receipt. If the proceeds of the sale may be used for other types of investment, the overall effect is equivalent to a negative holding of [the borrowed asset]" (p. 500).

6. In general, we use lowercase subscripts to refer to a generic security and uppercase subscripts to refer to particular entities. Thus, for example, the subscript $i$ indicates that the variable under consideration is an unspecified security $i$. The subscript $B$ refers to a particular chosen benchmark, and $P$ refers to the particular portfolio.

7. Regulation T represents an institutional friction. In this analysis, it conveniently drops out of the specification of the problem, and the analysis continues to be consistent with the assumption in Note 5. For a review of the institutional aspects of the market, see Jacobs and Levy (1997).

8. It can be shown that the proportional change in utility when the portfolio is constrained to be dollar neutral is $\Delta U/U = -(1^T Q^{-1} r)^2 / [(1^T Q^{-1}])(r^T Q^{-1} r)]$. This change has a maximum value of zero (which occurs when the condition for dollar neutrality is satisfied), and is otherwise always negative.

9. Strictly, the excess return is $r_E = [(1 + r_A)/(1 + r_B)] - 1$, but the two measures of excess return are similar for small constituent returns and the expression used in the text is more convenient arithmetically.

10. Sponsors are often content with a specification of residual risk and are concerned with risk taking that exceeds the specified level or with closet indexing, where risk is below the intended level. Jacobs and Levy (1996a) showed that enhanced passive searches that consider exclusively managers having risk of a certain level or less are suboptimal.

11. Our approach is valid for the usual case in which the benchmark return cannot be expressed as a linear combination of the returns of the individual securities in the portfolio. If the benchmark return can be expressed in such a way (for example, if the portfolio consists of every single one of the securities used to construct the benchmark), then the augmented covariance matrix is singular and an analogous but slightly different approach must be taken to find the optimal portfolio.

12. A Hermitian matrix is one that is equal to its transpose (or conjugate transpose if it is complex). Because $Q$ is Hermitian, $(Q^{-1})^T Q$ is equal to the identity matrix and cancels out during derivation of Equation 16.24.

# REFERENCES

Arnott, R. D., and D. J. Leinweber. 1994. "Long–Short Strategies Reassessed." Letter to the editor. *Financial Analysts Journal*, vol. 50, no. 5 (September/ October):76–80.

Black, F. 1972. "Capital Market Equilibrium with Restricted Borrowing." *Journal of Business*, vol. 45, no. 3 (July):444–55.

Brush, J. S. 1997. "Comparisons and Combinations of Long and Long–Short Strategies." *Financial Analysts Journal*, vol. 53, no. 3 (May/June):81–89.

Elton, E. J., M. J. Gruber, and M. W. Padberg. 1976. "Simple Criteria for Optimal Portfolio Selection." *Journal of Finance*, vol. 31, no. 5 (December): 1341–57.

Jacobs, B. I., and K. N. Levy. 1995. "More on Long–Short Strategies." Letter to the editor. *Financial Analysts Journal*, vol. 51, no. 2 (March/April):88–90.

———. 1996a. "Residual Risk: How Much Is Too Much?" *Journal of Portfolio Management*, vol. 22, no. 3 (Spring):10–15.

———. 1996b. "20 Myths about Long–Short." *Financial Analysts Journal*, vol. 52, no. 5 (September/October):81–85.

———. 1997. "The Long and Short on Long–Short." *Journal of Investing*, vol. 6, no. 1 (Spring):73–86.

Kailath, T. 1980. *Linear Systems*. Englewood Cliffs, NJ: Prentice-Hall.

Levy, H., and H. Markowitz. 1979. "Approximating Expected Utility by a Function of Mean and Variance." *American Economic Review*, vol. 69, no. 3 (June):308–17.

Magnus, J. R., and H. Neudecker. 1988. *Matrix Differential Calculus with Applications in Statistics and Econometrics*. Chichester, U.K.: John Wiley & Sons.

Markowitz, H. 1952. "Portfolio Selection." *Journal of Finance*, vol. 7, no. 1 (March):77–91.

Michaud, R. O. 1993. "Are Long–Short Equity Strategies Superior?" *Financial Analysts Journal*, vol. 49, no. 6 (November/December):44–49.

Sharpe, W. F. 1991. "Capital Asset Prices with and without Negative Holdings." *Journal of Finance*, vol. 46, no. 2 (June):489–509.

———. 1994. "The Sharpe Ratio." *Journal of Portfolio Management*, vol. 21, no. 1 (Fall):49–58.

Treynor, J. L., and F. Black. 1973. "How to Use Security Analysis to Improve Portfolio Selection." *Journal of Business*, vol. 46, no. 1 (January):66–86.

von Neumann, J., and O. Morgenstern. 1944. *Theory of Games and Economic Behavior*. Princeton, NJ: Princeton University Press.

# CHAPTER 17

# The Efficiency Gains of Long/Short Investing

**Richard C. Grinold**
Managing Director
Barclays Global Investors

**Ronald N. Kahn**
Managing Director
Barclays Global Investors

*Long/short strategies have generated controversy and institutional interest for more than 10 years. We analyzed the efficiency gains of long/short investing, where we defined efficiency as the information ratio (IR) of the implemented strategy (the optimal portfolio) relative to the intrinsic IR of the alphas. The efficiency advantage of long/short investing arises from the loosening of the (surprisingly important) long-only constraint. Long/short and long-only managers need to understand the impact of this significant constraint. Long/short implementations offer the most improvement over long-only implementations when the universe of assets is large, asset volatility is low, and the strategy has high active risk. The long-only constraint induces biases (particularly toward small stocks), limits the manager's ability to act on upside information by not allowing short positions that could finance long positions, and reduces the efficiency of traditional (high-risk) long-only strategies relative to enhanced index (low-risk) long-only strategies.*

Institutions in the United States have used long/short (or market-neutral) strategies investing since at least the late 1980s. These strategies have generated controversy but, over time, have gained increasing acceptance as a worthwhile innovation. According to the *Pensions & Investments* May 18, 1998 issue, 30 investment management firms were then offering market-neutral strategies, up from the 21 firms listed one year earlier.[1] The popularity of long/short strategies arises from the distinct advantage they offer over long-only strategies: the potential for more efficient use of information, particularly (but not exclusively) downside information.

Long/short investing refers to a method for implementing active management ideas. Any strategy can be implemented as long/short or long only. Long/short investing is general. It does not refer to a particular source of information. Every long-only portfolio has an associated active portfolio with zero net investment and often zero beta. Therefore, every long-only portfolio has an associated long/short portfolio. But the long-only constraint has a significant impact on this associated long/short portfolio. Long/short strategies provide for more opportunities—particularly in the size of short positions in smaller stocks (assuming a capitalization-weighted benchmark is being used).

We present analysis of several important aspects of long/short strategies and, by implication, some important and poorly understood aspects of long-only strategies. The analysis is thus important to all managers—not solely those offering long/short strategies.

The long/short strategies we studied were defined specifically as equity market-neutral strategies. The strategies have betas of zero and equal long and short positions. Some databases group these strategies in the more general category of "hedge fund." The hedge fund category, however, can include almost any strategy that allows short positions. We focus much more specifically on risk-controlled equity strategies with zero beta and zero net investment.

## FRAMEWORK AND NOTATION

Before we can review past research and controversy, we need a basic framework for analyzing active strategies.[2] We use the framework of Grinold and Kahn (2000). We define asset residual returns, $\theta_n$, as

$$\theta_n = r_n - \beta_n r_B \tag{17.1}$$

where   $r_n$ = the asset's excess return (return above the risk-free rate)
  $\beta_n$ = the asset's beta with respect to the benchmark
  $r_B$ = the benchmark excess return

The residual return is the part of the asset's return unexplained by the benchmark return. The asset's expected residual return is

$$\alpha_n = E(\theta_n) \tag{17.2}$$

Its residual risk is

$$\omega_n = \text{std}(\theta_n) \tag{17.3}$$

where $\text{std}(\theta_n)$ is the standard deviation of the asset's residual return.

Grinold (1994) showed that $\alpha_n$ has the form:

$$\alpha_n = \omega_n I C z_n \tag{17.4}$$

where $IC$ is the information coefficient (the correlation of the forecasted $\alpha_n$ with the realization $\theta_n$) and $z_n$ is a dimensionless score with mean of 0 and standard deviation of 1 over time.

We build portfolios $\mathbf{h}_P$ to maximize utility:

$$U = \alpha_P - \lambda_R \omega_P^2$$
$$= (\mathbf{h}_P - \mathbf{h}_B)^T \alpha - \lambda_R (\mathbf{h}_P - \mathbf{h}_B)^T \mathbf{VR}(\mathbf{h}_P - \mathbf{h}_B) \tag{17.5}$$

where   $\lambda_R =$ the investor's aversion to residual risk
$\mathbf{h}_B =$ the benchmark portfolio
$\mathbf{VR} =$ the covariance matrix of the residual returns

The optimal positions are

$$(\mathbf{h}_P - \mathbf{h}_B) = \left(\frac{1}{\lambda_R}\right) \mathbf{VR}^{-1} \alpha \tag{17.6}$$

A key statistic for measuring active strategies is the IR:

$$IR = \frac{\alpha_P}{\omega_P} \tag{17.7}$$

This statistic is important because the maximum possible utility depends on the IR of the strategy:

$$U_{max} = \frac{(IR)^2}{4\lambda_R} \tag{17.8}$$

Grinold (1989) showed that the IR depends on the strategy's IC and its breadth,

$$IR = IC\sqrt{BR} \qquad (17.9)$$

where the breadth, $BR$, measures the number of independent bets per year. Basically, Equation 17.9 states that strategies earn high IRs by applying their forecasting edge many times over.

## PREVIOUS RESEARCH AND CONTROVERSY

Proponents of long/short investing offer several arguments in its favor. What was probably the original argument claims that the complete dominance of long-only investing has preserved short-side inefficiencies; hence, the short side may offer higher alphas than the long side.

The second argument depends on diversification. A long/short implementation includes, effectively, a long portfolio and a short portfolio. If each of these portfolios separately has an information ratio of $IR$ and the two portfolios are uncorrelated, then the combined strategy, simply through diversification, should exhibit an information ratio of $IR\sqrt{2}$. The problem with this argument is that it applies just as well to the active portfolio associated with any long-only portfolio. So, this argument cannot be the justification for long/short investing.

The third, and most important, argument for long/short investing is the enhanced efficiency that results from the loosening of the long-only constraint. The critical issue for long/short investing is not diversification but, rather, constraints.

These arguments in favor of long/short investing have generated considerable controversy. The first argument, short-side inefficiency, is difficult to prove and brings up the issue of the high implementation costs associated with shorting stocks. The second argument, based on diversification, is misleading, if not simply incorrect. Not surprisingly, it has attracted considerable attack. The third argument is the critical issue, and it has implications for both long/short and long-only investors.

The first criticism of long/short investing was by Michaud (1993). He criticized the diversification argument as overstated because the long and short portfolios are not uncorrelated. He pointed out that long-only investors also exploit short-side information. He questioned the cost of shorting. He also questioned whether risk-control technology was up to the task of building market-neutral portfolios.

From this opening, the debate moved to Arnott and Leinweber (1994), Michaud (1994), Jacobs and Levy (1995), and participants at a conference of the Institute for Quantitative Research in Finance (the Q-Group) on Long/Short Strategies in Equity and Fixed Income.[3] These articles and reports provide a point/counterpoint debate on several issues, especially the costs and risks of long/short strategies. Jacobs and Levy (1995) provided the first criticism of the diversification argument. Jacobs and Levy (1996), Freeman (1997), Jacobs, Levy, and Starer (1998, 1999), and Levin (1998) published further detailed analyses of aspects of long/short investing.

Other recent work has examined how long/short strategies fit into overall pension plans (Brush, 1997) and the performance of long/short managers (Kahn and Rudd, 1998).

## Surprising Impact of the Long-Only Constraint

We set out to investigate the costs imposed by the most widespread institutional constraint—the restriction on short sales—or equivalently, the benefits of easing that constraint. How does the long-only constraint restrict the investor's opportunity set? To answer that question, we ignored transaction costs and all other constraints and focused on how this constraint affects the active frontier—the trade-off between exceptional return $\alpha$ and risk $\omega$.

A very simple model will provide some insight before we tackle the more realistic case. This model consists of $N$ assets and an equal-weighted benchmark. In addition, all assets have identical residual risk $\omega$ and uncorrelated residual returns. This model opens a small window on the workings of the long-only constraint.

With these assumptions, Equation 17.5 dictates that the active position for asset $n$ is

$$h_P(n) - h_B(n) = \frac{\alpha}{2(\lambda_R)\omega^2} \qquad (17.10)$$

The overall residual (and active) risk, $\omega_p$, is

$$\omega_P^2 = \frac{1}{4(\lambda_R^2)\omega^2} \sum_{n=1}^{N} \alpha_n^2 \qquad (17.11)$$

From Equations 17.4 and 17.9, the active positions and portfolio active risk become

$$h_P(n) - h_B(n) = \frac{IRz_n}{2(\lambda_R)\omega\sqrt{N}} \tag{17.12}$$

and

$$\omega_P = \frac{IR}{2\lambda_R}\sqrt{\left(\frac{1}{N}\right)\sum_{n=1}^{N} z_n^2}$$

$$\approx \frac{IR}{2\lambda_R} \tag{17.13}$$

where the number of stocks, $N$, is used for the strategy breadth because this illustration assumes uncorrelated residual returns (and annual portfolio construction).

Equations 17.12 and 17.13 can be used to link the active position with the desired level of active risk, $\omega_p$, the stock's residual risk, $\omega$, and the square root of the number of assets to produce

$$h_P(n) - h_B(n) = \frac{\omega_P z_n}{\sqrt{N}\omega} \tag{17.14}$$

The limitation on short sales becomes binding when the active position plus the benchmark holding is negative. Surprisingly, Exhibit 17.1 shows that it also handles the positions. For an equal-weighted benchmark, this moment occurs when

$$z_n \le -\frac{\omega_P}{\sqrt{N}\omega_P} \tag{17.15}$$

Exhibit 17.1 shows this information boundary as a function of the number of stocks for various levels of active risk. Information is wasted if the Z-score falls below the minimum level. The higher the minimum level, the more information an investor is likely to leave on the table. For example, suppose we have a strategy with 500 stocks, active risk of 5 percent, and typical residual risk of 25 percent. Whenever the Z-score falls below −0.22, we will waste information. Assuming normally distributed scores, this lost opportunity will occur 41 percent of the time.

This rough analysis indicates that an aggressive strategy involving a large number of low-volatility assets should reap the largest benefits from easing

Minimum *Z*-Score

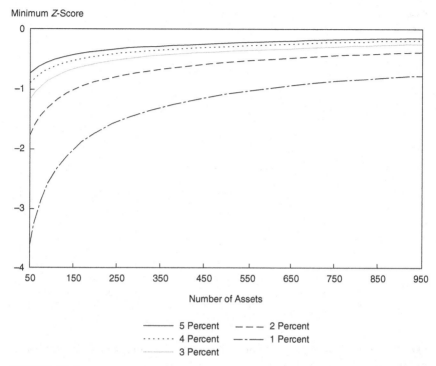

Number of Assets

——— 5 Percent    – – – 2 Percent

······· 4 Percent    —·— 1 Percent

———— 3 Percent

**EXHIBIT 17.1**   Sensitivity of Minimum Z-Score to Active Risk
*Note:* Curve labels indicate level of active risk.

the restriction on short sales. The more aggressive the strategy, the more likely it is to hit bounds. The lower the asset volatility, the larger the active positions the investor would desire. The more assets in the benchmark, the lower the average benchmark holding and the more likely that the investor will hit the boundary.

In a long-only optimization, the restriction against short selling has both a direct and an indirect effect. The direct effect precludes exploiting the most negative alphas. The indirect effect grows out of the desire to stay fully invested. In this case, the investor must finance positive active positions with negative active positions. Hence, a scarcity of negative active positions can affect the long side: Overweights require underweights. Put another way, without the long-only constraint, an investor could take larger underweights relative to the benchmark. But because underweights and overweights balance, without the long-only constraint, the investor will take larger overweights as well.

Active Holding (%)

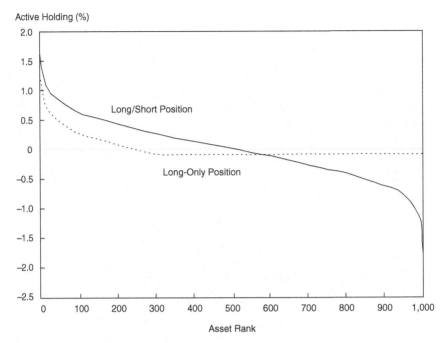

**EXHIBIT 17.2** Long–Only and Long/Short Active Positions with Assets Ordered by Highest of Lowest Alphas

A simple case will illustrate this knock-on effect. Suppose we start with an equal-weighted benchmark and generate random alphas for each of the 1,000 assets in it. Then, we construct optimal portfolios in the long-only and long/short cases. Exhibit 17.2 displays the active positions in the long/short and long-only cases with assets ordered by their alphas from highest to lowest. In the long/short case, a rough symmetry exists between the positive and negative active positions. The long-only case essentially assigns all assets after the first 300 the same negative alpha. We expected that the long-only portfolio would handle negative alphas less efficiently than the long/short portfolio, but largest positive alphas less efficiently.

## IMPORTANCE OF THE BENCHMARK DISTRIBUTION

The impact of the long-only constraint depends on the weighting of the benchmark and can be more dramatic than shown in the previous section if the benchmark is not equally weighted. To calculate the impact in realistic

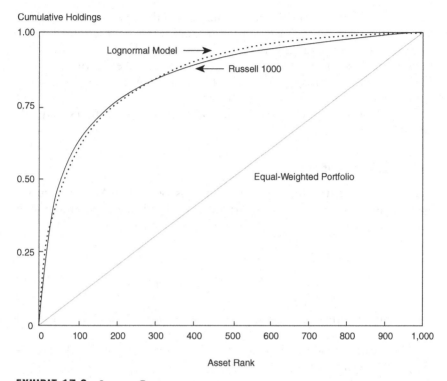

**EXHIBIT 17.3** Lorenz Curves

environments, we need a model of the capitalization distribution. And this model requires a short detour.

We use Lorenz curves to measure distributions of capitalization. By definition, to construct the curves, we

- Calculate benchmark weight as a fraction of total capitalization,
- Order the assets from highest to lowest weight, and
- Calculate the cumulative weight of the first $n$ assets as $n$ moved from largest to smallest.

Such a Lorenz curve plots the series of cumulative weights. It starts at 0 and increases in a concave fashion until it reaches 1. If all assets have the same capitalization, it will be a straight line. Exhibit 17.3 shows Lorenz curves for the Russell 1000 Index, for a model portfolio designed (as described later) to resemble the Russell 1000, and for an equal-weighted portfolio.

One summary statistic for the Lorenz curve is the Gini coefficient, which is twice the area under the curve less the area under the equal-weighted curve. Gini coefficients must range between 0 (for equal-weighted benchmarks) and 1 (for single-asset benchmarks). So, Lorenz curves can be drawn for benchmarks with any arbitrary distribution of capitalization and any distribution can be summarized with a Gini coefficient.

Further progress requires a specific form for the distribution of capitalization.

## Capitalization Model

Assume that the distribution of capitalization is lognormal. A one-parameter model that will produce such a distribution is as follows: First, order the $N$ assets by capitalization from largest ($n = 1$) to smallest ($n = N$).

Define

$$P_n \equiv 1 - \left( \frac{1}{2N} + \frac{n-1}{N} \right) \tag{17.16}$$

These values resemble probabilities: They start close to 1 and move toward 0 as capitalization decreases.

Next, calculate a normally distributed quantity $y_n$ such that the probability of observing $y_n$ is $p_n$:

$$P_n = \Phi(y_n) \tag{17.17}$$

where $\Phi(\bullet)$ is the cumulative normal distribution.

So far, linear ranks have been converted to normally distributed quantities $y_n$. The next step is to generate capitalizations:

$$\mathrm{CAP}_n = \exp(cy_n) \tag{17.18}$$

The constant $c$ can be generated to match the desired Gini coefficient or to match the Lorenz curve of the market.[4]

We used this model to match the Russell 1000 in Exhibit 17.3. Exhibit 17.4 contains similar results for several markets covered by Morgan Stanley Capital International (MSCI) as of September 1998. It also includes equal-weighted and cap-weighted examples from the hypothetical land of "Freedonia,"[5] whose market consists of 1 stock comprising 99 percent of total capitalization and 100 other stocks, each with 0.01 percent of capitalization. To analyze the loss in efficiency as a result of the long-only constraint, we used the value 1.55 for the constant $c$ because $c$ ranges from

**EXHIBIT 17.4** Modeling Capitalization Distributions, September 1998

| Index | Assets | Gini | Constant $c$ |
|---|---|---|---|
| United States | | | |
|   Russell 1000 | 1,000 | 0.71 | 1.55 |
|   MSCI | 381 | 0.66 | 1.38 |
| MSCI United Kingdom | 135 | 0.63 | 1.30 |
| MSCI Japan | 308 | 0.65 | 1.35 |
| MSCI Netherlands | 23 | 0.64 | 1.38 |
| Freedonia | | | |
|   Equal weighting | 101 | 0.00 | 0.00 |
|   Cap weighting | 101 | 0.98 | 11.15 |

1.30 to 1.60 in a large number of countries, but the MSCI indexes necessarily trim out a great many of the smaller stocks in a market.

Armed with this one-parameter model of the distribution of capitalization, we could derive our rough estimates of the potential benefits of long/short investing.

## Estimate of Long/Short Benefits

We could not derive any analytical expression for the loss in efficiency resulting from the long-only constraint because the problem contains an inequality constraint. But we could use a computer simulation to obtain a rough estimate of the magnitude of the impact.

As our previous simple analysis showed, the important variables in the simulation are the number of assets and the desired level of active risk. We considered 50, 100, 250, 500, and 1,000 assets, with desired risk levels from 1 percent to 8 percent by 1 percent increments and from those increments to 20 percent by 2 percent increments.[6]

For each of the five levels of assets and the 14 desired risk levels, we solved 900 randomly generated long-only optimizations. For each case, we assumed uncorrelated residual returns, identical residual risks of 25 percent, a full investment constraint, and an IR of 1.5. We ignored transaction costs and all other constraints. We generated alphas using

$$\alpha_n = \omega \left( \frac{IR}{\sqrt{N}} \right) z_n \qquad (17.19)$$

Forecasted Active Return (%)

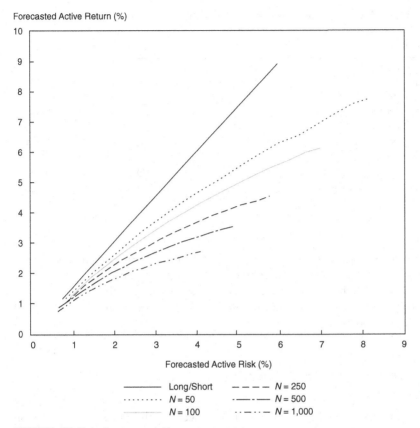

Forecasted Active Risk (%)

|                | Long/Short | — — — — $N$ = 250 |
|----------------|------------|-------------------|
| ·········      | $N$ = 50   | —·—·— $N$ = 500   |
|                | $N$ = 100  | ··—··— $N$ = 1,000 |

**EXHIBIT 17.5**   The Active Efficient Frontier

Exhibit 17.5 shows the active efficient frontier—the alpha as a function of active risk. Each observation point in Exhibit 17.5 displays the mean active return and mean active risk from a sample of 900 simulations.

The efficient frontiers in Exhibit 17.5 can be roughly estimated as[7]

$$\alpha(\omega, N) = 100IR \left\{ \frac{\left[1 + \frac{\omega}{100}\right]^{1-\gamma(N)} - 1}{1 - \gamma(N)} \right\} \tag{17.20}$$

where

$$\gamma(N) = (53 + N)^{0.57} \tag{17.21}$$

and $\alpha$ and $\omega$ are measured in percentages.

As anticipated, with the IR held constant, long-only implementations become less and less effective as the number of assets increases. Also clear is that higher desired active risk lowers efficiency. In fact, efficiency can be *defined* as the shrinkage in the IR (and IC):

$$\text{Efficiency} = \left\{ \frac{\left[ \frac{\alpha(\omega,\, N)}{\omega} \right]}{IR} \right\}$$

$$= \left( \frac{100}{\omega} \right) \left\{ \frac{\left[ 1 + \frac{\omega}{100} \right]^{1 - \gamma(N)} - 1}{1 - \gamma(N)} \right\} \qquad (17.22)$$

Exhibit 17.6 illustrates the dependency of efficiency on risk and number of assets. For typical U.S. equity strategies—500 assets and 4.5 percent risk—the efficiency is 49 percent according to Equation 17.22, which agrees with Exhibit 17.6. The long-only constraint has enormous impact: It cuts IRs for typical strategies in half![8]

Equation 17.22 also allows quantification of the appeal of enhanced index (i.e., low-active-risk) strategies. The efficiency is 71 percent for a long-only strategy involving 500 assets with only 2 percent active risk. At this low level of risk, an investor loses only 29 percent of the original IR.

At high levels of active risk, long/short implementations can have a significant advantage over long-only implementations. At low levels of active risk, this advantage disappears. And, given the higher implementation costs of long/short strategies (e.g., the uptick rule, costs of borrowing), at low levels of active risk, long-only implementations may offer an advantage.

With a large number of assets and the long-only constraint, achieving high levels of active risk is difficult. From Equation 17.20, an empirical analog of Equation 17.13 can be derived (see Appendix A for details):

$$\lambda_R = \frac{IR}{2\omega \left( 1 + \frac{\omega}{100} \right)^{\gamma}} \qquad (17.23)$$

To corroborate the validity of our results on efficiency, we analyzed the sensitivities of the empirical results to the assumptions used for the efficient frontiers in Exhibits 17.5 and 17.6: an inherent IR of 1.5; a lognormal size distribution constant, $c$, of 1.55; and identical and uncorrelated residual risks of 25 percent. Changing the inherent IR did not affect our conclusions at all. As Equation 20 implies, the efficient frontier simply scales with the IR.

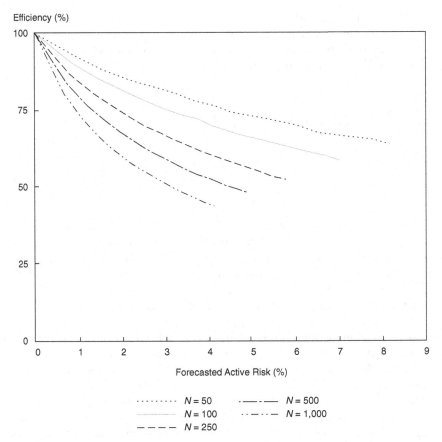

**EXHIBIT 17.6**   Efficiency as a Function of Risk and Number of Assets

Changing the lognormal size distribution constant through the range from 1.2 to 1.6, which is a wider range than we observed in examining several markets, had a minor impact. Lower coefficients were found to be closer to equal weighting, so the long-only constraint was less restrictive in those cases. At 4.5 percent active risk and 500 assets, however, as we varied this coefficient, the efficiency ranged only from 0.49 to 0.51.

Exhibit 17.7 shows how our results changed with changing asset residual risk. Our base-case assumption of 25 percent asset residual risk is very close to the median U.S. equity residual risk, but an investor may be investing in a particular universe of assets with higher or lower average residual risk. As asset residual risk increases, the investor can achieve more risk with

Efficiency (%)

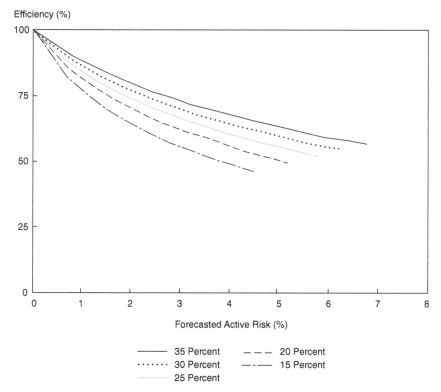

Forecasted Active Risk (%)

——— 35 Percent   – – – 20 Percent
······· 30 Percent   —·— 15 Percent
——— 25 Percent

**EXHIBIT 17.7** Sensitivity of Efficiency to Asset Residual Risk (250 Assets)

smaller active positions, thus making the long-only constraint less binding. At the extremely low level of 15 percent, the long-only constraint has a considerable impact. In the (more reasonable) range of 20 to 35 percent, the efficiency at 4.5 percent active risk and 250 assets ranges from 65 to 54 percent.

We also analyzed the assumption that every asset has equal residual risk. Given an average residual risk of 25 percent and assuming 500 assets, we analyzed possible correlations between size (as measured by the log of capitalization) and the log of residual risk. We expected a negative correlation because larger stocks tend to exhibit lower residual risks. Examination of large U.S. equities (the Barra HICAP universe of roughly the largest 1,200 stocks) shows that the correlation between cap size and residual risk has varied from roughly −0.51 to −0.57 in the past 25 years. This negative correlation improves efficiency in general because it implies that smaller-cap

Efficiency (%)

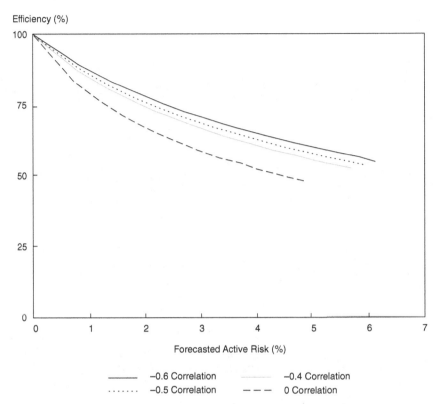

Forecasted Active Risk (%)

——— −0.6 Correlation ········· −0.4 Correlation
········· −0.5 Correlation − − − 0 Correlation

**EXHIBIT 17.8** Sensitivity of Efficiency to Correlations between Size and Residual Risk (500 Assets; 25 Percent Average Residual Risk)
*Note:* Correlations measured for log of capitalization and log of residual risk.

stocks (for which the long-only constraint is most binding) are riskier than larger-cap stocks, which leads to smaller desired active positions in small-cap stocks). Exhibit 17.8 shows the frontier as we varied that correlation from 0 to −0.6. With a correlation of 0, we found an efficiency of 49 percent at 4.5 percent active risk. With a correlation of −0.6, the situation improved to an efficiency of 0.63.

Finally, Exhibit 17.9 displays the size bias that we anticipated for various correlations between size and residual risk. The correlation did not significantly change the result. We measured size as log of capitalization, standardized to a mean of 0 and standard deviation of 1. So, an active

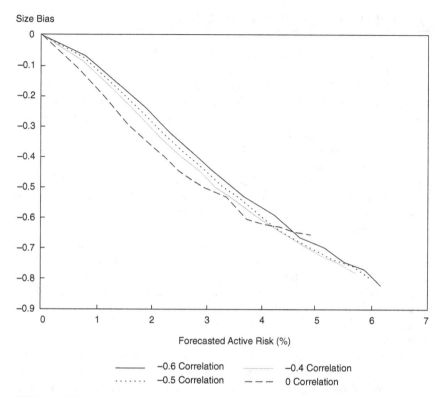

**EXHIBIT 17.9** Sensitivity of Size Bias to Correlations between Size and Residual Risk (500 Stocks)
*Note:* Correlations measured for log of capitalization and log of residual risk.

size exposure of −0.3 means that the active portfolio had an average size exposure 0.3 standard deviations below the benchmark.

These size biases are significant. Exhibit 17.9 implies that a typical manager following 500 stocks and targeting 4.5 percent risk will have a size exposure of −0.65.[9] In the United States, from October 1997 through September 1998, the size factor in the Barra U.S. equity model exhibited a return of 1.5 percent: Large stocks outperformed small stocks. This set of circumstances would have generated a 98 basis point (bp) loss simply as a result of this incidental size bet. From September 1988 through September 1998, the same size factor experienced a cumulative gain of 361 bps, generating a loss of 235 bps over that 10-year period.

## THE APPEAL OF LONG/SHORT INVESTING

Who should offer long/short strategies? Who should invest in them? Clearly, long/short strategies are a pure active management bet. The consensus expected return to long/short strategies is zero because the strategies have betas of zero. Put another way, the consensus investor does not invest in long/short strategies. Therefore, the most skillful active managers should offer long/short strategies: Such strategies allow them the freedom to implement their superior information most efficiently.

Long/short strategies offer no way to hide behind a benchmark. A long-only manager delivering 15 percent while the benchmark is delivering 20 percent is arguably in a better position than a long/short manager losing 5 percent. Although not an intrinsic benefit of long-only strategies, this aspect can be a practical benefit for investment managers.

Long/short strategies do offer investment managers the freedom to trade *only* on their superior information. They can build a long/short market-neutral portfolio by using only utility stocks if this is how they can add value. They have no need to buy stocks just because the stocks are members of the benchmark. Both the long and the short sides of the portfolio may have large active risk relative to the S&P 500 Index, just not to each other.

Long/short strategies offer the most benefit to those investors who are best able to identify skillful managers. Long/short strategies are quite appealing because of the (engineered) low correlations such strategies have with equity market benchmarks. Long/short strategies can in this way successfully compete against bonds.

Long/short investing also offers the appeal of easy alpha portability. Futures contracts can move active return from one benchmark to another. If an investor starts with a strategy managed relative to the S&P 500 and sells S&P 500 futures and buys Financial Times Stock Exchange (FTSE) 100 futures, the investor will transfer the alpha to the FTSE 100. In a conventional long-only strategy, this transfer requires an extra effort. It is not the natural thing to do. With a long/short strategy, the investor starts with the pure active return and must choose a benchmark. The potential for transfer is thrust upon the investor. So, long/short strategies place the notion of a portable alpha in center stage.

Finally, long/short investing offers the possibility of more-targeted active management fees than does traditional investing. Long-only portfolios largely contain the benchmark stocks. Long-only investors pay active fees for that passive core.[10] Long/short investors pay explicitly for the active holdings.

## EMPIRICAL OBSERVATIONS

We have only preliminary observations about long/short strategies. The strategies do not have a sufficiently long track record to allow us to definitively compare their performance with the performance of long-only strategies. But understanding can begin with long/short strategies' risk profile and initial performance record.

For this purpose, we studied the performance of 14 U.S. long/short strategies with histories of varying lengths (but all in the 1990s) ending in March 1998.[11] These 14 strategies are those of large, sophisticated quantitative managers. Most of these managers are Barra clients. Exhibit 17.10 shows the relevant observations. (Keep in mind the small and potentially nonrepresentative sample behind these data.)

First, note that the risk levels shown for these strategies do not differ substantially from the typical active risk levels of about 4.5 percent.[12] So, at least based on these 14 sophisticated implementations, long/short strategies do not exhibit substantially higher levels of risk than long-only strategies.

Second, according to Exhibit 17.10, these strategies achieved market neutrality. Their realized betas and market correlations are close to zero. In fact, the highest observed correlations with the S&P 500 correspond to managers with the shortest track records. No statistical evidence indicates that any of these strategies had true betas different from zero, and the realized numbers are all quite small. This (admittedly limited) sample thus refutes the argument that achieving market neutrality is difficult.

Third, at least in this historical period, these long/short strategies *as a group* provided remarkable performance. Although the performance results of 14 strategies over a particular market period do not prove that long/short implementations boost IRs,[13] the results do help explain the increasing popularity of these strategies.

**EXHIBIT 17.10** Performance of 14 Long/Short Strategies, 1990s

| Percentile | History (months) | Volatility | Beta | S&P 500 Correlation | Information Ratio |
|---|---|---|---|---|---|
| 90 | 96 | 10.90% | 0.10 | 0.23 | 1.45 |
| 75 | 86 | 6.22 | 0.06 | 0.15 | 1.23 |
| 50 | 72 | 5.50 | 0.02 | 0.04 | 1.00 |
| 25 | 50 | 4.12 | −0.03 | −0.07 | 0.69 |
| 10 | 28 | 3.62 | −0.16 | −0.20 | 0.44 |

## SUMMARY

Long/short investing is an increasingly popular approach to implementing active strategies. Long/short strategies offer the potential to implement superior information more efficiently than long-only strategies. Because the long-only constraint is an inequality constraint and because its impact depends on the distribution of benchmark holdings, we could not derive many detailed analytical results on exact differences in efficiency. But both simple models and detailed simulations showed that the benefits of long/short investing can be significant, particularly when the universe of assets is large, asset volatility is low, and the strategy has high active risk.

From the opposite perspective, long-only managers should understand the surprising and significant impact of the long-only constraint on their portfolios. Among the surprises: This constraint induces a significant negative size bias; it affects active long as well as short positions; and enhanced index (low-risk) long-only strategies are more efficient than traditional (high-risk) long-only strategies.

Empirical observations on long/short investing are preliminary but should certainly inspire further interest and investigation.

## ACKNOWLEDGMENTS

We thank Naozer Dadachanji, Uzi Levin, Bruce Jacobs, and Bill Jacques for helpful comments and suggestions. Andrew Rudd contributed to the section on the appeal of long/short investing.

## APPENDIX A. FURTHER EXPLANATIONS

Here, we present details about four items from the "Framework and Notation" section, especially underlying validation for Equations 17.4, 17.5, 17.8, and 17.9, and details of the derivation of Equation 17.23, the risk aversion required to achieve a given level of risk.[14]

### General Form of an Alpha (Equation 17.5)

We define a stock's alpha as its expected residual return, $E(\theta)$, conditional on information, which we represent as a signal, $g$, so that

$$\alpha = E(\theta|g) \qquad (17.A1)$$

The best linear unbiased estimate of $\theta$ conditional on $g$ is

$$E(\theta|g) = E(\theta) + \text{cov}(\theta, g)\text{var}^{-1}(g)[g - E(g)] \qquad (17.A2)$$

Assuming the unconditional expected residual return, $E(\theta)$, is zero, we can write Equation 17.A1 as the desired result,

$$\alpha = \omega(IC)z \qquad (17.A3)$$

where the information coefficient is

$$IC \equiv \text{corr}(\theta, g) \qquad (17.A4)$$

the residual risk is

$$\omega \equiv \text{std}(\theta) \qquad (17.A5)$$

and the Z-score is

$$Z \equiv \frac{g - E(g)}{\text{std}(g)} \qquad (17.A6)$$

## Utility Function (Equation 17.5)

Start with a general mean–variance utility function of the form,

$$U = f_P - \lambda\sigma_P^2 \qquad (17.A7)$$

where $f_P$ is the expected excess (above the risk-free) return and $\rho_P$ is the standard deviation of that return.

This form of utility makes no reference to the benchmark. But we can express the excess return as a component driven by the benchmark and an independent component. When we do so, and then substitute these expressions into Equation 17.A7 and delete terms that should be zero or are irrelevant to utility maximization (e.g., are constants), the utility simplifies to

$$U = \alpha_P - \lambda\omega_P^2 + \left(\beta_{PA}\Delta f_B - \lambda\beta_{PA}^2\sigma_B^2\right) \qquad (17.A8)$$

where  $\beta_{PA} =$ the portfolio's active beta $(\beta_P - 1)$
$\lambda =$ the investor's risk aversion (trade-off between expected return and risk)
$\Delta f_B =$ the exceptional expected return to the benchmark

The benchmark has zero alpha by definition. For a portfolio that optimizes this utility, the first two terms on the right-hand side of Equation 17.A8 determine stock selection and the last two terms determine only the overall portfolio beta in response to any expected exceptional benchmark return. For purposes of our study, we assumed no benchmark timing. Therefore, we set $\Delta f_B$ and $\Delta_{PA}$ to zero and were left with the utility function of Equation 17.5.

When we optimize this resulting utility function, we still face a budget constraint—for example, the full investment constraint, $h_P e = 1$, where $h_P$ is the portfolio and e is a vector of 1. Adding this constraint and assuming a fully invested benchmark leads to optimal holdings,

$$(\mathbf{h}_P - \mathbf{h}_B) = \left(\frac{1}{2\lambda}\right) \left[ \mathbf{VR}^{-1}\alpha - \left(\frac{\alpha^T \mathbf{VR}^{-1}\mathbf{e}}{\mathbf{e}^T \mathbf{VR}^{-1}\mathbf{e}}\right) \mathbf{VR}^{-1}\mathbf{e} \right] \qquad (17.A9)$$

where $\mathbf{h}_B$ is the benchmark portfolio and $\mathbf{VR}$ is the covariance matrix of the residual returns.

To reach Equation 17.6, we made the reasonable assumption that our alphas were cash neutral:

$$\alpha^T \mathbf{VR}^{-1}\mathbf{e} = 0 \qquad (17.A10)$$

For the simple model discussed in the text (in which residual returns were independent and of equal volatility), Equation 17.A10 requires that the alphas have a mean of zero.

### Importance of the Information Ratio (Equation 17.8)

Substituting the information ratio, $IR$, into our utility function produces

$$U = IR\omega_P - \lambda\omega_P^2 \qquad (17.A11)$$

Optimizing Equation 17.A11 as a function of risk leads to the first-order condition,

$$IR - 2\lambda\omega_P^* = 0 \qquad (17.A12)$$

with

$$U(\omega_p^*) = \frac{(IR)^2}{4\lambda}$$ (17.A13)

where $\omega^* p$ is the optimal level of risk. Equation 17.A13 is Equation 17.8 in the text.

### Information Ratios, Skill, and Breadth (Equation 17.9)

The mathematical derivation of Equation 17.9 is too long to include here, but we can summarize the argument in spirit. It begins with the alpha forecasts and builds an optimal portfolio. It then analyzes the expected IR of that optimal portfolio, ultimately expressing it on the basis of the correlations between alpha forecasts and subsequent realized returns (the IC) and on the number of independent forecasts (typically, the number of stocks in the portfolio). Intuitively, the IR measures expected return per unit of risk, the IC is a component of the expected return, and the breadth is a measure of potential risk diversification.

### Risk Aversion and Target Risk Level (Equation 17.23)

Generalizing on Equation 17.A11, we express utility in terms of risk as

$$U = \alpha(\omega) - \lambda_R \omega^2$$ (17.A14)

Using Equation 20, Equation 17.A14 becomes

$$U = 100IR \left\{ \frac{\left[1 + \frac{\omega}{100}\right]^{1-\gamma(N)} - 1}{1 - \gamma(N)} \right\} - \lambda_R \omega^2$$ (17.A15)

We solve for the optimal level of risk by taking the derivative of $U$ with respect to $\omega$ and setting the result equal to zero,

$$IR \left[1 + \frac{\omega}{100}\right]^{-\gamma(N)} = 2\lambda_R \omega$$ (17.A16)

which leads directly to Equation 17.23.

# NOTES

1. See various articles on market-neutral strategies in the May 12, 1997, and May 18, 1998, issues of *Pensions & Investments*.
2. Appendix A expands on several points in this section, in particular, the details behind Equations 17.4, 17.5, 17.8, and 17.9.
3. Refer to Dadachanji (1995) and Jacobs (1997).
4. As an alternative, set the constant $c$ to the standard deviation of the log of the capitalization of all the stocks. The two criteria mentioned in the text place greater emphasis on fitting the larger-cap stocks.
5. Freedonia appeared in the 1933 Marx Brothers movie, *Duck Soup*. During a 1994 Balkan eruption, when asked if the United States should intervene in Freedonia, several U.S. congressmen laughed, several stated that it would require further study, and several more were in favor of intervention if Freedonia continued its policy of ethnic cleansing.
6. We used Equation 17.13 to convert desired risk levels to risk aversions. We required extremely high levels of desired risk because the long-only constraint severely hampered our ability to take risk.
7. Equations 17.20 and 17.21 are estimates based on computer simulations. You may obtain slightly different results if you repeat the experiment yourself.
8. This is a best-case analysis assuming we have efficiently used our information. Poor portfolio construction will only reduce the efficiency.
9. Note that this analysis did not include size as a risk factor. Adding that would mitigate (but not eliminate) the bias.
10. See Freeman.
11. See Kahn and Rudd.
12. See Grinold and Kahn (2000) for empirical observations on long-only risk levels. The standard error of the mean risk level for these long/short strategies is 0.64 percent So, although the medians displayed here exceed 4.5 percent, the difference is not significant at the 95 percent confidence level.
13. In fact, several of these managers struggled in 1999.
14. Even this technical appendix is insufficient to thoroughly cover the items in "Framework and Notation." Readers who would like the full treatment should refer to Chapters 4, 5, 6, and 10 of Grinold and Kahn (2000).

# REFERENCES

Arnott, R. D., and D. J. Leinweber. 1994. "Long–Short Strategies Reassessed." *Financial Analysts Journal*, vol. 50, no. 5 (September/October):76–78.
Brush, J. S. 1997. "Comparisons and Combinations of Long and Long–Short Strategies." *Financial Analysts Journal*, vol. 53, no. 3 (May/June):81–89.
Dadachanji, N. 1995. "Market Neutral Long–Short Strategies: The Perception versus the Reality." Presentation at the October 1995 Q-Group Conference, La Quinta, CA.

Freeman, J. D. 1997. "Investment Deadweight and the Advantages of Long–Short Portfolio Management." *VBA Journal* (September):11–14.

Grinold, R. C. 1989. "The Fundamental Law of Active Management." *Journal of Portfolio Management*, vol. 15, no. 3 (Spring):30–37.

———. 1994. "Alpha Is Volatility Times IC Times Score, or Real Alphas Don't Get Eaten." *Journal of Portfolio Management*, vol. 20, no. 4 (Summer):9–16.

Grinold, R. C., and R. N. Kahn. 2000. *Active Portfolio Management*. 2nd ed. New York: McGraw-Hill.

Jacobs, B. I. 1997. "The Long and Short on Long–Short." *Journal of Investing*, vol. 6, no. 1 (Spring):73–86. (Also presented at the October 1995 Q-Group Conference, La Quinta, CA.)

———. 1998. "Controlled Risk Strategies." In *Alternative Investing*. Charlottesville, VA: AIMR.

Jacobs, B. I., and K. N. Levy. 1995. "More on Long–Short Strategies." *Financial Analysts Journal*, vol. 51, no. 2 (March/April):88–90.

———. 1996. "20 Myths about Long–Short." *Financial Analysts Journal*, vol. 52, no. 5 (September/October):81–85.

Jacobs, B. I., K. N. Levy, and D. Starer. 1998. "On the Optimality of Long–Short Strategies." *Financial Analysts Journal*, vol. 54, no. 2 (March/April):40–51.

———. 1999. "Long–Short Portfolio Management: An Integrated Approach." *Journal of Portfolio Management*, vol. 25, no. 2 (Winter):23–32.

Kahn, R. N., and A. Rudd. 1998. "What's the Market for Market Neutral?" *Barra Preprint* (June).

Levin, A. 1998. "Long–Short Investing—Who, Why, and How." In *Enhanced Index Strategies for the Multi-Manager Portfolio*. Edited by Brian Bruce. New York: Institutional Investor.

Michaud, R. O. 1993. "Are Long–Short Equity Strategies Superior?" *Financial Analysts Journal*, vol. 49, no. 6 (November/December):44–49. (Also presented at the October 1995 Q-Group Conference, La Quinta, CA.)

———. 1994. "Reply to Arnott and Leinweber." *Financial Analysts Journal*, vol. 50, no. 5 (September/October):78–80.

# CHAPTER 18

# Toward More Information-Efficient Portfolios

## Relaxing the Long-Only Constraint

**Roger G. Clarke**
Chairman
Analytic Investors

**Harindra de Silva**
President
Analytic Investors

**Steven Sapra**
Portfolio Manager
Analytic Investors

In an environment of lower-than-normal systematic market returns, many investors are trying to improve their returns from active management (see, e.g., Thomas, 2000). Some have turned to absolute return strategies to enhance portfolio returns. Market-neutral managers focus on the delivery of pure alpha by relaxing portfolio constraints in order to put information to work more efficiently in their portfolios. Whereas market-neutral strategies may not be suitable for all investors, the ability to take even modest short positions is an important structural advantage that can be used to improve the information efficiency of traditional long-only portfolios.

This article originally appeared in the Fall 2004 issue of *The Journal of Portfolio Management*, published by Institutional Investor, Inc.

Thus, investors do not need to relax the long-only constraint completely in order to reap substantial benefits. Relaxing the constraint by just 10 percent to 20 percent can be advantageous.

Grinold and Kahn (2000), Jacobs, Levy, and Starer (1998), and Brush (1997) describe the impact of the long-only constraint in structuring portfolios and the loss of efficiency that can occur. We use an empirical analysis to illustrate the extent of this efficiency loss.

We demonstrate the impact of various constraints, showing that the long-only constraint is often the most significant in terms of information loss. Lifting this constraint is critical to improving information transfer from the security valuation model to active portfolio weights. Finally, we show that relaxing this constraint even modestly can lead to a significant improvement in information efficiency.

## IMPACT OF CONSTRAINTS

When investors have valuable information, portfolio constraints usually limit the investor's ability to fully capitalize on the value of that information. Some limitations have more impact than others. To illustrate the impact of various constraints, we construct a series of optimized portfolios with *ex ante* annualized tracking error (TE) of 4 percent relative to the S&P 500.[1]

The first optimized portfolio, which we call the *fully constrained* portfolio, is subject to all these constraints relative to the S&P 500:

- Market capitalization neutrality,
- Industry neutrality,
- Sector neutrality,
- ±3% maximum position limits relative to index weights,
- No short sales.

To ensure full market exposure, we also constrain the portfolio to have a beta of 1 relative to the S&P 500 benchmark. This beta-neutrality constraint is maintained for every optimization. We maximize a value-based expected return signal, subject to all these constraints. We then remove each constraint one-by-one to determine the impact of each.[2]

The impact is represented by the change in the portfolio transfer coefficient (TC) developed by Clarke, de Silva, and Thorley (2002) as an extension of the fundamental law of active management articulated by Grinold (1989). The TC is calculated as the correlation between the risk-adjusted expected returns and the risk-weighted active exposures of securities in the portfolio.

It measures the degree of information transfer from a security-ranking signal into active portfolio weights for each security. A higher TC implies a more efficiently constructed portfolio, all these equal.[3]

The TC captures the effect of portfolio constraints on the expected information ratio (IR) of a portfolio strategy. The equation shows the relationships among the portfolio's information coefficient (IC), defined as the expected correlation between predicted and actual returns, the TC, and the number of independent securities to choose from (N) as

$$IR = TC \; IC \; \sqrt{N}$$

The fundamental law indicates that the expected IR is a product of how effectively the investor's information is transferred into portfolio weights, how good the information is, and how widely it can be applied.

A TC of 1.0 would characterize a portfolio whose risk-adjusted active weights are perfectly proportional to their risk-adjusted expected returns. This would give the maximum expected IR. Less informationally efficient portfolios would have a TC of less than 1.0. The change in TC measures the gain in information transfer from removing a particular constraint.

Exhibit 18.1 shows the TCs and corresponding TC gain for each optimization. The fully constrained portfolio shows a TC of only 0.332, implying that only 3 percent of the information in security rankings is transferred into active portfolio positions.

The greatest change in the TC comes from elimination of the long-only constraint. Removing this constraint results in a 108 percent improvement in information transfer. The second most significant constraint is the market capitalization neutrality constraint. Eliminating this constraint increases the TC by 4 percent.

**EXHIBIT 18.1** Change in TC by Removing Constraints

| | All Constraints | Constraint Removed | | | | |
|---|---|---|---|---|---|---|
| | | Industry | Sector | PosLimit | Mcap | Long-Only |
| TC | 0.332 | 0.347 | 0.346 | 0.298 | 0.471 | 0.678 |
| TC Percentage Change | | 8.4% | 7.9% | −6.5% | 45.6% | 108.1% |

These results are typical of the impact of constraints when portfolios are constructed relative to a concentrated capitalization-weighted benchmark. In the case of the long-only constraint, because most of the names in the benchmark represent a very small percentage holding, a manager has limited ability to underweight most securities. The market cap constraint forces the manager to hold a balanced proportion of the larger and smaller names in the benchmark, thereby producing a significant amount of dead weight in the portfolio.

Although the sector and industry constraints appear to have a rather small impact individually, when both sector and industry constraints are removed at the same time, the TC improvement is more significant.[4]

Exhibit 18.2 shows the scatterplots of active weights and standardized expected returns from each optimization. These scatterplots show that eliminating the long-only constraint and to a lesser extent the market cap constraint leads to more balanced portfolio active weights, resulting in a more efficient use of the investor's stock-ranking information.

## IMPROVING INFORMATION EFFICIENCY BY ALLOWING SHORT SALES

The stocks with the greatest weightings in a capitalization-weighted index provide substantial opportunity for underweighting in a long-only portfolio. The problem is that most of the stocks in a capitalization-weighted index represent such small weights that there is little opportunity to underweight them. The inability to short stocks that are deemed unattractive significantly restricts the investment manager's ability to take full advantage of the value of the information in a stock-ranking system.

Although the S&P 500 index includes 500 names, two-thirds of its weight is concentrated in the top 100. In fact, the *effective number of names* in the S&P 500 is only 114.[5]

Exhibit 18.3 shows the cumulative weights of the top 20 names in the S&P 500 benchmark.

It is not a coincidence that the greatest improvement in the TC occurs when we remove constraints that are directly related to the cap-weighted nature of the S&P 500 benchmark. The 20 stocks in the largest third of the index capitalization have an average weight of 1.7 percent. Moving beyond the 20 largest stocks to the second third, the average weight for the next 76 stocks drops to 0.4 percent. Finally, the average weight drops to a mere 0.1 percent for the 404 stocks in the final third. The net effect of these low average weights for the 480 stocks below the largest 20 in the index is that

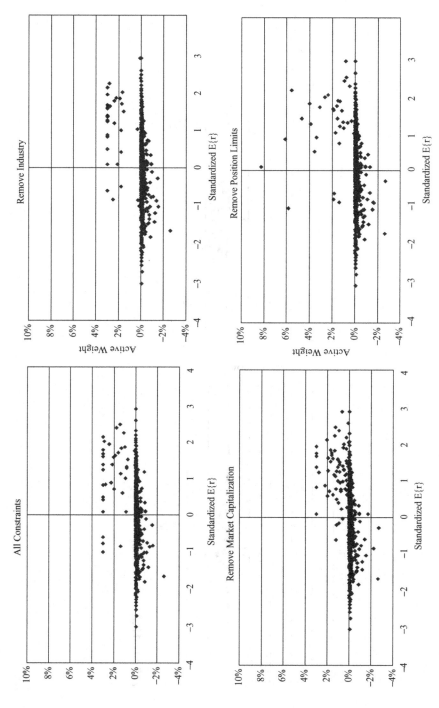

**EXHIBIT 18.2**   Active Portfolio Weights versus Expected Returns

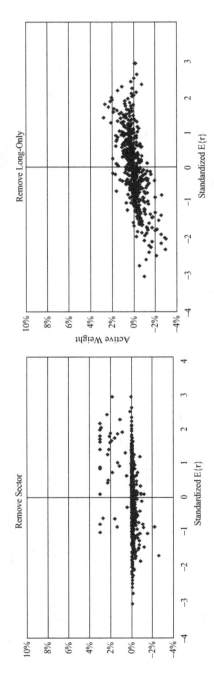

**EXHIBIT 18.2** *(Continued)*

**EXHIBIT 18.3** Largest Capitalization Stocks in S&P 500 Index as of Year-End 2003

| Name | Weight | Cumulative Weight |
|------|--------|-------------------|
| General Electric Co | 3.0% | 3.0% |
| Microsoft Corp | 2.6% | 5.6% |
| Exxon Mobil Corp | 2.6% | 8.2% |
| Pfizer Inc | 2.6% | 10.8% |
| Citigroup Inc | 2.5% | 13.3% |
| Wal-Mart Stores Inc | 2.4% | 15.7% |
| American International Group Inc | 1.9% | 17.5% |
| Intel Corp | 1.7% | 19.3% |
| Cisco Sys Inc | 1.6% | 20.8% |
| Bank of America Corp | 1.6% | 22.4% |
| IBM | 1.5% | 23.9% |
| Johnson & Johnson | 1.4% | 25.3% |
| Procter & Gamble Co | 1.3% | 26.6% |
| Coca-Cola Co | 1.2% | 27.8% |
| Altria Group Inc | 1.1% | 28.9% |
| Verizon Communications | 1.0% | 29.8% |
| Merck & Co Inc | 0.9% | 30.8% |
| Wells Fargo & Co | 0.9% | 31.7% |
| Chevron Texaco Corp | 0.9% | 32.6% |
| Pepsico Inc | 0.9% | 33.5% |
| | **Average Weight** | **Index Weight** |
| Top 20 Names | 1.7% | 33.5% |
| Next 76 Names | 0.4 | 33.1 |
| Bottom 404 Names | 0.1 | 33.4 |

managers have little room to underweight any individual stock (0.1% on average for 404 stocks) when they deem the stock to be unattractive.

Another way to visualize this limitation is to realize that if two stocks are deemed to be equally unattractive (i.e., have the same expected relative return), and one falls in the first group (1.7% index weight) and the other in the third group (0.1% index weight), a manager can underweight the larger-cap stock by on average 17 times the permitted underweight of the smaller stock.

Lorenz curves show the dramatic difference between a traditional capitalization-weighted benchmark such as the S&P 500 and an equally weighted benchmark. The curved line in Exhibit 18.4 represents the

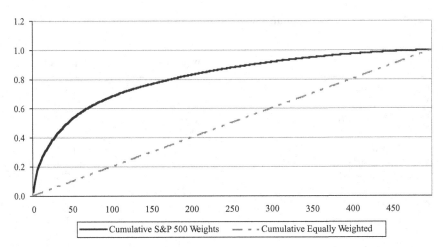

**EXHIBIT 18.4** Cumulative Weights for Equally Weighted Portfolio and S&P 500 Index

cumulative benchmark weight of the S&P 500. The straight line represents a 500-stock equally weighted benchmark.

The top-heavy nature of cap-weighted benchmarks makes it hard to exploit negative-alpha information. Consequently, the improvement in information transfer from relaxation of the long-only constraint is most likely to occur from active positions in the stocks with lower benchmark weights.

## OPTIMAL LEVEL OF SHORTING

Relaxing the long-only constraint can have a dramatic benefit in improving the portfolio's TC. The majority of the benefit occurs because a portfolio manager can take more active positions in the names that constitute lower weights in the benchmark.

We next examine the optimal amount of shorting for a given level of TE in order to maximize the TC and subsequently maximize the expected IR.

Increasing the level of TE but not allowing the portfolio to take any short positions naturally forces the portfolio manager to take greater active weights in the larger-cap names. Thus, active decisions driven by the desire for higher TE force more activity into capitalization segments of the portfolio where it may or may not be most efficiently used.

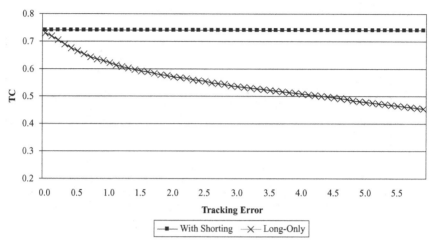

**EXHIBIT 18.5** TC versus TE with and without Long-Only Constraints

We run two series of optimizations to show the impact of the long-only constraint on information transfer. The first set of optimizations does not allow for short positions. Although we impose a beta = 1.0 constraint to ensure full-market exposure, we do not impose any additional constraints other than the targeted TE. Running this same optimization for successively higher levels of *ex ante* active risk traces out a TC curve. The second set of optimizations allows for short positions, but we do not restrict the degree of shorting.

The lines in Exhibit 18.5 show the relationship between active risk and TC for these two sets of optimizations.

In the presence of a long-only constraint, the TC declines as the TE increases. This is a natural consequence of holding more concentrated port-folios in order to get greater TE. As the TE rises, the effect of the long-only constraint intensifies, thus resulting in a lower TC.

For the optimization that does not constrain the level of short sales, we see that the TC stays essentially constant at every level of TE. The optimizer constructs the best TC portfolio possible, and then scales the size of positions to achieve the desired TE. Naturally, the ability to maintain a constant (and very high) TC leads to portfolios that dominate the long-only portfolio at each comparable level of TE.

The reason that the portfolio that allows for short sales can maintain a constant TC throughout the TE range is that the level of short sales is

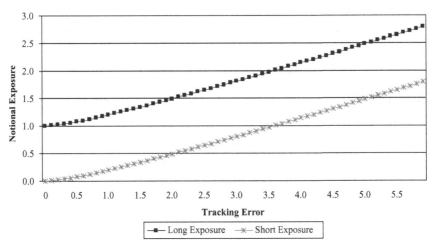

**EXHIBIT 18.6** Long/Short Level that Optimizes IR

*endogenously* determined. The degree of short sales is a consequence of the targeted TE rather than an explicit constraint.

Exhibit 18.6 shows the endogenously determined long/short level in the optimized portfolio in Exhibit 18.5. Because the degree of shorting is allowed to vary and is not a hard constraint, it does not affect the portfolio's TC.

Notice that the optimal level of shorting for a 2 percent TE portfolio in this example would require a structure of approximately 150 percent long exposure and 50 percent short exposure (+150/−50). Higher levels of shorting are required to maintain the maximum TC for higher levels of TE. Very little shorting is required to maintain the TC at low TE levels, because the long-only constraint is a less serious limitation.

Grinold and Kahn (2000) confirmed this effect in earlier work. They note that the more aggressive a given strategy (i.e., the higher the desired level of TE), the more likely that the long-only constraint would be binding. Thus, the long-only constraint will have a greater impact on information transfer for more aggressive portfolios. Hence, we need more shorting as we increase the desired level of active risk.

Because the long-only TC line declines in Exhibit 18.5 as TE increases, the expected IR will drop as well. The constant TC line for the unconstrained case implies that the IR is also constant across the TE continuum. This is easily seen from the relationships in the extended fundamental law derived by Clarke, de Silva, and Thorley (2002), as in the equation $IR = TC \, IC \, \sqrt{N}$. Both the IC and breadth are constant for the portfolio, making the IR directly proportional to the TC. Unlike the unconstrained portfolio, the declining TC in the long-only portfolios implies that the IR falls as TE rises.[6]

## TRADE-OFFS AMONG TRACKING ERROR, DEGREE OF SHORTING, AND TRANSFER COEFFICIENT

In practice, it is probably not possible to (1) maintain the maximum TC, (2) target a typical level of TE, and (3) use a limited amount of shorting simultaneously. The investor will need to make trade-offs among the TE, the level of shorting, and the TC. For example, Exhibit 18.6 suggests that to maintain the maximum TC at TEs higher than 3 to 4 percent, a level of shorting higher than 50 percent will be required. Limiting the degree of shorting to 20 to 30 percent while trying to maintain typical levels of TE will reduce the TC below the maximum, although it will still be higher than the long-only portfolio.

To illustrate this effect, we generate six different optimal portfolios with different degrees of targeted long/short constraints: long-only, +110/−10, +120/−20, +130/−30, +140/−40, and +150/−50, where the (+) and (−) amounts represent the notional exposure of the long and the short sides. For example, +110/−10 signifies a portfolio that is 110 percent long and 10 percent short. Note that all six of these strategies result in fully invested portfolios (i.e., 100% market exposure). Each portfolio is subject to a 4 percent *ex ante* annualized active risk constraint and its respective long/short constraint only.

Exhibit 18.7 shows the significant impact of a long-only constraint on the creation of active portfolios. In both panels, we plot active weights on the y-axis and securities sorted by benchmark weights on the x-axis in descending order (i.e., the benchmark weight gets smaller moving left to right).

In the long-only graph, we see meaningful negative active weights only in the farthest left portion. Positive active weights, on the other hand, look to be somewhat more uniformly distributed. In the +150/−50 graph, however, it appears that active weights are nearly evenly distributed across all benchmark weights. This is true for both positive and negative active weights.

We also measure the correlation between the absolute value of active weights and benchmark weights for both portfolios. The correlation for the

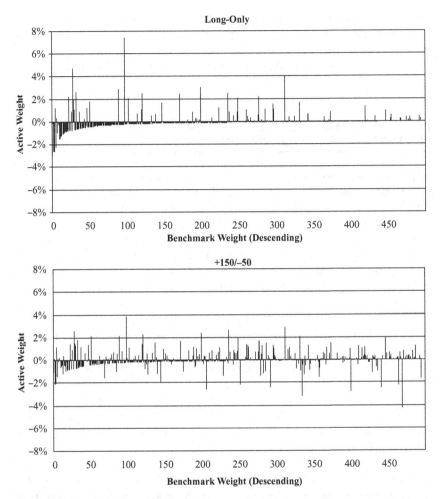

**EXHIBIT 18.7**    Active Portfolio Weights Ranked by Descending Benchmark Weights

long-only portfolio is 0.44 but only 0.19 for the +150/−50 portfolio. Thus, benchmark weight plays a much smaller role in the portfolio when some shorting is allowed.

Next, we segregate the S&P 500 universe into five size quintiles, from Q1 for the smallest-cap names to Q5 for the largest-cap names, and compute the TC for each portfolio within its size quintile. Exhibit 18.8 shows the TC within each quintile for successive degrees of shorting.

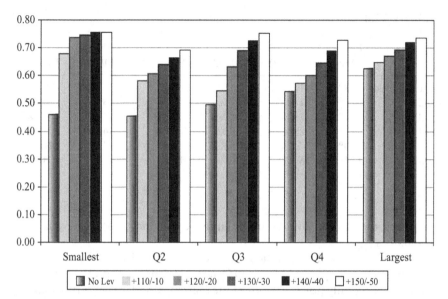

**EXHIBIT 18.8** TC by Size Quintile for Various Degrees of Shorting

The long-only portfolio shows a dramatic drop-off in TC moving from the largest names to the smallest names (from right to left). This is expected because as the benchmark weight becomes smaller, a manager's ability to meaningfully underweight a stock diminishes. Allowing even a minimal amount of shorting of 10 percent, there is a dramatic pickup in TC, particularly for quintiles 1, 2, and 3. This improvement in TC continues as the degree of shorting allowed rises, although the majority of the improvement occurs at the initial relaxing of the long-only constraint and then increases moderately at each successive level.

Exhibit 18.9 shows the cumulative sum of the absolute value of active weights in each size quintile. For example, the sum of the absolute value of active weights in the smallest stocks (Q1) for the long-only portfolio is 8 percent.

Two things should be apparent from Exhibit 18.9. First, increasing the degree of shorting increases the activity of the portfolios. This effect is shown by the increasing sum of active weights (last line) as we move to the right. Even though all the portfolios have an *ex ante* annualized TE of 4.0 percent, increasing the degree of shorting allows the optimizer to build a much more active portfolio. Second, as the allowed level of shorting

**EXHIBIT 18.9** Cumulative Value of Absolute Active Weights

| | Long-Only | +110/−10 | +120/−20 | +130/−30 | +140/−40 | +150/−50 |
|---|---|---|---|---|---|---|
| Q1-Smallest | 8% | 15% | 21% | 27% | 31% | 35% |
| Q2 | 13% | 18% | 22% | 25% | 28% | 32% |
| Q3 | 24% | 29% | 34% | 39% | 42% | 45% |
| Q4 | 29% | 29% | 29% | 31% | 34% | 37% |
| Q5-Largest | 80% | 76% | 74% | 68% | 64% | 61% |
| Sum | 154% | 167% | 180% | 190% | 199% | 210% |

increases, the activity shifts from the largest-cap names (Q5) to the smallest-cap names (Q1).

For the long-only portfolio, 52 percent (0.80/1.54) of the sum of its absolute active weights resides in Q5 and only 5 percent in Q1. This is because the long-only portfolio cannot meaningfully underweight the smallest names. Conversely, the +150/−50 portfolio has only 29 percent of the sum of its absolute active weights in Q5 and nearly 17 percent in Q1, reflecting broader information transfer across all market cap groups. Removing the long-only constraint results in a more active portfolio for a given level of *ex ante* TE, and a more balanced transfer of information across securities in the benchmark.

Grinold and Kahn (2000) note that increasing a manager's ability to take short positions enhances not only the underweight positions on the short side but also the overweight positions on the long side. Because short sales finance buys, and underweights and overweights must sum to zero, this allows larger underweight positions to accommodate larger overweight positions. Hence, allowing for short sales not only allows a manager to better exploit negative alpha information, but also produces an overall more active portfolio for a given level of *ex ante* active risk.

Although we have targeted specific shorting levels here, it is clear that doing so is not necessarily optimal in terms of maximum information transfer. Forcing any degree of shorting generally improves the portfolio TC (the exception to this is a portfolio with very low TE). TC will typically reach a maximum at some point for a given TE, however, and then subsequently decline.

The TC curves in Exhibit 18.10 show TC as a function of *ex ante* TE. As expected, TCs for each of the portfolios that allow shorting rise above and remain above that of the long-only portfolio. Each also has an

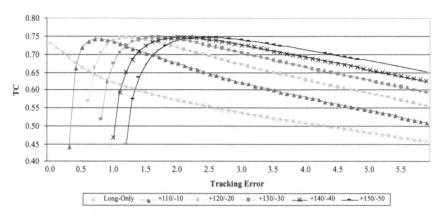

**EXHIBIT 18.10** TC versus TE

optimal, or maximum, TC that peaks and then declines as the TE increases. This occurs because the increasing concentration of securities required to achieve higher and higher levels of TE becomes restricted by the maximum long/short constraint.

Thus, as TE increases, it is clear that allowing for more shorting leads to more information-efficient portfolios, in terms of both TC and expected return. Interestingly, for investors with very low active risk targets, say, 1 percent (enhanced indexing), a minimal reduction in the long-only constraint to only 10 percent actually results in a more information-efficient portfolio than forcing a higher level of shorting, say, 50 percent.[7]

Two things become apparent from the graph in Exhibit 18.10. First, there is indeed an optimal TE-shorting combination that maximizes TC. Second, higher TE strategies are better off if they allow higher levels of shorting. For example, an investor would not want to run a 1.5 percent TE strategy using a +150/−50 portfolio because a higher TC can be achieved with less shorting. The +150/−50 portfolio does not become more attractive until TE is higher than 2.0 to 2.5 percent.

Exhibit 18.11 shows the TC of each given strategy as a percentage of the TC for a full +200/−100 portfolio with a typical 4 percent TE. Whereas a long-only portfolio achieves only 68 percent of the TC of the +200/−100 portfolio, a +120/−20 portfolio achieves 85 percent. Thus, relaxing the long-only constraint by only 20 percent results in a substantial pickup in TC compared to the more aggressive case.

**EXHIBIT 18.11** TC as Percent of Full +200/−100 Strategy for 4% TE Portfolio

| | Long-Only | +110/−10 | +120/−20 | +130/−30 | +140/−40 | +150/−50 | +200/−100 |
|---|---|---|---|---|---|---|---|
| Transfer Coefficient | 0.510 | 0.584 | 0.633 | 0.668 | 0.695 | 0.715 | 0.745 |
| Percentage of +200/−100 TC | 68.4% | 78.3% | 84.9% | 89.6% | 93.2% | 95.9% | 100% |

## PRACTICAL IMPLICATIONS

Part of the attraction of market-neutral portfolios is the increased potential to add value by fully eliminating the long-only constraint. It is not uncommon for a market-neutral portfolio to have nearly double the TC of a typical long-only portfolio, implying a much more efficient use of the manager's information.[8] For those wanting to maintain broad equity market exposure, pure market-neutral portfolios can be overlaid with equity market futures contracts or equity index total return swaps. Combining the two pieces gives the alpha, or value added, from the market-neutral portfolio plus the beta exposure, or long-only index returns, on the broad equity market.

Many investors may be unfamiliar with full market-neutral strategies or may feel uncomfortable with a derivatives-based overlay to obtain the beta exposure they desire. Using only physical assets and relaxing the long-only constraint at the margin, however, can recapture much of a manager's information content lost in the long-only portfolio. Hence, we can modify the long/short solution: Allow a limited amount of shorting in the portfolio, and use the cash generated to invest a similar amount in long positions. This approach enables the investor to maintain 100 percent market exposure (e.g., 120% long less 20% short) while using the information embedded in the manager's ranking system much more efficiently.[9]

Relaxing the long-only constraint delivers several advantages to investors. First, relaxing the constraint increases the TC and thus the IR considerably. Much of the loss in information efficiency between a market-neutral portfolio and the long-only portfolio can often be restored with even a modest ability to short stocks. The investor is nevertheless forced to make trade-offs among the TE, the level of shorting, and the improvement in TC. Not all can be controlled simultaneously.

Second, for limited amounts of shorting, the investor can implement the strategy without having to use derivatives to maintain the long-only market exposure required for an overlay strategy. This is an advantage for investors who are uncomfortable with derivatives or whose policies preclude their use.

Third, the modest use of short positions is less aggressive and may be more acceptable to many investment committees than a full market-neutral structure. The ability to short a modest amount allows a skilled manager to increase the expected active return with no commensurate increase in active risk and with no major commitment to short-selling.

# NOTES

1. We use Barra's USE3 risk model to calculate portfolio parameters.
2. Expected active returns are generated using the standard Grinold (1989, 1994) framework, $E\{r\} = IC \times$ Volatility $\times$ Score. IC is assumed constant at 0.05; volatility is Barra's specific risk variable (USE3); and scores are generated on the basis of a company's book-to-price ratio.
3. TC is computed as $\rho(E\{r\}\Omega^{-1}, \Delta w\Omega)$, where $\rho$ is the correlation coefficient operator; $E\{r\}$ is an $N \times 1$ vector of expected returns; $\Omega$ is an $N \times N$ diagonal matrix of idiosyncratic risk; and $\Delta w$ is an $N \times 1$ vector of active weights.
4. The optimization removing both sectors and industries results in a TC of 0.422 or an increase of 27 percent.
5. Effective weights are computed as 1/(sum of the squared benchmark weights). For the S&P 500 as of the end of 2003, this would be $1/0.0087 = 114$. The effective weights roughly estimate what the number of names would be if the benchmark were equally weighted, given the weight distribution of the benchmark. For an equally weighted portfolio of 500 stocks, the effective weights would equal exactly 500. See Strongin, Petsch, and Sharenow (1999).
6. For portfolios with additional constraints such as position size limits, even the IR for a portfolio allowing short sales will drop at some point, but the short-sale case will still dominate the long-only portfolio.
7. Curves allowing for shorting initially lie below the curve of a traditional long-only portfolio. This effect occurs because for lower levels of TE, the optimization is dominated by the need to restrict TE at a forced level of shorting. At these low TEs, expected returns are basically ignored. As the TE is allowed to increase, its effect becomes less dominant, thus enabling the optimizer to better exploit expected returns. Hence, TC eventually rises above the long-only curve.
8. In practice, TCs for market-neutral portfolios are usually lower than 1.0 because many portfolios still constrain the portfolio to maintain industry or sector neutrality as well as limit the size of individual positions. Additionally, the use of a risk model will affect the portfolio's TC.
9. One might suppose this would be equivalent to constructing a long-only portfolio while investing 20 percent of the value in a pure market-neutral strategy. In fact, a fully integrated optimization is generally better than optimizing the pieces separately because it allows for more efficient risk management.

# REFERENCES

Brush, J. S. 1997. "Comparisons and Combinations of Long and Long-Short Strategies." *Financial Analysts Journal*, vol. 53, no. 3 (May/June):81–89.

Clarke, R., H. de Silva, and S. Thorley. 2002. "Portfolio Constraints and the Fundamental Law of Active Management." *Financial Analysts Journal*, vol. 58, no. 5 (September/October):48–66.

Grinold, R. C. 1999. "Alpha is Volatility Times IC Times Score." *The Journal of Portfolio Management*, vol. 20, no. 4 (Summer):9–16.

"The Fundamental Law of Active Management." 1989. *The Journal of Portfolio Management*, vol. 15, no. 3 (Spring):30–37.

Grinold, R. C., and R. N. Kahn. 2000. "The Efficiency Gains of Long-Short Investing." *Financial Analysts Journal*, vol. 56, no. 6 (November/December):40–53.

Jacobs, B. I., K. N. Levy, and D. Starer. 1998. "On the Optimality of Long-Short Strategies." *Financial Analysts Journal*, vol. 54, no. 2 (March/April):40–51.

Strongin S., M. Petsch, and G. Sharenow. 1998. "Beating Benchmarks: A Stock Picker's Reality: Part II." Goldman, Sachs, November.

Thomas, L. R. "Active Management." 2000. *The Journal of Portfolio Management*, vol. 26, no. 2 (Winter):25–32.

# CHAPTER 19

# Allocation Betas

**Martin L. Leibowitz**
Managing Director
Morgan Stanley, Research

**Anthony Bova**
Vice President
Morgan Stanley, Research

*The complexities of standard optimization can obscure the intuitive decision process that should play a major role in asset allocation. The use of allocation alphas and betas—with U.S. equity as the beta source—facilitates an intuitive approach and greatly simplifies the decision process. A portfolio's assets are separated into two groups: Swing assets are the traditional liquid asset classes, such as U.S. bonds and equity; the alpha core is all other assets, which are subject to more stringent limits. After the nontraditional assets are combined to form an alpha core, the result is a three-part efficient frontier: (1) a cash-to-core segment, (2) a fixed-core segment, and (3) an equity extension. The boundaries lead to a sweet spot on the efficient frontier where most U.S. institutional portfolios are clustered.*

The market assumptions behind the standard asset allocation studies embed a set of expected returns and covariance relationships of the relevant assets. These assumed relationships are often not consistent with either equilibrium conditions or an efficient market view. This article deconstructs the relationships in an illustrative set of market assumptions into beta components that are correlated with U.S. equities and alpha components that are independent of equities. The term "allocation beta" is used to underscore that these values are derived from a covariance matrix intended as the starting point for an allocation study.

The selection of U.S. equity as the beta source is motivated by its role as the dominant risk factor in U.S. institutional portfolios. In addition, the beta measure relative to a U.S. equity index is a familiar and intuitive concept (even though it is not typically used in an allocation context). When this asset-based analysis is applied to representative U.S. institutional portfolios, roughly 90 percent or more of their volatility is explained by their beta sensitivity to U.S. equities. Moreover, for a wide range of U.S. institutional portfolios, the beta values (and the overall volatilities) tend to be surprisingly tightly clustered around a beta of 0.60 and a volatility of 10 percent.

This framework provides a simplified approach to the allocation process. A portfolio's assets can be decomposed into two groups—swing assets and an alpha core. Swing assets are the traditional liquid assets—U.S. equity, U.S. bonds, and cash—whereas the alpha core consists of all other assets—non-U.S. equity, real estate, hedge funds, private equities, and so on—that are potential alpha sources but are generally subject to relatively tight portfolio constraints. The allocation process can then be viewed as a three-step process. First, maximum acceptable amounts are determined for each nontraditional asset class. Second, these alternative assets are combined into a subportfolio—the alpha core. The aim is to include this alpha core in the portfolio at its maximum allowed percentage. The third step is to adjust the composition of the swing assets to achieve the desired risk level for the overall fund. (In essence, this process reverses the usual allocation path, whereby a portfolio of traditional assets is established and then incrementally deployed into alternatives.)

The assumption of a fixed percentage weight devoted to the alpha core leads to a three-part efficient frontier: (1) a cash-to-core segment, (2) a fixed-core segment, and (3) an equity extension to 100 percent equity. The first and third segments are tied to the fixed points of, respectively, 100 percent cash and 100 percent equity.

## STANDARD MEAN–VARIANCE FRONTIERS

Standard asset allocation is based on the mean–variance approach first suggested by Markowitz in the 1950s (see Markowitz, 1959). In it, a covariance matrix characterizes the volatility behavior of the various asset classes and a computer algorithm then generates an efficient frontier that represents the highest-return portfolios for a range of volatilities. The frontier is, of course, highly dependent on the assumptions in the covariance matrix and also on any constraints or limits established for each asset class.

These optimizations provide exact efficient portfolios based on the return and covariance data used as inputs, but the reliability of various market assumptions and the black box characteristics of the optimization make it difficult for many asset managers to evaluate intuitively the validity or robustness of the resulting portfolios. Indeed, a classic problem with any optimization is that the computer will seize upon any inconsistent or illogical input parameter and use it to force an unintended but significant position in the solution. Such out-of-the-box optimization results should always serve as a basis for reconsidering the reliability, consistency, and/or applicability of the original market assumptions. Another common problem is the sequential manipulation—or torturing—of the constraints to achieve portfolios that are not only theoretically optimal, but also satisfy the more intuitive criterion of being palatable.

## THE ALLOCATION BETA

The concept of beta as market risk stretches far back into the beginnings of modern financial market theory. It is commonly used to risk-adjust stock portfolios or individual stocks, but it is seldom applied to individual asset classes in the context of asset allocation. This neglect is curious because the underlying covariance matrix actually contains all the information needed to tease out the implied beta values. Moreover, this beta calculation is quite simple: the correlation between equities and the asset class in question multiplied by the ratio of their respective volatilities.

We presented this process in its earliest form in 2004 (see Leibowitz, 2004b). Subsequent studies have expanded on this theme along a number of dimensions (see Leibowitz and Bova, 2004a–2004f, 2005). The present article goes beyond the earlier formulation to show how the alpha/beta framework can be used to address a number of issues related to the development of policy portfolios and efficient frontiers (see the Leibowitz and the Leibowitz–Bova articles). For illustrative market assumptions, we drew on a standard return–covariance matrix, depicted in Exhibit 19.1, from a consulting firm involved in asset allocation studies. These return–covariance values do not purport to represent either an efficient market or a set of equilibrium conditions. In fact, they are not globally efficient in any sense. Moreover, the following numerical results derived from this particular covariance matrix are presented here solely for the purpose of illustrating the analytical framework. In this section, international equity is the example alternative asset class, so it has been shaded in tables and figures.

**EXHIBIT 19.1** Illustrative Return—Covariance Matrix

| | Expected Return | Standard Deviation | U.S. Equity | International Equity | Emerging Market Equity | Absolute Return | Equity Hedge Funds | Venture Capital | Private Equity | REITs | Real Estate | Commodities | U.S. Bonds | Cash |
|---|---|---|---|---|---|---|---|---|---|---|---|---|---|---|
| U.S. equity | 7.25% | 16.50% | 1.00 | 0.65 | 0.45 | 0.50 | 0.85 | 0.35 | 0.70 | 0.55 | 0.10 | −0.25 | 0.30 | 0.35 |
| International equity | 7.25 | 19.50 | 0.65 | 1.00 | 0.60 | 0.55 | 0.55 | 0.30 | 0.60 | 0.40 | 0.15 | −0.10 | 0.20 | 0.20 |
| Emerging market equity | 9.25 | 28.00 | 0.45 | 0.60 | 1.00 | 0.50 | 0.65 | 0.35 | 0.30 | 0.25 | −0.30 | −0.05 | −0.15 | 0.00 |
| Absolute return | 5.25 | 9.25 | 0.50 | 0.55 | 0.50 | 1.00 | 0.65 | 0.10 | 0.35 | 0.55 | −0.05 | −0.05 | 0.15 | 0.20 |
| Equity hedge funds | 5.75 | 12.75 | 0.85 | 0.55 | 0.65 | 0.65 | 1.00 | 0.50 | 0.60 | 0.50 | 0.00 | −0.15 | 0.15 | 0.35 |
| Venture capital | 12.25 | 27.75 | 0.35 | 0.30 | 0.35 | 0.10 | 0.50 | 1.00 | 0.65 | −0.05 | 0.15 | 0.20 | −0.25 | 0.05 |
| Private equity | 10.25 | 23.00 | 0.70 | 0.60 | 0.30 | 0.35 | 0.60 | 0.65 | 1.00 | 0.20 | 0.20 | −0.05 | −0.10 | 0.25 |
| REITs | 6.50 | 14.50 | 0.55 | 0.40 | 0.25 | 0.55 | 0.50 | −0.05 | 0.20 | 1.00 | 0.00 | −0.20 | 0.30 | 0.20 |
| Real estate | 5.50 | 12.00 | 0.10 | 0.15 | −0.30 | −0.05 | 0.00 | 0.15 | 0.20 | 0.00 | 1.00 | −0.05 | 0.00 | 0.40 |
| Commodities | 5.25 | 19.00 | −0.25 | −0.10 | −0.05 | −0.05 | −0.05 | 0.20 | −0.05 | −0.20 | −0.05 | 1.00 | −0.10 | −0.20 |
| U.S. bonds | 3.75 | 7.50 | 0.30 | 0.20 | −0.15 | 0.15 | 0.15 | −0.25 | −0.10 | 0.30 | 0.00 | −0.10 | 1.00 | 0.45 |
| Cash | 1.50 | 0.00 | 0.35 | 0.20 | 0.00 | 0.20 | 0.35 | 0.05 | 0.25 | 0.20 | 0.40 | −0.20 | 0.45 | 1.00 |

*Source:* Morgan Stanley Research

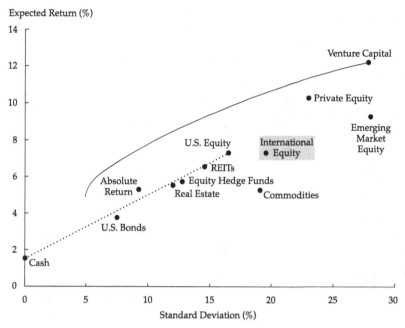

Expected Return (%)

**EXHIBIT 19.2** Expected Return versus Volatility: Standard Format
*Source:* Morgan Stanley Research

Exhibit 19.2 depicts the 12 asset classes in the standard format of expected return versus standard deviation. The straight line connecting cash and U.S. equity shows that most asset classes fall below this line (or its extension).

The beta calculation is carried out with the matrix values of (see Exhibit 19.1) 0.65 for the correlation between U.S. equity and international equity and 16.50 percent and 19.50 percent for their respective volatilities. The beta for international equity, $\beta_{IE}$, can then be determined by multiplying its 0.65 correlation with U.S. equity by the ratio of the two volatilities:

$$\beta_{IE} = \rho_{IE,EQ}\left(\frac{\sigma_{IE}}{\sigma_{EQ}}\right)$$

$$= 0.65\left(\frac{19.50}{16.50}\right)$$

$$= 0.77$$

**EXHIBIT 19.3**  Allocation Betas for Asset Classes

| Asset Class | Expected Return, $E(r_i)$ | Standard Deviation, $\sigma_i$ | Correlation, $\rho_{i,EQ}$ | Allocation Beta, $\beta_i = \rho(\sigma_i/\sigma_{EQ})$ |
|---|---|---|---|---|
| U.S. equity | 7.25% | 16.50% | 1.00 | 1.00 |
| International equity | 7.25 | 19.50 | 0.65 | 0.77 |
| Emerging market equity | 9.25 | 28.00 | 0.45 | 0.76 |
| Absolute return | 5.25 | 9.25 | 0.50 | 0.28 |
| Equity hedge funds | 5.75 | 12.75 | 0.85 | 0.66 |
| Venture capital | 12.25 | 27.75 | 0.35 | 0.59 |
| Private equity | 10.25 | 23.00 | 0.70 | 0.96 |
| REITs | 6.50 | 14.50 | 0.55 | 0.48 |
| Real estate | 5.50 | 12.00 | 0.10 | 0.07 |
| Commodities | 5.25 | 19.00 | −0.25 | −0.29 |
| U.S. bonds | 3.75 | 7.50 | 0.30 | 0.14 |
| Cash | 1.50 | 0.00 | 0.35 | 0.00 |

*Source:* Morgan Stanley Research

The same procedure is used to calculate the beta value for each asset class. The results are displayed in Exhibit 19.3, where $E(r_i)$ is expected return on asset class $i$, which is not U.S. equity, and $\rho_{i,EQ}$ is the correlation of asset class $i$ with U.S. equity. We refer to the values in the last column as allocation betas to, again, emphasize that they are derived from the covariance matrix that formed the starting point for the allocation study.

Next, the axis on which risk was defined as standard deviation in the return–risk diagram of Exhibit 19.2 is replaced by a horizontal axis on which risk is defined as the allocation beta as shown in Exhibit 19.4. In switching from standard deviation to the beta dimension to define risk, *all* the asset classes shift to positions above the cash-to-U.S.-equity line. The explanation for this transformation is that beta captures only one component of total risk. Therefore, the move to beta values related to U.S. equities creates a left-hand shift from the picture of the standard risk–return diagram of Exhibit 19.2.

## RETURN DECOMPOSITION: ASSET CLASS

To find the component of, for example, international equity volatility that can be ascribed to U.S. equity, its risk point must be shifted to 12.68 percent,

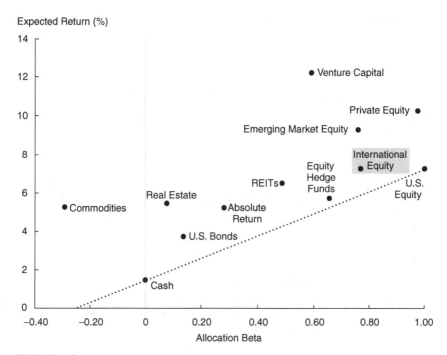

**EXHIBIT 19.4** Expected Return versus Allocation Beta
*Source:* Morgan Stanley Research

a figure computed by multiplying the international equity allocation $\beta$ of 0.77 by the 16.50 percent volatility of U.S. equity. Exhibit 19.5 isolates the cash-to-U.S.-equity line and the position of international equity from Exhibit 19.2 and shows this shift.

The expected return of 7.25 percent for international equity can now be decomposed into three components:

1. The risk-free rate, $r_f$, of 1.50 percent;
2. The expected return premium, $\beta r_p$, that would be associated with a U.S. equity and cash portfolio having a beta of 0.77 (this beta-based expected return is 4.42%, the product of international equity's beta of 0.77 and the 5.75% risk premium, $r_p$, assumed for U.S. equity);
3. The remaining return of 1.33 percent that lies above the cash-to-U.S.-equity line and is derived from sources other than U.S. equity risk.

This 1.33 percent of excess expected return is based on the assumed results of a passive investment in international equities as an asset class.

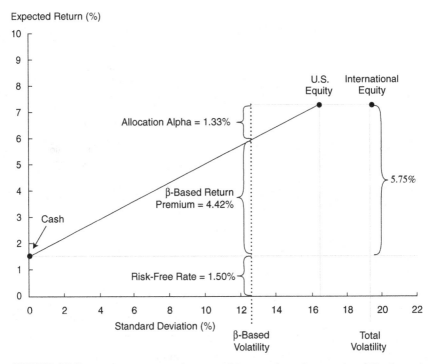

Expected Return (%)

**EXHIBIT 19.5** Decomposition of Expected Return from International Equity
*Source:* Morgan Stanley Research

It is derived from the inefficiencies embedded in the market assumptions, the diversification structure of typical institutional portfolios, and our deliberate selection of U.S. equities (rather than a global market index or a policy portfolio baseline) as the fundamental risk factor. Thus, this alpha is alpha-like in the sense that it represents expected return components that are not related to the dominant risk factor in typical U.S. portfolios. There is no presumption of positive outcomes from the selection of superior managers or from direct active investment by the asset manager. Thus, an allocation alpha does not represent an *active* alpha in any sense and we will use the term "allocation alpha" to underscore this distinction.

In Exhibit 19.6, the return decomposition described here is applied to the 12 illustrative asset classes, listed in order of decreasing allocation alpha.

**EXHIBIT 19.6** Return Decomposition by Asset Class

| Asset Class | Total Expected Return, $E(r_i)$ | Beta Relative to U.S. Equity | Risk-Free Rate, $r_f$ | Beta Expected Return, $\beta r_p$ | Allocation Alpha Component, $\alpha$ |
|---|---|---|---|---|---|
| Venture capital | 12.25% | 0.59 | 1.50 | 3.38 | 7.37 |
| Commodities | 5.25 | −0.29 | 1.50 | −1.66 | 5.41 |
| Real estate | 5.50 | 0.07 | 1.50 | 0.42 | 3.58 |
| Emerging market equity | 9.25 | 0.76 | 1.50 | 4.39 | 3.36 |
| Private equity | 10.25 | 0.98 | 1.50 | 5.61 | 3.11 |
| REITs | 6.50 | 0.48 | 1.50 | 2.78 | 2.22 |
| Absolute return | 5.25 | 0.28 | 1.50 | 1.61 | 2.14 |
| U.S. bonds | 3.75 | 0.14 | 1.50 | 0.78 | 1.47 |
| International equity | 7.25 | 0.77 | 1.50 | 4.42 | 1.33 |
| Equity hedge funds | 5.75 | 0.66 | 1.50 | 3.78 | 0.47 |
| U.S. equity | 7.25 | 1.00 | 1.50 | 5.75 | 0.00 |
| Cash | 1.50 | 0.00 | 1.50 | 0.00 | 0.00 |

*Source:* Morgan Stanley Research

## RISK DECOMPOSITION: ASSET CLASS

The allocation alpha of 1.33 percent for international equity is not without its own sources of risk. International equity's allocation alpha carries an implicit volatility of 14.82 percent, which represents (see Exhibit 19.5) the volatility required to take the beta-based volatility of 12.68 percent to international equity's total volatility of 19.50 percent [i.e., $(14.82)^2 + (12.68)^2 = (19.50)^2$]. Appendix A provides the basic formulas for the allocation alpha and beta variables. This allocation alpha risk, which will always have a zero correlation with U.S. equity, may itself be composed of other risk factors, such as currency risk, interest rate risk, or liquidity concerns. In certain contexts, these other factors must be explicitly taken into account (e.g., in an asset/liability framework).

The allocation alphas are an intrinsic component of the total expected return from each asset class and, as such, would be incorporated in any standard optimization procedure. Carving them out explicitly, however, can provide insight into how these sources of incremental return interact with the portfolio's overall risk profile. With more clarity about these fundamental return–risk trade-offs, the portfolio manager may see options for return enhancement (and perhaps for greater caution) that may be obscured by the standard black-box optimization.

It should again be emphasized that the specific values of this return–risk decomposition are totally dependent on inputs from the illustrative return–covariance matrix assumptions.

## PORTFOLIO-LEVEL ANALYSIS

Exhibit 19.7 displays four portfolios representing a range of allocations, as shown in Panel A. Portfolio C may be considered a broadly diversified modern portfolio, and Portfolio D, an extreme alternative-centric portfolio.

**EXHIBIT 19.7** Illustrative Portfolios

| Measure | A | B | C | D |
|---|---|---|---|---|
| *A. Asset-class weights* | | | | |
| U.S. equity | 60% | 60% | 20% | |
| International equity | | | 15 | |
| Emerging market equity | | | 5 | |
| Absolute return | | | 10 | 20% |
| Equity hedge funds | | | | |
| Venture capital | | | 10 | 20 |
| Private equity | | | 10 | |
| REITs | | | | |
| Real estate | | | 10 | 20 |
| Commodities | | | | 20 |
| U.S. bonds | | 40 | 20 | 20 |
| Cash | 40 | | | |
| *B. Results* | | | | |
| Expected return (%) | 4.95 | 5.85 | 7.08 | 6.40 |
| Exact standard deviation, $\sigma$ (%) | 9.90 | 11.17 | 10.83 | 8.04 |
| Portfolio $\alpha$ | 0.00 | 0.59 | 2.28 | 3.99 |
| Portfolio $\beta$ | 0.60 | 0.65 | 0.57 | 0.16 |
| $\beta$-Based $\sigma$ (%) | 9.90 | 10.80 | 9.45 | 2.61 |
| Ratio of $\beta$-based $\sigma$ to exact $\sigma$ | 100.00 | 96.70 | 87.20 | 32.40 |
| $\sigma_\alpha$-Plus (%) | 0.00 | 2.86 | 4.48 | 7.13 |
| $\beta$-Plus $\sigma$ (%) | 9.90 | 11.17 | 10.45 | 7.59 |
| Ratio of $\beta$-plus $\sigma$ to exact $\sigma$ | 100.00 | 100.00 | 96.50 | 94.50 |

*Source:* Morgan Stanley Research

These portfolios were chosen strictly for illustrative purposes and are not optimal or efficient in any sense.

Panel B of Exhibit 19.7 shows the expected return of each portfolio and exact volatilities as generated by the covariance matrix in Exhibit 19.1. For example, because the simplest allocation, Portfolio A, consists of 60 percent U.S. equity and 40 percent cash, the allocation beta is a combination of 60 percent of $\beta = 1$ for U.S. equities and 40 percent of $\beta = 0$ for cash, netting to $\beta = 0.60$ for the portfolio. On the basis of this beta, Portfolio A's beta-based volatility is 9.90 percent—the product of its 60 percent equity exposure and the equity volatility of 16.50 percent. In this simple case, the beta-based volatility estimate accounts for fully 100 percent of the exact volatility.

Portfolio B has the same 60 percent equity exposure as Portfolio A, but now has 40 percent bonds replacing Portfolio A's 40 percent cash. From Exhibit 19.3, bonds have a beta of 0.14. When 40 percent of this beta is added to the beta contribution of 0.60 from the direct equity exposure, the result is a Portfolio B beta of 0.65, slightly greater than Portfolio A's beta. The product of the beta of 0.65 and the equity volatility of 16.50 percent gives a beta-based approximation of 10.80 percent, which accounts for approximately 97 percent of the exact volatility of 11.17 percent. (This 97% figure also corresponds to the portfolio's correlation with U.S. equities.)

The allocation represented by Portfolio C is based on the trend among many institutions toward using a broad array of asset classes in an attempt to diversify risk. Portfolio C has greatly reduced exposure to U.S. equities and U.S. bonds, but each asset class in the portfolio has some correlation with U.S. equities, which creates an implicit equity exposure that is reflected in each class's respective beta value.

Applying the allocation betas in Exhibit 19.3 to the weights composing Portfolio C produces the portfolio beta of 0.57. This beta, even though it is for the modern Portfolio C with its broad diversification of asset classes, is surprisingly close to the traditional Portfolio B's beta of 0.65. The closeness of these two beta values demonstrates that, in spite of its diversification across a wider range of asset classes, Portfolio C is similar to traditional Portfolio B in certain basic risk characteristics.

As an approximation to the overall volatility, Portfolio C's beta-based volatility is $0.57 \times 16.50$ percent $= 9.45$ percent. This estimate is not quite as good an approximation as the 97 percent approximation for Portfolio B, but it still captures 87 percent of the exact volatility of 10.83 percent.

In spite of the similarity in their volatilities, Portfolio C's return is significantly superior to Portfolio B's return. Thus, *if one accepts all the assumptions in the return–covariance matrix*, Portfolio C is superior to Portfolio B: For a roughly comparable level of risk, it provides an extra 1.23 percentage points of return. The source of the higher return is clearly the many non-U.S.-equity and non-U.S.-bond assets that provide significantly positive allocation alphas. Moreover, because the risks associated with the allocation alphas are submerged under the dominant beta factor, this additional return is attained without much change in portfolio volatility. Thus (again, given the assumptions), these sources of allocation alpha provide a highly desirable ratio of incremental return to incremental risk at the portfolio level.

It is surprising that the first three portfolios have such similar risk characteristics: (1) allocation betas within 0.05 of $\beta = 0.60$, (2) exact volatilities within $\pm 1$ percentage point of 10.50 percent, and (3) beta-based volatilities that account for 87 percent or more of the exact volatility. In fact, however, these same volatility characteristics apply to a wide range of U.S. institutional portfolios.

Portfolio D has been provided because it illustrates, for completeness and full disclosure, that one can construct portfolios in which this beta-based approach fails to account for a significant portion of the total volatility. Portfolio D has five equal-weighted asset classes and no direct exposure to U.S. equities or several other asset classes. Portfolio D's return comes overwhelmingly from return sources that are orthogonal to U.S. equities; these sources account for almost 4 percentage points of the total 6.40 percent return. Portfolio D also has a vastly different risk structure from the other portfolios; its allocation beta is only 0.16, and its beta-based volatility is 2.61 percent, which accounts for only 32 percent of the exact volatility of 8.04 percent. Clearly, most of my comments about the first three portfolios do not apply to Portfolio D. I included Portfolio D to make the cautionary point that some portfolios are not beta dominated.

## ALPHA INDEPENDENCE AND BETA-PLUS

The non-beta-dominated Portfolio D provides an opportunity to address the important issue of allocation alpha independence. Statistically independent alphas open up many avenues for direct analysis and clear intuitions. Without alpha independence, matters quickly become complex and intuitions become entangled. In the method described here, the allocation alphas and betas for each asset class are independent of each other by construction. There is no assurance, however, that the allocation alphas are independent across the various asset classes. In fact, most covariance matrices will lead to alpha variables that have some degree of cross correlation.

The approach we followed up to this point was pragmatic; in recognition that the starting set of market assumptions was itself an approximation (at best), the search at this point was not for precise results but for findings that could serve as useful and intuitive approximations. In this spirit, we tried to determine whether the alpha variables are sufficiently uncorrelated that they can be treated as independent—at least within some range of portfolios.

To this end, we developed an alpha-based volatility measure to supplement the earlier beta-based estimate. As presented in the Appendix for a given portfolio, this supplement is the simple sum of the asset classes' allocation alpha variances weighted by each class's respective percentage holding in the portfolio (i.e., a summation based on the presumption of zero correlation among the allocation alphas). When added to the beta-based volatility, this alpha supplement creates a beta-plus estimate that accounts for an even more surprising portion of the exact volatility (see the bottom rows of Exhibit 19.7) than the beta-based estimate. For example, for Portfolio A, the beta already accounted for 100 percent of the volatility, so the alpha supplement (which is zero) adds nothing. For Portfolios B and C, the beta-plus estimate, not surprisingly, improves the volatility estimates to 100 percent and 96.5 percent, respectively. The major surprise is Portfolio D, with its low beta value and the beta-based estimate that accounted for only 32 percent of the exact volatility. With the beta-plus measure, the volatility estimation for Portfolio D rises to 94.5 percent of the exact value. Thus, even for the highly aberrant Portfolio D, the result is not far off if the allocation alpha variables are treated as uncorrelated. In this case, Portfolio D is, literally, the exception that proves the rule!

Appendix A also shows the development of the covariance structure that would have to hold for the independence assumption to be strictly true. Many of the original covariance entries differ significantly from these values. Nevertheless, in a wide range of portfolio contexts, the independence assumption appears to provide a reasonable approximation.

## ALPHA CORES AND EFFICIENT FRONTIERS

The allocation beta framework can be used to develop highly simplified efficient frontiers. Exhibit 19.8 shows the computer-generated long-only efficient frontier based on Exhibit 19.1's return–covariance matrix. Return–risk positions for Portfolios A, B, and C are also denoted. This graphical context demonstrates the narrow range of volatilities spanned by these three portfolios.

Now, the allocation alpha/allocation beta approach can be used to decompose a portfolio's assets into two groups, the swing assets and the alpha core. Swing assets are the traditional liquid assets—U.S. equity, U.S. bonds, and cash—that are typically used relatively freely to help shape the portfolio's overall risk structure. The alpha core consists of other assets that

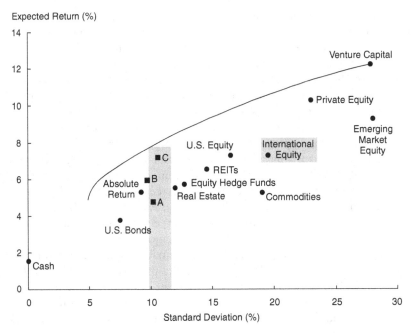

**EXHIBIT 19.8**   Unconstrained Efficient Frontier
*Source:* Morgan Stanley Research

are potential sources of alpha and that tend to be subject to relatively tight position limits for one reason or another.

The position limits may be based on regulatory or organizational constraints, difficulty of access to satisfactory investment vehicles or managers, underdeveloped financial markets, excessive transaction costs, problematic fee structures, liquidity concerns, peer-based standards, headline risk, insufficient or unreliable historical data, and so on. Many of these issues fall under the category that may be called "dragon risk"—that is, legitimate fears about moving into uncharted waters where unknown dangers lurk (see Leibowitz and Bova, 2004d). In essence, one may not be able to trust the return–risk assumptions for these nontraditional assets to the same extent one can trust the estimates for the more traditional asset classes.

Markets and institutional positions clearly evolve over time, but today's alpha cores generally include such assets as international equity, real estate, emerging market equity, and recently, various hedge funds and (sometimes) even commodity funds. In spite of the position constraints, these asset classes can aggregate to serve as valuable sources of incremental alpha return.

The alpha core approach assumes that the fund will first determine the maximum acceptable limits for each asset class that is outside the basic swing assets. The next decision will be to combine these asset choices into a coherent subportfolio—the alpha core. The composition of this subportfolio will generally involve intuitive and qualitative considerations that go well beyond the explicit quantitative characteristics embedded in the return–covariance matrix. Structuring the alpha core demands concentrated research, judgment, and deliberation—on the part of both fund sponsors and their managers.

When an acceptable alpha core has been formed, one (admittedly heroic) assumption is then needed to achieve a major further simplification: that the fund will try to include this specific alpha core at some maximum allowed percentage within any final portfolio. When the desired overall risk falls outside the volatility range where this maximum percentage can be sustained, the assumption is that the fund will maintain the alpha core's internal structure even as its percentage within the overall portfolio has to be reduced. The basic idea here is that the fund has already made a qualitative determination about how much of the alpha core assets can be accommodated within the overall portfolio. Because the core acts as a return enhancer, the fund would like to maintain the maximum acceptable core contribution whenever possible.

The allocation problem then breaks down into three basic steps: (1) determining the size limits for asset classes that can be used to form the alpha core, (2) developing an optimal alpha core within these constraints, and (3) incorporating the swing assets to form a portfolio that best represents the desired balance of return and risk. In some ways, this process represents a reversal of the typical portfolio evolution, in which allocations based on traditional assets are established first, followed by extensions into the nontraditional classes.

Given the respective roles of the alpha core and the swing assets, the entire efficient frontier takes on a relatively simple form:

1. A basic fixed alpha core consisting of the core at its maximum weight, with risk levels determined by varying mixtures of bonds and equity,
2. A lower-risk cash-to-core segment with varying levels of cash, and
3. A higher-risk equity extension segment that trades off the alpha core weight for greater equity exposure.

In practice, most allocations will fall within the fixed alpha core, where the maximum core is mixed with bonds and equity.

As an example, Exhibit 19.9 shows how the asset structure in Portfolio C can be used to develop an alpha core and an efficient frontier based on

**EXHIBIT 19.9** Alpha Core Frontier Based on Portfolio C

| | Cash Extension | Fixed-Core Segment | | | Equity Extension |
|---|---|---|---|---|---|
| | | Low-Risk Point | Portfolio C | High-Risk Point | |
| Composition/Measure | 0% | 60% | 60% | 60% | 0% |
| *A. Composition* | | | | | |
| Alpha core | | | | | |
| International equity | | | 15% | | |
| Emerging market equity | | | 5 | | |
| Absolute return | | | 10 | | |
| Venture capital | | | 10 | | |
| Private equity | | | 10 | | |
| Real estate | | | 10 | | |
| Swing assets | | | | | |
| U.S. equity | | 0% | 20 | 40% | 100% |
| U.S. bonds | | 40 | 20 | 0 | |
| Cash | 100% | 0 | 0 | 0 | |
| *B. Overall portfolio performance* | | | | | |
| Expected return (%) | 1.50 | 6.38 | 7.08 | 7.78 | 7.25 |
| $\alpha$ (%) | 0.00 | 2.58 | 2.28 | 1.99 | 0.00 |
| $\beta$ | 0.00 | 0.40 | 0.57 | 0.75 | 1.00 |
| $\beta$ return (%) | 0.00 | 2.30 | 3.29 | 4.28 | 5.75 |
| Standard deviation (%) | 0.00 | 8.35 | 10.83 | 13.01 | 16.50 |

*Source:* Morgan Stanley Research

this core. The alpha core positions shown in Panel A for Portfolio C are the maximum acceptable positions for those assets.

Exhibit 19.10 is a graph of the three-segment efficient frontier based on Exhibit 19.9's fixed 60 percent core. The fixed-core segment comprises the 60 percent core, with the remaining 40 percent weight deployed into varying mixes of U.S. bonds and equities. At the lowest-risk point on this segment, corresponding to the Low-Risk Point column in Exhibit 19.9, Panel B shows that the return is 6.38 percent and the volatility is 8.35 percent, with the volatility being derived from a combination of volatilities of the 60 percent core and the 40 percent bonds. As one moves along the frontier to the right, equities replace bonds. When the mix reaches a 20 percent equity/20 percent

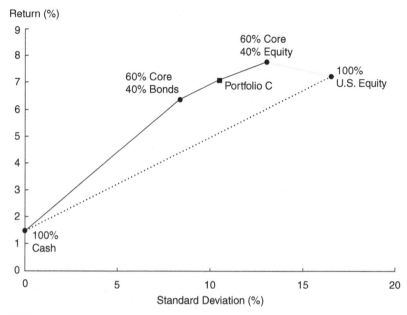

Return (%)

**EXHIBIT 19.10** The Three-Segment Frontier
*Source:* Morgan Stanley Research

bond point, this position is that of the original Portfolio C. Farther to the right, the equity concentration grows until it reaches 40 percent. At this right-most High-Risk Point, the expected return is 7.78 percent and the volatility is 13.01 percent.

In summary, to achieve portfolio risk levels that lie higher or lower than the fixed-core segment, the swing portfolios can be mixed with greater concentrations of cash or equity. Thus, at low levels of risk, varying levels of cash can be mixed with the 60 percent core/40 percent bond portfolio. At the higher-risk end of the fixed-core segment, the portfolio may have 60 percent core and 40 percent equity. To attain still higher levels of risk, the frontier must move into the equity extension, where equity replaces the alpha core until the portfolio reaches 100 percent equity.

Exhibit 19.11 combines the computer-generated unconstrained frontier of Exhibit 19.4 with the three-segment fixed-core frontier from Exhibit 19.11 and shows the placement of the original Portfolios A, B, and C. Clearly, the three-segment frontier covers a much more limited volatility range and has expected returns that are significantly lower than the unconstrained frontier, but the unconstrained frontier contains portfolios that fall well outside of

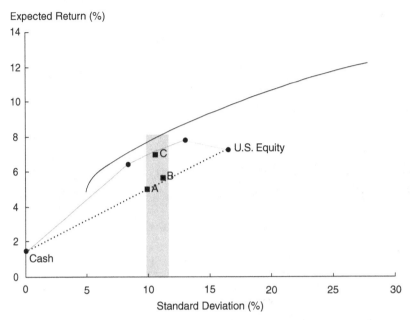

**EXHIBIT 19.11** The Three-Segment Frontier versus the Unconstrained Frontier
*Source:* Morgan Stanley Research

what is viable for the portfolios of most U.S. investors. For example, the unconstrained portfolio lying above Portfolio C has 24 percent invested in venture capital and 24 percent invested in real estate. In the standard allocation process, this out-of-the-box portfolio would be whittled down by the application of sequential constraints. Ultimately, the portfolio would probably end up somewhere near the region where Portfolios A, B, and C are clustered—that is, in the middle of the fixed-core segment.

## CONCLUSION

This article has demonstrated how allocation alphas and betas simplify the portfolio allocation process and facilitate an intuitive approach to asset allocation. The key is to separate a portfolio's assets into the swing assets (traditional U.S. asset classes) and the alpha core of all other assets. Although the alpha core can be viewed as a way to diversify the volatility of the swing assets, its real benefit tends to be return enhancement.

After a fund determines the maximum limits acceptable for the nontraditional assets, it then combines these assets to form the alpha core. This procedure leads to a three-part efficient frontier consisting of a cash-to-core line, a fixed-core segment, and an extension to 100 percent equity. Because the outside segments are tied to the fixed points of 100 percent cash on the left and 100 percent equity on the right, the shape of the entire frontier is determined by the fixed-core segment.

Not surprisingly, most allocations fall—rather tightly—within the fixed core. Long-term funds apparently have an incentive to move beyond the cash line and an incentive to not pursue the equity extension. The fixed-core segment thus forms a sweet spot on the efficient frontier, a spot where most real-life portfolios are likely to cluster.

Alternative asset classes in the alpha core may not have investment channels that reliably reflect the fundamental returns of the asset class as a whole. In addition to the intrinsic return volatility embedded in the assets, therefore, there can be a "channel risk" associated with the selection of investment vehicles and/or management teams. Consequently, a specified level of allocation alpha returns may not be available, as a passive investment, to all funds. Funds thus need to be as realistic as possible in evaluating, implementing, and effectively monitoring alternative assets as prospective sources of return.

## APPENDIX A: ALLOCATION ALPHAS AND BETAS

First, the return of the $i$th asset class, $\tilde{r}_i$, is characterized in terms of its regression coefficient, $\beta_i$, on the U.S. equity return, $\tilde{r}_e$, in excess of the risk-free rate, $r_f$, where $\tilde{\alpha}_i$ is the orthogonal term,

$$\tilde{r}_i = \tilde{\alpha}_i + \beta_i \left( \tilde{r}_e + r_f \right) \qquad (19.A1)$$

Given the covariance of $\tilde{r}_i$ and $\tilde{r}_e$, which is $\sigma_{i,e}^2 = \rho_{i,e}\sigma_i\sigma_e$, the regression coefficient can be viewed as an allocation beta,

$$\beta_i = \rho_{i,e} \left( \frac{\sigma_i}{\sigma_e} \right) \qquad (19.A2)$$

For simplicity of notation, set

$$\tilde{\alpha}_i = \alpha_i + \tilde{\varepsilon}_i \qquad (19.A3)$$

where $\alpha_i$ is the mean orthogonal term, $\tilde{\varepsilon}$ is the residual, and the expected value of the residual is zero:

$$E(\tilde{\varepsilon}_i) = 0 \qquad (19.A4)$$

The standard formulation then takes the form,

$$\tilde{r}_i = \alpha_i + \beta_i(\tilde{r}_e - r_f) + \tilde{\varepsilon}_i \tag{19.A5}$$

and

$$\bar{r}_i = \alpha_i + \beta_i(\bar{r}_e - r_f) \tag{19.A6}$$

so

$$\alpha_i = \bar{r}_i - \beta_i(\bar{r}_e - r_f) \tag{19.A7}$$

With this notation, note that

$$
\begin{aligned}
\sigma_{\alpha_i} &= \sigma_{\varepsilon_i} \\
&= \sqrt{\sigma_i^2 - (\beta_i \sigma_e)^2} \\
&= \sigma_i \sqrt{1 - \rho_{i,e}^2}
\end{aligned}
\tag{19.A8}
$$

### Alpha Independence

By construction, the residual, $\tilde{\varepsilon}_i$, is orthogonally independent of equity return, $\tilde{r}_e$, so

$$E(\tilde{r}_e \tilde{\varepsilon}_i) = 0$$
$$i \neq e \tag{19.A9}$$

The residuals of different asset classes will not, in general, however, be uncorrelated. In this section, we explain the conditions required to treat these residuals as approximately uncorrelated and thereby allow the allocation alpha returns to be treated as independent of each other.

The covariance between any two distinct assets, $\sigma_{i,j}^2$, with random returns $\tilde{r}_i$ and $\tilde{r}_j$ and mean returns $\bar{r}_i$ and $\bar{r}_j$ can be expressed as

$$
\begin{aligned}
\sigma_{i,j}^2 &= E(\tilde{r}_i \tilde{r}_j) - E(\tilde{r}_i) E(\tilde{r}_j) \\
&= E\left\{ \left[ \alpha_i + \beta_i(\tilde{r}_e - r_f) + \tilde{\varepsilon}_i \right] \left[ \alpha_j + \beta_j(\tilde{r}_e - r_j) + \tilde{\varepsilon}_j \right] \right\} - \overline{r_i r_j} \\
&= \alpha_i \alpha_j + \alpha_i \beta_j(\tilde{r}_e - r_f) + \alpha_j \beta_i(\tilde{r}_e - r_f) \\
&\quad + \beta_i \beta_j E\left[ (\tilde{r}_e - r_f)^2 \right] + E(\tilde{\varepsilon}_i \tilde{\varepsilon}_j) - \overline{r_i r_j}
\end{aligned}
$$

$$= \beta_i \beta_j E\left[\left(\tilde{r}_e - r_f\right)^2\right] + E(\tilde{\varepsilon}_i \tilde{\varepsilon}_j) - \beta_i \beta_j (\tilde{r}_e - r_f)^2$$

$$= \beta_i \beta_j \sigma_e^2 + \rho_{\varepsilon_i, \varepsilon_j} \sigma_{\varepsilon_i} \sigma_{\varepsilon_j}$$

$$= \rho_{i,e} \rho_{j,e} \sigma_{r_i} \sigma_{r_j} + \rho_{\varepsilon_i, \varepsilon_j} \sigma_{\varepsilon_i} \sigma_{\varepsilon_j} \qquad (19.A10)$$

Because

$$\sigma_{\varepsilon_i} = \sigma_{r_i} \sqrt{1 - \rho_{i,e}^2} \qquad (19.A11)$$

Equation 19.A10 can be expressed as

$$\sigma_{i,j}^2 = \sigma_{r_i} \sigma_{r_j} \left( \rho_{i,e} \rho_{j,e} + \rho_{\varepsilon_i, \varepsilon_j} \sqrt{1 - \rho_{i,e}^2} \sqrt{1 - \rho_{j,e}^2} \right) \qquad (19.A12)$$

The correlation between $r_i$ and $r_j$ is

$$\rho_{i,j} = \frac{\sigma_{i,j}^2}{\sigma_{r_i} \sigma_{r_j}} \qquad (19.A13)$$

$$= \rho_{i,e} \rho_{j,e} + \rho_{\varepsilon_i, \varepsilon_j} \sqrt{1 - \rho_{i,e}^2} \sqrt{1 - \rho_{j,e}^2}$$

From this formulation, one can see that even nonzero cross correlations $\rho_{\varepsilon_i, \varepsilon_j}$ will have relatively little effect on $\rho_{i,j}$, when either $\rho_{i,e}$ or $\rho_{j,e}$ is close to 1 (i.e., when either of the assets has a sufficiently large correlation with equities). Because this result holds for portfolios as well as individual assets, it suggests that the cross correlations are not likely to play a major role when dealing with beta-dominated portfolios. In other words, the correlation can be treated as if

$$\rho_{i,j} = \rho_{i,e} \rho_{j,e} \text{ for } i \neq j \qquad (19.A14)$$

and

$$i, j \neq e \qquad (19.A15)$$

## The Beta-Plus Volatility Approximation

Consider a portfolio $p$ with asset holdings having weight $\omega_i$, beta $\beta_i$, and orthogonal residual volatility $\sigma_{\alpha_i}$. Then, the beta of the portfolio can be defined as

$$\beta_p = \sum_i \omega_i \beta_i \qquad (19.A16)$$

and the portfolio's residual variance can be defined as

$$\sigma_{\alpha_p}^2 = \sum_i \omega_i^2 \sigma_{\alpha_i}^2 \qquad (19.A17)$$

The "beta-plus" approximation then becomes

$$\sigma_p^2 \cong \beta_p^2 \sigma_e^2 + \sigma_{\alpha_p}^2 \qquad (19.A18)$$

corresponding to the assumption that $\rho_{\varepsilon_i, \varepsilon_j} \cong 0$.

## REFERENCES

Leibowitz, M. 2004a. "The Changing Role of the Policy Portfolio." In *Points of Inflection: New Directions for Portfolio Management*. Charlottesville, VA: CFA Institute:30–38.

———. 2004b. "The $\beta$-Plus Measure in Asset Allocation." *Journal of Portfolio Management*, vol. 30, no. 3 (Spring):26–36.

Leibowitz, M., and A. Bova. 2004a. "Structural Betas: The Key Risk Factor in Asset Allocation." Morgan Stanley Research Notes (June 21).

———. 2004b. "Structural Alphas and Portfolio Triage." Morgan Stanley Research Notes (July 7).

———. 2004c. "Triaged Alpha Risk and the Beta-Plus Measure." Morgan Stanley Research Notes (July 16).

———. 2004d. "Beyond Diversification: Dragon Risk." Morgan Stanley Research Notes (July 21).

———. 2004e. "Increasing Relative Returns with Structural Alphas." Morgan Stanley Research Notes (October 14).

———. 2004f. "Relative Returns within a Constant-Beta Framework." Morgan Stanley Research Notes (November 14).

———. 2005. "The Efficient Frontier Using 'Alpha Cores'." Morgan Stanley Research Notes (January 7).

Markowitz, H. 1959. *Portfolio Selection: Efficient Diversification of Investments*. New York: John Wiley & Sons.

# CHAPTER 20

# Alpha Hunters and Beta Grazers

**Martin L. Leibowitz**
Managing Director
Morgan Stanley, Research

*Active alphas are derived from exploiting acute and chronic ineffi-
ciencies. They are hard to capture, but the great investors have been
able to do so over many, many years.*

There is a great philosophical divide between passive, efficiency-based beta
grazers and active alpha hunters. The explosive growth of hedge funds,
of both the traditional and the long-only format, has contributed to this
widening chasm between intensely proactive investors and those funds that
are indexed or semi-indexed.

This chapter presents my personal observations on the general subject of
active investing and on the nature, persistence, and discernibility of various
market inefficiencies that could give rise to such investment opportunities.
Ironically, these behavioral biases can act as frictions as well as opportunities, and this ambiguity may help explain why a few notable investors
appear to be almost continuously successful while other active investors fall
well short of their alpha targets.

At the outset, we should note that there is a middle ground where
relatively passive, non-zero-sum forms of alpha return can be found. As described in a series of articles (Leibowitz, 2004; Leibowitz and Bova, 2005a,
(2005c), these allocation alphas arise because the volatility risk of typical
institutional portfolios is overwhelmingly dominated by their home-market
equity exposure. By tilting their strategic allocations toward a more balanced allocation, institutions can often garner enhanced expected returns

---

with only modest increases in marginal volatility. The level of expected benefit obviously depends on the institution's specific return–risk assumptions.

Unlike truly active alphas, *allocation* alphas are broadly accessible through a semipassive process of moving toward an effective strategic allocation. As such, they are akin to the civilized sort of protein-seeking found in shopping at the local supermarket, with the selections determined by personal taste and dietary constraints. These readily available allocation alphas serve a critical and valuable role in moving a fund toward optimal strategic allocation. Allocation alphas are quite distinct, however, from the truly active alphas derived from tracking down—and bagging—the fleeting and elusive opportunities that arise from market inefficiencies. Both forms of alpha offer the potential for enhanced return, and they can sometimes be combined to create exceptional opportunities. They are quite different concepts, however, and are pursued in different ways. Having made this distinction, I focus the remainder of this article on the truly active skill-based investments that are intended to add alpha above and beyond the returns passively available in any asset class or strategic portfolio.

## TRULY ACTIVE ALPHAS

Much of the literature on truly active investing has focused on so-called anomalies—sources of incremental return that appear to have some degree of persistence. In addition, a number of elegant formalizations have been developed for incorporating active return–risk prospects into the investment decision process (Sharpe, 1991; Grinold and Kahn, 2000; Waring and Siegel, 2003; Asness, 2004). This discussion should be broadened, however, to include consideration of all frictions and behavioral biases—persistent as well as occasional—that might serve as fundamental sources of inefficiency. Such inefficiencies are not always exploitable: They may take the form of overshoots at certain times and undershoots at other times, their exploitation may be blocked by counterforces or technical restrictions of various sorts, or they may resolve themselves very slowly—or never.

We need to understand, however, that these sources of inefficiency are multifold, broad based, and continually renewing themselves. Most importantly, we need to understand that they really do exist—even if they are not always available, discernible, or directionally consistent. Such pockets of inefficiency at times become reasonably discernible and actionable—to certain active investors. Thus, their very existence becomes one facet of an argument (albeit, an admittedly still incomplete argument) for the possibility of successful active investing.

Another argument (also incomplete) is the historical fact that a handful of investors has produced extraordinary performance over a span of many years—often together with equally extraordinary cross-sectional success in their choices of disparate investments. The approaches of these great investors—Warren Buffett, Bill Miller, Leon Levy, Dave Swensen, Jack Meyer—differ in numerous aspects, but as pointed out by Peter Bernstein (2005), the investors share the common feature of not being in the mainstream (i.e., they are all contrarians in one way or another). The great ones share a number of positive characteristics—focus, patience, a clear-cut philosophy, a willingness to go beyond the diversification mantra and accept high concentration risks, an innovation-prone attitude, the organizational sponsorship and personal fortitude to endure significant periods of underperformance, and a disciplined process for pursuing their goals. And in various ways and at various points in time, they have all been willing to stake significant chips on their convictions.

With respect to this latter point, one may well recall Charles Ellis's (1998) wonderful characterization of most investors as playing what in tennis parlance is called "the loser's game." In the loser's game, weekend players, with their readily returnable forehands and backhands, square off against each other and the one who misses the last return loses. The message is to play a consistent game and to avoid miss-hits. It is generally good advice for B players—and beta grazers.

The great ones, however—in tennis and in investing—go one big step beyond. They play a disciplined game until the moment they see what looks like a grand opportunity. At that moment, they move into *carpe diem* mode, gather up their prowess, and take a calculated risk to proactively and aggressively force a win.[1]

Even the great Fischer Black was fascinated by the potential for exploitable inefficiency, although he certainly knew that such opportunities would not be easy, widespread, or available to all. He once famously answered a question about how his view of the investing world had evolved after moving from the Massachusetts Institute of Technology to Goldman Sachs with "the view is much clearer from the banks of the Charles than from the banks of the Hudson." Earlier in his career, he had delivered a wonderful talk at the University of Chicago under the title "Yes, Virginia, There Is Hope," which was later published in the *Financial Analysts Journal* (Black 1973). In that talk, he reported on his study of the Value Line Ranking System, which would have produced superior performance over a long span of years if followed religiously (and with transactional-cost efficiency!).

## CHRONIC AND ACUTE INEFFICIENCIES

Some of my pet sources of inefficiencies are behavioral and organizational distortions that I have observed over the years. I certainly do not mean to imply that they are exploitable anomalies, but they do represent the raw nuclear material out of which discernible opportunities could arise.

In perfectly efficient markets, all information would be immediately embedded in prices. The market would go through a sequence of quantum leaps from one equilibrium value to another. Investors would have no need to trade except for liquidity purposes. It would be hard to make a living working in such an idealized world. Fortunately, for those of us in the financial arena, the reality is that the markets are always in transition from one state of inefficiency to... maybe equilibrium but, more likely, a new state of inefficiency.

Inefficiencies come in many forms and subforms, but they can be roughly classified as either chronic or acute. *Acute inefficiencies* are the discernible opportunities that can be exploited by accessible arbitrages. With acute inefficiencies, the surrounding uncertainties can be hedged or minimized. Their resolution occurs quickly, well within the relevant time frame of arbitraging participants. *Chronic inefficiencies* tend to be less discernible, more ambiguous, more resistant to rapid resolution from available market forces, and generally longer term in nature. This distinction relates to Jack Treynor's (1976) wonderfully suggestive concept of fast ideas versus slow ideas.

Obviously, one would prefer to hurl fast ideas at acute inefficiencies, but by their very nature, fast ideas have a short half-life. And that half-life may be condensing with the explosive growth in hedge funds. But even in this era of the hedge fund, only a small minority of market participants spend their days in a high-performance hunt for acute inefficiencies. The vast majority of investors, and certainly the bulk of the assets, swim with the broad currents, while looking for less-fleeting incremental opportunities.

Within this mainstream, one has expanses of apparent efficiency coexisting with pockets of chronic inefficiencies. Chronic inefficiencies arise from structural and behavioral sources, such as trading frictions, organizational barriers, imbalances in capital flows, valuation ambiguities, lack of catalysts for resolution, convoy or herding behavior, artificial peer comparisons, rebalancing inconsistencies, compulsive confirmation seeking, filtering of conflicting data, misreading of market signals, inertia, formulaic action plans, and overly rigid policy portfolios. These types of chronic inefficiencies can be quite persistent. Few arbitrageurs have mandates that allow them to pursue long-term opportunities, and their absence contributes to the longevity of such inefficiencies. As the well-known saying goes: The market can remain irrational far longer than you can hang onto your position—or your career.

## Process versus Outcome

A much-discussed behavioral bias is the tendency to overemphasize recent historical results. As every mutual fund prospectus states: "Past performance should not be taken as a guide to future performance." That warning, although true, is not much help when few other hard facts are available. A more ominous rephrasing would be: "Past performance is not even a good guide to the *quality of the decisions* that went into that past performance." Yet, the ultimate issue is the soundness of the decision process itself: Was all knowable information incorporated? Was the reasoning thorough and sound? Were alternative scenarios considered and contrary views sought? Was a well-planned implementation and monitoring program established—and then followed? Was there a routine postmortem analysis of lessons learned? And are organizational discipline and staff continuity sufficient to achieve consistency in the decision process itself?

Unfortunately, the sort of retrospective analysis that includes these questions occurs more often when the outcomes are bad than when they are good. Participants would be well advised to conduct such postmortems even when the outcomes are happy ones, however, and to ask what *really* led to success. Was the positive result achieved for the reasons thought, or was it simply good fortune in this particular instance?

Even when presented with a regime that has every evidence of success—but only a probabilistic success—few investors are able to bring themselves or their organizations to consistently follow its path. The pressures of benchmarks, peer comparisons, standard accounting, liability and expenditure demands, limited organizational risk tolerance, managerial self-doubt—all can lead to lurching departures from prescribed disciplines, even ones with a high—but probabilistic—success prospect. After all, even a strategy whose success is mathematically provable will generate long runs of underperformance. Indeed, a topic in probability theory deals specifically with the risk of ruin—and the ultimate odds of ruin always favor the infinitely resourced casino.

## Convoy Behavior

Traditional modes of investing in the financial markets involve absolute or relative valuations of various market segments or securities—a process in which ambiguities, complexities, and externalities abound. Inefficiencies and opportunities do exist in this area, but they are far from clearly discernible and can only be seen "through a glass darkly."

Many chronic inefficiencies have their roots in the behavioral biases of mainstream participants. For example, consider the herding behavior of institutional funds. Participants in the financial markets find themselves on a sea of ambiguity. They may try to climb up the mast to see what lies ahead, to look for islands of opportunity, but they are always battered by the waves, the weather, and the uncertainties of navigating in uncharted waters. Is there any surprise that one sees so many sailing in convoys?

It is no coincidence that most institutional portfolios are tightly clustered, with total volatilities falling in the 10 to 11 percent range—regardless of the fund's mission, liability structure, sponsor strength, or funding status (Leibowitz and Bova, 2004). When such ambiguity abounds, people naturally assume that their peer groups may just have the right idea. This behavior is not totally irrational where theory is more art than science and where the expertise-to-luck ratio is often tilted in favor of luck. Moreover, a sufficient critical mass of investors with a common belief, even an erroneous one, can forge a pricing consensus that becomes a de facto reality that must be taken seriously.

Another issue is the valuation horizon of the average investor. The true efficient marketeer may argue that the market is continuously efficient over time. It is interesting to speculate, however, whether most investors have some specific span of time—perhaps from six months to three years—on which they focus their investment and valuation decisions. If so, investors with longer horizons may reap a somewhat larger risk premium than average investors do. In terms of Treynor's fast–slow dichotomy, the advantage may go to investors who are either faster or slower than this hypothetical norm.

Another behavioral bias is the tendency to seek the opinions of other experts who can confirm one's own views, which results in what may be called a "compounding consensus." Actually, instead of seeking confirmation, one should actively solicit *contrary* views, hear them out, consider them objectively, and then try to recognize that the financial markets themselves always reflect some balance of conflicting views. In theory, one should always start with the hypothesis that the market is well priced. Then, before acting on any potential opportunity, one should (1) try to ascertain why the market is priced where it is, (2) become convinced that the basis for this current price does not fully reflect the true opportunities, (3) believe that there is some process whereby one's views of the true state of affairs will eventually come to be widely discernible (and in a more compelling fashion than has obviously happened to date), and (4) conclude that this discernment will transpire within a relevant time span.

## Bayesian Rigidity

The compulsion to seek confirmation also relates to how the unfolding of events is interpreted. The rigid Bayesians will relentlessly try to retain their old views in the face of new information. To help counter this all-too-human inclination, one could write down the explicit reasoning behind a projected outcome and then establish the milestones that would have to occur if events took the anticipated path. Such a write-up would be akin to the contingency plans military establishments routinely create for a wide spectrum of geopolitical scenarios.

A French marquis once said:

> *He who makes detailed plans about every potential course of action, and then decides—in advance and in great detail—how to respond to the various contingencies that might arise, and then further proceeds to address the subsequent situations that could follow each possible outcome, etc., etc.—this man will make very few mistakes [actually, I'm not sure that this part is true], but he will also do very little [I am sure that this part is true].*

Yet, although the market's fast pace may limit how much contingency planning makes sense, the investment management profession surely could devote more effort in this direction.

## Price-Target Revisionism

Another area of curious behavior has to do with price targets. When a long position is taken and the market moves favorably, the price rise tends to be taken as a confirmation of the wisdom of the purchase decision. To the extent that a price target was established at the outset, the investor may then be tempted to find some rationale for revising the target upward. This revisionism has some rather obvious dangers. A more rational approach would be to assume that as the price moves toward the original target, the prospect for further incremental return decreases while the risk increases. So, as a first cut, one should think in terms of selling off a portion of the position as it moves up. Thus, investors would be well advised to have a plan to reduce the positions as the original target is approached—the burden of proof (or at least the burden of argument) being placed on the investor who wishes to maintain the original position and/or revise the price target upward.

When the market moves against one's position, one may reasonably conclude that the market is giving a clear signal that one is wrong. A more common belief is that the market is wrong and that greater return is to be expected from the lower price. To counter the natural tendency to avoid a frontal look at deteriorating positions, a help, again, may be to have a series of adverse-event milestones that could act as trip wires to signal serious reconsideration. A substantive adverse move should be the basis for asking what the market is trying to reveal and for vigorously seeking those contrary views.

## The Ebullience Cycle

Another common behavior is the unopened envelope syndrome. Back in the old days when physical envelopes were the primary delivery vehicle for individuals' portfolio statements, a persistently dreary market would lead to these envelopes being redelivered—unopened—into the circular file. Such a state of denial when the market moves against one is totally human, especially when deciding what to do about it, if anything, is not easy. The unopened envelope reinforces individuals' propensity for inaction in the face of losing positions.

The opposite phenomenon is, of course, that when the markets are moving up, the incoming envelope is eagerly awaited and ripped open with great vigor. High spirits are rampant, and risks are more comfortable. In this ebullient atmosphere, both individual and institutional investors are inclined to hold on firmly to their winning positions, which are shining examples of their brilliance. They may even invest more aggressively, leading to the phenomenon that Jack Bogle (2005) cited of markets providing one return, the mutual funds providing something less, and the investors getting even less (a number that is rarely measured, except by the individuals in pain). This problem of making ever-greater investments as the market rises is a classic cycle that is not likely to abate.

## Rebalancing Behavior

Market movements typically elicit different responses from four types of actors: holders, rebalancers, valuators, and shifters (Leibowitz and Hammond, 2004).

**Holders.**  As noted, in a deteriorating market, individuals tend to leave their envelopes unopened and positions unchanged. This holding pattern effectively reduces their equity allocations.

**Rebalancers.** Institutions behave very differently from holders. When the market pushes an institutional fund away from its policy portfolio allocation, it usually quickly rebalances back to the original percentage weights. In essence, institutions act as formulaic rebalancers.

**Valuators.** Valuators take positions based on the belief that the market is either cheap (or rich) or that it will continue (or reverse) its recent direction. Valuators can obviously play in two directions. As the market moves down, they may, based on the belief that the market has become cheap and will reverse itself, act as contrarians. As momentum players, they may view the market's decline—on either a technical or a fundamental basis—as a harbinger of further downward pressure.

**Shifters.** This category really represents a transient reaction rather than an ongoing style. Investors in any of the first three categories may find themselves becoming shifters at some point in time. Shifting occurs when a fundamental change in asset allocation is required because of circumstances intrinsic to a fund's or an individual's situation rather than because of their assessment of the market's valuation.[2] That is, shifting is a fundamental move from one strategic stance to another. For example, individuals may increase their short-term fixed-income allocations when suddenly faced with an imminent liquidity need—loss of a job, an upcoming move, a looming major purchase, medical contingencies, and so on.

Institutions are more resistant to shifting behavior. Most institutional funds have a policy portfolio that serves as an anchor for their overall strategy. The policy portfolio is intended to be the best possible passive portfolio that encapsulates all relevant information about the nature of the fund, its purpose, and how it interacts with prospective returns and risks in the financial markets. Policy portfolios have great organizational value in forming a baseline for structuring and controlling the investment management process. Following normal market movements, institutions try to rebalance back to their policy portfolios. Significant shifts tend to take place only after a major reallocation study or under extreme organizational duress. A downside to policy portfolios is that they tend to be defined somewhat arbitrarily, to be specified in greater detail than is justified, to be sustained over a longer time than is appropriate, and to form a high barrier for any tactical departure. Bill Jahnke (1999), Rob Arnott (2004), and Bernstein (2004) have written eloquently about the behavioral distortions that can arise from an overly rigid commitment to policy portfolios.

## MARKET IMPACT

These different responses may either exacerbate or moderate market movements. Obviously, the holders will have little effect on the market; they are out of the game, so to speak. The rebalancers will tend to have a smoothing effect: As the market goes down, they buy more; as the market goes up, they sell. Within the valuator category, the contrarians and reversionists will act as moderators whereas those pursuing momentum strategies will have an exacerbating effect. Because shifting tends to become more urgent (and probably more widespread) in adverse conditions, shifters will generally exacerbate market moves.

This four-part categorization also indicates something about how new flows are invested. Holders and rebalancers will usually invest their new funds congruently with their existing allocations. (However, individuals do seem to exhibit somewhat more proactive flexibility in investing their new funds than with their existing allocations. This behavior is rather curious.) Valuators, of course, will make fresh decisions about where to deploy new funds, but this type represents a relatively small part of overall new fund flows. The bulk of flows is concentrated in holders and rebalancers—those with relatively rigid channels who tend to direct new investments largely toward their current allocations.[3]

## REBALANCING AND MARKET EFFICIENCY

The rebalancing behaviors themselves may become sources of market inefficiency. Consider which of the behaviors really make sense. Suppose a fund starts with a portfolio that mirrors the market as a whole. One could argue that, in a strictly efficient market, price movements would move the fund's portfolio in concert with the evolving equilibrium, and in this case, holding behavior may make eminent sense. Most funds do not, however, have a portfolio that reflects the market as a whole (certainly not on purpose). Moreover, at least in the case of individuals, holding behavior is more likely to be the result of inertia, not sophisticated reasoning.

Some formulaic rebalancers believe they are adhering to an appropriate response in an efficient market. There is some inconsistency, however, in reestablishing the same allocation after an efficient market has made a major alteration in global asset weights. After all, a downward move reduces the asset's weight in the market portfolio, which argues for rebalancing back to an allocation somewhat lower than the original policy portfolio weight.

One sometimes hears the rationale for formulaic rebalancing presented in terms of buying cheaper after a decline and selling expensive assets after a rise. But if one really believes that the market has become discernibly cheaper as a result of a decline, should not the right move be to establish an even larger position rather than to rebalance back to the original position? After all, if the policy allocation were done afresh (given the newly cheaper valuation), the revised allocation should be even more aggressive than before. Thus, one can reasonably argue that rebalancing should, in general, lead not to a resurrection of the original allocation but, rather, to a higher or lower percentage weighting.

Ideally, rational rebalancing should not be rigidly tethered to a fixed-policy portfolio, but should respond more fluidly to market signals—to the extent they are interpreted either as an efficient restructuring of the global portfolio or as a *discernible* change in valuation. The problem, of course, is that large investment organizations are not designed to facilitate such judgmental flexibility. And as one astute chief investment officer put it, "Better to have a rigid rebalancing by prior agreement than a portfolio that deteriorates into a holding pattern because the organization lacks the confidence or the will to reestablish the policy portfolio weightings—or to even move back in that direction."

The behavior of valuators is integrally tied into the issue of *discernibility*. To the extent that discernible valuation opportunities truly exist, why not try to take advantage of them? Of course, with valuators, the big question is whether their business models *compel* them to make tactical and timing decisions even when no market opportunities meet this test of reasonable discernibility.

## RISK AS RISK TO THE POLICY PORTFOLIO

A fund's strong reluctance to being forced to shift away from its policy portfolio may play an underappreciated role in setting the fund's risk tolerance and in shaping its policy portfolio in the first place. When an institution shifts to a lower-risk allocation, it departs from the policy portfolio that was previously considered to represent an optimal allocation. Institutional funds are understandably reluctant to move away from pre-established policy portfolios. Indeed, their rebalancing behavior is specifically geared toward sustaining this portfolio structure. Most institutional managers view it as most unfortunate if the fund is forced by an extreme market movement—or by the fund's investment committee—to abandon the presumably optimal approach and shift into a lower-risk strategy.

Potential trigger points for such mandated shifts lurk in the background of every investor's mind, however, acting as fence posts that define the outer limits of tolerable risk. These fence posts may also play a feedback role in setting the policy portfolio's overall risk level in the first place. For example, suppose adverse movements of 15 to 20 percent are considered to be the tolerable outer limit of the risk envelope. Then, a fund may reasonably want to control the prospect of any such triggering event by reducing its probability to a minimal level (say, 10%). This shortfall constraint implies a portfolio volatility (risk) level in the 10 to 11 percent range, which happens to be exactly where most institutional funds are clustered.

Two further observations on this issue of risk: One is that the standard measure of risk, volatility, is an estimate of the range of returns *at a given horizon*. As pointed out by Mark Kritzman (2000) and by Kritzman and Don Rich (2002), this end-of-horizon distribution is not the same as the distribution of outcomes that could occur at some intermediary time. That distribution is much wider. And, logically, this riskier intermediary distribution should determine when trigger points may be activated.[4]

## THE ILLUSION OF GROWTH ETERNAL

Participants in the financial markets are intrinsically oriented toward an optimistic view of a world with a continuously compounding growth of value. Reality reminds us, however, that wealth can also be destroyed—both by whimpers and by bangs. Sidney Homer and I (2004) once posed the following question: If a Roman soldier put just one drachma in a savings account and let it compound at 4 percent throughout the ages, how much money would his descendants have today? The answer turned out to be so many drachmas that, at virtually any exchange rate, it would amount to far more than the total existing wealth in the world. This outcome led to a follow-up question: What happened to it all? The sobering answer is that wealth is destroyed by war, inflation, devaluation, pandemic, political collapse, repudiation, obsolescence, virulent competition, bankruptcy, financial debacle, revolutionary technology, nonproductive investment, and so on. The natural inclination to deny the phantom of such discontinuities may be necessary for moving things forward, but it may also be a chronic source of inefficiency.

## CONCLUSION

Participants in the financial markets often find themselves sailing on a sea of ambiguity through broad patches of fog, bouts of heavy weather, and occasional balmy periods that may prove only to be the center of passing storms. One can elect the passive approach—fly the beta flag and allow one's portfolio to float on the index currents. Or one can choose to be an active alpha-seeking investor and try to chip away at the many chronic inefficiencies and behavioral biases that we know exist, even though we cannot clearly discern how they are priced and whether they will profitably regress toward equilibrium within a reasonable time. With chronic inefficiencies, by their very definition, discernibility will always be somewhat clouded. (Otherwise, they would become acute—and would be long gone.) So, with these opportunities, one is always acting on imperfect knowledge and playing the odds. But without actively scanning the horizon and being poised to move on reasonably discernible opportunities, investors will surely have no chance of reaping the incremental return inherent in the grand continuous march toward efficiency.

The great investors are like the great sailors: They have the courage to set forth, they know where they want to go, they have a strong gyroscope to keep them on course, they have appropriate respect for the dangers of the sea and its potential for radical shifts in weather and currents, and they are not afraid to be alone for long stretches.

## NOTES

1. Although I argue for the possibility of successful active investing, I do not wish to suggest that everyone can be a winner. Indeed, they cannot. And the narrowness of the list of great investors attests to that dour fact. The great mass of investors should treat the market as being highly efficient and should start with the null hypothesis that all assets are fairly priced.
2. In some cases, market movements do ultimately lead to a portfolio shift. For example, a rule of thumb says that many individuals will let their allocations drift until a 15 to 20 percent decline from some high-water mark forces them to seriously reconsider their risk tolerances. I am drawing a distinction, however, between shifts based on a market-driven change in risk tolerance and those reallocations that are directly valuation motivated.
3. The large majority of existing dollar assets are also controlled by holders and formulaic rebalancers, which leads to the interesting question of whether the key risk premiums between asset classes are being priced by a relatively minor segment of the investing universe.
4. An even more severe criterion would be based on the range of declines from a high-water mark (Leibowitz and Bova, 2005b).

## REFERENCES

Arnott, Robert D. 2004. "Managing Assets in a World of Higher Volatility and Lower Returns." In *Points of Inflection: New Directions for Portfolio Management* (Charlottesville, VA: CFA Institute):39–52.

Asness, C. 2004. "An Alternative Future." *Journal of Portfolio Management* (Special Anniversary Issue):94–103.

Bernstein, P. L. 2004. "Overview: A Fifth Point of Inflection." In *Points of Inflection: New Directions for Portfolio Management* (Charlottesville, VA: CFA Institute):1–5.

———. 2005. "Alpha: The Real Thing, or Chimerical?" *Economics and Portfolio Strategy* (March 5).

Black, F. 1973. "Yes, Virginia, There Is Hope: Tests of the Value Line Ranking System." *Financial Analysts Journal*, vol. 29, no. 5 (September/October):10–14.

Bogle, J. 2005. "The Mutual Fund Industry 60 Years Later: For Better or Worse?" *Financial Analysis Journal*, vol. 61, no. 1 (January/February):15–24.

Ellis, C. 1998. *Winning the Loser's Game*. New York: McGraw-Hill.

Grinold, R. C., and R. N. Kahn. 2000. *Active Portfolio Management*. 2nd ed. New York: McGraw-Hill.

Homer, S., and M. L. Leibowitz. 2004. *Inside the Yield Book*. Princeton, NJ: Bloomberg Press.

Jahnke, W. 1999. "Why Setting an Asset Allocation Policy Is a Bad Idea." *Journal of Financial Planning* (February). Available online at www.fpanet.org/journal/articles/1999_Issues/jfp0299-art5.cfm.

Kritzman, M. P. 2000. *Puzzles of Finance*. New York: John Wiley & Sons.

Kritzman, M. P., and D. Rich. 2002. "The Mismeasurement of Risk." *Financial Analysis Journal*, vol. 58, no. 3 (May/June):91–99.

Leibowitz, M. L. 2004. "The $\beta$-Plus Measure in Asset Allocation." *Journal of Portfolio Management*, vol. 30, no. 3 (Spring):26–36

Leibowitz, M. L., and A. Bova. 2004. "Structural Betas: The Key Risk Factor in Asset Allocation." Morgan Stanley Research Notes (June 21).

———. 2005a. "The Efficient Frontier Using 'Alpha Cores'." Morgan Stanley Research Notes (January 7).

———. 2005b. "Convergence of Risk." Morgan Stanley Research Note (April).

———. (2005c. "Allocation Betas." *Financial Analysts Journal*, vol. 61, no. 4) (July/August):70–82.

Leibowitz, M. L., and P. B. Hammond. 2004. "The Changing Mosaic of Investment Patterns." *Journal of Portfolio Management*, vol. 30, no. 3 (Spring): 10–25.

Sharpe, W. F. 1991. "From the Board: The Arithmetic of Active Management." *Financial Analysts Journal*, vol. 47, no. 1 (January/February):7–9.

Treynor, J. L. 1976. "Long-Term Investing." *Financial Analysts Journal*, vol. 32, no. 3 (May/June):56–59.

Waring, M. B., and L. B. Siegel. 2003. "The Dimensions of Active Management." *Journal of Portfolio Management*, vol. 29, no. 3 (Spring):35–52.

# CHAPTER 21

# Gathering Implicit Alphas in a Beta World

## New Questions about Alternative Assets

**Martin Leibowitz**
Managing Director
Morgan Stanley, Research


**Anthony Bova**
Vice President
Morgan Stanley, Research

In recent years, U.S. institutional funds have trended toward diversification into a broad range of asset classes. For the most part, this diversification has turned out to be quite productive, helping to materially increase their returns over time. Yet, with the proliferation of asset classes, it has become increasingly difficult to gain a clear insight into fundamental risk characteristics of increasingly complex policy portfolios.

In a search for such a risk measure, we have examined a number of institutional-style allocations, from the traditional 60/40 equity/bond approach to more modern allocations, some with as many as 12 different asset classes.

The first step is to identify a primary risk factor. Although the natural candidate is the exposure to U.S. equities, the equity percentage by itself is clearly an inadequate risk gauge for highly diversified funds. Some way is needed to capture the *implicit* beta effects contributed by growing allocations to alternative asset classes.

This article originally appeared in the Spring 2007 issue of *The Journal of Portfolio Management*, published by Institutional Investor, Inc.

**EXHIBIT 21.1** Sample Return/Covariance Matrix

| | | | Correlations | | | |
|---|---|---|---|---|---|---|
| | Expected Return | Volatility | REITs | U.S. Equity | U.S. Bonds | Cash |
| REITs | 6.50 | 14.50 | 1.00 | 0.55 | 0.30 | 0.00 |
| U.S. Equity | 7.25 | 16.50 | 0.55 | 1.00 | 0.30 | 0.00 |
| U.S. Bonds | 3.75 | 7.50 | 0.30 | 0.30 | 1.00 | 0.00 |
| Cash | 1.50 | 0.00 | 0.00 | 0.00 | 0.00 | 1.00 |

*Source:* Morgan Stanley Research

## IMPLICIT BETAS AND TOTAL FUND BETAS

One path to these implicit betas led us to the covariance matrix that funds (or their consultants) use to develop recommended allocations. In essence, these covariance matrices represent market models for the statistically anticipated comovements among asset classes.

Exhibit 21.1 presents a sample of the components that might constitute such a covariance matrix.

From the assumed comovement of an asset class with U.S. equities, it is possible to calculate an implicit beta measure as in Exhibit 21.2. Then, for a given allocation, all the weighted beta values—both implicit and explicit—would be rolled up to arrive at a *total* beta sensitivity for the fund as a whole.

Exhibit 21.3 is representative of the results when this total beta analysis is applied to a wide range of institutional allocations. Four surprises immediately emerge.

The first surprise is that virtually every U.S. pension, endowment, and foundation fund has a total volatility in the 10.00 to 11.50 percent range.

**EXHIBIT 21.2** Beta: REITs

$$Beta = Correlation\ with\ U.S.\ Equity \left[ \frac{Volatility\ of\ REITs}{Volatility\ of\ U.S.\ Equity} \right]$$
$$= 0.55 \left[ \frac{14.50}{16.50} \right]$$
$$= 0.48$$

*Source:* Morgan Stanley Research

**EXHIBIT 21.3**  Model Portfolios with Clustered Betas and Volatilities

|  | A | B | S | C |
|---|---|---|---|---|
| **Swing Assets** | | | | |
| U.S. Equity | 60% | 60% | 45% | 20% |
| U.S. Bonds | | 40% | 35% | 20% |
| Cash | 40% | | | |
| Total Swing Assets | 100% | 100% | 80% | 40% |
| **Alpha Core** | | | | |
| International Equity | | | 20% | 15% |
| Emerging Mkt Equity | | | | 5% |
| Absolute Return | | | | 10% |
| Venture Capital | | | | 10% |
| Private Equity | | | | 10% |
| Real Estate | | | | 10% |
| Alpha Core % | 0% | 0% | 20% | 60% |
| Total Beta | | | | |
| Expected Return | 4.95 | 5.85 | 6.03 | 7.08 |
| Total Volatility | | | | |
| Beta × Equity Volatility (16.5%) | 9.90 | 10.80 | 10.75 | 9.45 |
| % Volatility from Beta | | | | |

*Source:* Morgan Stanley Research

Whereas most funds knew their own volatility level, they were quite surprised to find that other funds, some of them looking very different, are also clustered within this same narrow volatility band.

The second surprise is that roughly 90 percent or more of this total volatility is explained by the correlation with U.S. equity. Thus, in spite of their diversification into multiple asset classes, most funds' volatility characteristics remain fundamentally unchanged—that is, dominated totally by equity risk.

The third surprise comes from calculating a total beta by combining the explicit equity percentage with the implicit betas based on the correlation of each asset class with equities. The resulting total beta values all fall into a common range between 0.55 and 0.65. When the total beta values are multiplied by the volatility of equity, the resulting beta-based volatility accounts for 90 percent or more of the allocation's total volatility. This volatility dominance applies even to the most highly diversified allocations with as little as 20 percent direct exposure to equities.

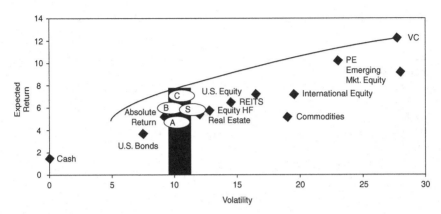

**EXHIBIT 21.4** Unconstrained Efficient Frontier with Model Portfolios
*Source:* Morgan Stanley Research

The fourth surprise is that the diversification into a broader range of asset classes does not significantly reduce a fund's total volatility, but it does materially improve the expected return.

Exhibit 21.4 displays a computer-generated efficient frontier based on a return/covariance matrix. This graph confirms the narrow range of volatilities, even though the four model portfolios represent very different levels of diversification. Thus, we see that, contrary to conventional wisdom, diversification as typically pursued improves expected returns but has a relatively minor impact on fund volatility.

The early work on this total beta concept is described in Leibowitz and Hammond (2004) and Leibowitz (2005a).

## NEW QUESTIONS

These findings raise several questions:

- Why is fund volatility not reduced by the standard form of diversification?
- What is the nature of the incremental expected return derived from diversification?
- If these incremental returns can be achieved without increased volatility risk, why not pursue them more aggressively?
- Can such incremental return be stable in an increasingly competitive market?

- Why do funds appear to set their volatility risks at roughly the same level?
- What are the implications for the construction and monitoring of a fund's policy portfolio?

In this chapter, we attempt to provide some answers.

## BETA-PRESERVING DIVERSIFICATIONS

The natural tendency is to equate diversification with risk reduction. Yet diversification can take many forms; some reduce a fund's risk, whereas others may actually increase it.

Exhibit 21.5 illustrates three ways to diversify a standard 60/40 portfolio into an allocation that is 20 percent real estate investment trusts (REITs). First, with 20 percent equities as the funding source, both the beta and the volatility are obviously reduced. Second, funding with 20 percent bonds increases both the beta and the total volatility. The third case, however, is more representative of the actual practice among institutional funds—the funding source is some combination of high-beta equity and low-beta bonds.

This exchange of a mid-beta funding package for a new mid-beta asset results in a relatively unchanged portfolio beta. With the total beta preserved, the volatility remains about the same, even as the expected return increases.

**EXHIBIT 21.5** Diversification and Total Volatility

| | Portfolio Allocation | | | Risk/Return Characteristics | | | |
| | Equity | Bonds | REITs | Total Beta | Total Volatility | Total Return | % Vol. from Beta |
|---|---|---|---|---|---|---|---|
| Diversifying Move into | | | | | | | |
| 20% REITs Funded with: | | | | | | | |
| 20% Equity | 40% | 40% | 20% | 0.55 | 9.82 | 5.70 | 92.4% |
| 20% Bonds | 60% | 20% | 20% | 0.72 | 12.26 | 6.40 | 97.3% |
| 10% Bonds 10% Equity | | | | | | | |

*Source:* Morgan Stanley Research

## IMPLICIT ALPHAS

The incremental returns in Exhibit 21.5 are derived from the return/risk characteristics of REITs.

As shown in Exhibit 21.6, one component (2.88%) of REITs' expected 5.00 percent return premium can be ascribed to its implicit beta value of 0.48 and its corresponding co-movement with U.S. equities. After this beta-based return is deducted, the residual return of 2.22 percent can be viewed as an implicit alpha, in the sense that this incremental return can be obtained without significant increases in the fund-level volatility.

These implicit alphas are passive in that there is no presumption of positive outcomes from the selection of superior managers or from direct active investment by an asset manager.

By definition, these implicit alphas will always have a zero correlation with U.S. equity. At the same time, the original covariance model may imply that these implicit alphas themselves are subject to a high level of non-equity-related volatility risk. Because of the generally fragmented allocation and weak cross correlations, however, the sum total of these model-based alpha volatilities will typically have a minimal impact at the portfolio level.

Thus, allocation to such an alternative asset will directly add its weighted alpha to the fund's return and its weighted beta to the fund's beta, but its model-based alpha volatility will have only a minimal impact at the total fund level.

## HUNTING ACTIVE ALPHAS, GATHERING IMPLICIT ALPHAS

The term *alpha* has multiple meanings in the financial literature. One common usage refers to the hoped-for incremental return derived from superior

**EXHIBIT 21.6**  Implicit Passive Alpha: REITs

| | |
|---|---|
| Total Return | 6.50 |
| Less Risk-Free Rate | (1.50) |
| REIT Risk Premium | 5.00 |
| Less (REIT Beta 0.48* Equity Risk Premium 5.75) | (2.78) |
| Implicit REIT Alpha | 2.22 |

*Source*: Morgan Stanley Research

security selection, accessing the best-performing managers, or successful timing strategies. Such active alphas call for a higher skill level or a greater flexibility to achieve favorable outcomes.

In Leibowitz (2005b), we use the metaphor of a *beta grazer* to describe index funds that seek simply low-cost index-like exposure to the traditional equity and fixed-income markets. The term *alpha hunter* is used to characterize the highly proactive effort needed to track down and capture the fleeting opportunities derived from market inefficiencies and anomalies. These active alphas are intrinsically zero-sum in the sense that for every gain by one market participant, there must be a corresponding loss (or forgone opportunity) taken from some other participant.

Unlike these active alphas, the implicit alphas described earlier are broadly accessible through a semipassive process of moving incrementally toward a more effective strategic allocation. These implicit alphas can serve a valuable role in acting as vectors that point the fund toward more optimal allocations. They are, thus, not zero-sum, in that they need not be direct takeaways from other market participants.

In a sense, taking advantage of the implicit alphas that are truly available—and digestible—lies somewhere between passive beta grazing and aggressive hunting for active alphas. To push the metaphor one step further, implicit alphas can enrich the diet of herbivores who are willing to raise their sights to include a limited amount of low-hanging fruit and berries (and maybe even nuts). Going even further into the metaphoric wilderness, it perhaps should be noted that some berries could be poisonous. Finally, although omnivores are fairly rare in nature, they may be the most popular species in the financial markets.

Implicit alphas are, thus, quite distinct from active alphas. Both forms of alpha offer the potential for enhanced return, and they can sometimes be combined to create exceptional opportunities. All the same, they are quite different concepts, and are pursued in different ways.

- Active alphas must be hunted.
- Implicit alphas can be gathered.

## THE ALPHA WALL

The term *alpha core* can be used to refer to the subportfolio of alternative assets. We have said that the beta risk in most institutional portfolios tends to overwhelm any volatility impact from an alpha core. Thus, rather than the oft-cited diversification argument, the alpha core's real benefit is return enhancement.

The nature of this beta domination and the core's return-enhancing role can be dramatically illustrated by transforming the standard return/risk diagram into the alpha *wall* format shown in Exhibit 21.7. The dashed line is the cash/equity line. The wall coming from this point represents the added return derived from an increasing weight assigned to the alpha core. When this assigned core percentage reaches 30 percent. we have a portfolio with an enhanced total return at the prescribed 10 percent volatility.

The key point of the alpha wall diagram is to show how the addition of the core enhances the return/risk characteristics of the overall portfolio. With a low core percentage and a high level of beta domination, the fund return climbs almost vertically up the alpha wall, reflecting the significant return enhancement obtainable with only minimal added volatility.

Exhibit 21.7 also shows how the portfolio's return and risk will shift if additional weight can theoretically be added to the given core structure. As the core weight moves beyond 30 to 60 percent, the wall bends increasingly to the right, as the incremental volatility addition becomes more significant—but the total volatility can be kept at a specified 10 percent target level by a modest reduction in the fund's total beta exposure.

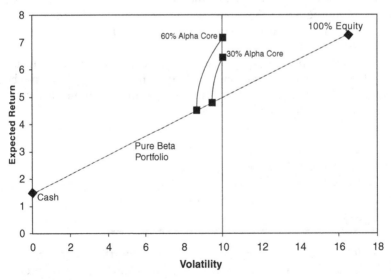

**EXHIBIT 21.7**   The Alpha Wall
*Source*: Morgan Stanley Research

## ALPHA CONSTRAINTS AND BEYOND-MODEL RISKS

Asset classes with positive implicit alphas can provide the fund with a higher expected return with little impact on total volatility. Why not pursue this apparently free lunch more vigorously? A related question is why not concentrate the alternative allocation on the single highest alpha source, rather than scattering the weight over multiple alpha assets?

In practice, the allowable allocation into any alternative asset is always subject to constraints. These constraints play a fundamental role in the ultimate outcome of any allocation study. The position limits may be based on a variety of factors: underdeveloped financial markets, liquidity concerns, limited access to acceptable investment vehicles or first-class managers, problematical fee structures, regulatory or organizational structures, peer-based standards, headline risk, or insufficient or unreliable historical data. Regardless of any optimization results based upon a given return/covariance matrix, it is these beyond-model risks that determine the percentage weight ultimately assigned to the various alpha sources.

Some limits placed on acceptable asset classes may be due to a lack of familiarity, unfounded fears, or absence of peer support. Other constraints may have a very rational basis in valid beyond-model considerations, even when a precise articulation of the reasoning may be elusive. Whatever the reason, at any given point in a fund's evolution, some of these constraints will be binding and thereby limit the available allocations. Consequently, moving to higher percentages in the alpha core may not be possible if it tips one or more asset classes over their set limits.

Thus, unlike the simple example illustrated in Exhibit 21.7, a given alpha core may not be scalable in a continually proportional fashion, whether by increased allocation weighting or by leveraging. At some point, one or more of the asset classes will approach its limit, requiring a revision in the core's percentage composition as it grows in weight or aggregate exposure.

It should also be noted that, although the total volatility is the standard measure of fund risk, there are other risk concerns that deserve mention. In addition to the beyond-model risks, there are other risks associated with the fund's ultimate ability to meet its (possibly complex) set of liabilities. (This issue of surplus risk is a critically important factor in many settings, but it is beyond our asset-only focus.)

Fund-level tracking error (TE) represents the statistical deviation of returns measured relative to the passive policy portfolio. The year-by-year deviations between any two funds can be significantly different even when both funds have the same level of total volatility over time. These year-by-year deviations may also have to be considered in assessing the various concerns associated with peer group comparisons.

## THE ALPHA/BETA MATRIX

The alpha/beta matrix in Exhibit 21.8 attempts to classify the various forms of portfolio management styles using an alpha/beta template.

- The *beta grazers* are the index funds that passively feed off the return premiums that are broadly available to all.
- The *gatherers* are funds that expand their allocation by diversifying, but passively, into a wider range of asset classes with the intention of accessing the implicit alphas.
- The alpha *hunters* are the active managers who aggressively seek excess returns from the exercise of superior investment skill. Unlike gathering, hunting is an intrinsically zero-sum activity.
- Then there are the *foragers*, who venture forth and seek returns wherever they can be found.

All of these return-seeking pursuits can prove valuable if pursued successfully, but they differ materially in the character of the risks entailed—and the nature of their fund-level effects.

Benchmark-centric alpha hunting should ideally have risks that take the form of a moderate level of uncorrelated TE. Benchmark-sensitive alpha hunting will involve higher levels of TE and some degree of beta variability.

The gathering of implicit alphas in new asset classes may entail a substantial degree of uncorrelated TE, but the more significant risk in expanded diversification arises from the beyond-model risks. Although these risk factors may not be formalized, they reveal themselves at the fund level through the de facto limits imposed on the nontraditional asset classes.

Free-range foraging can incur any and all of these forms of risk. The fund-level impact depends on the intensity of the risks and the percentage of the overall allocation deployed in each form of active management.

Clearly, these activities can be mixed and matched. For example, an alpha-gatherer fund may well elect—at the outset or subsequently—to become a hunter and pursue active alphas—as well as the passive alphas—implicit within the new asset classes.

## REVERSING THE STANDARD OPTIMIZATION

The allocation process has historically proceeded from a basic equity/fixed-income allocation and then evolved step-by-step toward some alternative

**EXHIBIT 21.8** Fund-Level Alpha/Beta Structures

| Metaphor | Betas | Management Styles | Nature of Alphas | Fund Level Effects | | |
|---|---|---|---|---|---|---|
| | | | | Fund Volatility | Model Risk | TE vs. Policy |
| Beta Grazing | Stapled | Passive Investing in Broad Equity/Fixed Income Markets | Risk Premium | Fundamental Source | Very Low | Zero |
| Alpha Hunting | Beta-Targeted | Risk-Controlled Active Equity Market Neutral Active Extension | Active Management | Low | Low | Low |
| Alpha Gathering | Correlation-Based | Diversification into New Asset Classes Concentrated Long-Only Some Hedge Funds | Implicit Correlation-Based Passive Alphas and Selection Alphas | Low | High | Low/High |
| Alpha Foraging | Free Range Betas | Beta-Agnostic Opportunistic Investment Some Hedge Funds Macro Funds | Hyper Active | High | High | High |

*Source*: Morgan Stanley Research

assets. Now the central role of the alpha core in determining the fund's expected return argues for consideration of a reversal of the conventional approach.

One problem with any formal mean-variance analysis is that it often devolves into a tortured optimization process. Using the raw input of returns, volatilities, and correlations for different asset classes, the initial computer-based solution will usually be unacceptable. Certain asset classes will be given weights that far exceed credible limits. The typical next step is to impose a sequence of ad hoc constraints, until repeated optimization produces a portfolio that becomes palatable.

There is nothing fundamentally wrong with this procedure when a reasonable portfolio is the final outcome. Yet the mathematical and computer complexities involved in the standard optimization can obscure the more intuitive decision process that should play a fundamental role in the final outcome.

One way to address this problem is to accept some approximations to obtain a simpler and more naturally intuitive framework. It turns out that the alpha/beta framework can provide a path to this simplification. Moreover, this alpha/beta approach may even better reflect how portfolios are structured in practice.

The underlying philosophy is that any set of market assumptions is inherently imprecise—at best. Therefore, it is far better to develop approximate guidelines than to become enmeshed in a complex methodology that promises theoretically refined solutions, but obscures the role that should be played by intuition, judgment, and common sense.

The key is to use the alpha/beta approach to decompose a portfolio's assets into two groups: (1) the alpha core, and (2) the swing assets, that is, the traditional liquid assets—U.S. equity, U.S. bonds, and cash—that are used relatively freely to help shape the portfolio's overall risk structure.

The alpha core approach presumes that the fund will first determine the maximum acceptable limits for each asset class outside the basic swing assets. The next decision will be to combine these asset choices into a coherent alpha core subportfolio. The composition of this subportfolio will generally involve both intuitive and qualitative considerations that go well beyond the explicit quantitative characteristics embedded in the return/covariance matrix.

For modern portfolios, structuring the alpha core demands concentrated research, judgment, and deliberation, both by fund sponsors and by their managers. Although they might not use the specific term, alpha core, we believe large funds already devote major effort to this decision, at both the allocation and the implementation levels.

When an acceptable alpha core has been formed, its return and risk characteristics can be transformed into basic alpha/beta terms. Taken together, these core assumptions then allow the allocation problem to be decomposed into three basic steps: (1) determining the size limits for asset classes that can be used to form the alpha core; (2) developing an optimal alpha core, given these constraints; and (3) incorporating the swing assets to adjust the portfolio's desired balance of return and risk.

The basic idea is that, rather than using the standard optimization procedure with its sequential constraints, a better portfolio may be obtained from a more deliberate (and perhaps more deliberated) confrontation of the many issues that go into forming an acceptable alpha core.

## RISK AS RISK TO THE POLICY PORTFOLIO

One question raised by this analysis is why most funds have total fund volatilities that fall within the same 10 to 11 percent range.

A fund's strong reluctance to being forced to shift away from its policy portfolio may play an underappreciated role in setting the fund's risk tolerance and in shaping its policy portfolio in the first place. When an institution shifts to a lower-risk or higher-risk allocation, it departs from the policy portfolio that it has considered to represent an optimal allocation.

Institutional funds are understandably reluctant to move away from these preestablished policy portfolios. Indeed, a fund's rebalancing behavior is specifically geared toward sustaining this portfolio structure. Most institutional managers would view it as particularly unfortunate if the fund were forced by an extreme market movement—or by the fund's investment committee—to abandon its presumably optimal approach and shift into a lower-risk strategy.

Potential trigger points for such mandated shifts lurk in the background of every investor's mind, however, acting as fence posts that define the outer limits of tolerable risk. These fence posts may also play a feedback role in setting the policy portfolio's overall risk level in the first place.

For example, suppose adverse movements of 15 to 20 percent are considered the tolerable outer limit of the risk envelope. Then, a fund might reasonably want to control the prospect of any such triggering event by reducing this probability to a minimal level. It can be shown that a combination of reasonable shortfall constraints leads total betas toward the 0.55 to 0.65 range and portfolio volatilities of 10 to 11 percent; that is exactly where risk levels are located in practice.

Under the banner of diversification, funds adopt different mixes of active alpha hunting or implied alpha gathering that they find suitable as a way to enhance their expected return. Yet there seems to be a surprising commonality in their determination to avoid roughly the same level of catastrophic risk. With the equity beta serving as the dominating risk factor for virtually all institutional funds, it is likely that any such catastrophic event would be the result of—or at least associated with—a major equity downturn. Consequently, it may not really be too surprising that total fund betas are generally found to lie in the narrow range of 0.55 to 0.65.

## STRESS BETAS

A fund's beta essentially determines its total volatility level, but the implied betas and the fund's volatility are both based on the probability distribution of overall returns. In fact, the critical risk event may actually be an adverse market move so severe as to force a reconsideration of the current policy allocation. Such a sharp market movement would likely create short-term technical conditions leading to tightened correlations and higher betas across virtually all financial assets.

Moreover, any persistent downturn is likely to be driven by a significant decline in equities. In this case, the conditional correlations and betas would tend to remain quite high—even after relaxation of the shorter-term technical tightening described earlier. In other words, in a persistent severe downturn, even a highly diversified portfolio is likely to exhibit a much higher equity correlation than normal. This persistent effect is quite distinct from the more frequently mentioned sudden-move tightenings.

A severe stress situation may be the defining risk scenario that determines the structure of a fund's policy portfolio. Thus, to the extent that the total fund beta is a precursor of these higher stress betas, it may prove to be a better gauge of the fundamental risk characteristics than the fund's standard volatility measure.

## ALPHA EROSION UNDER BETA DOMINATION

The growing acceptance (and even fashionability) of alternative asset classes engenders new dollar flows that could lead to a reduction in prospective alpha returns. When the source of an alpha is limited, return erosion would be the natural evolution as a market moves toward a rational equilibrium under the pressure of such new demand.

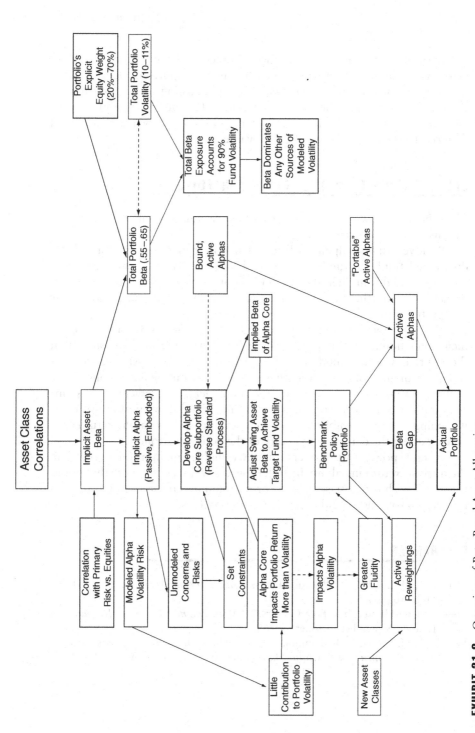

**EXHIBIT 21.9** Overview of Beta-Based Asset Allocation
*Source:* Morgan Stanley Resarch

In reality, there are always multiple sources of demand for a given asset class. As the alphas are pushed down by one new source of demand, they will at the same time be driving away other preexisting sources of support. At some point, the net effect of attracted new demand (or supply) will just balance the exit of the earlier supporters, and going-forward returns will then reach some non-zero equilibrium value.

## GREATER FLUIDITY IN THE POLICY PORTFOLIO

The schematic flowchart in Exhibit 21.9 traces out a number of the implications of this beta-based analysis.

Positive implicit alphas will act as a powerful magnet for any beta-dominated fund. As funds that control large pools of assets become increasingly flexible in their allocation philosophy, they can deploy significant dollar flows into these positive alpha sources, and almost surely lower the prospective alpha returns.

This dynamic environment has major implications for the development and monitoring of policy portfolios. One such implication is that the return/covariance models may become increasingly unstable, with the rapidly evolving role of alternative assets in institutional portfolios. The return/covariance assumptions are the fundamental ingredients that shape the fund's policy portfolio at any given time. Fund flows that are so overwhelming as to discernibly depress an asset's prospective alpha returns can quickly affect the continuing validity of the policy portfolio.

A stable policy portfolio serves many valuable organizational needs, but the intrinsic return instability in alpha sources will seem to argue that policy portfolios with broad-based alpha cores should be subject to more frequent review and to a more fluid decision-making process.

## REFERENCES

Leibowitz, M. L. 2005a. "Allocation Betas." *Financial Analysts Journal*, vol. 61, no. 4 (July/August):70–82.

—— "Alpha Hunters and Beta Grazers." 2005b. *Financial Analysts Journal*, vol. 61, no. 5 (September/October):32–39.

Leibowitz, M. L., and P. B. Hammond. 2004. "The $\beta$-Plus Measure in Asset Allocation." *The Journal of Portfolio Management*, vol. 30, no. 3 (Spring):26–36.

CHAPTER **22**

# Optimal Gearing

## Not All Long/Short Portfolios Are Efficient

**Seanna Johnson**
Head, Japan Active Equity
Barclays Global Investors

**Ronald N. Kahn**
Global Head, Advanced Equity Strategies
Barclays Global Investors

**Dean Petrich**
Head, Proprietary Analytics
Barclays Global Investors

**W**ith the developments in quantitative finance over the past 50 years, investors have increasingly understood the importance of engineering portfolios to represent their views effectively. Markowitz (1959) began this process in the 1950s by specifying a clear mathematical approach to trading off expected return and risk. Sharpe (1963), Treynor and Black (1973), Rosenberg (1976), and others advanced the process by focusing active investors on how to build portfolios to beat specific performance benchmarks.

More recent work by Grinold and Kahn (2000a) and Clarke, de Silva, and Thorley (2002) has proposed specific measures of implementation efficiency—especially the transfer coefficient (TC)—to capture precisely how well portfolios represent underlying views. This work has improved our understanding of how constraints and costs impact portfolios.

---

This article originally appeared in the Summer 2007 issue of Institutional Investor's *Journal of Portfolio Management*.

One particular application has been an analysis of the impact of the long-only constraint, quantifying the advantages of long/short investing. Clarke, de Silva, and Sapra (2004) have further analyzed the advantages of partial long/short investing.

Most investors today understand that long/short portfolios reflect manager views more accurately than long-only portfolios. But is that the end of the story? Do all long/short portfolios exhibit similar efficiencies? Or, do even long/short portfolio managers face choices that can significantly impact their efficiency?

This article describes another important dimension—gearing—along which to consider implementation efficiency. Consider an equity market-neutral portfolio manager designing a $100 million product to deliver the maximum possible expected alpha at 10 percent risk. She can invest $100 million in a 10 percent risk portfolio. Or, she can use $100 million to collateralize a $300 million portfolio run at 3.3 percent risk. Or she can choose among a continuum of possible combinations of active risk and leverage.

As we will show, portfolio efficiency and the expected alpha of the portfolio vary in surprising, interesting, and important ways along that continuum. There is an optimal level of gearing to maximize efficiency, but, conversely, a poor choice of gearing can make a poor long/short implementation even less efficient than long-only.

We introduce the method using a simple model and embellishments. We provide both a rule of thumb to judge whether a portfolio is overgeared or undergeared and an analysis of an actual portfolio facing exactly this issue.

## SIMPLE MODEL

We first find the optimal relation between gearing and risk in a simple model, using the general framework of Grinold and Kahn (2000b). Later, we generalize this model to investigate the efficiency loss due to incompatible gearing and risk levels.

We start with an investment universe consisting of $N$ stocks, with uncorrelated residual returns, $\theta_n$, and identical residual risk levels, $\omega_0$. We assume individual stock expected residual returns have the form:

$$E\{\theta_n\} \equiv \alpha_n = IC \cdot \omega_0 \cdot z_n \qquad (22.1)$$

with the same information coefficient, $IC$, for each stock. The terms $\{z_n\}$ are independent, normally distributed, random variables with mean 0 and standard deviation 1.

Combining Equation 22.1 with the active management utility function:

$$U = \mathbf{h}^T \cdot \alpha - \lambda \mathbf{h}^T \cdot \mathbf{VR} \cdot \mathbf{h}$$

$$\Rightarrow \sum_{n=1}^{N} h_n \cdot \alpha_n - \lambda h_n^2 \cdot \omega_0^2 \tag{22.2}$$

where **h** represents portfolio holdings, and **VR** is the covariance matrix of residual returns, leads to optimal holdings:

$$h_n^* = \frac{\alpha_n}{2\lambda\omega_0^2} \Rightarrow \left(\frac{IC}{2\lambda}\right) \cdot \left(\frac{z_n}{\omega_0}\right) \tag{22.3}$$

Using Equation 22.3, we can calculate the portfolio alpha and risk as

$$\alpha^* = \left(\frac{IC^2}{2\lambda}\right) \cdot \sum_{n=1}^{N} z_n^2$$

$$\omega^* = \left(\frac{IC}{2\lambda}\right) \cdot \sqrt{\sum_{n=1}^{N} z_n^2} \tag{22.4}$$

Where does gearing enter here? We define as *unlevered* a market-neutral portfolio that is 100 percent long and 100 percent short, with 100 percent deposited in a collateral account. For example, an unlevered $100 million market-neutral portfolio has $100 million long, $100 million short, and $100 million deposited in a collateral account.

Although this is our definition in this article—and it is a common definition—others define this as two-times levered. With our view, we more generally define portfolio leverage, or *gearing*, as

$$G \equiv \frac{1}{2} \sum_{n=1}^{N} |h_n| \tag{22.5}$$

According to Equation 22.5, a portfolio 100 percent long and 100 percent short has a gearing of one. In our simple model, the portfolio gearing is related to the z-scores by

$$G^* = \frac{1}{2} \left(\frac{IC}{2\lambda\omega_0}\right) \cdot \sum_{n=1}^{N} |z_n| \tag{22.6}$$

If $N$ is reasonably high, we can replace the sums in Equations 22.4 and 22.6 by their expectations. Using $E\{z^2\} = 1$ and $E\{|z|\} = \sqrt{\frac{2}{x}}$, we find

$$\alpha^* = \frac{IC^2 \cdot N}{2\lambda}$$

$$\omega^* = \frac{IC \cdot \sqrt{N}}{2\lambda}$$

$$G^* = \frac{IC \cdot N}{\sqrt{2\pi}\lambda\omega_0} \tag{22.7}$$

A critical point is that there is only a single degree of freedom in Equation 22.7; if the investor fixes the risk aversion, that in turn fixes *all three* of the expected alpha, risk, and gearing. If the investor fixes the expected alpha instead, that determines the risk aversion, risk, and gearing. Attempting to specify any two of these independently runs the risk of pushing the portfolio away from the optimal relations among the expected alpha, risk, and gearing, with negative consequences for the information ratio (IR).

In practice, investors typically fix the risk level. Eliminating the risk aversion in favor of the risk, we find a relation between risk and gearing at optimality,

$$G^* = \left(\frac{\omega^*}{\omega_0}\right) \cdot \sqrt{\frac{N}{2\pi}} \tag{22.8}$$

What can we learn from Equation 22.8? First, at a high level, it relates the optimal gearing to the ratio of target portfolio residual risk, $\omega^*$, to $\omega_0/\sqrt{N}$, the residual risk of an equal-weighted portfolio of $N$ stocks, each with residual risk, $\omega_0$. The higher that ratio, the higher the optimal gearing.

Consider an example. Our investment universe comprises 250 stocks, each with 25 percent residual volatility, and we build an optimal portfolio with 5 percent risk. According to Equation 22.8, that portfolio has a natural gearing of 1.26. That is, a completely unconstrained portfolio naturally ends up with gearing of 1.26. We can also use Equation 22.8 to show that an unlevered portfolio ($G = 1$) has a natural volatility of 3.96 percent.

Now let us consider two different situations mentioned earlier. What if our portfolio manager builds a 10 percent risk portfolio with a gearing of 1? Forcing the gearing to be exactly 1, that is, imposing a gearing constraint, leads to a suboptimal portfolio. The natural ungeared portfolio has 3.96 percent risk. To increase that to 10 percent, while keeping gearing fixed, requires dropping assets to reach that higher-risk level. At the extreme, the portfolio could end up with only one stock long and one stock short. In these undergeared portfolios, we are giving up on diversification, and on our IR, to reach a target risk level.

The second situation involves building a 3.3 percent risk portfolio and gearing it three times. That involves overgearing. Our 3.3 percent portfolio must ignore some alpha information to reach that artificially low risk level. At the extreme, we build equally weighted long and short portfolios (given that each stock has identical and independent residual risks). This solution, forcing the gearing of 3, also leads to suboptimal portfolios.

## SIMPLE MODEL EXTENDED: GEARING PENALTIES

Of course, in the real world, portfolios may not have an optimal trade-off between risk and gearing. Suboptimal gearing has a cost.

To analyze its impact, we can extend the simple model's utility function, Equation 22.2, to include a penalty for gearing. To do this, we will account separately for long positions, $l_n$, and short positions, $s_n$, defining $l_n$ and $s_n$ as non-negative. In this simple model with uncorrelated residual returns, no transaction costs, and symmetric alphas, a positive alpha will on average result in $s_n = 0$, and a negative alpha will on average result in $l_n = 0$. In what follows, we will enforce that explicitly.

Our extended utility function is

$$U \Rightarrow \sum_{n=1}^{N} \alpha_n \cdot (l_n - s_n) - \lambda \cdot \omega_0^2 \cdot \sum_{n=1}^{N} (l_n - s_n)^2$$

$$- IC \cdot \omega_0 \cdot \phi \cdot \sum_{n=1}^{N} l_n - IC \cdot \omega_0 \cdot \phi \cdot \sum_{n=1}^{N} s_n$$

$$- \sum_{n=1}^{N} \eta_n^l \cdot l_n - \sum_{n=1}^{N} \eta_n^s \cdot s_n \tag{22.9}$$

The first two terms in Equation 22.9 represent the alpha and risk as before. Remember that, depending on the sign of the alpha, we know that for any particular asset, either $l_n$ or $s_n$ is zero. The (new) third and fourth terms penalize or encourage gearing, depending on whether $\phi$, the gearing penalty, is positive or negative. We multiply these terms by $IC \cdot \omega_0$ to ease the notational burden later. As a beneficial side effect, this also gives the gearing penalty a natural scale; for instance, $\phi = 1$ creates a gearing penalty equal to a one-standard deviation alpha. The last two terms—asset-specific holdings penalties—provide degrees of freedom necessary to satisfy the basic conditions that long and short holdings are non-negative.

Note that the gearing penalty does not force our solution to a specific gearing. The penalty approach can do this on average, but different samples of alphas lead to different gearing levels that vary around an average.

Our game plan is to solve for the optimal holdings, and see how our alpha, risk, gearing, and IR change as we vary the gearing penalty. We present the results here; further details of the calculations are in Appendix A.

For the portfolio alpha, $\alpha_p$, we find

$$\frac{\alpha_P}{\alpha^*} = \sqrt{\frac{2}{\pi}} \cdot [I_2(\phi_+) - \phi I_1(\phi_+)] \tag{22.10}$$

where

$$I_n(x) \equiv \int_x^\infty \exp\left\{\frac{-\gamma^2}{2}\right\} \gamma^n dy \tag{22.11}$$

and

$$\phi_+ \equiv \begin{cases} 0 & \phi < 0 \\ \phi & \phi \geq 0 \end{cases} \tag{22.12}$$

The quantity $\alpha^*$ is defined in Equation 22.7, and is the alpha of the gearing-unconstrained ($\phi = 0$) portfolio.

Similarly, we can estimate portfolio risk, $\omega_p$, and gearing as

$$\frac{\omega_P}{\omega^*} = \left(\frac{2}{\pi}\right)^{1/4} \sqrt{I_2(\phi_+) - 2\phi I_1(\phi_+) + \phi^2 I_0(\phi_+)} \tag{22.13}$$

$$\frac{G}{G^*} = I_1(\phi_+) - \phi I_0(\phi_+) \tag{22.14}$$

where, again, we computed $\omega^*$ and $G^*$ in Equation 22.7.

The intrinsic *IR* follows from the Fundamental Law of Active Management (Grinold, 1989), and is

$$IR_{int} = \frac{\alpha^*}{\omega^*} = IC \cdot \sqrt{N} \tag{22.15}$$

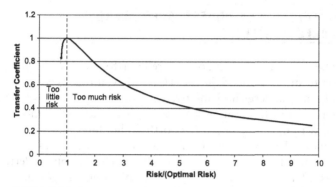

**EXHIBIT 22.1**   TC at Fixed Gearing

The implemented IR is simply the ratio of the alpha and risk estimates. From these, we can calculate the transfer coefficient, *TC*, as the ratio of implemented IR to intrinsic IR:

$$TC = \frac{\left(\alpha_P/\omega_P\right)}{\left(\alpha^*/\omega^*\right)} = \frac{IR}{IC \cdot \sqrt{N}}$$

$$= \left(\frac{2}{\pi}\right)^{1/4} \left[\frac{I_2(\phi_+) - \phi I_1(\phi_+)}{I_2(\phi_+) - 2\phi I_1(\phi_+) + \phi^2 I_0(\phi_+)}\right] \qquad (22.16)$$

Notice that, unlike the *IR*, the TC is independent of N. With a gearing penalty of zero, the optimization naturally chooses the optimal gearing, and the TC is 1.

Exhibit 22.1 shows the TC at a fixed gearing, and Exhibit 22.2 shows the TC at a fixed risk.

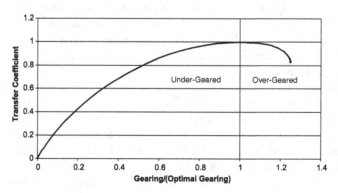

**EXHIBIT 22.2**   TC at Fixed Risk

## CHARACTERISTICS OF UNDERGEARED VERSUS OVERGEARED PORTFOLIOS

Interestingly, undergeared and overgeared portfolios are quite different, and this leads to an asymmetry in the TC for deviations away from optimal gearing. In fact, undergeared and overgeared portfolios are so different that it is possible to distinguish between severely undergeared and overgeared portfolios with only a glance at the portfolio holdings.

Exhibit 22.1 shows how the TC varies as a function of risk, with the portfolio held at fixed gearing throughout. This graph is derived from Equations 22.13, 22.14, and 22.16 by eliminating the gearing penalty $\phi$ in terms of the gearing level and the risk aversion $\lambda$ in terms of the risk level.

In the original portfolio manager example, we used Equation 22.8 to show that if the manager is constrained to $G = 1$, the ideal risk level is 3.96 percent. In Exhibit 22.1, the horizontal axis is measured in multiples of the ideal risk, and for a multiple of 1, the TC is at its maximum of 1. In this simple model, changes in the target gearing $G$ would change the optimal risk level but not the shape of Exhibit 22.1.

At the right-hand side of Exhibit 22.1, the portfolio bears too much risk for the given level of gearing. To increase the risk, more and more portfolio weight is concentrated in high-alpha names, and assets with low alphas are forced out of the portfolio entirely (thereby discarding all the information in those alphas). In the limiting case, we end up with a single name on the long side and a single name on the short side. This may be fine from an alpha perspective, but it is devastating from a risk perspective, and the huge increase in risk causes the TC to drop to zero in our simple model. More plausibly, a portfolio with three times the ideal risk level has a TC of only about 0.6, the same ballpark as an otherwise unconstrained long-only implementation.

Another perspective is that these high-risk, concentrated portfolios are undergeared, a point we return to below. A key characteristic of an undergeared portfolio is the collection of assets at exactly zero weight; this characteristic persists even in more realistic optimizations that include bounds, transaction costs, and so on.

At the left-hand side of Exhibit 22.1, the portfolio experiences too little risk for the level of gearing. The TC drops off more quickly, but it proves impossible to reduce the risk beyond a certain point, and at that point the TC is still over 80 percent of the maximum. The lower bound on the risk is a consequence of Hölder's Inequality, which relates the risk level and the gearing level (see Appendix B). As we force the portfolio to lower and lower risk levels, it overdiversifies by taking substantial positions even in assets with low alphas. In the limiting case, the portfolio consists of two equal-weighted portfolios: All the assets with positive alphas are held with equal weight on the long side, and all the assets with negative alphas are held with equal weight on the short side. The portfolio ignores all but the sign of the alpha, but because there is still information in the sign alone, the *IR* approaches a positive constant as the portfolio approaches the minimum risk.[1]

Again, another perspective is that these low-risk portfolios are overgeared, and, given the earlier interpretation, it is clear that an identifying characteristic of an overgeared portfolio is the absence of assets in a region around zero weight, and, again, this characteristic persists even in more realistic optimizations.

Exhibit 22.2 displays the TC as a function of gearing, for fixed risk. On the right, the portfolios are overgeared, and tend to have equal-weighted long and short sides, with no assets near zero weight. On the left, the portfolios are undergeared, and tend to have a collection of assets at exactly zero weight. The TC drops off more rapidly for overgeared portfolios, but is bounded below, whereas severe undergearing can reduce the TC all the way to zero.

To summarize the differences, undergeared portfolios tend to show an abnormally large number of holdings at exactly zero weight; overgeared portfolios tend to show an abnormal absence of assets in an entire region around zero weight; and perfectly geared portfolios show a smooth distribution of portfolio weights. In our simple model with no transaction costs and normally distributed alphas, the portfolio weights (Equation 22.3) are normally distributed when the portfolio is optimally geared.

For completeness, Exhibit 22.3 shows the efficient frontier for three different levels of gearing, as well as the gearing unconstrained line. The form of the efficient frontiers follows from the analysis so far. There is a point of highest *IR*, where the gearing, expected risk, and expected return are all compatible. To the left of that point, the portfolio is overgeared, and the efficient frontier terminates at the maximally overgeared portfolio, in this case an equal-weighted portfolio. To the right of the point of maximum *IR*, the portfolios are undergeared. Although our simple model shows no upper bound on the risk, in principle at the far right the efficient frontier also terminates, at the risk and return characteristics of the maximum alpha asset.

Exhibit 22.3 also clarifies that the scenarios we are considering here are not simply movements along the capital market line. The capital market line is straight precisely because gearing varies with risk as we move along it. If we fix the gearing, the efficient frontier curves are as shown in Exhibit 22.3.

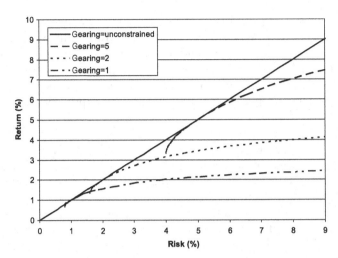

**EXHIBIT 22.3**   Efficient Frontiers

## EMPIRICAL ANALYSIS

We now want to verify aspects of this analysis under more realistic conditions. We can show how gearing affects implemented IRs by generating random alphas, and building optimal market-neutral portfolios at different risk and gearing levels. For this case, we ignore all constraints other than the gearing constraint, and ignore transaction costs, but include a realistic covariance between assets.

Exhibit 22.4 shows the subsequent active efficient frontiers based on the expected risk and return. Despite widely differing underlying parameters, the behavior displayed in Exhibit 22.4 very closely matches the pattern in Exhibit 22.3.

The distance between the straight line and the curved frontier is the loss in *IR* from the gearing constraint and, as we saw before, this can be very high. To achieve levels of risk beyond the optimal point, the portfolio reduces diversification and concentrates in only a few names. At risk levels below optimal, the portfolio overdiversifies, ignoring information available in the alphas to reduce risk.

Exhibit 22.5 shows the results of more realistic analysis, including alpha, risk, transaction costs, asset-level bounds, and, in three of the four cases, a gearing constraint. The graph is again based on expected alpha and risk, and the risk is allowed to go to extremely high levels only to indicate that even the gearing-unconstrained curve dips for high enough risk levels.

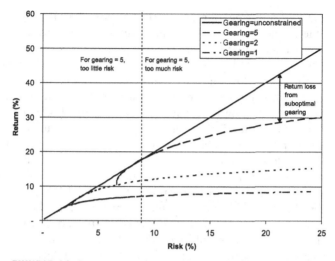

**EXHIBIT 22.4**   Efficient Frontiers—No Other Constraints

A crucial difference between Exhibits 22.4 and 22.5 is that in Exhibit 22.5 the gearing-constrained portfolios have negative expected returns for some risk levels. This is due entirely to expected transaction costs, indicating that the cost of suboptimal gearing is potentially much higher for portfolios that bear significant transaction costs.

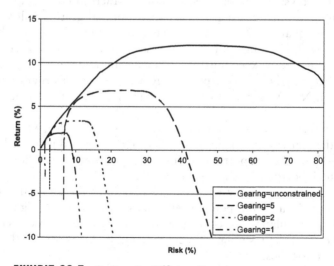

**EXHIBIT 22.5**   In Practice Efficient Frontiers

In Exhibit 22.5, the gearing-unconstrained curve has the highest return for any value of the risk because the portfolio is allowed to naturally find the level of gearing compatible with the risk. The other curves have a shape similar to those generated by our extended model, but have somewhat different behavior at very low and very high risk.

In our simplified model, without transaction costs, the minimum-risk portfolio at a fixed gearing is an equal-weighted portfolio. The minimum-risk portfolios in Exhibit 22.5 are very similar to those in our simple model, but when the portfolios are subject to transaction costs, it is costly for assets to flip from the long side to the short side or vice versa. The net result is that for minimum-risk portfolios and the level of transaction costs we have chosen, the transaction costs overcome the alpha, leading to a negative expected *IR*. In the middle of each fixed-gearing curve, there is a more normal balance among alpha, risk, transaction costs, and gearing, resulting in *IR*s that are positive, but still lower than the gearing-unconstrained *IR*. As before, at a fixed gearing there is a single optimal risk level, or at a fixed risk there is a single optimal gearing level. Finally, to the far right in Exhibit 22.5, at very high risk levels, the performance drops precipitously again as excessive transaction costs are incurred in order to reach the risk target.

## OTHER REAL-WORLD ISSUES

Empirical analysis inevitably identifies other practical issues important for determining optimal gearing. For instance, optimal gearing will vary over time. From Equation 22.8, we know that gearing depends on the risk target, the asset risk levels, and number of the assets in the opportunity set. As asset risk levels change, to keep portfolio risk constant and the TC high requires changing gearing in a compatible way. As volume patterns change, or funds grow, even $N$ can change as less liquid names move out of the investment universe.

Our models so far have assumed stock borrowing is free, which does not hold in the real world. If analysis implies that we should increase leverage, for example, and run a portfolio at lower risk, we must also account for the higher stock borrowing costs that will entail.

Finally, the regulatory environment may limit the allowed values for the gearing, even to the point of eliminating the point of highest IR. In particular, if regulations force the portfolios to be undergeared (as opposed to overgeared), the resulting TCs can potentially be as low as the TCs of long-only portfolios.

## CONCLUSION

In constructing investment products, managers may set risk targets according to client preferences, and meet those risk targets by altering the asset mix suboptimally. In products that use leverage, managers typically set gearing independent of choice of risk. Yet, as we have shown, risk and gearing incompatibility have a surprisingly high cost. This efficiency loss is asymmetric; undergearing is ultimately more costly than overgearing. Overgeared portfolios are identified by their equal weighting of assets, with no assets near absolute weight of zero; undergeared portfolios are identified by an abnormal collection of assets at exactly zero weight.

Although this analysis has focused on the costs of ignoring the connection between risk and gearing in market-neutral portfolios, it is only one example of a more general issue beyond market neutral—compatibly setting portfolio risk, gearing, and shorting when we can freely specify all three.

## APPENDIX A

### Portfolios Subject to Gearing Penalties

Maximizing utility leads to the holdings:

$$l_n = \frac{1}{2\lambda\omega_0^2}(\alpha_n - IC \cdot \omega_0 \cdot \phi - \eta_n^l)$$

$$s_n = \frac{1}{2\lambda\omega_0^2}(-\alpha_n - IC \cdot \omega_0 \cdot \phi - \eta_n^s) \tag{22.A1}$$

where we choose $\eta_n^l$ and $\eta_n^s$ to enforce $l_n \geq 0$ and $s_n \geq 0$. For instance, if $(\alpha_n - IC \cdot \omega_0 \cdot \phi) \leq 0$ for a positive alpha, we set $\eta_n^l$ to exactly $(\alpha_n - IC \cdot \omega_0 \cdot \phi)$, to pin the asset at $l_n = 0$. If $(\alpha_n - IC \cdot \omega_0 \cdot \phi) \geq 0$ for a positive alpha, we need not enforce $l_n \geq 0$ explicitly, and can set $\eta_n^l$ to zero.

Given the optimal portfolio, Equation 22.A1, we can calculate its characteristics—alpha, residual risk, and gearing—and how they vary as we change the risk aversion and the gearing penalty.

Whereas we must separately analyze the cases of positive and negative penalties, $\phi$, for gearing, we can summarize the results with single formulas. To calculate the expected portfolio alpha, we estimate the expected average contribution per stock (active position times stock alpha), and multiply by the number of stocks.

Three integrals arise in the following calculations. They are all of the type described in Equation 22.11. Some of these integrals can be done explicitly. A few particular values of use are: $I_0(0) = I_2(0) = \sqrt{\frac{\pi}{2}}$ and $I_1(0) = 1$.

We will calculate the portfolio risk in detail, starting with the simpler $\phi \leq 0$ case. The short and long sides give the same contribution, so we need to calculate only one. The expected variance of an asset on the long side is

$$\omega_0^2 E[l_i^2] = \omega_0^2 \int_0^\infty P(\alpha) l^2 \, d\alpha$$

$$= \omega_0^2 \int_0^\infty \frac{1}{2\pi IC^2\omega_0^2} \exp\left\{\frac{-\alpha^2}{2IC^2\omega_0^2}\right\} \left(\frac{1}{2\lambda\omega_0^2}\right)^2 \times (\alpha - IC \cdot \omega_0 \cdot \phi)^2 \, d\alpha$$

$$= \frac{IC^2}{4\lambda^2\sqrt{2\pi}} \int_0^\infty \exp\left\{\frac{-x^2}{2}\right\} (x - \phi)^2 \, dx$$

$$= \frac{IC^2}{4\lambda^2\sqrt{2\pi}}[I_2(0) - 2\phi I_1(0) + \phi^2 I_0(0)] \tag{22.A2}$$

When $\phi \geq 0$, the gearing penalty forces the long side assets toward zero, and if the alpha is low enough the gearing penalty will force the asset out of the portfolio entirely. Then,

$$\omega_0^2 E[l_i^2] = \omega_0^2 \int_0^\infty P(\alpha) l^2 \, d\alpha$$

$$= \omega_0^2 \int_0^\infty \frac{1}{2\pi\omega_0^2} \exp\left\{\frac{-\alpha^2}{2IC^2\omega_0^2}\right\} \left(\frac{1}{2\lambda\omega_0^2}\right)^2 \times (\alpha - IC \cdot \omega_0 \cdot \phi)^2 \, d\alpha$$

$$= \frac{IC^2}{4\lambda^2\sqrt{2\pi}} \int_\phi^\infty \exp\left\{\frac{-x^2}{2}\right\} (x - \phi)^2 \, dx$$

$$= \frac{IC^2}{4\lambda^2\sqrt{2\pi}}[I_2(\phi) - 2\phi I_1(\phi) + \phi^2 I_0(\phi)] \tag{22.A3}$$

The $\phi \geq 0$ and $\phi \leq 0$ cases together can be written as

$$\omega_0^2 E[l_i^2] = \frac{IC^2}{4\lambda^2\sqrt{2\pi}}[I_2(\phi_+) - 2\phi I_1(\phi_+) + \phi^2 I_0(\phi_+)] \tag{22.A4}$$

Recalling that both the long and short sides contribute to the risk, the total portfolio risk is

$$\frac{\omega_P}{\omega^*} = \left(\frac{2}{\pi}\right)^{1/4} \sqrt{I_2(\phi_+) - 2\phi I_1(\phi_+) + \phi^2 I_0(\phi_+)} \qquad (22.A5)$$

in terms of the $\phi = 0$ risk level, $\omega^* = \frac{IC\sqrt{N}}{2\lambda}$.

The expected gearing and alpha calculations are similar to the expected variance calculation, and so are omitted. The formula for the gearing is

$$\frac{G}{G^*} = I_1(\phi_+) - \phi I_0(\phi_+) \qquad (22.A6)$$

in terms of the $\phi = 0$ gearing,

$$G^* = \frac{N \cdot IC}{2\lambda\omega_0\sqrt{2\pi}}$$

The formula for the alpha is

$$\frac{\alpha_P}{\alpha^*} = \sqrt{\frac{2}{\pi}}[I_2(\phi_+) - \phi I_1(\phi_+)] \qquad (22.A7)$$

in terms of the $\phi = 0$ alpha,

$$\alpha^* = \frac{N \cdot IC^2}{2\lambda}$$

# APPENDIX B

## Hölder's Inequality and the Upper Bound on Gearing

Hölder's inequality is

$$\sum_{i=1}^{N} |x_i y_i| \leq \left(\sum_{i=1}^{N} |x_i|^p\right)^{\frac{1}{p}} \left(\sum_{i=1}^{N} |y_i|^q\right)^{\frac{1}{q}} \qquad (22.B1)$$

where $\frac{1}{p} + \frac{1}{q} = 1$.

Plugging $p = q = 2$, $x_i = \frac{1}{\omega_i}$, and $y_i = \omega_i h_i$ into Hölder's inequality yields

$$\sum_{i=1}^{N} |h_i| \leq \sqrt{\sum_{i=1}^{N} \frac{1}{\omega_i^2}} \sqrt{\sum_{i=1}^{N} \omega_i^2 h_i^2}$$

or

$$G \leq \frac{\sqrt{N}}{2} \frac{\omega^*}{\overline{\omega}} \tag{22.B2}$$

where $\omega_i$ is the specific risk of asset $i$, $\omega^*$ is the portfolio specific risk, and $\overline{\omega}$ is a typical asset risk, defined by

$$\overline{\omega} \equiv \left( \frac{1}{N} \sum_i 1 \Big/ \omega_i^2 \right)^{-1/2}$$

Combining the upper bound with the calculation of optimal gearing in our simple model shows that the ratio of the maximum gearing to the optimal gearing satisfies

$$\frac{G_{\max}}{G^*} = \sqrt{\frac{\pi}{2}} \approx 1.25 \tag{22.B3}$$

This ratio is a pure number, independent of the risk level, $IC$, and so on. Notice that the maximum gearing produced by our extended simple model satisfies this relation.

Finally, note that similar bounds can be found by applying the Cauchy-Schwarz inequality, which is obviously related to Hölder's inequality.

## NOTES

1. The equal-weighting follows from our assumption that all assets have equal risk and are uncorrelated. More generally, overgearing should, in the limit, lead to long and short portfolios built to minimize risk.

## REFERENCES

Clark, R., H. de Silva, and S. Sapra. 2004. "Toward More Information-Efficient Portfolios." *The Journal of Portfolio Management* (Fall): 54–62.

Clark, R., H. de Silva, and S. Thorley. 2002. "Portfolio Constraints and the Fundamental Law of Active Management." *Financial Analysts Journal*, vol. 58, no. 5 (September/October):48–66.

Grinold, R. C. 1989. "The Fundamental Law of Active Management." *The Journal of Portfolio Management*, vol. 15, no. 3. 30–37.

Grinold, R. C., and R. N. Kahn. 2000a. *Active Portfolio Management*, 2nd ed. New York: McGraw-Hill.

———. 2000b. "The Efficiency Gains of Long-Short Investing." *Financial Analysts Journal*, vol. 56, no. 6 (November/December).

Markowitz, H. M. 1959. *Portfolio Selection: Efficient Diversification of Investment.* New Haven, CT: Yale University Press.

Rosenberg, B. 1976. *Security Appraisal and Unsystematic Risk in Institutional Investment.* Proceedings of the Seminar on the Analysis of Security prices, Chicago: University of Chicago Press:171–237.

Sharpe, W. F. 1963. "A Simplified Model for Portfolio Analysis." *Management Science*, vol. 9, no. 1 (January):277–293.

Treynor, J., and F. Black. 1973. "How to Use Security Analysis to Improve Portfolio Selection." *Journal of Business*, vol. 46, no. 1:68–86.

# CHAPTER 23

# 20 Myths about Enhanced Active 120/20 Strategies

**Bruce I. Jacobs**
Principal
Jacobs Levy Equity Management

**Kenneth N. Levy**
Principal
Jacobs Levy Equity Management

*Enhanced active equity strategies, including 120/20 and 130/30 long/short portfolios, have become increasingly popular as managers and investors search for new ways to expand the alpha opportunities available from active management. But these strategies are not always well understood by the financial community. How do such strategies increase investors' flexibility both to underweight and overweight securities? How do they compare with market-neutral long/short strategies? Are they significantly riskier than traditional, long-only strategies because they use short positions and leverage? This article sheds light on some common myths regarding enhanced active equity strategies.*

Enhanced active equity strategies, such as 120/20 or 130/30 portfolios, have short positions equal to some percentage of capital (generally 20% or 30% but possibly 100% or more) and an equal percentage of leveraged long positions.[1] Enhanced active equity strategies are facilitated by modern *prime brokerage* structures, which allow the proceeds from short sales to be

---

used to purchase long equity positions. Long positions in excess of capital can be bought without the use of margin loans.

A 120/20 portfolio with initial capital of $100, for example, sells $20 of securities short and uses the proceeds from the short sales plus the initial $100 to purchase $120 of securities long. The $20 in short positions offsets the $20 in leveraged long positions, leaving a net market exposure of $100. The portfolio retains full sensitivity to underlying market movements (a beta of 1) and participates fully in the equity market return.

If a portfolio manager is able to distinguish between securities that will perform better than the underlying benchmark and those that will perform worse, the 120/20 portfolio will achieve a return higher than the return on the underlying benchmark (at a higher risk level). It can also be expected to outperform a long-only portfolio based on comparable insights; relaxation of the short-selling constraint allows the 120/20 portfolio to achieve security underweights that a long-only portfolio cannot attain, where the ability to invest the proceeds from short sales in additional long positions allows the portfolio to achieve security overweights that an unleveraged long-only portfolio cannot attain.[2] Compared with long-only portfolios, enhanced active equity strategies afford managers greater flexibility in portfolio construction, which allows for fuller exploitation of investment insights.[3] They also provide managers and investors with a wider choice of risk–return trade-offs.

Enhanced active equity strategies have become increasingly popular as managers and investors search for new ways to expand the alpha opportunities available from active management. The strategies build on the wave of interest in alternative strategies that followed the downturn in equity markets after 1999, which sent investors flocking to hedge funds and market-neutral (MN) strategies, such as convertible arbitrage, merger arbitrage, and long/short equity. Such strategies frequently use short selling to reduce market risk and improve performance.[4]

Enhanced active equity strategies differ in some fundamental ways from other active equity strategies, both long-only and long/short. As a result, the financial community has formed some misconceptions about these strategies.[5] An article in the *Wall Street Journal*, for example, suggested that the strategies are excessively risky because of their use of short positions (Patterson 2006). As we show, this and other myths about enhanced active equity strategies do not necessarily survive objective scrutiny.

**Myth 1. Long-only portfolios can already underweight securities by holding them at less than their benchmark weights, so short selling offers little incremental advantage.** Excess returns come from active security weights—portfolio weights that differ from benchmark weights. An active long-only portfolio holds securities expected to perform above average at higher-than-benchmark weights and those expected to perform below average at lower-than-benchmark weights. It can overweight any security by enough to achieve a significant positive active weight. Without short selling, however, it cannot underweight many securities by enough to achieve significant negative active weights. The long-only portfolio can underweight a security by, at most, the security's weight in the benchmark; it does so by not holding any shares of the security.

Consider that there are only about 15 stocks in the Standard & Poor's (S&P) 500, Russell 1000, or Russell 3000 indices that have index weights greater than 1 percent. Half the stocks in the S&P 500 have index weights below 0.10 percent, half the stocks in the Russell 1000 have index weights below 0.03 percent, and half the stocks in the Russell 3000 have index weights below 0.01 percent. Thus, meaningful underweights of most securities can be achieved *only* if short selling is allowed.

**Myth 2. Constraints on short selling do not affect the portfolio manager's ability to overweight attractive securities.** A 120/20 portfolio can sell short and use the proceeds from the short sales to purchase additional long positions. It can, therefore, take more and/or larger active overweight positions than a long-only portfolio with the same amount of capital (assuming the long-only portfolio does not increase its long positions via borrowing). The 120/20 portfolio's additional long positions, like its short positions, offer the opportunity for higher excess returns relative to the long-only portfolio.[6] Furthermore, the incremental overweights and underweights versus the long-only portfolio permit more diversification, which should result in greater consistency of performance.

Moreover, and more subtly, a portfolio manager's ability to overweight attractive securities may be limited by constraints on short selling. Consider, for example, a manager who has a strong belief that some companies in a given industry are significantly undervalued but desires a neutral industry weight for purposes of risk control. To maintain a market weight on the industry, the manager will have to offset overweights of the attractive securities with underweights of other securities in the industry. In the absence of short selling, the ability to establish sufficient underweights may be limited, especially if the overvalued securities have insignificant benchmark weights. This limitation may, in turn, constrain the portfolio's ability to overweight the attractive securities in the industry. The portfolio that can sell short can underweight in larger amounts, which also allows for larger overweights. This ability should translate into higher expected excess returns than a long-only portfolio can provide.

**Myth 3. A 120/20 equity portfolio can be constructed by combining two portfolios—a long-only 100/0 portfolio and a 20/20 long/short portfolio.** This type of construction is possible, but it negates most of the advantages of long/short construction. The real benefits of any long/short portfolio emerge only with an integrated optimization that considers all long and short positions simultaneously, together with any desired benchmark exposure, to produce a single portfolio:

> *The important question is not how one should allocate capital between a long-only portfolio and a long/short portfolio but, rather, how one should blend active positions (long and short) with a benchmark security in an integrated optimization. (Jacobs, Levy, and Starer, 1998, p. 40)*

**Myth 4. For portfolios that have only a limited amount in short positions (e.g., 120/20 portfolio), the ability to short must have only a small impact on performance.** For a large number of securities, insights regarding overvaluation cannot be meaningfully reflected in a long-only portfolio because the portfolio's ability to underweight the securities is so constrained. Short selling, even in limited amounts, can extend portfolio underweights substantially. For example, compared with a long-only portfolio, a 120/20 portfolio, which sells short an amount equal to 20 percent of capital, can augment the underweights of 80 stocks by an average of 0.25 percent (or 40 stocks by 0.50% each). Thus, the median stock in the S&P 500, with its weight of 0.10 percent, could be underweighted by 0.35 percent (or 0.60%), versus the maximum underweight of 0.10 percent attainable in a long-only portfolio. And the median stock in the Russell 3000, with a weight of 0.01 percent, could be underweighted by 0.26 percent (or 0.51%), versus an insignificant underweight in a long-only portfolio.

Note also that opportunities for shorting are not necessarily mirror images of opportunities for buying long. There is some theoretical foundation for believing that overvaluation is more common, and larger in magnitude, than undervaluation (Jacobs and Levy, 1993; Miller, 2001).[7] In addition, price reactions to good and bad news may not be symmetrical. Earnings disappointments, for example, may have a stronger impact on security prices than positive earnings surprises. Thus, the ability to underweight shares subject to earnings disappointments may be more valuable than the ability to overweight shares subject to positive earnings surprises.

Should an investor find a 120/20 structure too limiting in terms of performance opportunities, the strategy may be extended to include more short selling (and more long positions). An enhanced active portfolio can take short (and additional long) positions as large as the prime broker's policies on leverage allow. For example, the portfolio could short securities equal to 100 percent of capital and use the proceeds plus the capital to purchase long positions, resulting in a 200/100 portfolio.

**Myth 5. An enhanced active 200/100 strategy is the same as an equitized market-neutral long/short strategy with 100 percent of capital in short positions, 100 percent in long positions, and 100 percent in an equity market overlay.** An MN long/short portfolio holds approximately equal amounts in long and short positions with approximately equal sensitivities to market moves. The long and short positions cancel out underlying market risk (beta) and market return. The portfolio offers the return (and risk) associated with the individual securities held long and sold short; its positions are fully active. By combining an equity market overlay—stock index futures, swaps, or exchange-traded funds (ETFs)—with an MN long/short portfolio, the manager or investor can establish equity market exposure while retaining the active return benefits of an MN long/short strategy (Jacobs and Levy, 1999). The result is a portfolio that has 100 percent of capital in long stock positions, 100 percent in short stock positions, and 100 percent exposure to the market via the overlay. This portfolio may appear to be similar to an enhanced active 200/100 portfolio, but there are some significant differences.

The equity overlay is, by definition, passive; the investor cannot expect to receive a return in excess of the underlying index return and will generally receive a return that is, after costs, somewhat less. An enhanced active 200/100 strategy is more active. Full market exposure is established not by a passive overlay but by the 100 percent active net long investment in equities. For each $100 of capital, the investor has $300 in stock positions to use in pursuing return and controlling risk. Furthermore, because the enhanced active 200/100 portfolio uses individual securities to achieve market exposure, it is not, as is the equitized MN portfolio, confined to stock index benchmarks having liquid market overlays.

The cost of the enhanced active 200/100 structure is about the same as the cost of equitizing an MN portfolio with an overlay (Jacobs and Levy, 2006).[8]

**Myth 6. An equitized market-neutral long/short strategy is more flexible than an enhanced active equity strategy.** Some may think that an enhanced active equity portfolio offers less flexibility to overweight and underweight securities than an equitized MN long/short portfolio, which has fully active weights through its MN portion and full exposure to the equity market through the overlay. In theory, however, enhanced active and equitized MN portfolios are equivalent, having identical active weights and identical market exposures—hence, identical performance (Jacobs and Levy, 2007).[9]

An equitized MN long/short portfolio is typically an "untrim" portfolio.[10] In essence, an untrim portfolio is a portfolio that holds long and short positions in the same security. For example, a portfolio may have sold short a security in an amount equal to 0.60 percent of capital while at the same time holding, through the market overlay, a long position of 0.05 percent in the same security. The portfolio has an active underweight in the security of 0.55 percent. The remaining 0.05 percent of the short position overlaps the 0.05 percent long position, with neither contributing to portfolio return or portfolio risk control.

Untrim portfolios can be made trim if the overlap between long and short positions in each security can be eliminated without affecting the portfolio's overall performance. In the case of the security discussed in the preceding paragraph, reducing both the long and short positions by 0.05 percentage point results in a portfolio that holds a 0.55 percent active underweight in the security. Because this underweight is the same as the active weight held by the untrim equitized portfolio, portfolio risk and return remain unchanged.

In practice, trimming equitized portfolios is not feasible because market exposure is established with an equity market overlay, such as a futures contract or a swap. With an enhanced active equity portfolio, however, market exposure is established with individual security positions. The enhanced active portfolio can be constructed to be trim, with no overlapping long and short positions. The enhanced active portfolio is thus more compact and uses less leverage than the equivalent equitized MN long/short portfolio (Jacobs and Levy, 2007). Also, because the enhanced active portfolio obtains its benchmark exposure through individual security positions, the investor can achieve benchmark exposure even if liquid overlays are not available.

**Myth 7. Enhanced active equity portfolios are inherently much more risky than long-only portfolios because they contain short positions.** Whether a portfolio achieves an underweight by holding a security at less than the security's benchmark index weight or by not holding the security at all or whether it extends the underweight by selling the security short, the portfolio is in a risky position in terms of potential value added or lost relative to the benchmark index return. Of course, enhanced active equity strategies do involve risks not shared by unleveraged long-only strategies.

Losses on unleveraged long positions are limited because a security's price cannot drop below zero, but losses on short positions are theoretically unlimited because the security's price can rise without limit. In practice, however, this risk can be minimized by diversification and rebalancing. With proper diversification, losses in some positions should be mitigated by gains in others. And as noted earlier, short selling allows greater diversification among underweights and overweights than long-only investing allows. Trading to maintain security position sizes as prices change can also reduce the risk of unlimited losses, because short positions are scaled back or covered as their prices increase.[11]

**Myth 8. Enhanced active equity strategies provide investors a free lunch.** No investment strategy provides a free lunch. An enhanced active equity strategy has an explicit cost—namely, a stock loan fee paid to the prime broker. The prime broker arranges for the investor to borrow the securities that are sold short and handles the collateral for the securities' lenders.[12] The stock loan fee amounts to about 0.50 percent annually of the market value of the shares shorted (about 10 bps of capital for a 120/20 portfolio). An enhanced active strategy will usually incur a higher management fee than a long-only portfolio and, given the additional trading owing to portfolio leverage, higher transaction costs. The strategy may also incur incremental implicit costs in the form of additional risk from expanded underweights and overweights.

What the strategy offers in return for these costs is a more efficient way to manage equities than a long-only strategy allows. Expanding the manager's ability to underweight securities permits more comprehensive use of investment insights, which should translate into enhanced performance relative to a long-only portfolio based on the same insights. At the same time, the incremental underweights and overweights can lead to better diversification than in a long-only portfolio, which can translate into enhanced consistency of performance. Thus, enhanced active equity strategies, although they do not provide a free lunch, do provide a more complete lunch.

**Myth 9. The leverage in an enhanced active equity portfolio results in leveraged market return and risk.** A 120/20 portfolio is leveraged, in that it has $140 at risk for every $100 of capital invested. The market exposure created by the 20 percent in leveraged long positions is offset, however, by the 20 percent sold short. The portfolio has a 100 percent net exposure to the market and, with appropriate risk control, a marketlike level of systematic risk (a beta of 1). The leverage and added flexibility can be expected to increase excess return and residual risk relative to the benchmark. If the manager is skilled at security selection and portfolio construction, any incremental risk borne by the investor should be compensated for by incremental excess return.

**Myth 10. An enhanced active 120/20 portfolio is simply a long-only port-folio leveraged 1.4 times.** An investor can leverage a long-only portfolio by borrowing funds equal to 40 percent of the initial capital and investing in additional long positions. But the portfolio will still not be able to sell short, so its ability to underweight securities will be just as constrained as that of an unleveraged long-only portfolio. It will benefit from none of the added flexibility to underweight securities that gives the 120/20 portfolio the opportunity to enhance performance through more complete implementation of investment insights.[13] Furthermore, borrowing funds to leverage a long-only portfolio magnifies the portfolio's exposure to market risk by a factor of 1.4 and may leave an otherwise tax-exempt investor subject to taxes (see Myth 11).

**Myth 11. Because enhanced active equity strategies are leveraged, using the strategies subjects an otherwise tax-exempt U.S. investor to taxation.** One may expect that a portfolio with long positions of more than 100 percent of capital must have taken advantage of margin borrowing. The otherwise tax-exempt investor that borrows funds to invest in long positions incurs acquisition indebtedness and is subject to taxes on Unrelated Business Taxable Income (UBTI). With an enhanced active equity strategy, however, long positions established in excess of capital are purchased with the proceeds from the short sales; the longs are not purchased with a margin loan. U.S. IRS Ruling 95-8 concludes that borrowing shares to sell short does not give rise to UBTI because no acquisition indebtedness has been incurred (Jacobs and Levy, 1997).[14]

**Myth 12. Leverage is limited by Federal Reserve Board Regulation T, so 150/50 portfolios are the most leveraged enhanced active equity strategies available.** Mutual funds and other companies regulated under the Investment Company Act of 1940 cannot relinquish custody of their long positions to a broker. As a result, they may not be able to use stock loan accounts and may remain subject to the leverage limits of Reg T. These entities may be able to use enhanced active 120/20, or even 150/50 portfolios, but not portfolios with more leverage.[15]

In contrast, separate accounts and other types of investment vehicles can establish stock loan accounts with prime brokers. With a stock loan account, the investor is not a customer of the prime broker, as would be the case with a margin account, but is a counterparty to the stock lending transaction. In this arrangement, borrowing shares to sell short is not subject to Reg T limits on leverage. With a stock loan account, leverage is limited only by the broker's own internal lending policies.[16]

**Myth 13. Enhanced active equity strategies must provide cash collateral for the short positions, including meeting daily marks to market, which complicates trading and requires a cash buffer that can reduce returns.** With a traditional margin account, the lenders of any securities sold short must be provided with collateral at least equal to the current value of the securities. When the securities are first borrowed, the proceeds from the short sales usually serve as this collateral. As the short positions subsequently rise or fall in value, the investor's account provides to or receives from the securities' lenders cash equal to the change in value.

To avoid the need to borrow money from the broker to meet these collateral demands, the account usually maintains a cash buffer. It can use up to 10 percent of capital.[17] Long positions may sometimes need to be sold to replenish the cash buffer; in that case, an appropriate amount in short positions will also have to be covered to maintain portfolio balance. Neither the short-sale proceeds nor the 10 percent cash buffer earns investment profits (although they do earn interest).

With the enhanced brokerage structures available today, the investor's account must have sufficient equity to meet the broker's *maintenance margin requirements*—generally 100 percent of the value of the shares sold short plus some additional percentage determined by the broker. This collateral requirement is usually covered by the long positions. The investor does not have to meet cash marks to market on the short positions; the broker covers those needs and is compensated by the stock loan fee. Also, dividends received on long positions can be expected to more than offset the amount the account has to pay to reimburse the securities' lenders for dividends on the short positions. The investor thus has little need for a cash buffer in the account. An enhanced active portfolio will generally retain only a small amount of cash, similar to the frictional cash (the cash assets held between selling and buying) retained in a long-only portfolio.

**Myth 14. Short selling is problematic because of the possibility of short squeezes and the observance of uptick rules.** Short squeezes tend to be limited to illiquid stocks that are generally not candidates for institutional portfolios. If a security does become subject to a short squeeze, a reduction in the supply of shares available for borrowing is usually signaled by a decline in the rebate rate offered by prime brokers or by warnings from the prime brokers, so the position can be scaled back or covered in advance of any demand that borrowed shares be returned to the prime broker.

Short sales used to require a plus tick to execute (that is, the last price change had to have been positive). The U.S. Securities and Exchange Commission (SEC) recently rescinded the "tick test," however, and as of July 6, 2007, brokers are prohibited from applying any price tests to short sales.[18]

**Myth 15. The short selling in enhanced active equity strategies will drive equity market levels down.** Enhanced active portfolios have net market exposures of 100 percent. Their short sales are balanced by their leveraged long purchases. Any pressures put on individual security prices by the trading of enhanced active portfolios should net out at the aggregate market level. Thus, enhanced active equity strategies should not cause the aggregate market either to rise or to fall; the strategies are not inherently positive-feedback strategies, which can push prices up by buying as prices rise and push prices down by selling as prices fall.[19]

**Myth 16. Trading costs in an enhanced active equity portfolio are prohibitively high.** Turnover in an enhanced active equity portfolio should be roughly proportional to the leverage in the portfolio. With $140 in positions in a 120/20 portfolio, versus $100 in a long-only portfolio, turnover can be expected to be about 40 percent higher in the 120/20 portfolio. The portfolio optimization process should account for expected trading costs so that a trade does not occur unless the expected benefit in terms of excess risk-adjusted return outweighs the expected cost of trading.

The enhanced active portfolio may incur more trading costs than a long-only portfolio because, as security prices change, it needs to trade to maintain the balance between its short and long positions relative to the benchmark. Suppose, for example, that a 120/20 portfolio experiences adverse stock price moves so that its long positions lose S2 and its short positions lose $3, causing capital to decline from $100 to $95. The portfolio now has long positions of $118 and short positions of $23—not the desired portfolio proportions. To reestablish portfolio exposures of 120 percent of capital as long positions and 20 percent of capital as short positions, the manager needs to rebalance by selling $4 of long positions and using the proceeds to cover $4 of short positions. The resulting portfolio restores the 120/20 proportions (because the $114 long and $19 short are, respectively, 120 percent and 20 percent of the $95 capital).

**Myth 17. Converting long-only mandates to enhanced active equity has no effect on a manager's asset capacity.** In enhanced active equity strategies, investments in securities exceed the capital provided, so the strategies use more market liquidity than do unleveraged long-only strategies. Any strain on capacity may be exacerbated by the smaller average capitalization of securities in enhanced active portfolios. Because short selling facilitates portfolio underweights that cannot be attained in long-only portfolios, and the constraint on short selling will more frequently be binding for smaller-cap than for larger-cap securities, the short positions in an enhanced active portfolio will generally have a smaller average capitalization than the underlying benchmark. To hedge the smaller-cap short positions, the long positions in the portfolio will also generally have a smaller average capitalization than the benchmark (so that, on a net basis, the enhanced active portfolio's market capitalization is similar to the benchmark's).[20] Smaller-cap securities, whether they are sold short or purchased long, tend to be less liquid than large-cap securities.

Managers need to focus on their overall equity positions rather than on assets under management when determining their asset capacities. A measure of capacity that is based on the average trading volume of each position will naturally take each security's liquidity into account.

When evaluating a manager's capacity for assets, investors should realize that managers offering enhanced active equity strategies will hold security positions that exceed the amount of capital they manage.

**Myth 18. The performance of an enhanced active equity portfolio can be measured in terms of the excess return of the long positions relative to the benchmark index and the excess return of the short positions relative to the benchmark index, together with their associated residual risks.** If an enhanced active equity portfolio is constructed properly, with the use of integrated optimization, the performance of the long and short positions cannot be meaningfully separated. With integrated optimization, some or all of a short or long position may reflect a hedge of another position; it is not meaningful to look at such a position as a separate entity, just as it is not meaningful to look at a single stock within a long-only portfolio as a separate entity irrespective of its interactions with the other stocks in the portfolio. Furthermore, given that the average capitalization of the underlying benchmark will usually exceed the average of either the short positions or the long positions, the benchmark will provide a fair gauge of the portfolio's performance only when the portfolio is considered in its entirety. Its performance can be measured in terms of the entire portfolio's excess return and residual risk relative to the benchmark index.

**Myth 19. Enhanced active equity portfolios are a form of hedge fund.** Like hedge funds, enhanced active equity portfolios use short selling and leverage to expand return opportunities. There are significant differences, however, between enhanced active investing and hedge fund investing.

Hedge funds typically lack risk-adjusted performance benchmarks. As a result, their risk may be greater than expected and their fees may be higher than warranted. When incentive fees are levied on the basis of absolute portfolio return or portfolio return in excess of a T-bill rate, investors in hedge funds may find themselves paying for indexlike (passive) returns that could be obtained for lower fees or find themselves paying for returns that reflect short-term volatility rather than manager skill.

Enhanced active equity strategies, generally like equity portfolios, are managed relative to an underlying benchmark, such as the S&P 500 or Russell 1000. Investors thus have an objective, risk-adjusted yardstick against which to measure portfolio performance and determine performance fees. Performance fees should generally be levied only on that portion of return that exceeds the underlying benchmark return—that is, on alpha.

Compared with hedge funds, enhanced active strategies typically provide greater transparency of the investment process, portfolio holdings, and security pricing. Hedge funds are often opaque in terms of their processes and holdings. They may invest in assets for which market prices are not readily available. Enhanced active strategies, in contrast, usually rely on liquid, publicly traded assets. Finally, many hedge funds restrict their investors' ability to withdraw funds, whereas an enhanced active portfolio can provide daily liquidity.

**Myth 20. For purposes of asset allocation, investors should classify enhanced active strategies with hedge funds and other alternative investments.**    Enhanced active portfolios share some characteristics with hedge funds and other alternative investments. From the perspective of an investor's asset allocation, however, an enhanced active portfolio is simply a more flexible equity portfolio, not an alternative investment. It has the same equity benchmark as a comparable long-only portfolio but has the potential to improve upon the performance of the long-only portfolio by virtue of its ability to extend portfolio overweights and underweights of attractive and unattractive securities. It is an enhanced form of active equity management.

## NOTES

1. Enhanced active strategies can be developed for various equity benchmarks (large capitalization, small cap, growth, value) and for other asset classes, such as fixed income.
2. The constraint on short selling is a common constraint faced by equity investors (see Jacobs, Levy, and Starer, 1998). Other constraints are those on portfolio risk levels (Jacobs and Levy, 1996a) and on the investable universe (Ennis, 2001; Jacobs and Levy, 1995).
3. See Jacobs, Levy, and Starer, 1998, 1999; Clarke, de Silva, and Sapra, 2004; Jacobs and Levy, 2006.
4. *Market Neutral Strategies*, 2005, edited by Jacobs and Levy, provides a description of these strategies.

5. As they did with regard to long/short investing when it was first becoming popular (Jacobs and Levy, 1996b).

6. A long-only portfolio that is allowed to take more residual risk can take larger and/or more overweights in the most attractive stocks. The portfolio's ability to underweight the most unattractive stocks is still limited, however, by the short-sale restriction. No matter how skilled the manager, the restriction on short selling limits the manager's ability to take active (residual) risk and hence produce excess return. When skill is present, the ability to sell short increases risk and return potential. In general, shorting becomes more desirable as portfolio active weights and manager skill increase because more shorting allows for greater exploitation of under- and overvalued stocks.

7. If enhanced active equity strategies do reduce overvaluation of individual securities, use of the strategies will improve market efficiency and perhaps improve allocation of societal resources.

8. For an MN long/short portfolio using an enhanced prime brokerage structure, establishing an equity market exposure with futures involves moving either cash from the short-sale proceeds or U.S. T-bills (purchased with the cash proceeds) to the futures account to meet futures margin requirements. About 5 percent of the nominal futures value in cash or T-bill margin is needed, and the investor pays an annual stock loan fee of about 50 bps on this amount. The futures should provide a return approximating the return on the underlying market less an amount reflecting the difference between the LIBOR implicit in the futures value and the short rebate the investor earns on the proceeds of the short sale. This differential has recently averaged about 40 bps annually. Additionally, the investor incurs transaction costs to establish and roll the futures position. Establishing equity market exposure with ETFs involves an annual stock loan fee of about 50 bps applied to the amount invested, and the investor expects to receive the relevant stock index return less the transaction costs and management fees associated with the ETF. The cost of a swap is negotiated between the investor and the swap counterparty; it would presumably approximate the cost of alternative methods of equitization. The cost of an active equity overlay in a 200/100 portfolio is the annual stock loan fee of 50 bps applied to the value of the shorted securities.

9. Any equitized MN long/short portfolio can be transformed into an enhanced active equity portfolio via trimming, and any enhanced active equity portfolio can be transformed into an equitized long/short portfolio by adding an equity market overlay to its active weights.

10. Trim and untrim portfolios are defined in Jacobs, Levy, and Markowitz (2005, 2006).

11. Any leveraged portfolio can experience losses that exceed capital. With properly constructed enhanced active portfolios, such an outcome is unlikely because of the portfolio's benchmark orientation and given proper control of residual risk.

12. The investor is usually under no obligation to trade through the prime broker; trades can be executed through other brokers, with the prime broker handling clearing and settlement.

13. See Jacobs and Levy (2006) for an illustration of how short selling can enhance performance.
14. Also, legal opinion generally holds that the purchase of additional long positions with proceeds from short sales does not give rise to acquisition indebtedness; hence, it does not give rise to UBTI for a tax-exempt investor. Prospective participants in these types of transactions should consult their tax and legal advisers.
15. Although a mutual fund's long positions cannot be held at the prime broker, they can be pledged as margin for the short positions. Doing so requires a margin account, which is subject to Reg T limits on leverage. Reg T requires 50 percent initial margin for long positions and 150 percent initial margin for short positions. When securities are used as margin for the short positions, they are generally valued at 50 percent of their market price (as opposed to a valuation of 100% for cash). Initial capital of $100 can support no more than $50 in short positions (and $50 in additional long positions). The $50 in short positions will require $75 margin, which equals half the value of the $150 in long positions (representing the investment of the $100 in initial capital plus the $50 in short-sale proceeds). Thus, the most leveraged enhanced active equity portfolio permitted under the Investment Company Act would hold long positions of 150 percent of capital and short positions of 50 percent of capital (a 150/50 portfolio).
16. Prospective participants in these types of transactions should consult their legal advisers.
17. For equitized MN portfolios, the buffer is generally about half that percentage, with a comparable amount of cash used as collateral for the equity overlay (Jacobs and Levy, 1997).
18. In accordance with SEC Release No. 34-55970, dated June 28, 2007, all price test restrictions on short sales found in Rule 10a-1 under the Securities Exchange Act of 1934 were eliminated and self-regulated organizations were prohibited from having such price tests. This release became effective on July 3, 2007, with compliance mandated by July 6, 2007.
19. For the possibly adverse effects of positive-feedback strategies, see Jacobs (2004).
20. To the extent that smaller-cap stocks are priced less efficiently, this migration down the capitalization spectrum for both long and short positions can result in greater active returns.

## REFERENCES

Clarke, R. G., H. de Silva, and S. Sapra. 2004. "Toward More Information-Efficient Portfolios." *Journal of Portfolio Management*, vol. 30, no. 1 (Fall):54–63.

Ennis, R. 2001. "The Case for Whole-Stock Portfolios." *Journal of Portfolio Management*, vol. 27, no. 3 (Spring):17–26.

Jacobs, B. I. 2004. "Risk Avoidance and Market Fragility." *Financial Analysts Journal*, vol. 60, no. 1 (January/February):26–30.

Jacobs, B. I., and K. N. Levy. 1993. "Long/Short Equity Investing." *Journal of Portfolio Management*, vol. 19, no. 1 (Fall):52–63.

———. 1995. "The Law of One Alpha." *Journal of Portfolio Management*, vol. 21, no. 3 (Summer):78–79.

———. 1996a. "Residual Risk: How Much Is Too Much?" *Journal of Portfolio Management*, vol. 22, no. 3 (Spring):10–16.

———. 1996b. "20 Myths about Long–Short." *Financial Analysts Journal*, vol. 52, no. 5 (September/October):81–85.

———. 1997. "The Long and Short on Long–Short." *Journal of Investing*, vol. 6, no. 1 (Spring):73–86.

———. 1999. "Alpha Transport with Derivatives." *Journal of Portfolio Management*, vol. 25, Special Issue (May):55–60.

———, eds. 2005. *Market Neutral Strategies*. Hoboken, NJ: John Wiley.

———. 2006. "Enhanced Active Equity Strategies: Relaxing the Long-Only Constraint in the Pursuit of Active Return." *Journal of Portfolio Management*, vol. 32, no. 3 (Spring):45–55.

———. 2007. "Enhanced Active Equity Portfolios Are Trim Equitized Long–Short Portfolios." *Journal of Portfolio Management*.

Jacobs, B. I., K. N. Levy, and H. M. Markowitz. 2005. "Portfolio Optimization with Factors, Scenarios, and Realistic Short Positions." *Operations Research*, vol. 53, no. 4 (July/August):586–599.

———. 2006. "Trimability and Fast Optimization of Long–Short Portfolios." *Financial Analysts Journal*, vol. 62, no. 2 (March/April):36–46.

Jacobs, B. I., K. N. Levy, and D. Starer. 1998. "On the Optimality of Long–Short Strategies." *Financial Analysts Journal*, vol. 54, no. 2 (March/April):40–51.

———. 1999. "Long–Short Portfolio Management: An Integrated Approach." *Journal of Portfolio Management*, vol. 25, no. 2 (Winter):23–32.

Miller, E. 2001. "Why the Low Returns to Beta and Other Forms of Risk?" *Journal of Portfolio Management*, vol. 27, no. 2 (Winter):40–55.

Patterson, S. 2006. "A Strategy Aiming to Pump Returns Gains Clout but May Be 'No Free Lunch'." *Wall Street Journal* October 13:C1.

# CHAPTER 24

# Active 130/30 Extensions: Alpha Hunting at the Fund Level

**Martin L. Leibowitz**
Managing Director
Morgan Stanley, Research

**Anthony Bova**
Vice President
Morgan Stanley, Research

*Active equity strategies that are highly benchmark-centric will generally have a minimal impact on fund-level volatility. Because most U.S. institutional portfolios are overwhelmingly dominated by their equity exposure, any incremental tracking error (TE) will be submerged by the beta effect. Positive alpha opportunities from tightly beta-targeted strategies can, therefore, be particularly valuable because they can significantly increase the fund's total return with only minor increases in the overall volatility or other beyond-model forms of risk.*

*Active extension (AE) strategies such as 130/30 portfolios are intrinsically benchmark-centric, and can potentially lead to higher levels of active alpha. The expanded footings open the door to a fresh set of actively chosen underweight positions and provide a wider range of alpha-seeking opportunities for both traditional and quantitative management.*

*Active extension strategies can be designed to fit within a sponsor's existing allocation space for active U.S. equity. With proper risk control, an AE may entail TE that is only moderately greater than that of a comparable long-only fund.*

*A carefully implemented AE can expand relationships with existing managers. A sponsor may want to draw upon those active managers that have already been vetted in terms of their alpha-seeking skills, organization infrastructure, and risk-control procedures.*

*The preconditions for realizing any of these benefits are a credible basis for producing positive alphas in both long and short portfolios, a high level of risk discipline, an ability to minimize and/or offset unproductive correlations, and an organizational ability to pursue AEs in a benchmark-centric, cost-efficient fashion.*

## INTRODUCTION

The general approach in this article consists of three parts: (1) development of an illustrative model for 120/20-type portfolios that describe the key features of AEs, (2) a beta-based analysis of the return/risk characteristics of the typical institutional fund, and (3) a discussion of the special niche occupied by AEs within the broad spectrum of management processes.

The strategy spectrum is characterized as progressing from the beta grazing of index funds, to the gathering of passive alphas through greater diversification, to hunting down active alphas, and finally ending with institutional foraging for return whenever and however can be found. Within this spectrum, it will be shown that the AEs provide a particularly broad hunting ground for seeking active alphas, whereas its benchmark-centric approach to risk can offer special benefits within the context of the typical beta-dominated fund.

The separation of alpha and beta is a topic that has garnered a tremendous amount of interest in recent years. There are several new types of active equity strategies that focus on providing alphas relative to some well-defined and closely tracked equity benchmark. These benchmark-centric funds differ in analytic approach, net exposures, target beta, tracking error (TE), and their ability to short stocks.

One of these new strategies is the AE, also referred to as a 120/20 portfolio. This term came from the early implementations that allowed up to 20 percent of the portfolio to be shorted, with the proceeds used to purchase 20 percent additional longs. Hence, the portfolios maintained their 100 percent net long exposure with gross footings of 120 percent long and

20 percent short. More recent AE launches have been in the 130/30 to 140/40 range as managers and sponsors have gained more comfort with this approach.

It is well known that virtually every equity market is highly concentrated, with a small number of stocks with very large capitalizations, a number of moderately large-cap issues, and a very large number of lesser capitalization companies. In a long-only portfolio, the ability to take significant underweight positions is limited to those few stocks with very large capitalizations. By allowing a limited facility to short stocks within a risk-controlled framework, AE strategies open the door to a fresh set of underweight positions in lesser-cap stocks. Additional potential benefits include the ability to offset unproductive correlations and to facilitate specific pair trades between long and short positions.

A growing body of studies has addressed the potential performance benefits that can be obtained by loosening the standard long-only constraint (Jacobs and Levy, 1993, 1995, 1999, 2006; Jacobs, Levy, and Starer, 1998; Grinold, 1989, 2005; Grinold and Eaton, 1998; Grinold and Kahn 2000a,b,c; Clarke, de Silva and Thorley, 2002, 2005; Clarke, 2005; Michaud, 1993; Arnott and Leinweber, 1994; Brush, 1997; Litterman, 2005; Markowitz, 2005). The early work of Jacobs and Levy (1993, 1995, 1999, 2006) on risk-controlled long/short equity portfolios created a body of literature that served as a foundation in this area. A further dimension was analytic framework for active management developed by Grinold (1989, 2005), Grinold and Eaton (1998), Grinold and Kahn (2000a,b,c). In recent years, the 120/20 strategy has been the direct focus for an increasing number of theoretical studies, including key papers by Clarke, de Silva, and Thorley (2002, 2005) and Clarke (2005) together with further contributions on this specific topic by Jacobs and Levy, Grinold and Kahn, as well as various studies by numerous other authors (Michaud, 1993; Arnott and Leinweber, 1994; Brush, 1997; Litterman, 2005; Markowitz, 2005; Bernstein, 2006; Emrich, 2006; Winston and Hewett, 2006).

Active extensions are based upon relaxation of this long-only constraint but have special features that maintain the basic risk characteristics of benchmark-centric long-only funds: (1) the percentage sold short is offset by reinvestment in beta-equivalent new longs so as to preserve both the 100 percent net long posture and the original beta target, and (2) the overweight and underweight positions are structured so as to keep the TE within reasonable bounds.

These risk-control characteristics enable AE funds to occupy a position close to active long-only funds while still having the ability to pursue a larger number of alpha opportunities. Thus, unlike other long/short strategies with beta values that are either untargeted or deliberately varied, an AE's well-defined beta value allows it to occupy the same allocation space as long-only equity funds.

The interest in AE strategies has grown significantly as both investment sponsors and asset managers have sought higher levels of positive alpha. The acceptance of these strategies has also been enhanced because they can be viewed as an extension of traditional equity management rather than as a quantum leap into the more limited space allocated to alternative assets.

A series of studies on asset allocations has shown that the total beta (equity exposure) accounts for over 90 percent of the overall volatility of most U.S. pension funds, foundations, and endowments (Leibowitz, 2004; Leibowitz and Bova, 2005a,b, 2007). Moreover, this total beta dominance occurs even with very highly diversified allocations having as little as 15 to 20 percent direct weight in U.S. bonds and equities.

Within this asset allocation context, benchmark-centric equity funds have some uniquely certain desirable risk characteristics: (1) the uncorrelated TE will only have a minimal impact on the fund's overall volatility risk, (2) because the beta value can be tightly specified, it can be readily incorporated into the desired total beta target for the overall fund, and (3) there is little of the "beyond-model" risk that surrounds nontraditional asset classes. With these desirable risk characteristics, the key issue then becomes the benchmark-centric strategy's ability to generate positive alpha outcomes on a credible and reliable basis.

While functioning within these benchmark-centric risk characteristics, a properly designed AE can materially expand the proactive long/short footings that form the alpha hunting ground for active alphas.

At the outset, it should be noted that shorting differs significantly from long-only management in a number of important ways, including somewhat higher transaction and maintenance costs, the available level and continuity of liquidity, the need for more intensive monitoring and risk control, and so on. To realize any of the benefits from AE, the management organization must have the ability to utilize negative alpha opportunities and be able to establish short positions in a risk-controlled, operationally secure, and cost-efficient fashion.

## ACTIVE EXTENSIONS

### Alpha Ranking and Weighting Models

This section is intended to describe the key features of AE strategies and highlight their potential for alpha enhancement within a fund-level context. The first step is to develop simple alpha ranking and position weighting models to characterize the active management process. A basic example of AE is then chosen for illustrative purposes. Although this approach represents an admittedly less comprehensive treatment than the referenced studies, it does capture the fundamental appeal of AE strategies for sponsors as well as for both traditional and quantitative active equity managers.

In a benchmark-centric management process, the portfolio is structured to maintain the targeted beta relative to the stated benchmark. An active position is then based on the expectation of a positive return in excess of the security's beta-adjusted return. Portfolio managers generally have some formal or informal process for classifying these prospective active positions in a descending sequence based upon their expected excess return. Alpha ranking models can be used to approximate such classifications.

Exhibit 24.1 represents the alpha ranking model that will be used in our base case example. The solid top line is modeled on an exponential alpha decay with a beginning alpha of 5 percent for the first most promising position, which then declines to 2.24 percent for the 25th position.

An active position is established by assigning a differential weight to the security that is above (or below) its weight in the benchmark. This differential weighting will depend on the security's alpha potential and the

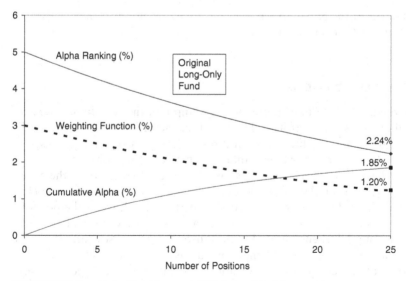

**EXHIBIT 24.1** Alpha Ranking and Weighting Models
*Source:* Morgan Stanley Research

residual volatility of its excess returns. With the assumption of a constant residual volatility, the optimal differential weighting for each position should be roughly proportional to its alpha ranking. The dotted middle line in Exhibit 24.1 is an exponential weighting function that begins at a maximum 3 percent weight and then follows approximately the same decay rate as the alpha ranking model. After the 25th position, the active weight from the extension process remains constant for any additional long positions added to the portfolio.

It should be noted that even in long-only portfolios, active positions can take the form of either overweights or underweights. However, the exposition is greatly simplified by treating the long-only active positions as if they were all overweights. The following discussion of the long-only portfolios adopts this "overweight-only" convention.

The alpha contribution of each active position is represented by the product of its alpha (from the alpha ranking model) and its differential weight (from the weighting model). The sum of all such alpha contributions adds up to the expected portfolio alpha.

Using the alpha ranking and exponential weighting models from Exhibit 24.1, the baseline example of a long-only portfolio is constructed with 25 active positions. The solid bottom curve in Exhibit 24.1 shows how the cumulative alpha builds as additional positions are incorporated into the portfolio. For the illustrative 25 position long-only portfolio, the cumulative alpha attains a level of 1.85 percent (the remaining "nonproactive" component of the portfolio serves as a source of funds as well as helping to maintain the fund's target beta).

## Tracking Error Models

With the target beta pinned down by assumption, the remaining source of volatility risk is the portfolio's TE. The three factors that determine the TE are the residual volatilities of each position, the portfolio weightings, and the correlations or factor effects that exist between the positions.

At the security level, the TE is just the residual volatility of the excess return (i.e., the standard deviation of the security's return above or below its beta-adjusted market return). At the portfolio level, when the portfolio beta is tightly targeted at 1, the TE measures the deviation of portfolio returns around the benchmark. For the illustrative base case example, the TE computation is based on the simplifying assumptions of a constant residual volatility of 23 percent for each position. Any interaction between positions is modeled as a pairwise correlation. The active weightings, together with

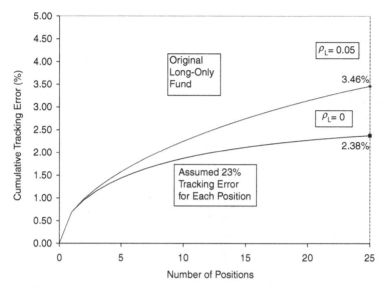

**EXHIBIT 24.2** TE Models
*Source:* Morgan Stanley Research

these two assumptions, then provide the basis for computing the portfolio TE (the development of the analytic expression for the portfolio TE becomes somewhat involved and, for that reason, has been relegated to the Technical Appendix).

Exhibit 24.2 shows how the TE grows as positions are added to the long-only portfolio under assumed pairwise correlations ($\rho_L$) of zero and 0.05. For the 25-position long portfolio, the TE ends up at 2.38 percent for the uncorrelated case, and at 3.46 percent for an assumed 0.05 pairwise correlation between all 25 active positions. It only takes a slight increase in pairwise correlation to generate significant increases in the TE.

## The Short Extension

The ability to take short positions provides access to a fresh set of underweights. In the following analysis, these new underweights are assumed to have alphas that coincide with the corresponding long-only alpha ranking model, less some given shorting cost, taken to be 0.50 percent in the base case example. The small-dashed line that starts at a 4.50 percent alpha in Exhibit 24.3 schematically depicts a 35 percent short extension. The base case

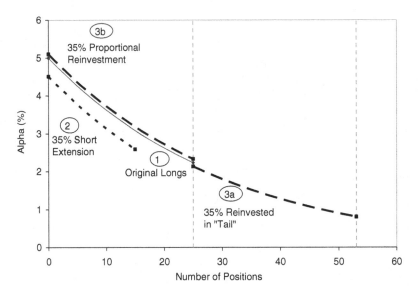

**EXHIBIT 24.3** AE with Proportional and Tail Reinvestment
*Source:* Morgan Stanley Research

also assumes that the short portfolio follows the same exponential weighting model as the long portfolio. The proceeds generated by the shorts are then reinvested into new long positions.

The proceeds from the shorts could theoretically be reinvested either in new longs or back into the original portfolio. In the first case, if the long-only portfolio had already reached its maximum allowable weight in the original 25 positions, then the proceeds would have to be reinvested in the "tail" positions (i.e., starting with the 26th ranked long position). In the second case, if the portfolio has been funding constrained in terms of its ability to achieve the desired active positions, the proceeds could be reinvested to proportionally augment the initial active weights.

Exhibit 24.4 displays the growth of the cumulative alpha from the initial 25 position long-only portfolio through a range of AEs.

The beginning single curve just reflects the accumulating alpha of the long-only portfolio as it grows to incorporate its 25 active positions. The lower of the subsequent three curves is the added alpha generated by the new short portfolio by itself (i.e., if the proceeds were reinvested into a zero-alpha set of new long). The shorts represent fresh opportunities and generate a significant alpha. However, as the short weight expands, the alphas follow the decay path of (literally) diminishing returns, leading to

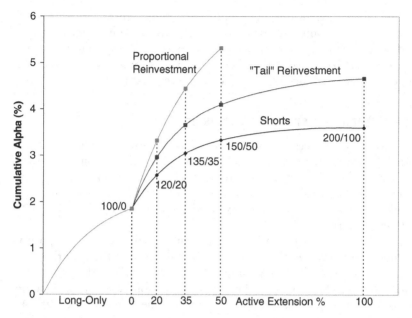

**EXHIBIT 24.4** AE with Proportional and Tail Reinvestment
*Source:* Morgan Stanley Research

a flattening alpha curve. Given the specific assumption in our illustrative model, the short alpha curve rises fairly sharply to a cumulative alpha level of 3.05 percent for a 35 percent extension, then begins to flatten, and obtains very little incremental alpha beyond a 50 percent short weight.

The middle curve shows the added benefit from reinvesting the proceeds in the tail positions that have lower alpha expectations. This curve is higher, but has roughly the same shape as the short-only curve, with the alpha for the 35 percent extension rising to 3.66 percent, 1.71 percent beyond the long-only's 1.85 percent. The curve then continues to ascend modestly upward, even beyond the 50 percent extension.

The top curve reflects the more aggressive proportional reinvestment case where the initial active weights are directly augmented by the short proceeds. At a 35 percent extension, the portfolio alpha reaches 4.44 percent (i.e., almost 2.60% beyond the long-only alpha of 1.85%). As the extension percentage grows, the tacit assumption is that the active weights can continue to be increased without encountering some upper bound of acceptability. Thus, in our example, at a 50 percent extension, the proportional reinvestment would push the active weight of the first ranked long position to 6 percent, which we take as being this ultimate upper bound.

At the higher extensions, the proportional reinvestment case is probably too aggressive, not only because of a bound on the maximum active weight, but also because it relies too heavily on a fixed alpha ranking model. For this reason, the base case in the later fund-level examples will focus on the more conservative results associated with tail reinvestment.

## Tracking Error under Active Extension

As the extension process adds new positions and/or augments the active weights, the TE increases accordingly. In the earlier discussion of the long-only portfolio, there were two different correlation assumptions: (1) totally uncorrelated, and (2) a pairwise correlation of +0.05 between all positions. The uncorrelated case is the most optimistic, leading to significantly smaller TEs than the correlated case.

In moving to the AE, the more conservative path is to assume positive correlations of +0.05 *within* the long portfolio ($\rho_L$) and *within* the short portfolio ($\rho_S$). By itself, this assumption leads to significantly greater TEs as the short weight expands. The impact of various correlation assumptions is shown in Exhibit 24.5 for tail reinvestment and in Exhibit 24.6

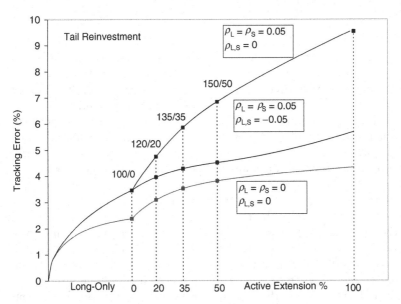

**EXHIBIT 24.5**   AE TE with Tail Reinvestment
*Source:* Morgan Stanley Research

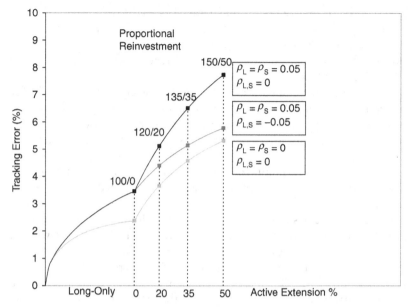

**EXHIBIT 24.6** AE TE with Proportional Reinvestment
*Source:* Morgan Stanley Research

for proportional reinvestment. In each graph, the lower curve represents the most optimistic case of totally uncorrelated residuals, whereas the top curve shows the significantly higher TEs resulting from even modest levels of pairwise correlation. However, with a long/short portfolio structure, one must also address the correlation that may exist between the long and the short portfolios. Indeed, one of the potential benefits of AE is that the short portfolio facilitates offsetting unproductive factor effects within the long portfolio, such as an excessive size or growth bias. The middle curves in Exhibits 24.5 and 24.6 reflect the TE benefit that can be derived from offsetting correlations of −0.05 *between* the short and long positions. Although still lying above the uncorrelated curve, these offsets materially reduce the TE levels associated with higher short weights. The subsequent baseline examples will be based on this assumed negative offset correlation ($\rho_{L,S}$) of −0.05 *between* the longs and shorts. This assumption provides a middle road, resulting in TEs that are lower than the case with only positive correlations, but considerably higher than the uncorrelated situation.

It should be recognized that, in general, AEs lead to TEs that are larger than those experienced in the original long-only portfolio. Thus, even for the tail-reinvestment case, where the augmented active weight is more broadly spread, the TEs rise from the long-only's 3 percent to the 4 percent region for 20 to 50 percent extensions.

The Appendix develops an analytic model for computing the TE for the general case of an AE with an exponential weighting function and any assumed set of pairwise correlations. Pairwise correlation assumptions may serve as proxies for the more complex factor effects that impact all portfolios, whether long or short. A successful extension process should include close attention to minimizing the impact of any unproductive or unintended factor effects other than those deliberately viewed as being return producing.

For the baseline assumptions cited earlier, Exhibit 24.7 compares the TE growth for the reinvestment models as a function of the short weight. With a 35 percent extension and tail reinvestment, the TE rises from 3.46 percent for the initial long-only portfolio to 4.29 percent. With proportional reinvestment, the TE increases much more rapidly because of the greater concentration of reinvested weight in the first 25 long positions. The

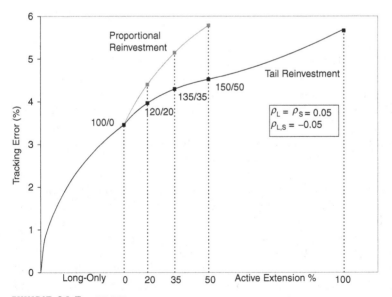

**EXHIBIT 24.7**   AE TE
*Source:* Morgan Stanley Research

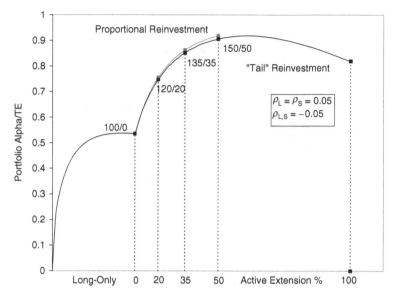

**EXHIBIT 24.8**  Portfolio Alpha/TE: The Standard Measure
*Source:* Morgan Stanley Research

proportional case attains a TE of 5.14 percent at a 35 percent extension and 5.78 percent at a 50 percent extension.

## The Alpha/Tracking Error Ratio

The alpha ranking models from Exhibit 24.3 can be combined with the TEs in Exhibit 24.7 to calculate the alpha/TE ratios displayed in Exhibit 24.8. With positive correlation of 0.05, the information ratio (IR) for the basic 25-position long-only portfolio ratio was 0.54. With the assumed offsetting −0.05 correlation, the ratios for the two reinvestment alternatives turn out to be surprisingly close, both rising to about 0.85 for 35 percent extensions and to 0.91 for 50 percent extensions. This striking result is due to the proportional reinvestment's higher alpha in the numerator being largely matched by a higher TE in the denominator. (The convergence in these ratios is the result of the specific parameter values in our baseline example, and should not be taken as an indication of any general principle.)

The alpha/TE ratio is an important metric, but it may not always be a sufficient gauge of a strategy's value. It also makes sense to look separately at the two individual components that comprise this ratio. The alpha versus

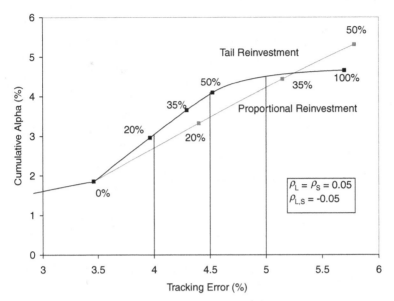

**EXHIBIT 24.9** Portfolio Alpha versus TE.
*Source:* Morgan Stanley Research

TE presentation in Exhibit 24.9 provides a deeper insight into the return/risk characteristics of the two investment modes. First, it becomes clear that, for greater short weights, both the alpha *and* the TE increase much faster in the proportional case than with tail reinvestment. Second, it is interesting to observe that the proportional reinvestment curve rises as virtually a straight line. Third, it becomes evident why the ratios converge because they correspond to the slope of the straight line drawn from the origin (0% TE and 0% alpha) to the curve values shown in Exhibit 24.9.

There is an even more important point to be made by the separation of the IR into an alpha numerator and a TE denominator as shown in Exhibit 24.9. The return/risk ratio is a standard measure for evaluating portfolio strategies. It is particularly useful in assessing the a priori—or *ex post*—ability of a strategy to generate positive alpha outcomes on a on a statically consistent basis. However, the ratio also implies a degree of comparability between the numerator and the denominator. In certain contexts, there may be significantly different utility value associated with alpha as an incremental return or with the TE as a gauge of risk. In such situations, this ratio approach could be highly misleading.

One such situation is the role of AEs and other benchmark-centric equity strategies at the level of the overall fund. For example, suppose a fund were able to tolerate a maximum TE of 4.50 percent. Thus, from Exhibit 24.9, this fund could accept a 50 percent extension with tail reinvestment and obtain a cumulative alpha of 4.13 percent, more than twice the long-only's 1.85 percent. Alternatively, it could be slightly more conservative, accept a 4.29 percent TE and obtain a 3.66 percent alpha from a 35 percent tail-based extension. In the following section, we explore how such a 35 percent tail-based extension would affect the typical institutional portfolio in terms of its fund-level risk and return characteristics.

## FUND-LEVEL RISK EFFECTS

### Three Volatility Surprises

The preceding sections have dealt with how AEs can lead to improvements in the equity portfolio's alpha at the cost of increasing TE. However, the discussion has, to this point, taken place strictly within the confines of the individual equity portfolio. From the point of the view of the asset owner or the fund sponsor, the situation is quite different and, in many ways, more compelling. As long as the risk-control discipline can assure that a beta of 1 is being maintained and that exogenous sources of risks are excluded, then the increased TE from the AE will be the only additional source of volatility risk at the fund level. In such a situation, the extension's alpha adds, on a weighted basis, to the overall fund return while the higher TE can be shown to be largely submerged within the beta risk that dominates the volatility of the overall fund.

The policy allocations of a wide range of institutional funds have surprisingly similar risk characteristics. Exhibit 24.10 shows two examples—a traditional 60/40 portfolio B and a modern portfolio C that is diversified into a wide range of asset classes.

The fund's risk characteristics in Exhibit 24.10 are derived from a standard return/covariance matrix developed by a well-known consultant.

The covariance matrix provides an estimation of the volatility of each asset class and the correlations between any two asset classes. In particular, it specifies the correlation of each asset class with a U.S. equity benchmark. This correlation can be combined with the ratio of the asset's volatility to the assumed equity volatility to develop an implicit beta. This implicit beta represents a correlation-based estimate of the asset's mean response to changing equity returns.

**EXHIBIT 24.10** Typical Diversification Does Not Materially Change Fund Volatility: 90 Percent Plus from Equity

| | Correlation-Based Implicit Beta | B | C |
|---|---|---|---|
| Passive U.S Equity | 1.00 | 60% | 20% |
| Passive U.S. Bonds | 0.14 | 40% | 20% |
| International Equity | 0.77 | | 15% |
| Emerging Mkt Equity | 0.76 | | 5% |
| Absolute Return | 0.28 | | 10% |
| Venture Capital | 0.59 | | 10% |
| Private Equity | 0.98 | | 10% |
| Real Estate | 0.07 | | 10% |
| Total | | 100% | 100% |
| Total Volatility | | 11.17 | 10.45 |
| Total Beta | | 0.65 | 0.57 |
| % Volatility from Beta | | 96.7% | 90.4% |

*Source:* Morgan Stanley Research

The correlation-based implicit betas for each asset class are shown in Exhibit 24.10. A total beta for a given fund can then be found by weighting the implicit betas by the percentage allocation. Thus, portfolio B has a total beta of 0.65, composed of its 60 percent explicit equity allocation together with 0.05 from the 40 percent bonds with an implicit beta of 0.14. In the highly diversified portfolio C, the total beta value of 0.57 is composed of 0.20 from the 20 percent direct equity and a further 0.37 from the weight in the other asset classes.

In comparing these fund-level risk characteristics of portfolios B and C at the bottom of Exhibit 24.8, three surprises immediately present themselves.

The first surprise is that, in spite of the vastly different levels of diversification, the two portfolios B and C have total volatilities that are nearly the same. Although portfolio C does have a somewhat lower volatility, 10.45 versus 11.17 for the 60/40 portfolio B, given the uncertainties in any covariance matrix, it is hard to believe that too much should be made of this minor difference.

The second surprise is that the total betas for these two very different funds again are quite close, 0.65 and 0.57, respectively, for B and C. If we were to look at a wide spectrum of asset allocations across U.S. pension funds, foundations, and endowments, total betas and total volatilities would both be found to fall within quite narrow ranges, 0.55 to 0.65 for the total betas, and 10 to 11.5 percent for the volatilities.

The third surprise is found by taking the total beta value and multiplying by the 16.50 percent volatility that the covariance model assigns to U.S. equities. When this product is divided by the fund volatility, the result is the percentage of the total volatility that can be ascribed to the fund's equity exposure. For B and C, these percentages are $(0.65 \times 16.50\%)/11.17\% = 97\%$, and $(0.57 \times 16.50\%)/10.45\% = 90\%$, respectively. Thus, an overwhelming percentage of the volatility risk in these two funds is derived from their co-movement relationship with equities. This dominating beta role can be seen across a wide swath of institutional portfolios.

The percentage of equity-based volatility can also be interpreted as the correlation of the fund with movements in the equity market. This powerful and pervasive beta dominance at the fund level has major implications for the potential role of AEs and other benchmark-centric strategies that are tightly targeted to a stated equity benchmark.

## Passive Implicit Alphas

Exhibit 24.11 shows how B's expected return of 5.85 percent and C's 7.08 percent is derived from the weighted expected return of the component assets. The return components can also be broken down a risk-free base rate of 1.50 percent and return premiums of 4.35 percent for fund B and the significantly higher 5.85 percent for fund C. The return premiums are then further parsed into one component associated with the asset's implicit beta component and a second component consisting of the remaining expected return specified in the return/covariance model. The beta-based return component is simply the multiple of the implicit beta and the equity return premium (5.75% in this example). The second component has the form of an "implicit alpha" (i.e., the remaining return that can be accessed by *passively* investing in the given asset class).

As seen in Exhibit 24.11, the weighted sum of these implicit alphas adds to only 0.59 percent in portfolio B. In contrast, the implicit alphas for portfolio C accumulate to a sizable 2.29 percent accounting for a large part of C's higher return relative to B.

It should be emphasized that these implicit alphas are quite different from active alphas. The implicit alphas are derived from passive investment in an asset class that receives just the expected return embedded in the return/ covariance model. The passive return from implicit alphas is obtainable without any unique skills or structural advantages. They represent a nonzero sum vector of rewards for moving the portfolio from its current allocation into a less constrained and more diversified posture that provides higher expected returns.

**EXHIBIT 24.11**  Diversification Raises Fund Return through Implicit Alphas

| | Expected Total Return | Correlation-Based Implicit Alpha | B | C |
|---|---|---|---|---|
| Passive U.S. Equity | 7.25 | | 60% | 20% |
| Passive U.S. Bonds | 3.75 | 1.47 | 40% | 20% |
| International Equity | 7.25 | 1.33 | | 15% |
| Emerging Mkt Equity | 9.25 | 3.36 | | 5% |
| Absolute Return | 5.25 | 214 | | 10% |
| Venture Capital | 12.25 | 7.37 | | 10% |
| Private Equity | 10.25 | 3.14 | | 10% |
| Real Estate | 5.50 | 3.58 | | 10% |
| Total | | | 100% | 100% |
| Expected Return | | | 5.85 | 7.08 |
| Total Beta × Equity Premium × Equity Premium | | | $0.65 \times 5.75$ | $0.57 \times 5.75$ |
| Beta Return | | | 3.76 | 3.29 |
| Risk-Free Rate | | | 1.50 | 1.50 |
| Implicit Alpha | | | 0.59 | 2.29 |

*Source:* Morgan Stanley Research

It should also be noted that Exhibits 24.10 and 24.11 have the somewhat startling implication that diversification as typically practiced by institutional funds does not really reduce total volatility, but rather enhances expected returns.

### Beyond-Model Dragon Risks

The preceding discussion suggests that, at the fund level, asset classes with positive implicit alpha can provide a higher expected return with little impact on total volatility. This raises the question as to why this apparently free lunch should not be pursued more vigorously. A related question is why allocations are not more concentrated on the single highest-alpha source, rather than having the weight to alternatives fragmented over multiple alpha assets. This same issue arises from an unconstrained optimization process that invariably produces initial allocations with overtly unacceptable concentrations in one or more alternative assets.

In practice, pension funds, endowments, and foundations often use a process that could be described as tortured optimization based on the mean/variance approach, first suggested by Harry Markowitz in the 1950s (Markowitz, 1959). The resulting allocations are naturally highly dependent on both the assumptions in the covariance matrix and on the constraints established for each asset class. Torturing refers to the common practice of sequentially manipulating these constraints to achieve portfolios that are theoretically optimal, but that also satisfy the more ephemeral criterion of being palatable. Whether determined in advance or as part of the process, the constraints play a key role in determining the ultimate allocation.

The allocation into any alternative asset is always subject to a variety of constraints, some well founded and well articulated, and others that may be more subtle and/or simply convention based. Some considerations that are frequently put forward for setting these position limits include: underdeveloped financial markets, liquidity concerns, limited access to acceptable investment vehicles or first-class managers, problematic fee structures, regulatory or organizational strictures, peer-based standards, "headline risk," insufficient or unreliable historical data, and so forth.

The term *dragon-risks* aptly captures the cornucopia of concerns that lead to these constraints. This expression is taken from a paper by Cliff Asness (2002), referring to the medieval mapmaker's characterization of uncharted territories as places where dragons may dwell. The basic issue here is the critical divide between modelable probabilities and the more fundamental uncertainty about the validity of any model. This distinction has been discussed at some length in the work of Peter Bernstein (1996) and Frank Knight (1964).

As funds diversify into alternative assets, they incur three forms of risk: (1) implicit betas, (2) modeled alpha volatility, and (3) the beyond-model dragon risks.

The implicit beta at the fund level is often preserved through the purchase of a mid-beta alternative asset using a mid-beta combination of bonds and equity. Indeed, this is why the typical diversification creates only minimal changes in the fund's total beta or overall volatility risk. To the extent that diversification initially results in a beta shift, the fund can easily reestablish the desired beta target by revising the percentage mixture in the remaining bonds and equity.

The modeled alpha volatility is a form of TE that is uncorrelated with the dominant beta exposure. However, with the alternative assets having such fragmented allocations, the fund's dominant beta risk will overwhelm the volatility effect from modeled TEs (as long as they remain uncorrelated with each other). The beyond-modeled risks are more problematic because they are harder to formally assess and control. The standard approach is to set what seems to be reasonable constraints on each alternative asset, and trust that the resulting fragmented allocation represents an acceptable balance of risk and return.

Thus, regardless of any optimization results based upon a given return/covariance matrix, it is these beyond-model dragon risks that determine the percentage weight ultimately assigned to the nontraditional asset classes.

## Active Alphas

To this point, we have not focused on any return/risk characteristics other than those associated with passive investments in the various asset classes. The associated implicit alphas are fundamentally different from the various forms of active alphas from superior security selection, better portfolio construction, uncovering high performing managers, unique access to desirable investment vehicles, and so on. Active alphas are intrinsically skill based and theoretically zero-sum in nature. Benchmark-centric and AE strategies depend upon skilled active management to generate their anticipated positive alphas.

A benchmark-centric strategy has a TE that is intended to be independent of the targeted beta volatility, and hopefully has few sources of beyond-model risk. This situation is quite different from the beyond-model concerns associated with nontraditional asset classes, where the standard covariance model will almost surely be viewed as only partially describing all the potential dimensions of risk. For example, any simple covariance assumptions for real estate or commodities can hardly be viewed as capturing the entire constellation of risks associated such with investments. However, a benchmark-centric process should be able to provide a high degree of assurance that its risks can be segregated into a targeted beta risk, an orthogonal TE component, and relatively few beyond-model concerns.

The first column in Exhibit 24.12 summarizes the return and risk characteristics for portfolio B with only passive investments. The second column, labeled B*, shows the case where the 60 percent passive equity is moved into the active long-only position with the earlier base case example earlier of an 1.85 percent alpha with 3.46 percent TE. The active equity increases the returns by $60\% \times 1.85\% = 1.11\%$, from 5.85 percent to 6.96 percent. The beta remains the same at 0.65 because one of the requirements for benchmark-centric active management is that the equity portfolio's beta retains the original target value of one. The 3.46 percent TE from active management on 60 percent of the assets is uncorrelated with the 0.65 beta exposure, so that B* total volatility can be found from the standard sum of

**EXHIBIT 24.12** Long-Only Active Equity Adds Active Alpha with Minimal Volatility Impact

|  | B | B* | B** |
|---|---|---|---|
| Passive U.S. Equity | 60% | 0% | 0% |
| Long-Only Active U.S. Equity | – | 60% | 40% |
| Active 35 Percent Extension | – | – | 20% |
| Passive U.S. Bonds | 40% | 40% | 40% |
| Total | 100% | 100% | 100% |
| Expected Return | 5.85 | 6.97 | 7.32 |
| Risk-Free Rate | 1.50 | 1.50 | 1.50 |
| Beta Return | 3.76 | 3.76 | 3.76 |
| Implicit Alpha | 0.59 | 0.59 | 0.59 |
| Active Alphas [1.85% Alpha on 60% Long-Only] | – | 1.12 | 1.12 |
| Total Volatility | 11.17 | 11.36 | 11.40 |
| Passive Volatility | 11.17 | 11.17 | 11.17 |
| With 3.46% TEV on 60% Long-Only | – | 0.19 | 0.19 |

*Source:* Morgan Stanley Research

squares equation,

$$B * vol = \sqrt{(Bvol)^2 + (0.60 * \text{TE})^2}$$
$$= \sqrt{(11.17)^2 + (0.60 * 3.46)^2}$$
$$= \sqrt{125 + 4.31}$$
$$= 11.36\%$$

Thus, because of the fund's volatility being dominated by the beta risk, the active TE raises B* volatility by only 0.19 percent to 11.36 percent from the passive portfolio B's 11.17 percent.

## Fund-Level Active Extensions

Now suppose 20 percent of B*'s 60 percent active equity is moved into an AE with a 35 percent short weight reinvested into the more conservative "tail"

**EXHIBIT 24.13** Long-Only Active Equity Adds Active Alpha with Minimal Volatility Impact

|  | B | B* | B** |
|---|---|---|---|
| Passive U.S. Equity | 60% | 0% | 0% |
| Long-Only Active U.S. Equity | – | 60% | 40% |
| Active 35 Percent Extension | – | – | 20% |
| Passive US Bonds | 40% | 40% | 40% |
| Total | 100% | 100% | 100% |
| Expected Return | 5.85 | 6.97 | 7.32 |
|   Risk-Free Rate | 1.50 | 1.50 | 1.50 |
|   Beta Return | 3.76 | 3.76 | 3.76 |
|   Implicit Alpha | 0.59 | 0.59 | 0.59 |
|     Active Alphas (1.85% Alpha on 60% Long-Only) | – | 1.12 | 1.12 |
|     AE Incremental Alpha (1.80% Alpha on 20% AE-35%) | – | – | 0.36 |
| Total Volatility | 11.17 | **11.36** | **11.40** |
|   Passive Volatility | 11.17 | 11.17 | 11.17 |
|   With 3.46% TEV on 60% Long-Only | – | 0.19 | 0.19 |
|   With 4.29% TEV on 20% AE-35% | – | – | 0.04 |

*Source:* Morgan Stanley Research

mode example. As shown in Exhibit 24.13, the return for this B** portfolio moves up from B's 5.85 percent for the purely passive case, to 6.97 percent for B*'s long-only active, to now 7.32 percent with B**'s AE. The total fund volatility moves up only slightly from B's 11.17 percent to B*'s 11.36 percent to B**'s 11.40 percent. Once again, this minimal volatility impact is based on the presumption that these TEs can be viewed as uncorrelated with the beta exposure.

Finally, Exhibit 24.14 shows that even for the highly diversified portfolio C, the same movement toward a 20 percent AE leads to similar results.

The return rises from C's 7.08 percent with the purely passive 20 percent equity, to 7.45 percent with the active long-only format, and then to 7.81 percent when the 20 percent equity is moved into an AE with a 35 percent short weight. As a result of C's lower overall equity exposure, the total volatility moves up even more slightly from C's 10.45 percent, to C*'s 10.48 percent, and finally to C**'s 10.49 percent.

**EXHIBIT 24.14** Long-Only Active Equity Adds Active Alpha with Minimal Volatility Impact

|  | C | C* | C** |
|---|---|---|---|
| Passive U.S. Equity | 20% | – | – |
| Active U.S. Equity | – | 20% | – |
| Active 35% Extension | – | – | 20% |
| Passive U.S. Bonds | 20% | 20% | 20% |
| Alpha Core | 60% | 60% | 60% |
| Expected Return | 7.08 | 7.45 | 7.81 |
| Risk-Free Rate | 1.50 | 1.50 | 1.50 |
| Beta Return | 3.29 | 3.29 | 3.29 |
| Implicit Alpha | 2.29 | 2.29 | 2.29 |
| Active Alphas (1.85% Alpha on 20% Long-Only) | – | 0.37 | 0.37 |
| AE Incremental Alpha (1.80% Alpha on 20% AE-35%) | – | – | 0.36 |
| Total Volatility | 10.45 | 10.48 | 10.49 |
| Passive Volatility | 10.45 | 10.45 | 10.45 |
| With 3.46% TEV on 60% Long-Only | – | 0.03 | 0.03 |
| With 4.29% TEV on 20% AE-35% | – | – | 0.01 |

*Source:* Morgan Stanley Research

## The Alpha/Beta Matrix

The alpha/beta matrix in Exhibit 24.15 attempts to classify the various forms of portfolio management styles using an alpha/beta template.

In an earlier series of papers, a rather anthropomorphic classification was used to describe different categories of alpha-seeking behavior.

The beta grazers are the index funds that passively feed off the return premiums that are broadly available to all.

The gatherers are funds that expand their allocation by diversifying, but passively, into a wider range of asset classes with the intention of accessing the implicit alphas.

The alpha hunters are the active managers that aggressively seek excess returns from the exercise of superior investment skill. In contrast to gathering, hunting is definitely an intrinsically zero-sum activity.

Then, there are the foragers, who venture forth and seek returns wherever these can be found.

**EXHIBIT 24.15** Fund-Level Alpha/Beta Structures

| Metaphor | Betas | Management Styles | Nature of Alphas | Fund Level Effects | | |
|---|---|---|---|---|---|---|
| | | | | Fund Volatility | Model Risk | TE vs. Policy |
| Beta Grazing | Stapled | Passive Investing in Broad Equity/Fixed Income Marketes | Risk Premium | Fundamental Source | Very Low | Zero |
| Alpha Hunting | Beta-Targeted | Risk-Controlled Active Equity Market Neutral Active Extension Some Hedge Funds | Active Management | Low | Low | Low |
| Alpha Gathering | Correlation-Based | Diversification into New Asset Classes | Implicit Correlation-Based Passive Alphas | Low | High | Low |
| Alpha/Beta Foraging | Free Range Betas | Beta-Agnostic Opportunistic Investment to Hyper Active Some Hedge Funds Macro Funds | Intense to Hyper Active | High | High | High |

*Source*: Morgan Stanley Research

All of these return-seeking pursuits can prove valuable if successfully pursued, but they differ materially in the character of the risks entailed—and nature of their fund-level effects.

Benchmark-centric alpha hunting should ideally have risks that take the form of a moderate level of uncorrelated TE. As evident from the preceding examples in Exhibits 24.12 to 24.14, these modest TE additions will have little impact at the fund level. Alpha hunting that is only benchmark sensitive will involve higher levels of TE. In addition, they may accept a degree of beta variability that could filter into the portfolio's beta and create more sources of drift in fund-level volatility.

The gathering of implicit alphas in new asset classes may entail a substantial degree of uncorrelated TE. However, the more significant risk in expanded diversification arises from the beyond-model dragon risks. These risk factors may not be formalized, but they reveal themselves at the fund level through the de facto limits imposed on the nontraditional asset classes.

Free-range foraging can incur any and all these forms of risk. However, the fund-level impact depends on the intensity of the risks and percentage of the overall allocation deployed in each form of active management.

Clearly, these activities can be mixed and matched. For example, an alpha-gatherer fund may well elect—at the outset or subsequently—to become a hunter and pursue active alphas within the new asset classes that exceed its passive return.

The basic message is that benchmark-centric active management will have only a minimal impact on fund-level volatility if its beta is (1) tightly stapled to the targeted value, (2) the TE is uncorrelated with the fund's dominant beta exposure, (3) there are no other significant sources of volatility risk that correlate with the TE, and (4) there are few, if any, sources of other nonmodeled risks.

Active extensions clearly fall into the benchmark-centric realm of alpha hunting, and must be assessed in terms of the ability to produce positive alphas over time.

If a reliably positive alpha can be accessed with such minimal effective risk at the fund level, it would seem to be desirable to accept some additional TE in exchange for further alpha enhancement. Relative to benchmark-centric long-only strategies, AEs move precisely in this direction.

## CONCLUSION

The volatility risk of U.S. institutional funds is 90 percent or more dominated by their explicit—and implicit—equity exposure. Active extensions are designed to maintain the targeted beta relative to the original long-only benchmark, with the primary source of additional risk being increased TE from the larger number of active positions. In a properly risk-controlled setting, such TE should be uncorrelated with equities. Because total equity exposure is overwhelmingly dominant at the fund level, the additional TE from AEs will be swamped in the standard sum-of-squares calculation. The net result is that the positive alphas derived from an AE will add to the fund's expected return, with only a minimal impact on the fund's overall volatility.

# REFERENCES

Arnott, R. D., and D. J. Leinweber. 1994. "Long–Short Strategies Reassessed." *Financial Analysts Journal*. September/October.

Asness, C. 2002. As cited in the "NACUBO Endowment Study." *NACUBO Business Officer*, April.

Bernstein, P. L. 1996. *"Against the God: The Remarkable Story of Risk."* John Wiley & Sons, Inc.

Bernstein, P. L. 2006. "The Points of Inflection Revisited." *Economics and Portfolio Strategy*. January.

Brush, J. S. 1997. "Comparisons and Combinations of Long and Long/Short Strategies." *Financial Analysts Journal*. May/June.

Clarke, R. 2005. "Portfolio constraints and the Fundamental Law of Active Management." *Society of Quantitative Analysts Half-Day Fall Seminar: Advances in Optimization and Portfolio Construction*. November.

Clarke, R., H. de Silva, and S. Thorley. 2002. "Portfolio Constraints and the fundamental Law of Active Management." *Financial Analysts Journal*. September/October.

Clarke, R., H. de Silva, and S. Sapra. 2004. "Towards More Information-Efficient Portfolios." *Journal of Portfolio Management*. Fall.

Clarke, R., H. de Silva, and S. Thorley. 2005. "Performance Attribution and the Fundamental Law." *Financial Analysts Journal*. September/October.

Emrich, S. 2006. "Alpha-Beta Separation and Short Extension Portfolios." *Morgan Stanley Quantitative and Derivatives Strategy*. June.

Grinold, R. C. 1989. "The Fundamental Law of Active Management. *Journal of Portfolio Management*. Spring.

Grinold, R. C. 2005. "Implementation Efficiency." *Financial Analysts Journal*. September/October.

Grinold, R. C., and K. Eaton. 1998. "Attribution of Performance and Holdings. *Worldwide Asset and Liability Modeling*.

Grinold, R. C., and R. Kahn. 2000a. "The Surprising Large Impact of the Long-Only Constraint." *Barclays Global Investors Investment Insights*. May.

Grinold, R. C., and R. Kahn. 2000b. "The Efficiency Gains of Long–Short Investing." *Financial Analysts Journal*. November/December.

Grinold, R. C., and R. Kahn. 2000c. "Active Portfolio Management: Quantitative Theory and Applications."

Jacobs, B. I., and K. N. Levy. 1993. "Long/Short Equity Investing: Profit from Both Winners and Losers." *Journal of Portfolio Management*. Fall.

Jacobs, B. I., and K. N. Levy. 1995. "More on Long–Short Strategies." *Financial Analysts Journal*. March/April.

Jacobs, B. I., K. N. Levy, and D. Starer. 1998. "On the Optimality of Long–Short Strategies." *Financial Analysts Journal*, vol. 54, no. 2 (March/April):40–51.

Jacobs, B. I., and K. N. Levy. 1999. "Long/Short Portfolio Management: An Integrated Approach." *Journal of Portfolio Management*. Winter.

Jacobs, B. I., and K. N. Levy. 2006. "Enchanced Active Equity Strategies: Relaxing the Long-Only Constraint in the Pursuit of Active Returns." *Journal of Portfolio Management*. Spring.

Knight, F. H. 1964. *Risk, Uncertainty, and Profit*, New York: Century Press. Originally Published in 1921.

Leibowitz, M. L. 2004. "The $\beta$-Plus Measure in Asset Allocation." *Journal of Portfolio Management*. Spring.

Leibowitz, M. L., and A. Bova. 2005a. "Allocation Betas." *Financial Analysts Journal*. July/August.

Leibowitz, M. L., and A. Bova. 2005b. "Alpha Hunters and Beta Grazers." *Financial Analysts Journal*. September/October.

Leibowitz, M. L., and A. Bova. 2007. "Gathering Implicit Alphas in a Beta World." *Journal of Portfolio Management*. Spring.

Litterman, B. 2005. "Are Constraints Eating Your Alpha?" *Pensions & Investments*. March.

Markowitz, H. 1959. *Portfolio Selection: Efficient Diversification of Investments*. Wiley.

Markowitz, H. M. 2005. "Market Efficiency: A Theoretical Distinction and So What?" *Financial Analysts Journal*.

Michaud, R. O. 1993. "Are Long–Short Equity Strategies Superior?" *Financial Analysts Journal*. November/December.

Winston, K., and T. Hewett. 2006. "Long–Short Portfolio Behavior with Barriers Part 1: Mechanism." *Q Conference Presentation*. Spring.

## APPENDIX

### The Long-Only Alpha and Weighting Model

One of the primary benefits cited for AEs is that they create access to a fresh set of opportunities for active underweights. Because there is a certain shorting cost associated with these new underweights, it is important to assess how these new shorts relate to the original long-only portfolio.

A second benefit from extensions is that the short proceeds can be reinvested back into new long positions. The alpha values of these reinvested longs must also be related to the original portfolio. For the initial analysis, we will treat the case of tail reinvestment, where the short proceeds are deployed into the remaining tail of available long opportunities. In a later section, we show how these expressions can be revised to handle the case of proportional reinvestment back into the original long portfolio.

Our approach to modeling these alpha ranking opportunities is to develop a function that declines exponentially with position rank. Thus, for the $i$th long position, the expected alpha would be

$$\alpha(i) = \alpha(1)\mu^{i-1}, \quad i = 1, 2, \ldots, N_{L_1}$$

where $N_{L_1}$ is the number of proactive positions in the original long portfolio. The weighting function is also assumed to follow some exponential decay path:

$$\omega_L(i) = \omega_L \lambda_L^{i-1}, \quad i = 1, 2, \ldots, N_{L_1}$$

The portfolio alpha then becomes

$$\alpha_L(N_{L_1}) = \omega_L \sum_{i=1}^{N_{L_1}} \alpha(i)$$

$$= \alpha(1)\omega_L \sum_{i=1}^{N_{L_1}} (\lambda_L)^{i-1}$$

$$= \alpha(1)\omega_L \left[ \frac{1 - (\lambda_L)^{N_{L_1}}}{1 - (\lambda_L)} \right]$$

$$0 < \mu < 1, \quad 0 < \lambda_L < 1$$

In a strictly literal accounting interpretation, the sum of all overweights and underweights must equal zero. However, $N_{L_1}$ long portfolio can be viewed as encompassing only those proactive positions that have a net positive alpha expectation that can add to the overall portfolio alpha. The remainder of the portfolio consists of nonproactive positions with zero-alpha expectations. These nonproactive positions may include both benchmark weights, overweights and underweights. In aggregate, they serve as sources of funds and play a role in helping to track the assigned benchmark (possibly in conjunction with some derivative overlays).

From this definition of a proactive position, we must have

$$\omega_L(i)\alpha(i) > 0 \qquad i = 1, 2, \ldots, N_{L_1}$$

Therefore, there is a no loss of generality if, for convenience all $\omega(i)$ and all $\alpha(i)$ are treated as positive values. Moreover, the $N_{L_1}$ position proactive portfolio then becomes theoretically free from any specific budget constraints.

## Alpha Functions for Active Extensions

The move to an AE portfolio entails $N_s$ short positions with weights $\omega_S(j)$:

$$\omega_S(j) = \omega_S \lambda_S^{j-1} \qquad j = 1, 2, \ldots, N_{L_1}$$

and total short weight:

$$W_S = \sum_{j=1}^{N_S} \omega_S \lambda_j$$

$$= \omega_S \left[ \frac{1 - (\lambda_S)^{N_S}}{1 - (\lambda_S)} \right]$$

$$0 < \mu < 1, \quad 0 < \lambda_L < 1$$

Two new alpha functions now come into play. The first is the cumulative alpha for the new $N_S$ short positions with weights $\omega_S$:

$$\alpha_S(N_S) = \sum_{j=1}^{N_S} \omega_S(j)[\alpha_{L_1}(j) - c]$$

$$= \sum_{j=1}^{N_S} \omega_S \lambda_S^{j-1}[\alpha_{L_1}\mu^{j-1} - c]$$

$$= \omega_S \alpha_{L_1} \left[ \frac{1 - (\lambda_S\mu)^{N_S}}{1 - (\lambda_S\mu)} \right] - cW_S$$

where $\alpha(i)$ is the original alpha function for the $i$th-ranked long position, and $c$ is the shorting cost. The assumption here is that the new short opportunities follow the same decay pattern as the longs, but with the deduction of shorting costs.

The next alpha function is associated with the reinvestment of the short proceeds $W_S$ into new long investments. As mentioned earlier, the first and more conservative approach is to apply these proceeds to the tail of the alpha function, so that

$$\alpha_{L_2}(N_{L_2}) = \sum_{i=N_{L_1}+1}^{N_{L_1}+N_{L_2}} \omega_L(i)\alpha(i)$$

$$= \left[ \sum_{i=1}^{N_{L_1}+N_{L_2}} \omega_L(i)\alpha(i) - \sum_{i=1}^{N_{L_1}} \omega_L(i)\alpha(i) \right]$$

$$= \omega_L\alpha(1) \left[ \frac{(\lambda\mu)^{N_{L_1}} - (\lambda\mu)^{(N_{L_1}+N_{L_2})}}{1-(\lambda\mu)} \right]$$

where the number of new long positions is determined by solving for $N_{L_1}$ in the expression:

$$(\omega_L\lambda)^{N_{L_2}} \left[ \frac{1-(\lambda_L)^{N_{L_2}}}{1-(\lambda_L)} \right] = W_S$$

The total number of active positions is therefore,

$$N = N_{L_1} + N_{L_2} + N_S$$

The total portfolio alpha $\alpha_p$ now becomes the sum of all three components:

$$\alpha_P(N) = \alpha_{L_1}(N_{L_1}) + \alpha_{L_2}(N_{L_2}) + \alpha_S(N_S)$$

## The Basic TE for Fixed Weights

The models used in this note assume a fixed residual volatility $\sigma$ attached to each active position, whether long or short. At the outset, the formula for the TE expression will be developed assuming a fixed weight for each position. For this basic case of $N$ active positions, each position is assumed to have the same weight $\omega$ for the moment, acting as an independent source of volatility, one would obtain the standard square root expression for the TE:

$$TE = \sqrt{N}\omega\sigma$$

For an AE portfolio, this result is obtained when $N$ is interpreted as the total of all positions (i.e., the original longs, the new shorts, and the new longs).

When a given pairwise correlation $\rho$ is assumed to exist across *all* positions, then the TE takes on the form:

$$TE = \omega \sqrt{ \sum_{i=1}^{N} \sigma^2 + \sum_{\substack{i \neq 1 \\ i,j=1}}^{N} \rho\sigma^2 }$$
$$= \omega\sigma\sqrt{N + N(N-1)\rho}$$

## The TE for Fixed Weights and Different Correlations

When the long and short portfolios have differentiated correlations, then the TE model becomes somewhat more complicated. To keep some level of manageability, we assume that the pairwise correlation $\rho_L$ exists *within* all the longs (i.e., both the original and new positions), a correlation $\rho_S$ exists *within* the shorts, and a correlation $\rho_{LS}$ exists *between* the longs and the shorts. (The choice of $\rho_{LS}$ is constrained to fall within a range set by the values for $\rho_L$ and $\rho_S$.)

Continuing with the fixed weight assumption, we can now let $N_L$ represent all the longs, that is,

$$N_L = N_{L_1} + N_{L_2}$$

and the correlation matrix then has the following structure.

Because all positions have a common variance $(\omega\sigma)^2$, the TE $(\rho_L, \rho_S, \rho_{LS})$ for a short extension portfolio can be found by simply enumerating all the pairs:

1. $N_L$ with $\rho_L = 1$,
2. $[N_L^2 - N_L]$ with $\rho = \rho_L$,
3. $N$ with $\rho_S = 1$,

|        |         | Longs |          |          |       |              | Shorts       |              |              |       |              |
|--------|---------|-------|----------|----------|-------|--------------|--------------|--------------|--------------|-------|--------------|
|        |         | 1     | 2        | 3        | · · · | $N_L$        | 1            | 2            | 3            | · · · | $N_S$        |
|        | 1       | 1     | $\rho_L$ | $\rho_L$ | · · · | $\rho_L$     | $\rho_{LS}$  | $\rho_{LS}$  | $\rho_{LS}$  | · · · | $\rho_{LS}$  |
|        | 2       | $\rho_L$ | 1     | $\rho_L$ |       |              | $\rho_{LS}$  | $\rho_{LS}$  | $\rho_{LS}$  |       |              |
|        | 3       | $\rho_L$ | $\rho_L$ | 1     |       |              | $\rho_{LS}$  | $\rho_{LS}$  | $\rho_{LS}$  |       |              |
|        | ·       |       |          |          |       |              |              |              |              |       |              |
| Longs  | ·       |       |          |          |       |              |              |              |              |       |              |
|        | ·       |       |          |          |       |              |              |              |              |       |              |
|        | $N_L$   | $\rho_L$ |       |          |       | 1            | $\rho_{LS}$  | $\rho_{LS}$  |              |       | $\rho_{LS}$  |
|        | 1       | $\rho_{LS}$ | $\rho_{LS}$ | $\rho_{LS}$ | · · · | $\rho_{LS}$ | 1         | $\rho_S$     | $\rho_S$     | · · · | $\rho_S$     |
|        | 2       | $\rho_{LS}$ | $\rho_{LS}$ | $\rho_{LS}$ |       |              | $\rho_S$     | 1            | $\rho_S$     |       |              |
|        | 3       | $\rho_{LS}$ | $\rho_{LS}$ | $\rho_{LS}$ |       |              | $\rho_S$     | $\rho_S$     | 1            |       |              |
| Shorts | ·       |       |          |          |       |              |              |              |              |       |              |
|        | ·       |       |          |          |       |              |              |              |              |       |              |
|        | ·       |       |          |          |       |              |              |              |              |       |              |
|        | $N_S$   | $\rho_{LS}$ | $\rho_{LS}$ |       |       | $\rho_{LS}$  | $\rho_S$     |              |              |       | 1            |

4. $[N_S^2 - N_S]$ with $\rho = \rho_S$,
5. $2 N_L N_S$ with $\rho = \rho_{LS}$.

This enumeration leads to the expression:

$$\text{TE}(\rho_L, \rho_S, \rho_{LS}) = (\omega\sigma)\sqrt{N_L + N_L(N_L - 1)\rho_L + N_S + N_S(N_S - 1)\rho_S + 2 N_L N_S \rho_{LS}}$$

It is interesting (and comforting) to see that, when all the $\rho$'s are the same, the above formula devolves to the simple one for a "homogenous" portfolio, that is

$$
\begin{aligned}
\text{TE}(\rho, \rho, \rho) &= (\omega\sigma)\sqrt{N_L + N_L(N - 1)\rho + N_S + N_S(N - 1)\rho + 2 N_L N_S \rho} \\
&= (\omega\sigma)\sqrt{(N_L + N_S) + \rho[N_L^2 - N_L + N_S^2 - N_S + 2 N_L N_S]} \\
&= (\omega\sigma)\sqrt{(N_L + N_S) + \rho[(N_L + N_S)^2 - (N_L + N_L)]} \\
&= (\omega\sigma)\sqrt{N + \rho[N(N - 1)]}
\end{aligned}
$$

where now $N = N_L + N_S$

Moreover, for extreme values of $\rho$, the formula provides the well-known result, that is,

$$\text{TE}(0, 0, 0) = (\omega\sigma)\sqrt{N}$$

$$\text{TE}(1, 1, 1) = (\omega\sigma)N$$

## Tracking Errors for Exponential Weights and Different Correlations

The above derivation assumes that all positions—long and short—have the same weight $\omega$. We now consider the situation where the weights follow an exponential pattern that declines continuously (without reaching any minimum limit), that is,

$$\omega_L(i) = \omega_L \lambda_L^{(i-1)} \qquad i = 1, 2, \ldots, N_L$$

$$\omega_S(j) = \omega_S \lambda_S^{(j-1)} \qquad j = 1, 2, \ldots, N_S$$

The correlation matrix with the embedded weights now has the more complex form,

| | | 1 | 2 | 3 | • | • | • | $N_L$ | 1 | 2 | 3 | • • • | $N_S$ |
|---|---|---|---|---|---|---|---|---|---|---|---|---|---|
| Longs | 1 | $(\omega_L^2 1 \lambda_L^0 \lambda_L^0)$ | | | | | | $(\omega_L^2 \rho_L \lambda_L^0 \lambda_L^{N_L-1})$ | $(\omega_L \omega_S \rho_{LS} \lambda_L^0 \lambda_S^0)$ | | | | $(\omega_L \omega_S \rho_{LS} \lambda_L^0 \lambda_S^{N_S-1})$ |
| | 2 | $(\omega_L^2 \rho_L \lambda_L^1 \lambda_L^0)$ | $(\omega_L^2 1 \lambda_L^1 \lambda_L^1)$ | | | | | | | | | | |
| | 3 | | | | | | | | | | | | |
| | • | | | [LL$_{11}$] | | | | | | | [SL$_1$] | | |
| | • | | | | | | | | | | | | |
| | • | | | | | | | | | | | | |
| | $N_L$ | $(\omega_L^2 \rho_L \lambda_L^{N_L-1} \lambda_L^0)$ | | | | | | $(\omega_L^2 1 \lambda_L^{N_L-1} \lambda_L^{N_L-1})$ | $(\omega_L \omega_S \rho_{LS} \lambda_L^{N_L-1} \lambda_S^0)$ | | | | $(\omega_L \omega_S \rho_{LS} \lambda_L^{N_L-1} \lambda_S^{N_S-1})$ |
| Shorts | 1 | $(\omega_L \omega_S \rho_{LS} \lambda_L^0 \lambda_S^0)$ | | | | | | | $(\omega_S^2 1 \lambda_S^0 \lambda_S^0)$ | | | | |
| | 2 | | | | | | | | $(\omega_S^2 \rho_S \lambda_S^1 \lambda_S^0)$ | $(\omega_S^2 1 \lambda_S^1 \lambda_S^1)$ | | | |
| | 3 | | | | | | | | | | | | |
| | • | | | [SL$_1$] | | | | | | | [SS] | | |
| | • | | | | | | | | | | | | |
| | $N_S$ | $(\omega_L \omega_S \rho_{LS} \lambda_L^{N_L-1} \lambda_S^0)$ | | | | | | $(\omega_L \omega_S \rho_{LS} \lambda_L^{N_L-1} \lambda_S^{N_S-1})$ | $(\omega_S^2 \rho_S \lambda_S^{N_S-1} \lambda_S^0)$ | | | | $(\omega_S^2 1 \lambda_S^{N_S-1} \lambda_S^{N_S-1})$ |

If we denote the sum of the four quadrants as LL$_{11}$ for long/long, SL$_1$ for the two short/long quadrants, and SS for short/short, then for $1 > \lambda_L > 0$ and $1 > \lambda_S > 0$,

$$\left( \frac{LL_{11}}{\omega_L^2} \right) = \left[ \sum_{i=0}^{(N_L-1)} \lambda_L^i \sum_{k=0}^{(N_L-1)} \lambda_L^k - \sum_{i=0}^{(N_L-1)} \lambda_L^{2i} \right] \rho_L + \sum_{i=0}^{(N_L-1)} \lambda_L^{2i}$$

$$= \left[ \left( \frac{1 - \lambda_L^{N_L}}{1 - \lambda_L} \right)^2 - \left( \frac{1 - \lambda_L^{2N_L}}{1 - \lambda_L^2} \right) \right] \rho_L + \left( \frac{1 - \lambda_L^{2N_L}}{1 - \lambda_L^2} \right)$$

$$= \rho_L \left( \frac{1 - \lambda_L^{N_L}}{1 - \lambda_L} \right)^2 + (1 - \rho_L) \left( \frac{1 - \lambda_L^{2N_L}}{1 - \lambda_L^2} \right)^2$$

Similarly for SS,

$$\left(\frac{SS}{\omega_S^2}\right) = \rho_S \left(\frac{1 - \lambda_S^{N_S}}{1 - \lambda_S}\right)^2 + (1 - \rho_S)\left(\frac{1 - \lambda_S^{2N_S}}{1 - \lambda_S^2}\right)$$

However, for each of the two $SL_1$ quadrants,

$$\left(\frac{SL_1}{\omega_L \omega_S}\right) = \rho_{LS} \sum_{i=0}^{(N_L-1)} \lambda_L^i \sum_{j=0}^{(N_S-1)} \lambda_S^i$$

$$= \rho_{LS} \left(\frac{1 - \lambda_L^{N_L}}{1 - \lambda_L}\right)\left(\frac{1 - \lambda_S^{N_S}}{1 - \lambda_S}\right)$$

$$TE(\rho_L, \rho_S, \rho_{LS}) = \sigma \sqrt{\omega_L^2(LL) + \omega_S^2(SS) + 2\omega_L\omega_S(SL_1)}$$

## Tracking Error for Exponential Weights Declining to Fixed Minimum Weights

In the case presented in this note, the weight declines to some minimum weight $\omega'$ and then remains fixed for all lower position ranks. For simplicity, suppose that the fixed weight region is only reached on the long side, and there are n such fixed weight positions. The total number of long positions becomes

$$N_L = N_{L_1} + N_{L_2}$$

and $N_{L_1}$ must be substituted for $N_L$ in the above expression for $LL_{11}$ and SS.

In addition, the following submatrices must be added to the preceding matrix:

These new submatrices have the fixed weights $\omega'$ for the $N_{L_2}$ long positions, so that they can be readily enumerated.

$$\left(\frac{LL_{12}}{\omega' \omega_L}\right) = N_{L_2} \rho_L \sum_{i=0}^{(N_{L_1}-1)} \lambda_L^{i-1}$$

$$= N_{L_2} \rho_L \left(\frac{1 - \lambda_L^{N_{L_1}}}{1 - \lambda_L}\right)$$

| | Longs | | Shorts |
|---|---|---|---|
| | 1 2 3 $\quad N_{L1}$ | 1 2 $\cdots$ $N_{L2}$ | 1 2 3 |
| Longs $\begin{array}{c}1\\2\\3\\\cdot\\\cdot\\\cdot\\N_{L1}\end{array}$ | $LL_{11}$ | $LL_{12}$ | $SL_1$ |
| $\begin{array}{c}1\\2\\\cdot\\\cdot\\N_{L2}\end{array}$ | $LL_{12}$ | $LL_{22}$ | $SL_2$ |
| Shorts $\begin{array}{c}1\\2\\3\\\cdot\\\cdot\\\cdot\\N_S\end{array}$ | $SL_1$ | $SL_2$ | $SS$ |

$$\left(\frac{SL_2}{\omega'\omega_S}\right) = N_{L_2}\rho_{LS}\left(\frac{1-\lambda_S^{N_S}}{1-\lambda_S}\right)$$

$$\left(\frac{LL_{22}}{\omega'^2}\right) = \rho_L\left(N_{L_2}^2 - N_{L_2}\right) + N_{L_2}$$

The TE now becomes

$$TE(\rho_{L.},\, \rho_S,\, \rho_{LS})$$

$$= \sigma \sqrt{\begin{array}{l} \omega_L^2(LL_{11}) + \omega_S^2(SS) \\ +2\omega_L\omega_S(SL_1) + 2(\omega')\omega_L(LL_{12}) \\ +2(\omega')\omega_S(SL_2) + (\omega')^2(LL_{22}) \end{array}}$$

## The Alpha/TE Ratio

The portfolio alpha and the TE functions are connected through a common position count and weightings. Thus, for a long-only portfolio with m positions, this ratio is simply

$$\frac{\alpha_P(m)}{TE(m)}$$

In moving to the AE portfolio, the long-only positions are set at $N_L$ and for a given weighting function, the short weight $W_S$ determines both the number of short positions $N_S$ and the corresponding number $n$ of new longs. Consequently, both the numerator and the denominator of the alpha/TE ratio now depend solely on $N_S$, so that the ratio takes the form:

$$\frac{\alpha_P(N_S)}{TE(N_S)}$$

for the various short weights.

## Proportional Reinvestment

The preceding analysis was based on the tail reinvestment where the $W_S$ proceeds from the shorts are reinvested into the $N_{L_2}$ lower ranked longs. With proportional reinvestment, the reinvested proceeds are added pro rata to the weights of the original long portfolio. Thus, in this case, the number of new longs is zero:

$$N_{L_2} = 0$$

and the total number of long positions remains the same, that is,

$$N_L = N_{L_1}$$

but the weight associated with these longs is now augmented to

$$\omega_L^*(i) = \omega_L(i)\left[1 + \frac{W_S}{W_L}\right]$$

where $W_L$ is the total active weight of the initial long portfolio.

Thus, the proportional reinvestment TE can be adjusted in the preceding equations by substituting $\omega_L^*$ for $\omega_L$:

$$\omega_L^* = \omega_L\left[1 + \frac{W_S}{W_L}\right]$$

Similarly, in the alpha equation, the portfolio return now becomes

$$\alpha_P = \left(1 + \frac{W_S}{W_L}\right)\alpha_{L_1}(N_{L_1}) + \alpha_S(N_S)$$

With these adjustments, the preceding formulations can be transformed to apply to proportional reinvestment.

## Implicit Betas and Alphas

If $\rho_{ij}$ is the correlation between asset $i$ and $j$, $r_i$ is the expected return for $I$, and $\sigma_i$ the standard deviation of $i$'s return, then the implicit $\beta_i$ for asset $i$ can be defined as

$$\beta_i = \rho_{ie}\frac{\sigma_i}{\sigma_e}$$

where $j = e$ is the equity benchmark.

The implicit $\alpha_i$ can then also be defined as

$$\alpha_i = r_i - r_o - \beta_i(r_e - r_o),$$

where $r_o$ is the return on cash, and $(r_c - r_o)$ is the risk premium for asset $i$.

With $\omega_1$ being the weight of the asset $I$ in a portfolio allocation, the total beta $\beta_P$ is

$$\beta_P = \sum \omega_i \beta_i$$

and the portfolio implicit alpha is

$$\alpha_P = \sum \omega_i \alpha_i$$

The portfolio's expected return $r_p$ can be expressed in terms of $\beta_P$ and $\alpha_P$,

$$\begin{aligned}
r_P &= \sum \omega_i r_i \\
&= \sum \omega_i \left[\alpha_i + r_o + \beta_i(r_e - r_o)\right] \\
&= \sum \omega_i \alpha_i + r_o \sum \omega_i + (r_e - r_o) \sum \omega\beta_i \\
&= \alpha_P + r_o + \beta_P(r_e - r_o)
\end{aligned}$$

The random return $\tilde{r}_i$ can be expressed as

$$\tilde{r}_i = \tilde{\alpha}_i + r_o + \beta_i(\tilde{r}_e - r_o)$$

where

$$r = E(\tilde{r}_i),$$

and

$$\alpha_i = E(\tilde{\alpha}_i)$$

The variance $\sigma_i^2$ can then be parsed into two orthogonal components:

$$\sigma_i^2 = \sigma_{\alpha i}^2 + \beta_i^2 \sigma_e^2$$

and the portfolio variance $\sigma_P^2$ is then comprised of the terms:

$$\sigma_P^2 = \sum \omega_i^2 \sigma_{\alpha_i}^2 + \sum \beta_i^2 \sigma_e^2 + \sum_{i \neq j} \omega_i \omega_j \rho_{ij} \sigma_i \sigma_j$$

In variance of typical institutional portfolios, the $\beta_i$ terms add so that

$$\frac{(\beta_P \sigma_e)^2}{\sigma_e} > 0.90$$

This dominance relationship arises because the $\tilde{\alpha}_i$ components are fragmented and semi-independent. When any new asset class is introduced into the allocation, it adds both $\alpha$-like and $\beta$-like components. In practice, for funds that pursue such diversification initiatives, the volatility $\sigma_P^2$ and the beta component $\beta_P$ appear to be generally kept constant or near constant. With $\beta_P$ maintained, the net contribution to both the portfolio level return and volatility is derived from the net change in the alpha components. The net alpha directly adds to (or detracts) from the portfolio return $r_p$, but the variance component continues to be dominated by the $\beta_P$ term, so that the volatility change is minimal.

A more detailed analysis of the volatility effects can be found in the Appendix of "Allocation Betas" (Leibowitz and Bova, 2005a).

**Keywords** Active extensions; 120/20 portfolios; 130/30 portfolios; long/ short portfolios; institutional portfolios; beta; alpha; tracking error.

# CHAPTER 25

# Long/Short Extensions: How Much Is Enough?

**Roger Clarke**
Chairman
Analytic Investors, Inc.

**Harindra de Silva**
President
Analytic Investors, Inc.

**Steven Sapra**
Portfolio Manager
Analyic Investors, Inc.

**Steven Thorley**
H. Taylor Peery Professor of Finance
Brigham Young University

*Long/short extension strategies, such as 130/30, allow portfolio managers to reduce the implementation inefficiencies associated with the long-only constraint. Ample research using benchmark-specific and time period-specific numerical analyses indicates that long/short extensions increase expected information ratios. What is lacking is a general theory or mathematical model of long/short extensions based on underlying assumptions about benchmark composition, the security covariance matrix, and the portfolio*

*optimization process. The analytical model developed here iden-*
*tifies the roles various parameters play in determining the size of*
*the long/short extension. The impact of changes in the model pa-*
*rameters over time and across markets is illustrated with the use of*
*historical and current equity benchmark data.*

One of the major innovations in portfolio construction during the past
several years has been the adoption of long/short extension strategies
that allow managers to fully exploit the cross-sectional variation in forecasted security returns. Generalizations of the Grinold and Kahn (1994)
theory of active management by Clarke, De Silva, and Thorley (2002) and
by others focused on the role of formal constraints in portfolio construction, particularly the negative impact of the long-only constraint. At the
same time, innovations in prime brokerage practices and the acceptance of
shorting by institutional fiduciaries led to a proliferation of long/short strategies and products. Because long/short extensions are new to many market
participants, Jacobs and Levy (2007) addressed misconceptions about the
strategies. The analytical model we develop here will further improve investors' conceptual understanding of the factors that determine the size of
the short (and equivalent long) extension in long/short strategies.

The short extension model is based on the concept of the expected short
weight for individual securities in the benchmark, similar to Sorensen, Hua,
and Qian (2006). We also use the assumption of a constant correlation matrix and other modeling techniques used in an early analytical treatment of
long/short strategies by Jacobs, Levy, and Starer (1998). In this chapter, we
describe how the expected short weight for a security depends on the relative
size of the security's benchmark weight and the active weight assigned to
that security by the portfolio management process. The formal mathematical
model and approximations enhance perspectives from previous studies that
depended on time period-specific numerical examples or on insights from
simulations.

The derivation of the long/short extension model rests on the assumption of an unconstrained portfolio optimization and, therefore, gives an
upper bound on possible long/short ratios in practice. In the language of
the fundamental law of active management, we assume a transfer coefficient
(TC) of 1 and thus the maximum possible expected information ratio (IR).[1]
As discretionary constraints are imposed, the long/short ratio declines from
the upper bound suggested by the model, with a corresponding decline in the
IR. As a result, empirical illustrations that use the S&P 500 Index and other
common equity benchmarks have long/short ratios that are generally higher
than applied strategies, in which a variety of additional constraints are often
used. In addition to being difficult to model mathematically, the incorpo-
ration of optional constraints that vary from manager to manager would

make our analysis less generic. Within the assumption of an unconstrained optimization process, we also discuss the special case of market-neutral or zero net-long portfolios, and use it to motivate a simple approximation of the general long/short extension model.

Our goal is to enhance past attempts to analyze the long/short ratio that relied on Monte Carlo simulation or numerical optimization using representative data. Such studies—by Sorensen, Hua, and Qian (2006) and Clarke, de Silva, and Sapra (2004)—allow for consideration of a wide range of implementation issues, including discretionary constraints, but lack the generality of an analytical model. For example, numerical analyses of S&P 500-benchmarked long/short extension portfolios that are only a few years old may already be outdated because of shifts in key market parameters.

## THE SHORT EXTENSION MODEL

Our analysis of the short extension in long/short portfolios is based on a decomposition of the security weights in the managed portfolio into benchmark and active weights. Specifically, the portfolio weight for the $i$th security, $w_{Pi}$, can be defined as the sum of the security's benchmark, weight, $w_{Bi}$, and active weight, $w_{Ai}$:

$$w_{Pi} = w_{Bi} + w_{Ai} \qquad (25.1)$$

The benchmark weight for any given security is set by the market, whereas the active weight is chosen by the manager. A basic tenet of portfolio theory is that the portfolio's expected active return (i.e., benchmark-relative alpha) and active risk (i.e., tracking error [TE]) are a function of the *active* security weights, not the benchmark weights.

For optimized portfolios, the set of active security weights is determined by forecasted security returns, the estimated security return covariance matrix, and the targeted level of active portfolio risk. As noted in Appendix A, a well-known solution exists for optimal active weights in the absence of portfolio constraints. We also assume a simplified covariance matrix in which the $N$ security risks are all equal to a single value, $\sigma$, and the $N(N-1)/2$ pairwise correlations are all equal to a single value, $\rho$. As shown in Appendix A, with this simplified covariance matrix, the optimal active weights are a scalar multiple, $c$, of a set of standard (zero mean and unit standard deviation) normal z-scores, $S_i$,

$$w_{Ai} = cS_i, \text{ with } c = \frac{\sigma_A}{\sigma\sqrt{1-\rho}\sqrt{N}} \qquad (25.2)$$

where $\sigma_A$ is the targeted level of active portfolio risk.

The zero-mean scores used in Equation 25.2 suggest that the active weight assigned to any given security can be thought of as a random variable with a mean of zero and standard deviation of $c$. Equation 25.2 shows that the range of active weights around zero increases with the portfolio's targeted active risk, $\sigma_A$, and decreases with $N$, the number of securities in the benchmark or investable set.[2] In addition, Equation 25.2 shows that in the simplified covariance matrix, the range of active weights decreases for higher security risk $\sigma$ and increases with higher correlation $\rho$ between security returns. The dependence of the absolute magnitude of the active weights on these parameters is critical to understanding the implications of parameter changes for the amount of shorting in the optimized portfolio.

Now consider the benchmark weights, $w_{Bi}$, in Equation 25.1. By definition, the $N$ benchmark weights are individually positive and sum to 1. For standard capitalization-weighted benchmarks, the distribution of weights is also fairly concentrated; a few securities have large weights whereas many other securities have relatively small weights. When market-cap weights are sorted in descending order, they generally decline in a geometric fashion, with the smallest benchmark weights approaching zero, as shown in Exhibit 25.1 for a portfolio with $N = 500$. We later formalize the assumption of a perfect geometric decline in benchmark weights, the concept of Effective

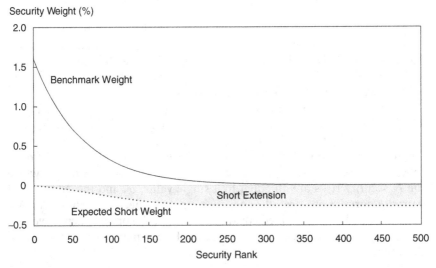

**EXHIBIT 25.1** Benchmark Weights and Expected Short Weights
*Note:* Active risk = 4 percent; security risk = 30 percent; security correlation = 0.200; $N = 500$; Effective $N = 125$

N, and other parameter values given in Exhibit 25.1, but for now, we simply focus on the intuition provided by sorting the benchmark weights from largest to smallest.

Consider a single security with a large benchmark weight on the far left-hand side of Exhibit 25.1 and the N possible active weights that may randomly be assigned to it by the manager's forecasting process. For a security with a large benchmark weight, the probability that the assigned active weight is negative and large enough to lead to a negative total weight, or short position, is relatively low. On the other hand, for a security with a small benchmark weight on the far right side of Exhibit 25.1, the probability of shorting is high, approaching 50 percent for benchmark weights of zero. Similarly, the magnitude (as opposed to simply the probability) of shorting depends on the relative magnitudes of the benchmark and active weights.

Thus, the expected short weight for each security in Exhibit 25.1 is based on the size of its benchmark weight and the range of all possible active weights as formalized below. Although much of the derivation for the material that follows is relegated to Appendix A, we have included the initial steps here to emphasize how expected shorting depends on the relative magnitudes of the benchmark and active weights.

From probability theory, a security's expected short weight is the expected value of the total weight, $w_{Pi}$, conditional on it being negative, times the probability of being negative:

$$E(short_i) = E(w_{Pi} | w_{Pi} < 0) \text{ prob } (w_{Pi} < 0) \tag{25.3}$$

Using Equations 25.1 and 25.2, we find that the probability of the total security weight being negative is the same as the probability that the z-score assigned to the security is negative enough to offset the benchmark weight divided by the scaling factor, $c$. In other words,

$$E(short_i) = \left[ w_{Bi} + cE \left( S | S < \frac{-w_{Ri}}{c} \right) \right] \text{ prob } \left( S < \frac{-w_{Bi}}{c} \right) \tag{25.4}$$

As described in Appendix A, applying well-known standard normal probability functions gives the final result for a security's expected short weight as

$$E(short_i) = c\varphi \left( \frac{-w_{Bi}}{c} \right) - w_{Bi} \Phi \left( \frac{-w_{Bi}}{c} \right) \tag{25.5}$$

where $\phi(\cdot)$ is the standard normal density function and $\phi(\cdot)$ is the standard normal *cumulative* density function. For ease of interpretation, the implicit short sale–induced negative sign in Equation 25.5 has been dropped, so larger positive values indicate more shorting. As illustrated in Exhibit 25.1, the expected short weight in Equation 25.5 is close to zero for securities with large benchmark weights. For securities with small benchmark weights, the expected short weight asymptotically approaches a maximum value of

$$E(short_i|w_{Bi} = 0) = \frac{\sigma_A}{\sigma\sqrt{1-\rho}\sqrt{N}\sqrt{2\pi}} \qquad (25.6)$$

Note that Equation 25.6 is not the largest possible short position; it is simply the average or *expected* short position for a zero-benchmark-weight security given all of the active weights that may be assigned to it by the manager's forecasting process.

The expected amount of shorting in the entire portfolio (e.g., the 30% implicit in a 130/30 portfolio) is the summation of Equation 25.5 across all $N$ securities:

$$S_0 = \sum_{i=1}^{N} c\varphi\left(\frac{-w_{Bi}}{c}\right) - w_{Bi}\Phi\left(\frac{-w_{Bi}}{c}\right) \qquad (25.7)$$

Equation 25.7 is the basic model for the expected amount of unconstrained portfolio shorting in the absence of costs. The actual short extension in any given optimization will vary around the expected value in Equation 25.7, depending on how the active weights are assigned to the benchmark weights. Although such assignments are certainly not random from the manager's perspective, Equation 25.7 is the average short extension across the very large number ($N$ factorial) of all possible assignments of $N$ active weights to $N$ securities. In other words, the size of the unconstrained short extension is a random variable, and we refer to the result in Equation 25.7 as the *expected* short extension for a given benchmark and active-risk target.

Exhibit 25.1 provides a geometric interpretation of the portfolio's expected short extension in Equation 25.7 for an active risk of 4.0 percent, $N = 500$, and other parameter values indicative of the S&P 500 in recent years.[3] The numbers on the horizontal axis in Exhibit 25.1 designate security rank when sorted in declining benchmark-weight order. The numbers on the vertical axis measure individual security weights, with benchmark weights as positive percentage values that decline from left to right and expected short weights as negative percentage values that become more negative for smaller securities. The expected short extension for the entire portfolio is the enclosed area below the horizontal axis at zero and above the curve of expected short weights, an area labeled "Short Extension." The long/short ratio depends on the size of this area compared with the area below the benchmark-weight curve and above the horizontal axis at zero, which must sum to 1 (100% for any benchmark size or concentration).

The geometry of Exhibit 25.1 illustrates how the long/short ratio varies with changes in the underlying parameter values. For example, if the benchmark becomes more concentrated in a few large securities, the curve of benchmark weights will become steeper (while still enclosing an area of 100% and the curve of expected short weights will shift to the left), increasing the area enclosed below the horizontal axis. Alternatively, an increase in the level of active risk does not affect the benchmark-weight curve, but does increase the depth of the short extension area, resulting in an increase in the long/short ratio.

The basic model of the short extension has at least one special case worth mentioning before we proceed with an analysis of costs. The focus of this chapter is the short extension in fully invested portfolios (i.e., portfolios in which the short weights are matched by long weights in excess of 100% of the portfolio's notional value). In market-neutral portfolios, where the benchmark weight is zero by definition for all securities, Equation 25.7 becomes

$$\text{Market-neutral } S_0 = \frac{\sigma_A \sqrt{N}}{\sigma \sqrt{1 - \rho} \sqrt{2\pi}} \qquad (25.8)$$

Equation 25.8 is simply the sum of Equation 25.6 across $N$ securities and provides a number of interesting perspectives on the construction of market-neutral portfolios. For example, the unconstrained amount of shorting in a market-neutral portfolio is linearly dependent on the active risk, $\sigma_A$, and the square root of the number of securities, $\sqrt{N}$. The form of the market-neutral special case in Equation 25.8 is similar to a recent model of portfolio leverage given by Johnson, Kahn, and Petrich (2007). Indeed, a major conclusion of Johnson et al. is that the gearing (leverage) of a market-neutral portfolio cannot be independently chosen once an active-risk target has been specified without reducing the transfer coefficient (TC). Equation 25.7 indicates that this property also holds in the more general case of netlong portfolios.

Further analysis of the model of portfolio shorting in Equation 25.7 requires a parameter that measures the degree to which benchmark weights are concentrated in a few securities. In this chapter, we use Effective $N$, popularized by Strongin, Petsch, and Sharenow (2000), which can be thought of as the number of *equal-weighted* securities that would have the same diversification implications as the N actual benchmark weights. As explained in Appendix A, Effective N is 1 over the sum of the benchmark weights squared and ranges from $N_E = N$ for an equally weighted benchmark to $N_E = 1$ for a portfolio that is completely concentrated in one security. For example, at the end of 2006, the $N_E$ of the largest 500 U.S. stocks was 125, but it had reached a low of about $N_E = 80$ in 1999 when the market was concentrated in technology stocks.

The expected shorting in a zero-benchmark-weight security shown in Equation 25.6 and the concept of Effective N motivate a simple approximation of the basic long/short model. Assume that the benchmark is equally distributed among $N_E$ large-cap securities that have no material potential for shorting, with zero weights on the other $(N - N_E)$ securities. In this step function assumption for the benchmark weights, the basic model in Equation 25.7 becomes

$$S_0 \approx \frac{\sigma_A \sqrt{N}(1 - N_E/N)}{\sigma \sqrt{1 - \rho}\sqrt{2\pi}} \tag{25.9}$$

which is completely closed form (i.e., has no probability functions or summations). The geometric interpretation of Equation 25.9 in Exhibit 25.1 is a rectangle of length $N - N_E$ that approximates the irregularly shaped short extension area.

Although the role of each of the parameters is simple and intuitive, Equation 25.9 is a good approximation of the amount of shorting only for low to moderate values of the ratio $N_E/N$. In Appendix A, we use the idea of an average benchmark security to derive a more robust approximation of the basic model in Equation 25.7. The more robust approximation for the portfolio expected short extension is

$$S_0 \approx (N - N_A)\frac{c}{\sqrt{2\pi}} - \frac{1}{2}\left(1 - \frac{2}{N_E}\right)^{N_A} \tag{25.10}$$

where

$$N_A \approx 1 - \frac{N_E}{2}\ln\left(\frac{c}{\sqrt{2\pi}}N_E\right)$$

is the rank of the average security.

We have derived the basic model for the expected level of shorting in long/short portfolios without considering costs or discretionary constraints.

Although the constraints applied to long/short portfolios are subject to managerial discretion, the costs of portfolio short extensions are dictated by market conditions and can substantially reduce the optimal level of shorting. We next introduce a simple adjustment to the no-cost expected shorting model in Equation 25.7 that produces levels closer to those seen in practice. Portfolio optimization problems in the presence of costs or constraints are mathematically intractable, and solutions generally require numerical optimization.

Although optimal active weights with costs for individual securities are difficult to model, we can determine the approximate level of portfolio shorting by using a "marginal benefit equals marginal cost" argument from the objective function. Using this approach, Appendix A shows that the expected short extension with costs is a function of the previously derived zero-cost short extension. Using the basic model in Equation 25.7 (or one of the approximations in Equations 25.9 or 25.10) to calculate $S_0$, we find the expected short extension with costs,

$$E(S) = S_0 \left( 1 - \frac{B + 2T}{IC\sqrt{N}\sigma_A} \right) \qquad (25.11)$$

where $IC$ is the manager's information coefficient and $B$ and $T$ are cost parameters as defined in the next paragraph. The IC is the expected cross-sectional correlation between forecasted and realized security alphas, a commonly used measure of forecasting accuracy. The IC becomes relevant when costs enter the picture because higher confidence in security return forecasts leads to a higher expected portfolio active return, as described in the Fundamental Law of Active Management (Grinold and Kahn, 1994). Indeed, the denominator of the second term in Equation 25.11 is simply the expected active portfolio return before costs, $E(R_A)$, as specified in the fundamental law equation.

Cost as a percentage of the dollar amount of shorting comes in two forms. First is the borrowing cost, $B$, or haircut difference between the interest rate paid to leverage long positions and the rate earned on short-sale proceeds. Borrowing costs vary with the difficulty the prime broker has in finding shares to lend out, but for S&P 500 securities, $B$ can be roughly approximated as 50 bps. In addition to the explicit borrowing costs, portfolio short extensions and the counterbalancing long extensions drive up the general cost of managing a portfolio. We make the simplifying but reasonable assumption that general operating costs increase linearly with leverage. For example, for any given level of transaction costs and turnover, a 130/30 strategy has approximately 160 percent of the operating cost of an equivalent long-only strategy. We use the notation $T$ for the percentage operating cost for an equivalent long-only strategy, which can vary widely depending on turnover, transaction costs, and other operational considerations. For portfolios benchmarked to the S&P 500 with 100 percent turnover per year and 40 bps of round-trip transaction costs, the value of $T$ is about 40 bps. The $T$ in Equation 25.11 is multiplied by 2 because the incremental costs associated with the short extension must be counterbalanced by an equivalent long extension. Thus, increases in the level of shorting have total *incremental* costs of $50 + (2 \times 40) = 130$ bps. Note that we use 130 bps only as a rough estimate of costs in the numerical examples in this study; our objective is not to precisely estimate the costs of shorting but to model how costs reduce the expected short extension.

The IC measures a portfolio manager's self-assessed accuracy in forecasting security returns; as such, it is easily overstated, as explained in Grinold and Kahn (1994). In practice, $IC$ is used by quantitative managers to properly scale the security alphas supplied to a numerical optimizer. Appropriate $IC$ values for modeling purposes should be calibrated to the number of securities by use of the fundamental law relationship, $IR = IC\sqrt{N}$, where $IR$ is the information ratio. The IR is defined as expected active return, $E(R_A)$, divided by active risk, $\sigma_A$. Grinold and Kahn argued that an $IR$ of 0.50 is good, an $IR$ of 0.75 is very good, and an $IR$ of 1.00 is exceptional. Goodwin (1998) adopted this framework in his review of uses and interpretations of the IR. For the base case, we use an active risk, $\sigma_A$, of 4.0 percent and choose an $IR$ of 0.75, so the $IC$ is 0.034 when $N = 500$. Under the cost assumption of $B + 2T = 1.3$ percent, Equation 25.11 indicates that the expected short extension with costs is

$$E(S) = S_0 \left( 1 - \frac{0.013}{0.75 \times 0.04} \right) = S_0(0.57)$$

or about 57 percent of the zero-cost model. Tests using a commercial optimizer with cost functionality generally confirmed Equation 25.11 for S&P 500 portfolios.

In practice, managers apply a wide variety of discretionary portfolio constraints that may also affect the level of shorting. For example, managers may explicitly constrain shorting under the assumption that moderate restrictions have only a minor effect on the expected active portfolio return, as measured by the TC (see Clarke, de Silva, and Sapra, 2004). Other common constraints, such as limits to individual active weights or style and sector neutrality constraints may indirectly reduce portfolio shorting. To keep the analysis as generic as possible, we do not consider constraints beyond the requisite budget and active-risk restrictions.

## MODEL PARAMETERS AND IMPLICATIONS

We now explore the impact of the various parameters identified in the short extension model, including the cost adjustment in Equation 25.11. The position of the portfolio active-risk parameter, $\sigma_A$, in the numerator of the simple approximation in Equation 25.9 verifies the common intuition that the size of the short extension increases with the manager's target for active risk (i.e., benchmark TE) in the optimization process. A higher active-risk target translates into larger absolute magnitudes for the active security weights, $w_{Ai}$, as shown in Equation 25.2. The larger negative active weights naturally lead to more shorting, with a commensurate increase in long security weights to keep the portfolio in a 100 percent net-long balance. The effect of active risk on the level of shorting is reinforced when costs are considered, as shown by the position of the $\sigma_A$ in the denominator of the last term in Equation 25.11. The active-risk parameter is unique in the long/short extension model as the only true choice variable selected by the manager. Most other model parameters (e.g., security risk, benchmark concentration, costs) are exogenous, in that they are forced on the manager by the market or choice of benchmark.

In Exhibit 25.2, we illustrate the impact of active risk on the expected level of shorting given by the general model in Equation 25.7 with the cost adjustment in Equation 25.11, under the assumption of a 1.3 percent total cost and other parameter values indicative of the S&P 500 in recent years.

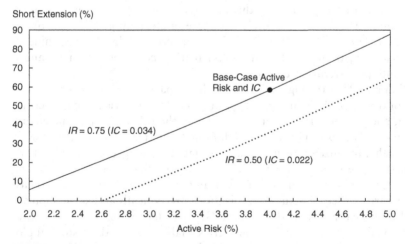

**EXHIBIT 25.2** Short Extension and Active Risk
*Note:* Security risk = 30 percent; security correlation = 0.200; $N = 500$; effective $N = 125$; cost = 1.3 percent

Exhibit 25.2 plots the short extension as a function of active portfolio risk for two values of the *ex ante* IR. For example, for the base-case IR of 0.75 (and associated *IC* of 0.034), the expected short extension at 3 percent active risk is about 30 percent (a 130/30 portfolio), but at the base-case active risk of 4 percent, the expected short extension is more than 50 percent. Although there is some slight curvature, the relationship between expected short extension and active risk in Exhibit 25.2 is nearly linear, in accord with the simple approximation in Equation 25.9.

Exhibit 25.2 also plots the short extension for various active risk levels at a lower IR of 0.50 to illustrate the impact of the *IC* parameter, which measures the manager's return-forecasting accuracy. According to the fundamental law, a lower *IC* leads to a lower expected active return before costs. A lower expected active return decreases the marginal benefit of the unconstrained optimal active security positions and thus lowers the level of shorting after costs, as illustrated by the lower curve in Exhibit 25.2. We note again that the model is for *unconstrained* portfolio optimizations and may produce expected short extensions that are higher than those for long/short strategies within the variety of additional discretionary constraints used in practice.

## A 500-Stock Benchmark

We next use the model to analyze how the unconstrained short extension changes with three market parameters: security risk, security correlation, and benchmark concentration. For this analysis, we use returns on the largest 500 common stocks in the CRSP database, a close approximation of the S&P 500. Our starting date of 1967 was determined by the beginning of complete (i.e., both NYSE and Amex) market coverage by CRSP and a 60-month prior-return requirement.

Exhibits 25.3 through 25.5 show the impact of historical changes in each of the three changing market parameters (security risk, security correlation, and benchmark concentration) while the other two parameters are held fixed. For example, the dark line in Exhibit 25.3 plots the trailing 60-month annualized return standard deviation, averaged across all 500 securities, as the security risk parameter. We note that in addition to being fully populated (i.e., having more than two parameters), estimated covariance matrices used in actual optimizations are typically based on sophisticated multifactor risk models and/or GARCH (generalized autoregressive conditional heteroscedasticity) time-series analysis. Thus, the historical plot in Exhibit 25.3 may overstate the variation in estimated security risk that would be produced by a more sophisticated model.

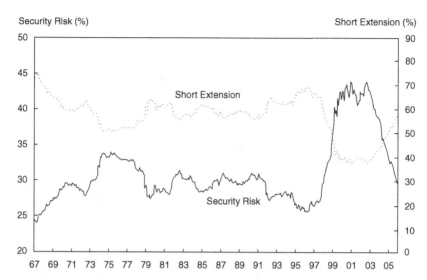

**EXHIBIT 25.3**  Security Risk and Short Extension: CRSP 500, 1967–2006
*Note:* Active risk = 4 percent; security correlation = 0.200; effective $N = 125$;
cost = 1.3 percent; $IC = 0.034$

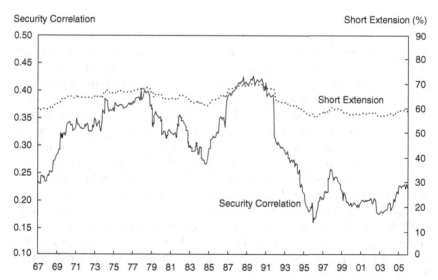

**EXHIBIT 25.4**  Security Correlation and Short Extension: CRSP 500, 1967–2006
*Note:* Active risk = 4 percent; security risk = 30 percent; effective $N = 125$; cost =
1.3 percent; $IC = 0.034$

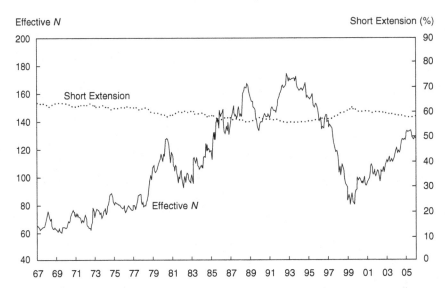

**EXHIBIT 25.5** Effective *N* and Short Extension: CRSP 500, 1967–2006
*Note:* Active risk = 4 percent; security risk = 30 percent; security correlation = 0.200; cost = 1.3 percent; *IC* = 0.034

The average security risk in Exhibit 25.3 (measured on the *left* vertical axis) varies over time between 25 percent and 35 percent, with the exception of the notable rise and fall associated with the build-up and bursting of the technology bubble in the late 1990s. As shown by the position of the security risk parameter, $\sigma$, in Equation 25.9, the long/short extension *decreases* with an increase in estimated security risk. Higher security risk decreases the absolute magnitude of the optimal active weights, shrinking the size of short positions and commensurately decreasing long weights.[4] The inverse relationship between estimated security risk and the size of the short extension (measured on the *right* vertical axis) is clearly evident in Exhibit 25.3. For example, the dramatic increase in security risk beginning in 1998 leads to a drop in the unconstrained expected short extension from about 70 percent to 40 percent (i.e., a 140/40 portfolio) by the year 2000, followed by a rise in expected shorting as individual security risk reverts back to long-term norms.

Exhibit 25.4 considers the impact of historical changes in the security correlation parameter, $\rho$, on the level of shorting. The dark line in Exhibit 25.4 shows the average pairwise security correlation from 1967 to 2006 based on a sample covariance matrix calculated from the trailing 60 months.

Although average security correlations at the end of 2006 are about 0.20, the levels have historically been higher, with a notable jump and then a drop five years later, which were associated with the inclusion and exclusion of the October 1987 stock market crash. The short extension *increases* with an increase in security correlation, as shown by the position of the $\rho$ parameter in Equation 25.9. Higher correlations between securities translate into lower breadth, in the Grinold and Kahn (1994) sense of number of independent bets a manager can take, so larger active weights are required to maintain the targeted level of active risk. For example, the higher security correlations in the five-year postcrash period are associated with higher levels of shorting in Exhibit 25.4. The short extension in Exhibit 25.4 moves between about 60 percent and 70 percent over the historical range of security correlation values, a much smaller range than in Exhibit 25.3 for changes in security risk.

Exhibit 25.5 considers the effect of historical changes in the benchmark concentration. The dark line in Exhibit 25.5 plots monthly observations of Effective $N$. Although the historical risk illustrations in Exhibits 25.3 and 25.4 may overstate the actual variation of a more sophisticated *ex ante* risk model, the Effective $N$ values shown in Exhibit 25.5 capture the actual concentration of the largest 500 U.S. stocks at each point in time. Exhibit 25.5 shows a generally decreasing level of concentration (increasing Effective $N$) over time—from an Effective $N$ of a little more than 60 in the late 1960s to about 170 by 1993. The trend to less concentration was reversed during the 1990s: the Effective $N$ dropped to about 30 in the late 1990s as the U.S. equity market became dominated by a relatively few large-cap technology stocks. With the bursting of the technology bubble at the turn of the century, the market has again moved to less concentration, with an Effective $N$ of about 125 in 2006.

Although the role of active risk in long/short extensions is perhaps the best understood of the model parameters, the impact of benchmark concentration on the size of the long/short extension may be one of the least understood. As more securities approach zero benchmark weight, they are prone to more shorting. For example, on the one hand, in a hypothetical set of 500 securities, where 100 have benchmark weights of 1 percent and the rest, 0, only 400 securities are subject to meaningful shorting. On the other hand, if all the benchmark weight is shifted to 10 securities with weights of 10 percent, then 490 securities are effectively subject to shorting. Note that Effective $N$ enters Equation 25.9 as a ratio to the actual number of securities, $N_E/N$, and that expected shorting is proportional to $1 - N_E/N$. Despite fairly dramatic changes in security concentration, the expected level of shorting in Exhibit 25.5, with other parameters held fixed, moves in a relatively narrow range around 60 percent. As indicated by the simple

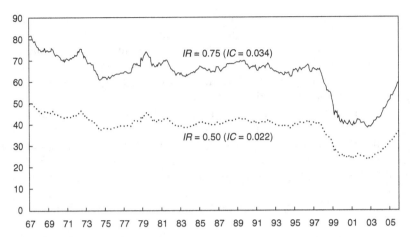

**EXHIBIT 25.6**   Combined Historical Parameters: CRSP 500, 1967–2006
*Note:* Active risk = 4 percent; cost = 1.3 percent

approximation in Equation 25.9, the short extension increases with an increase in benchmark concentration (i.e., decrease in Effective *N*), although the variation based on historical values of Effective *N* is relatively small.

Exhibit 25.6 shows the *simultaneous* effect of the three market parameters over time on the expected level of shorting for the CRSP 500 portfolio at 4 percent active risk. The variation in the short extension is dominated by the changes in security risk, but the combined effect of all three parameters shows greater variation in shorting than does any single parameter alone. Within recent history (i.e., 2003–2006), the short extension at the base-case active risk of 4 percent and an *IC* of 0.034 (*IR* of 0.75) increases from about 40 percent to 60 percent. Exhibit 25.6 also plots the historical short extension at the lower *IC* value of 0.022 to reemphasize the role of the manager's self-assessed forecasting skill. As shown in Exhibit 25.6, the level of shorting is smaller with the lower *IC*. In addition, the recent three-year range in short extensions has narrowed to between 25 and 40 percent (i.e., between 125/25 and 140/40 portfolios).

The substantial changes in the general level of shorting based on a manager-specific parameter, such as the IC, illustrate that the value of the analytical model is in identifying relevant parameters, direction of impact, and observed variation in value, not necessarily in specifying the exact level of shorting. Discretionary constraints, a lower assumed IC, and higher costs—all reduce the desirable level of shorting for a given strategy. A major implication of our analysis is that because relevant market parameters change over time, managers should allow the short extension to vary with market conditions, even though the targeted level of active risk is held constant.

## Other Benchmarks

In the prior examples, we focused on long/short strategies that used a close approximation to the S&P 500 to illustrate the effect of the security risk, security correlation, and benchmark concentration parameters on the size of the long/short extension. The analytical model is equally applicable to other equity benchmarks, however, and Exhibit 25.7 provides summary data for several U.S. and international benchmarks at the end of 2006.[5] The comparison of long/short extension levels for various benchmarks illustrates the impact of $N$ (number of investable securities) in the model and includes more variation in benchmark concentration than was observed in the historical CRSP 500 data.

In addition to the S&P 500 in the United States, we have included the Nikkei 225 for the Japanese market and the FTSE 100 for the U.K. market. The Nikkei and FTSE are both smaller than the S&P 500 in terms of number of securities in the index, but they have similar security concentrations as measured by the ratio of Effective $N$ to $N$. We have also included three MSCI regional indices, which also have a large range of $N$ values but, again, have similar concentrations and security risk parameters. The last section of Exhibit 25.7 provides data for four Russell Investment Group indices for the U.S. equity market—three large-cap indices and the small-cap

**EXHIBIT 25.7** Equity Benchmarks and Market Parameters, December 2006

| Index | No. of Securities | Effective $N$ | $N_E/N$ | Security Risk | Security Correlation |
|---|---|---|---|---|---|
| S&P 500 | 500 | 129 | 0.257 | 31.1% | 0.249 |
| Nikkei 225 | 225 | 88 | 0.329 | 33.9 | 0.363 |
| FTSE 100 | 101 | 35 | 0.349 | 28.6 | 0.277 |
| MSCI EAFE | 1,164 | 247 | 0.212 | 32.5 | 0.207 |
| MSCI Japan | 382 | 83 | 0.217 | 33.7 | 0.330 |
| MSCI Europe | 601 | 144 | 0.240 | 32.0 | 0.231 |
| Russell 1000 | 987 | 157 | 0.159 | 32.9 | 0.225 |
| Russell 1000 Value | 611 | 73 | 0.119 | 30.6 | 0.241 |
| Russell 1000 Growth | 683 | 130 | 0.191 | 35.2 | 0.230 |
| Russell 2000 | 1,972 | 1,255 | 0.636 | 44.4 | 0.186 |

Russell 2000 Index. The Russell 2000 is the only benchmark example in this study that specifically excludes large-cap securities and, consequently, has a markedly different concentration profile from the other indices. Although the Russell 2000 is a cap-weighted benchmark, the ratio of its Effective $N$ to $N$ ($1,255/1,972 = 0.636$) is much higher than the ratio for the other benchmarks. The concentration profile of the Russell 2000 approaches that of an equally weighted benchmark.

Exhibit 25.8 provides calculations of the expected short extension based on the parameter values in Exhibit 25.7. To make direct comparisons, we have used the S&P 500-based cost estimate of 1.3 percent for all benchmarks, although the borrowing and transaction costs will vary for different indices. We have also used a constant IR of 0.75 for all the benchmarks, which leads to different ICs for each benchmark according to the fundamental law relationship, $IR = IC\sqrt{N}$.

The first column in Exhibit 25.8 shows the expected short extension for each benchmark based on the general model in Equation 25.7 with the cost adjustment in Equation 25.11 and at a relatively low active-risk target, 3 percent. For example, the expected short extension for an S&P 500–benchmarked portfolio at 3 percent active risk is 31 percent (a long/short ratio of 131 to 31). The expected short extension for the other benchmarks range from a low of 12 percent for the FTSE ($N = 100$) to

**EXHIBIT 25.8**  Equity Benchmarks and Short Extensions, December 2006

| Index | Active Risk = 3% General Model (Equation 7) | Active Risk = 4 Percent | | |
| | | General Model (Equation 7) | Simple Approximation (Equation 9) | Robust Approximation (Equation 10) |
| --- | --- | --- | --- | --- |
| S&P 500 | 31% | 58% | 56% | 55% |
| Nikkei 225 | 17 | 33 | 30 | 30 |
| FTSE 100 | 12 | 23 | 24 | 22 |
| MSCI EAFE | 47 | 88 | 84 | 85 |
| MSCI Japan | 26 | 49 | 50 | 47 |
| MSCI Europe | 33 | 62 | 60 | 59 |
| Russell 1000 | 45 | 82 | 82 | 80 |
| Russell 1000 Value | 39 | 72 | 74 | 70 |
| Russell 1000 Growth | 33 | 61 | 62 | 59 |
| Russell 2000 | 39 | 76 | 36 | 72 |

highs of 47 percent for EAFE ($N = 1,164$) and 45 percent for the Russell 1000 ($N = 987$). A comparison of the results for the indices shows that the size of the expected short extension increases with the number of securities in the index. Specifically, when the ratio of $N_E/N$ is held constant, the remaining $\sqrt{N}$ term in Equation 25.9 is a result of two effects. First, an increase in $N$ decreases the size of the average benchmark weight (i.e., $1/N$), which increases the likelihood that the average security will be shorted. Second, as the size of the investable set increases, active weights decline by $\sqrt{N}$, as shown in Equation 25.2. The net effect is an increase in expected shorting.

Exhibit 25.8 next provides the expected short extension calculated at the base-case 4 percent active-risk level, with the use of the general model in Equation 25.7 and the two approximation in Equation 25.9 and 25.10—all with the cost adjustment in Equation 25.11. By comparing the second and third columns of Exhibit 25.8, we find that the simple approximation in Equation 25.9 provides a reasonably accurate estimate of the general model for most of the indices (e.g., 56% compared with 58% for the S&P 500). The one instance of poor accuracy for the simple approximation is the Russell 2000; the value is 36 percent from Equation 25.9 but 76 percent for the general model in Equation 25.7. As mentioned previously, the simple approximation in Equation 25.9 is not robust to the entire range of possible benchmark concentrations, and we recommend using the more robust approximation in Equation 25.10, which gives an estimate of 72 percent, closer to the 76 percent result for the general model.

## CONCLUSION

We have developed a mathematical model to analyze the parameters that affect the long/short ratio in unconstrained portfolios. We illustrated the relationships by using historical examples of a 500-stock domestic equity portfolio and a variety of other equity benchmarks. The analytical model of the short extension is based on simplifying assumptions about the structure of the security covariance matrix used to optimize the active portfolio and on the concentration profile of the benchmark. Under these simplifying assumptions, we derived equations that specify the expected size of the short extension for long/short portfolios in the absence of constraints. Although practitioners use live data, numerical optimizers, and a variety of constraints in actual application, the analytical model provides a clear understanding of the factors that affect the size of the short extension. For example, the mathematical model provides important insights to investors who are considering applying long/short strategies to alternative equity benchmarks.

The mathematical model captures two parameters that are intuitively important in determining the size of the short extension: active risk and costs. The short extension increases with the active risk of the strategy and decreases with the cost of shorting. In addition, the model identifies the role of three market parameters that change over time: security risk, security correlation, and the concentration of the benchmark as measured by Effective $N$. The unconstrained expected short extension decreases with security risk, increases with security correlation, and increases with benchmark concentration (low values of Effective $N$). In addition to identifying the relevant parameters, the derivation of the model based on benchmark and active weights helps explain *why* these parameters influence the amount of shorting. Of the three market parameters, the application of the model to a portfolio of the 500 largest U.S. stocks indicates that changes in security risk have historically been the most important.

When costs are considered, the analytical model also includes the assumed accuracy of the return forecasting process as measured by the IC. An increase in the *ex ante* IC means the manager can be more confident about offsetting the increased costs of shorting.

Finally, application of the analytical model to a variety of U.S. and international equity benchmarks illustrated the impact of the number of securities in a benchmark. All else being equal, a benchmark with more securities requires a larger short extension in a long/short strategy. Furthermore, differences in the concentration profile of small-cap benchmarks compared with large-cap benchmarks can lead to substantial differences in the size of the long/short extension.

Even under the simplifying assumptions needed for mathematical tractability, the final form of the basic model is complex and refers to computationally intensive probability functions summed over the investable set of securities. We thus provided a simple approximation of the general model to illustrate the intuition behind the role of each parameter and provided a more robust but closed-form approximation that allows for a wide range of portfolio concentration values.

## APPENDIX A: MODEL DEVELOPMENT

This appendix contains technical derivations and explanations that support the long/short extension model and approximations. We review optimal active security weights in the absence of constraints and the associated Fundamental Law of Active Management, the two-parameter covariance matrix assumption, our use of conditional normal probability functions, an expansion equation for securities outside the benchmark, the market-neutral special case, geometrically declining benchmark weights and Effective $N$, the robust approximation, and the logic behind our cost adjustment for optimal long/short extensions.

## OPTIMAL ACTIVE SECURITY WEIGHTS AND THE FUNDAMENTAL LAW

The objective in an active (as opposed to total) mean–variance portfolio optimization is to maximize the portfolio's expected active return under the budget constraint that the active weights sum to zero and that active risk (i.e., TE) be less than or equal to some value $\sigma_A$. The formal description of the optimization problem is

$$\max E(R_A) = \alpha' \mathbf{w_A} \text{ subject to} \\ \mathbf{w'_A} \mathbf{1} = 0 \text{ and } \mathbf{w'_A} \mathbf{\Omega} \mathbf{w_A} \leq \sigma_A^2 \tag{25.A1}$$

where $\alpha$ is an $N \times 1$ vector of forecasted security returns, $\mathbf{w_A}$ is an $N \times 1$ vector of active security weights, $\mathbf{1}$ is a $N \times 1$ vector of 1s, and $\mathbf{\Omega}$ is an $N \times N$ return covariance matrix. The general solution to this optimization problem gives an active weight vector of

$$\mathbf{w_A} = \frac{\sigma_A}{\sqrt{\alpha' \mathbf{\Omega}^{-1} \alpha}} \mathbf{\Omega}^{-1} \alpha \tag{25.A2}$$

We use the full covariance matrix version of Grinold's (1994) alpha generation process:

$$\alpha = IC \mathbf{\Omega}^{1/2} \mathbf{S} \tag{25.A3}$$

where $IC$ (the *ex ante* IC) is a scalar parameter and $\mathbf{S}$ is an $N \times 1$ vector of standard normal scores.[6] The substitution of Equation 25.A3 into Equation 25.A2 gives the optimal active weight vector in terms of security scores:

$$\mathbf{w_A} = \frac{\sigma_A}{\sqrt{N}} \mathbf{\Omega}^{-1/2} \mathbf{S} \tag{25.A4}$$

The vector of optimal active weights in Equation 25.A4 times the security alpha vector in Equation 25.A3 gives an expected active portfolio return of

$$E(R_A) = IC\sqrt{N}\sigma_A \qquad (25.A5)$$

which is known as the Fundamental Law of Active Management (Grinold and Kahn, 1994).

## SIMPLE TWO-PARAMETER COVARIANCE MATRIX

We assume a two-parameter security return covariance matrix in which all the variances are equal to a single value $\sigma^2$ and all the pairwise correlation coefficients are equal to a single value $\rho$. In matrix notation, the assertion is that

$$\mathbf{\Omega} = \sigma^2(1 - \rho)\mathbf{I} + \sigma^2\rho\mathbf{11}' \qquad (25.A6)$$

where $\mathbf{I}$ is the $N \times N$ identity matrix.

Under the covariance matrix assumption in Equation 25.A6, it can be shown that the optimal active weight vector in Equation 25.A4 reduces to the simple scalar result in Equation 25.A2. Specifically, the budget constraint is met because the scores sum to zero, and with Equation 25.A6 the active portfolio risk squared is

$$\mathbf{w'}_A\mathbf{\Omega}w_A = c^2\sigma^2(1 - \rho)S'IS + c^2\sigma^2\rho S'11'S \qquad (25.A7)$$

For standard normal scores, we have the matrix products $E(S'IS) = N$ and $E(S'11'S) = 0$. Note that the expectation operator is not required in these identities if the scores, as a group, are perfectly standard normal. The value of $c$ in Equation 25.A2 is based on these substitutions into Equation 25.A7.

## NORMAL PROBABILITY FUNCTIONS IN THE SHORT EXTENSION MODEL

The expression in Equation 25.A5 for the expected short weight of a single security is based on well-known integral solutions in conditional probability theory—as in probit regression analysis, for example. Using the notation

$\Theta\left(\cdot\right)$ for the standard normal cumulative density function and $\Phi(\cdot)$ for the standard normal density function, these solutions are

$$\text{prob}\left(S_i < \frac{-w_{Bi}}{c}\right) = \int_{-\infty}^{-w_{Bi}/c} \frac{1}{\sqrt{2\pi}} e^{-S^2/2} ds \qquad (25.\text{A}8)$$

$$= \Phi\left(\frac{-w_{Bi}}{c}\right)$$

and

$$E\left(S_i | S_i < \frac{-w_{Bi}}{c}\right) = \frac{1}{\Phi(-w_{Bi}/c)} \int_{-\infty}^{-w_{Bi}/c} S \frac{1}{\sqrt{2\pi}} e^{-S^2/2} ds \quad (25.\text{A}9)$$

$$= -\frac{\varphi(-w_{Bi}/c)}{\Phi(-w_{Bi}/c)}$$

For the specific argument of $W_{Bi} = 0$, cumulative standard normal function $\Theta(\cdot)$ has a value of $1/2$ and density function $\Phi(\cdot)$ has a value of $1/\sqrt{2\pi}$. With these two values in Equation 25.A5, the expected short weight for a zero-benchmark-weight security is $c/2\pi$, as shown in Equation 25.A6.

## EXPANSION EQUATION FOR SECURITIES OUTSIDE THE BENCHMARK

As explained in Note 2, the basic model in Equation 25.A7 can be used in the general case when the manager's investable universe is larger than the benchmark set. The parameter $N$ becomes the number of securities in the larger universe, where nonbenchmark securities are assigned a zero benchmark weight, with the expected short weight given in Equation 25.A6.

Alternatively, for notational precision, one can disaggregate Equation 25.A7 into benchmark and nonbenchmark components. Let $N_{BMK}$ be the number of securities in the benchmark and $N_{INV}$ be the number of securities in the investable universe. Under the assumption that the benchmark is a subset of the investable universe, Equation 25.A7 becomes

$$S_0 = \frac{c(N_{INV} - N_{BMK})}{\sqrt{2\pi}} + \sum_{i=1}^{N_{BMK}} c\varphi\left(\frac{-w_{Bi}}{c}\right) - w_{Bi}\Phi\left(\frac{-w_{Bi}}{c}\right) \qquad (25.\text{A}10)$$

The first term of Equation 25.A10 represents the contribution to portfolio shorting from nonbenchmark securities; the second term is the contribution from securities contained in the benchmark.

## MARKET-NEUTRAL SPECIAL CASE AND THE SIMPLE APPROXIMATION

An important special case of the basic long/short model is a market-neutral portfolio for which the benchmark weights are all zero. Using Equation 25.A6 and substituting $w_{Bi} = 0$ for all $i$ in Equation 25.A7 gives Equation 25.A8 of this chapter. The expected short weight of zero-benchmark-weight securities also motivates the simple approximation in Equation 25.A9 of this chapter For a hypothetical benchmark with equal weights on the first $N_E$ securities and zero on the other $N - N_E$, the shape of the "Benchmark Weight" curve in Exhibit 25.1 becomes a step function. The "Short Extension" area is a rectangle under the assumption that the benchmark weights on the first $N_E$ securities are large enough that their expected short weights can be ignored. The height of the rectangle is the expected short weight for zero-benchmark-weight securities, as given in Equation 25.A6, and the length of the rectangle is the number of zero-benchmark-weight securities, $N - N_E$. We note that ignoring the potential shorting of the first $N_E$ securities for large $N_E$-to-$N$ ratio benchmarks (i.e., Russell, 2000) can substantially understate expected portfolio shorting using Equation 25.A9, and in these cases, we suggest using the more robust approximation in Equation 25.A10.

## CAP-WEIGHTED BENCHMARK MODEL AND EFFECTIVE *N*

To provide a simple analytical model of benchmark weights, we assume that when benchmark weights are sorted by declining magnitude, each benchmark weight is equal to the prior weight multiplied by a parameter $\lambda$,

$$w_{Bi} = \lambda w_{Bi-1} \qquad (25.A11)$$

$$= w_{B0} \lambda^i$$

The restriction that the benchmark weights sum to 1 and the well-known finite geometric sum formula give a solution for $w_{B0}$ in Equation 25.A11, and the benchmark weight for security $i$ is

$$w_{Bi} = \frac{\lambda^{i-1}(1-\lambda)}{1-\lambda^N} \qquad (25.A12)$$

One measure of concentration used in economics is the Herfindahl Index, which is, in a security portfolio context, the sum of the benchmark weights squared. Effective $N$ is the inverse of the Herfindahl Index,

$$N_E = \frac{1}{\sum_{i=1}^{N} w_i^2} \qquad (25.A13)$$

Larger values of $N_E$ indicate *less* portfolio concentration. For example, Effective $N$ is 1 for a fully concentrated portfolio (all the weight on a single security) and $N$ for an equally weighted benchmark. The substitution of the analytical benchmark weights in Equation 25.A12 into Equation 25.A13 gives the relationship between the geometric decline parameter, $\lambda$, and Effective $N$ as

$$N_E = \frac{(1+\lambda)(1-\lambda^N)}{(1-\lambda)(1+\lambda^N)} \qquad (25.A14)$$

## ROBUST APPROXIMATION

The robust approximation in Equation 25.A10 is based on the rank of an average security, which we designate $N_A$. The absolute value of the expected active weight conditional on it being negative is

$$|E(cS|S < 0)| = \frac{c\varphi(0)}{\Phi(0)} = \frac{2c}{\sqrt{2\pi}} \qquad (25.A15)$$

Setting Equation 25.A15 equal to the benchmark-weight model in Equation 25.A12 and solving for $i$ (with the approximation that $\lambda^N \approx 0$) gives the stock rank of the average security when sorted in declining magnitude as

$$N_A \approx 1 + \frac{1}{\ln \lambda} \ln \left[ \frac{\left( 2c/\sqrt{2\pi} \right)}{1-\lambda} \right], 0 \le N_A \le N \qquad (25.A16)$$

With the result in Equation 25.A15 defined as $\overline{w}_A$, the probability that $\overline{w}_A$ results in a short position is

$$\text{prob}\,[\overline{w}_A > w_B(N_A)] \approx 1 - \frac{N_A}{N} \tag{25.A17}$$

Using the model benchmark weights in Equation 25.A12 and the formula for the finite geometric sum, we can compute the expected benchmark weight conditional on the benchmark weight being less than $w_B(N_A)$ as

$$E[w_B | w_B < w_B(N_A)] \approx \frac{1}{N - N_A}\left(1 - \frac{1 - \lambda^{N_A}}{1 - \lambda^N}\right) \tag{25.A18}$$

Using Equations 25.A15, 25.A17, and 25.A18, and sorting the z-scores in ascending order, we can define shorting for the overall portfolio as the sum over the first $N/2$ (negative) z-scores:

$$S_0 \approx \sum_{i=1}^{N/2}\left[\frac{1}{N - N_A}\left(1 - \frac{1 - \lambda^{N_A}}{1 - \lambda^N}\right) + cS_i\right]\left(1 - \frac{N_A}{N}\right) \tag{25.A19}$$

Then, by using the approximation $\lambda^N \approx 0$ and multiplying through by $-1$, so that the expected portfolio shorting will be a positive number, we arrive at a closed-form approximation for the expected short extension:

$$S_0 \approx (N - N_A)\frac{c}{\sqrt{2\pi}} - \frac{1}{2}\lambda^{N_A} \tag{25.A20}$$

We want to express Equations 25.A16 and 25.A20 in terms of Effective $N$ rather than $\lambda$, so we use the approximation $\lambda^N \approx 0$ to rearrange Equation 25.A14 to obtain

$$\lambda \approx \frac{N_E - 1}{N_E + 1} \tag{25.A21}$$

Substituting Equation 25.A21 into Equations 25.A16 and 25.A20 and using the approximations $\ln(1 - x) - \ln(1 + x) \approx -2x$ and $\ln(1 + N) \approx \ln(N)$ for large $N$, we express expected portfolio shorting as a function of Effective $N$ as given in Equation 25.A10 of this chapter.

## ADJUSTMENT FOR SHORTING COSTS

Optimal active weights in the presence of costs are difficult to model, but we can determine the general level of expected shorting by expanding the objective function in Equation 25.A1. The expanded objective function adjusts the active weights to maximize the portfolio expected active return *after* costs. The expected active portfolio return after costs is the expected return before costs minus the expected short extension times costs:

$$\max E(R_A) - E(S)(B + 2T) \qquad (25.A22)$$

subject to the same two conditions as Equation A1 (i.e., a budget constraint and a limit on the portfolio active risk). As explained previously, $B$ represents borrowing costs and $T$ is general portfolio operating costs as determined by turnover and transaction costs.

Even without an analytical solution to the active weights specified by Expression 25.A22, we know that the expected short extension will be adjusted until the marginal value of additional shorting equals the marginal cost. In other words, a first-order or equilibrium condition for the optimal solution is that the change in expected active return with respect to the level of shorting be equal to the cost of shorting:

$$\frac{\partial E(R_A)}{\partial E(S)} = B + 2T \qquad (25.A23)$$

Although the exact functional relationship between expected active return and expected shorting is unknown, we know a particular point on the function, the zero-cost active portfolio return and expected shorting, and we know this point is a maximum. The zero-cost expected active portfolio return is $IC\sqrt{N}\sigma_A$ as shown in Equation 25.A5, and the zero-cost expected shorting is $S_0$ in Equation 25.A7. We assume a simple second-order (i.e., parabolic) functional form, which leads to a linear relationship between costs and optimal shorting. Setting the zero-cost point, $(IC\sqrt{N}\sigma_A, S_0)$, as the vertex, we find the general parabolic function with a maximum to be

$$E(R_A) = IC\sqrt{N}\sigma_A - \frac{D}{2}[E(S) - S_0]^2 \qquad (25.A24)$$

in which $D$ is the rate of change of the slope (i.e., the second derivative). A natural assumption that properly scales the parabola is that

$$D = \frac{IC\sqrt{N}\sigma_A}{S_0} \qquad (25.A25)$$

With this substitution, we set the derivative of Equation 25.A24 with respect to expected shorting equal to costs, as shown in Equation 25.A23, to arrive at Equation 25.A11 in the body of this chapter.

## NOTES

1. The fundamental law introduced by Grinold and Kahn (1994) describes the relationship between expected portfolio performance and basic parameters that measure skill, breadth, and implementation efficiency. The IR is defined as the portfolio's expected active return divided by active risk. The TC is the cross-sectional correlation coefficient between security active weights and forecasted returns (i.e., the degree to which the manager's forecasts are translated into active weights).
2. We generally refer to the $N$ securities in the benchmark portfolio (e.g., $N = 500$ for the S&P 500 benchmark), but if the investor's universe is larger than the benchmark and nonbenchmark securities are given weights of zero, then $N$ can refer to the number of securities in the investable set.
3. The benchmark weights used for illustration in Exhibit 25.A1 are hypothetical weights with a perfect geometric decline, as discussed in Appendix A, rather than actual security weights. The hypothetical weights were constructed to have the same degree of security concentration as the largest 500 common stocks in the CRSP database at the end of 2006.
4. Note that an increase in security risk increases the magnitude of security alphas in the Grinold (1994) prescription, but the optimization process that translates security alphas into optimal active weights effectively divides by $\sigma^2$, so the net effect is a decrease in the size of active weights.
5. The data in Exhibit 25.7 are from the Barra Morgan Stanley Global Equity Model on December 29 2006. The security correlation number was inferred from the average security risk value and the Barra estimated risk of an equally weighted benchmark portfolio.
6. See Clarke, de Silva, and Thorley (2006) for a discussion of the mathematics of the full-covariance-matrix fundamental law, including the use of the matrix square root function. Although the derivation is more complicated, the results of this chapter also hold for the original scalar version of Grinold's (1994) alpha-generation process, $\alpha_i = IC\sigma_i, S_i$, under the maintained assumption of equal pairwise correlation coefficients for all securities.

## REFERENCES

Clarke, R., H. de Silva, and S. Sapra. 2004. "Towards More Information-Efficient Portfolios." *Journal of Portfolio Management*, vol. 31, no. 1 (Fall): 34–63.

Clarke, R., H. de Silva, and S. Thorley. 2002. "Portfolio Constraints and the Fundamental Law of Active Management." *Financial Analysts Journal*, vol. 58, no. 5 (September/October):48–66.

———. 2006. "The Fundamental Law of Active Portfolio Management." *Journal of Investment Management*, vol. 4, no. 3 (Third Quarter):54–72.

Goodwin, T. H. 1998. "The Information Ratio." *Financial Analysts Journal*, vol. 54, no. 4 (July/August):34–43.

Grinold, R. C. 1994. "Alpha Is Volatility Times IC Times Score, or Real Alphas Don't Get Eaten." *Journal of Portfolio Management*, vol. 20, no. 4 (Summer): 9–16.

Grinold, R., and R. Kahn. 1994. "Active Portfolio Management." 2nd edition. New York: McGraw-Hill.

Jacobs, B., and K. Levy. 2007. "20 Myths about Enhanced Active 120–20 Strategies." *Financial Analysts Journal*, vol. 63, no. 4 (July/August):19–26.

Jacobs, B., K. Levy, and D. Starer. 1998. "On the Optimality of Long–Short Strategies." *Financial Analysts Journal*, vol. 54, no. 2 (March/April):40–51.

Johnson, S., R. Kahn, and D. Petrich. 2007. "Optimal Gearing." *Journal of Portfolio Management*, vol. 33, no. 4 (Summer):10–18.

Sorensen, E., R. Hua, and E. Qian. 2006. "Aspects of Constrained Long–Short Equity Portfolios." *Journal of Portfolio Management*, vol. 33, no. 2 (Winter):12–22.

Strongin, S., M. Petsch, and G. Sharenow. 2000. "Beating Benchmarks." *Journal of Portfolio Management*, vol. 26, no. 4 (Summer):11–27.

# About the Authors

## MARTIN L. LEIBOWITZ

Martin L. Leibowitz is a managing director of Morgan Stanley Research Department's global strategy team. Over the past four years, he and his associates have produced a series of studies on such topics as beta-based asset allocation, active extension 130/30 strategies, asset/liability management, stress betas, and the need for greater fluidity in policy portfolios.

Before joining Morgan Stanley, Mr. Leibowitz was vice chairman and chief investment officer of TIAA-CREF (1995–2004), and was responsible for the management of over $300 billion in equity, fixed income, and real estate assets. Previously, he had a 26-year association with Salomon Brothers, where he became director of global research—covering both fixed income and equities—and was a member of the firm's Executive Committee.

Mr. Leibowitz received his A.B. and M.S. degrees from The University of Chicago and his Ph.D. in Mathematics from the Courant Institute of New York University.

He has written more than 150 articles on various financial and investment analysis topics, and is the most frequently published author in the *Financial Analysts Journal* (*FAJ*) and the *Journal of Portfolio Management* (*JPM*). Ten of his *FAJ* articles have received the Graham and Dodd Award for excellence in financial writing. In February 2008, an article written by Mr. Leibowitz and his associate Anthony Bova was voted Best Article in the 9th Annual Bernstein Fabozzi/Jacobs Levy Awards by the readers of *JPM*.

In 1992, *Investing*, a collection of his writings, was published with a foreword by William F. Sharpe, the 1990 Nobel Laureate in Economics. In 1996, his book *Return Targets and Shortfall Risks* was published by Irwin Co. In 2004, two of his books were published: a compilation of studies on equity valuation, titled *Franchise Value* (John Wiley & Co.), and a revised edition of his study on bond investment, *Inside the Yield*

*Book* (Bloomberg Press). The first edition of *Inside the Yield Book* was published in 1972, went through 21 reprintings, and remains a standard in the field. The new edition includes a foreword by noted economist Henry Kaufman.

The CFA Institute presented Mr. Leibowitz with three of its highest awards: the Nicholas Molodowsky Award in 1995, the James R. Vertin Award in 1998, and the Award for Professional Excellence in 2005. In October 1995, he received the Distinguished Public Service Award from the Public Securities Association, and in November 1995, he became the first inductee into The Fixed Income Analyst Society's Hall of Fame. He has received special Alumni Achievement Awards from The University of Chicago and New York University, and, in 2003, was elected a Fellow of the American Academy of Arts and Sciences.

Mr. Leibowitz is chairman of the Institute for Advanced Study in Princeton, New Jersey. He is also a member of the Rockefeller University Council and of the Board of Overseers of New York University's Stern School of Business. Mr. Leibowitz serves on the investment advisory committee for the Harvard Management Corporation, The University of Chicago, the Carnegie Corporation, the Rockefeller Foundation, and the International Monetary Fund. He is a past chairman of the board of the New York Academy of Sciences and a former vice chairman of the Carnegie Corporation.

## ANTHONY BOVA

Anthony Bova is a vice president with Morgan Stanley Equity Research's Global Strategy team, which focuses on institutional portfolio strategy. Prior to his current role, he spent four years covering commodity chemicals at Morgan Stanley. Mr. Bova received a B.S. in Economics with a minor in Mathematics from Duke University and holds the CFA designation. He recently won Best Article in the ninth annual Bernstein Fabozzi/Jacobs Levy Awards presented by *The Journal of Portfolio Management* for his co-authoring of "Gathering Implicit Alphas in a Beta World," which ran in its Spring 2007 issue.

## SIMON EMRICH

Simon Emrich is head of Quantitative and Derivative Strategies North America at Morgan Stanley, based in New York. Mr. Emrich has been with Morgan Stanley for seven years. His work has focused on optimal portfolio construction, quantitative alpha generation, and the use of derivatives in portfolio management. Most recently, he worked on issues related to alpha-beta separation and the optimization of alpha views in a benchmark-relative portfolio context, as well as on the implications of the quant meltdown of the second half of 2007. He holds degrees from the London School of Economics and Université Catholique de Louvain-la-Neuve in Belgium.

# Index